Temperamental differences in infants and young children

Ciba Foundation symposium 89

1982

Pitman
London

ISBN 0 272 79653 0

Published in June 1982 by Pitman Books Ltd, London. Distributed in North America by CIBA Pharmaceutical Company (Medical Education Administration), Summit, NJ 07006, USA.

Suggested series entry for library catalogues:
Ciba Foundation symposia.

Ciba Foundation symposium 89
x + 310 pages, 7 figures, 42 tables

British Library Cataloguing in publication data:
Temperamental differences in infants and young
   children.—(Ciba Foundation symposium series; 89)
   1. Temperament—Congresses   2. Child psychology
   —Congresses
   I. Porter, Ruth   II. Collins, Geralyn M.
   III. Series
   155.4'18   BF811

ISBN 0–272–79653–0   73891

Text set in 10/12 pt Linotron 202 Times, printed and bound
in Great Britain at The Pitman Press, Bath

Temperamental differences in infants and young children

Contents

Symposium on Temperamental differences in infants and young children held at the Ciba Foundation, London, 22–24 September 1981
Editors: Ruth Porter (Organizer) and Geralyn M. Collins

v

Participants

J. E. BATES Department of Psychology, Indiana University, Bloomington, Indiana 47405, USA

R. Q. BELL Department of Psychology, University of Virginia, Charlottesville, Virginia 22901, USA

M. BERGER Department of Child Psychiatry, St George's Hospital, Blackshaw Road, London SW17 0QT, UK

W. B. CAREY 319 West Front Street, Media, Pennsylvania 19063, USA (and Department of Pediatrics, University of Pennsylvania Medical School, Philadelphia, USA)

S. CHESS Millhauser Laboratories, Department of Psychiatry, New York University Medical Center, School of Medicine, 550 First Avenue, New York, New York 10016, USA

J. F. DUNN MRC Unit on the Development and Integration of Behaviour, University Sub-Department of Animal Behaviour, Madingley, Cambridge CB3 8AA, UK

D. W. FULKER Animal Psychology Laboratory, Institute of Psychiatry, The Bethlem Royal Hospital, Monks Orchard Road, Beckenham, Kent BR3 3BX, UK

P. J. GRAHAM Department of Child Psychiatry, Institute of Child Health, The Hospital for Sick Children, Great Ormond Street, London WC1N 3JH, UK

R. A. HINDE MRC Unit on the Development and Integration of Behaviour, University Sub-Department of Animal Behaviour, Madingley, Cambridge CB3 8AA, UK

C.-C. HSU   Children's Mental Health Center, Department of Psychiatry, National Taiwan University Hospital, No. 1, Chang-Te Street, Taipei 100, Taiwan

M. O. HUTTUNEN   Department of Psychiatry, University of Helsinki, Helsinki, Finland

B. K. KEOGH   Moore Hall, Department of Education, University of California at Los Angeles, 405 Hilgard, Los Angeles, California 90024, USA

G. A. KOHNSTAMM   Department of Developmental Psychology, University of Leiden, Hooigracht 15, 2312 KM Leiden, The Netherlands

I. KOLVIN   Nuffield Psychology and Psychiatry Unit, Fleming Memorial Hospital, Great North Road, Newcastle Upon Tyne NE2 3AX, UK

T. F. McNEIL   Department of Psychiatry, University of Lund, Malmö Allmänna Sjukhus, S-214 01 Malmö, Sweden

R. PLOMIN   Institute for Behavioural Genetics, University of Colorado, Campus Box 447, Boulder, Colorado 80309, USA

R. O. ROBINSON   Newcomen Centre, Guy's Hospital, St Thomas Street, London SE1 9RT, UK

M. RUTTER   Department of Child and Adolescent Psychiatry, Institute of Psychiatry, De Crespigny Park, Denmark Hill, London SE5 8AF, UK

J. E. STEVENSON   Department of Human Biology and Health, University of Surrey, Guildford, Surrey GU2 5XH, UK

J. STEVENSON-HINDE   MRC Unit on the Development and Integration of Behaviour, University Sub-Department of Animal Behaviour, Madingley, Cambridge CB3 8AA, UK

A. THOMAS   Millhauser Laboratories, Department of Psychiatry, New York University Medical Center, School of Medicine, 550 First Avenue, New York, New York 10016, USA

A. M. TORGERSEN   Department of Child Psychiatry, avd.18, Ullevål Hospital, Oslo 1, Norway

J. S. WERRY Department of Psychiatry, School of Medicine, University of Auckland P. B., Auckland, New Zealand

R. S. WILSON Department of Pediatrics, Child Development Unit, Health Sciences Center, University of Louisville, Louisville, Kentucky 40292, USA

S. N. WOLKIND Family Research Unit, The London Hospital Medical College, Turner Street, London E1 2AD, UK

Temperament: concepts, issues and problems

MICHAEL RUTTER

Department of Child and Adolescent Psychiatry, Institute of Psychiatry, De Crespigny Park, Denmark Hill, London SE5 8AF, UK

Abstract There are marked individual differences in children's temperamental styles—differences thought to be constitutionally determined in part. The importance of temperamental features is evident in their links with various forms of psychopathology and in their effects on the manner in which other people respond to the child. For these and other reasons it has rightly come to be accepted that greater attention needs to be paid to temperamental issues in consideration of the processes of development, children's responses to stress situations, and the genesis of emotional, behavioural and learning disorders. However, major conceptual, methodological and theoretical problems remain. Problems of measurement are considered in terms of the relativity of measures, whether or not to take social context into account, the functional equivalence of measures at different ages, the circumstances to use in assessing temperament, the choice of measuring instrument and the categorization of temperamental features. The issues involved in the meaning of temperamental differences are discussed with respect to consistency, developmental change, genetic influences, brain damage and mental retardation, sex differences and the mechanisms by which temperamental variables exert their effects.

The general concept of *temperament* goes back to at least mediaeval times, when it was used to refer to a person's mental disposition, as determined by the combination of the four cardinal humours. Its usage today retains much of that emphasis. That is, the term usually implies reference to the basic elements of behavioural functioning rather than to complex or idiosyncratic aspects of a person's emotional or social style; the concept applies to those elements that show substantial consistency over time and over space; and it is assumed that, to a considerable extent, the elements are constitutionally determined. Most notably, temperament refers to a preponderant style in *how* an individual does things or how he or she responds to people and to situations, rather than to *what* the individual does (i.e. the content of behaviour), or to *why* he or she does it (i.e. motivation), or to the behavioural

1982 Temperamental differences in infants and young children. Pitman Books Ltd, London (Ciba Foundation symposium 89) p 1-19

1

capacities or abilities that he or she manifests (Thomas & Chess 1977). Temperamental characteristics are abstractions, rather than directly observable discrete behaviours (Rutter et al 1964), and the questions with which we need to start therefore concern the empirical evidence that justifies the abstraction and shows its utility.

Although the concepts and terms are centuries old, the scientific study of temperamental attributes began much more recently. Gesell's (1937) analysis of film records of children—to assess characteristics such as activity level or energy output, adaptability, and liveliness of emotional expression—constituted one of the earliest studies. He concluded that . . . 'certain fundamental traits of individuality, whatever their origin, exist early, persist late and assert themselves under varying environmental conditions'. This view contrasted starkly with the prevailing popular impression that all young babies were much alike and that individual differences in early childhood were of little importance. Over the next two decades, a steady trickle of studies indicated important individual differences in a wide range of behavioural functions in infancy and early childhood. Then, a most important stimulus to research on temperament came from the New York longitudinal study started by S. Chess, A. Thomas and H. G. Birch in the mid-1950s. One of their early papers (Chess et al 1959) included the statement . . . 'We believe that the data indicate that the individual specific reaction pattern appears in the first few months of life, persists in a stable form thereafter, and significantly influences the nature of the child's response to all environmental events, including child care practices'. In subsequent years they somewhat modified their claims regarding temporal consistency, but the findings from their longitudinal study (see Thomas & Chess 1977) have otherwise generally supported their initial hypotheses on the importance of individual differences in temperamental characteristics. Moreover, as shown by a variety of recent reviews (Rutter 1977, Dunn 1980, Keogh & Pullis 1980, Bates 1980)—as well as by the papers in this symposium—the claims and findings from the New York study stimulated a mass of research by other investigators. We are consequently in a much stronger position now than we were 20 years ago to assess the concept of temperament. In reviewing what we know, we need to sharpen the hypotheses and clarify the issues in order to consider the utility of the current notions, and to identify the empirical questions and theoretical problems that remain to be tackled.

The utility of the concept of temperament

The empirical evidence that points to the utility of the concept of temperament may be considered under three main headings: (a) the demonstration of behavioural individuality; (b) the findings on constitutional determinants; and (c) the predictive power of temperamental measures for children's development of disorder and for children's responses to potentially stressful situations.

Behavioural individuality

The question of behavioural individuality can be quickly dealt with in view of the entirely consistent and extensive data showing that, far from all infants being the same, babies and young children differ strikingly in their behavioural characteristics (Buss & Plomin 1975, Rutter 1977, Bates 1980, Dunn 1980, Keogh & Pullis 1980). This has been shown, for example, for features as varied as activity level, autonomic reactivity, fussiness or irritability, soothability, visual alertness, regularity of sleep–wake patterns, adaptability to change and social responsiveness. Moreover, numerous investigators have shown that these characteristics can be measured reliably by questionnaire, interview, and by observational and mechanical means.

Constitutional basis

The question of the 'constitutional' basis of these individual differences raises more complex matters. The utility of the concept of temperament does not depend on the demonstration that it has its origins in genetically determined or any other kind of constitutional factors. If consistent individual differences in temperamental style were found, and these differences reliably predicted how children would respond to stressful situations, or how their course of later personality development would proceed, or whether they were likely to develop psychiatric problems, it would not matter if it were shown also that a child's temperament was largely shaped by early life experiences. In that case, temperament would still be viewed as a relatively enduring individual characteristic that reflected the personal qualities that a child brought to any new experience he or she encountered. The behavioural features would be 'constitutional' in the sense that they reflected an intrinsic aspect of personal functioning, even though their origins were experiential rather than genetic. Nevertheless, most workers have considered it important to claim and to demonstrate that temperament has a substantial genetic component.

The evidence on this point is limited and not free from difficulties. Even so, the empirical findings from twin studies (see Buss & Plomin 1975, Torgersen & Kringlen 1978, Matheny 1980, Goldsmith & Gottesman 1981) are reasonably consistent in showing that genetic factors play a significant part in individual variability for at least some temperamental features. This is most evident, perhaps, for activity level and task orientation, but it applies in varying degree to many other characteristics.

Another key aspect of the 'constitutional' notion concerns the consistency of temperamental functioning over time and space. If a feature is to be considered 'constitutional', it might be expected that the individual should exhibit the attribute in similar fashion across a range of different situations and over lengthy periods of time. In fact, this supposition is not quite so self-evident as it appears at first sight (a point to which I will return), but the evidence on consistency is still of some relevance. Several longitudinal studies have examined the question of temporal stability (Buss & Plomin 1975, Thomas & Chess 1977, Moss & Susman 1980) and found that children's temperamental style shows substantial consistency over periods of several months up to a year or so, but that correlations extending over several years between the pre-school period and middle childhood are generally quite low. The question of consistency across situations is at least as important, but there is surprisingly little evidence on the matter. There is moderate, but not high, agreement between measures based on parental reports, teacher reports and direct observations (Dunn & Kendrick 1980, Billman & McDevitt 1980, Buss et al 1980). The overall evidence therefore suggests that temperamental characteristics show some features associated with 'constitutional' variables.

Prediction to other aspects of functioning

The evidence considered so far partly substantiates the notion that the abstraction of temperament has some validity, but it does not attest to its utility. That is shown by the power of temperamental measures as predictors of how children are likely to respond in various situations. It is that power that provides the main reason for regarding temperament as a crucial variable for any research in the field of developmental psychopathology.

The relevant evidence falls under three main headings. Firstly, it has been shown that children with amodal temperamental characteristics on such variables as irregularity of functioning, negative mood, non-adaptability, high emotional intensity, and low fastidiousness have a substantially increased risk of developing emotional or behavioural disorders during the next few years (see reviews by Rutter 1977, Keogh & Pullis 1980). This has been found in groups of children that might be considered both low risk (Rutter et al 1964, Thomas & Chess 1977) and high risk (Graham et al 1973) in terms of their psychosocial situation. There is also evidence linking temperamental attributes with scholastic performance (see Keogh & Pullis 1980).

Secondly, it has been found that a child's temperamental features constitute an important predictor of how that child will respond to the birth of a sibling. Dunn et al (1981) found that high emotional intensity and a tendency towards negative mood were the two temperamental features associated with adverse reactions. Little is known about the importance of temperamental variables with respect to children's responses to other potentially stressful life situations or to changes of circumstances requiring adaptation of some kind, but there are various pointers to their probable relevance (see Rutter 1981a).

Thirdly, several naturalistic and experimental studies have shown that the behavioural characteristics of children have an important effect in determining how other people respond to them (see Rutter 1977, Dunn 1980). Children with different temperamental features *elicit* different behaviours from those with whom they interact. For example, in our study of families with a mentally ill parent, we found that children with adverse temperamental characteristics were twice as likely as other children to be the target of parental criticism (Rutter 1978). In contrast, easily adaptable children tended to be protected even in a stressful home environment, precisely because much of the hostility and discord was focused on other members of the family. Similarly, it has been found that weak malnourished children receive less parental attention than well-fed children and, probably because they elicit more caretaking, highly active babies are less likely to show developmental retardation in a depriving institutional environment (see Rutter 1977). Dunn found, in addition, that children's reactivity in infancy was linked with maternal responsiveness to them a year later (see Dunn 1980).

The temperamental qualities brought by a child to the interactions and situations that he or she encounters therefore play an important part in determining how that encounter proceeds and whether it is likely to result in the development of some form of maladaptive response or emotional–behavioural disturbance. The empirical evidence on those points provides ample justification for regarding the concept of temperament as theoretically important and practically useful.

Problems in measurement

The most immediate issue that bedevils the study of temperament concerns the question of how to measure temperament—not necessarily which particular instrument or measuring device to use but, rather, how to conceptualize and operationalize the characteristics to be assessed.

Relativity

For example, some problems stem from the use of relative rather than absolute measures. Nearly all instruments (other than strictly quantitative bits of gadgetry, such as actometers or stabilimeters to assess activity level) compare children with other children on some behavioural feature. For example, the parental questionnaire developed by the New York group (Thomas & Chess 1977) includes items such as 'my child splashes hard in the bath and plays actively' or 'if my child is angry or annoyed, he gets over it quickly' or 'my child is highly sensitive to changes in the brightness or dimness of light'. Adverbs such as 'hard', 'actively', 'quickly' or 'highly' all demand a knowledge of what is the 'norm'. Almost inevitably, a person's norm consists of other children of the same age that he or she happens to know. The consequence is that little confidence can be placed on comparisons across ages or across sociocultural groups. A lack of difference may simply mean that the person who is rating the child has adjusted the ratings to a different set of norms.

On the other hand, for some purposes, a relative measure may be more useful, provided that there is a known and constant norm. Thus, age-standardized Intelligence Quotient scores are used to remove the massive effects of age. As Kagan (1980) points out: 'When text books say that children's intelligence is stable from 5 to 10 years of age, they do not mean that cognitive ability is stable; it is not. They mean that the differences in test scores among a cohort of children remain stable, despite dramatic changes in the abilities that accompany growth'.

Social context

Whether or not to take social context into account constitutes a further variant of the same issue. For example, which is the higher activity level—wandering around aimlessly on the wing in a soccer match or fidgeting and squirming vigorously in a chair in front of the television set? The first may well involve greater energy output, but that is a function of the demands of the situation rather than of how the child responds to it. However, the situation may well reflect the child's *choice* of activities that suit his or her temperamental style. Precisely how to deal with social context, within a single narrow age span, is not obvious; it is even more difficult across age periods—the content of the activities of a 14-week-old baby bear little resemblance to those of a 14-year-old adolescent.

Functional equivalence

A third question concerns the issue of functional equivalence. Crying in a six-month-old and crying in a 16-year-old, for example, are both real reflections of emotional expression. But do they have the same functional meaning, and is it sensible to regard correlations between the two as if they were reflections of continuity or discontinuity in development? Conversely, because behaviours appear different in form, does it follow that in functional (or genotypic) terms they are dissimilar? Obviously not (see Kagan 1980, Moss & Susman 1980)—developmental changes may modify or alter the particular manner in which a characteristic is manifest. But how does one determine what is functional equivalence for temperamental features?

Situations for measurement

A further issue stems from the question of which situations or circumstances to use when attempting to assess temperament. Is it preferable to measure an individual's temperamental qualities in terms of his or her response to new situations or new demands or, rather, is it better to assess them in terms of his or her behaviour in more habitual circumstances? Of course, some characteristics (such as adaptability) can be assessed only in relation to new situations because it is the nature of the child's response to novelty that reflects the characteristic. But that does not necessarily apply to other characteristics (such as emotional intensity). On the other hand, the routine of day-to-day activities may reduce the opportunity for individuality to be shown. But how does one decide what is novel? Is an outing to Hyde Park novel because previous outings have been to St. James' Park or do the park-like qualities of each make them comparable and hence non-novel? Is the coming of a different baby-sitter a new experience, or does it matter whether the child has previously had one or 43 baby-sitters?

Measuring instrument

Having decided on the answers to these questions, one faces the further issue of what sort of measuring instrument to use—should it be direct observation, questionnaire, interview or some form of mechanical measurement? The crucial point here concerns the need to sample behaviour over a wide range of situations and over a reasonably long span of time. Obviously, it would be pointless to attempt to assess adaptability or regularity of functioning on a single episode, because the very definition of the variable requires knowledge of a person's behaviour over time.

It was this consideration that led the New York group to choose the parent as the observer. They argued that the parent represented a potential source of extensive direct observations of the child over many situations and over a prolonged time and, hence, that if this experience could be adequately assessed it would constitute a rich and economical source of information on temperamental style. They, and those of us who have utilized interview measures (see Graham et al 1973, Thomas & Chess 1977), have relied on careful questioning about actual behaviour (rather than generalizations about supposed traits), and on detailed descriptions of specific examples in order to get an account of what the child *actually* does—an account that is as free from the biases of selective reporting or attitudinally influenced pre-judgements as skilled questioning can make it. There is no doubt that this method provides vivid and detailed accounts of temperamental style which give rise to measures that reflect individuality in the way intended.

There are, however, three main queries regarding interview assessments. The first concerns the validity of the reports. Do the differences in temperament reported by mothers simply reflect biased perceptions of their children? Dunn & Kendrick (1980) have investigated this issue, comparing mother's and observer's ratings and contrasting each with detailed observational measures. On the whole, the results are reassuring in that they indicate satisfactory validity for most variables. It seems most *un*likely that the differences are solely a function of biased perceptions, but more data are required before firm conclusions should be drawn.

The second query concerns the fact that the mother's information is necessarily limited to situations when she has been present. With older children, this is likely to mean that she has not observed behaviour in many of the situations of most interest. With pre-school children, of course, this is not as much of a problem, provided that the mother is the main caretaker (but it would be a problem with children in full-time day-care). However, to an important extent, everyone's behaviour is relatively situation-specific (see Mischel 1979, Bem & Funder 1978, Epstein 1979). The reported behaviour of the child may therefore be influenced as much by the pressure stemming from the family interaction patterns as by any qualities intrinsic to the child. The only satisfactory solution to that problem is to tap the child's behaviour by interviewing more than one informant. The third query stems from the fact that this form of detailed interviewing with cross-questioning and the eliciting of multiple examples is immensely time-consuming. Could not the whole process be streamlined by using a standard questionnaire?

Several investigators have developed questionnaires that show as much individuality as do the interview measures, with moderately satisfactory re-test reliability and with reasonable agreement between the scores on questionnaires completed by mothers and by fathers (see e.g. Persson-Blennow & McNeil 1979, Bates et al 1979). So far, so good—but there remains the major concern about whether questionnaires are more prone than interviews to the effects of perceptual or attitudinal distortions. The data on this point are sparse indeed but Bates et al (1979) found not only a low level of agreement between questionnaire measures and observational measures but also that the questionnaire measures showed associations with maternal characteristics whereas the observational measures did not. As this group points out, their finding is open to several different interpretations, depending in part on the weight attached to the observational data. The question of possible biases in questionnaire completion remains open and the matter requires further study.

Observational measures constitute a third possibility for the measurement of temperament. In some respects, they are more objective than either interview or questionnaire measures but they are the most time-consuming of all methods and are severely limited in their scope. By their nature, they can sample only one situation at a time and only certain sorts of situations at that. Because there are important situation-specificities in people's behaviour, it is only by taking *multiple* samples of behaviour that the investigator can maximize the chances of obtaining a valid appraisal of general response dispositions or temperamental attributes (Epstein 1979). For this reason, although observational data constitute valuable checks on interview and questionnaire measures, they cannot necessarily be assumed to constitute validating criteria and it is unlikely that they will prove to be the best general means of assessing temperamental features.

Categorization of temperamental features

Several questions need to be raised here but I shall focus on just three. The first is whether to concentrate on variations within the normal range or to focus on the few individuals showing extreme patterns. In an attempt to improve the psychometric properties of temperamental measures some investigators have rejected items applying to only small proportions of the population (Persson-Blennow & McNeil 1979) but perhaps it is precisely those extremes that predict best. The possibility requires examination.

The next two questions—how far to reduce the separate temperamental variables to a smaller number of factors or summary measures, and what criterion to use in deciding this matter—are most conveniently considered together. Different investigators have given different answers. Garside et al (1975) argued that the intercorrelations between the items (as reflected in a principal components analysis) should constitute the criterion. That is a statistically tidy solution, but is it sensible? I would suggest that it is not, for three rather different reasons: (a) especially with a questionnaire the intercorrelations are strongly influenced by the particular constructs (organization of ideas regarding behaviour) used by the rater; (b) the specific factors obtained tend to vary according to the statistical method employed and the sample studied (for example, the New York group derived factors of strikingly different composition); and (c) the fact that particular items intercorrelate with each other in a normal population may have little bearing on the grouping of items that predict best how an individual will respond to stress situations, or indeed to any other kind of outcome variable such as cognitive impairment, learning difficulties, or the development of psychiatric disorders (see e.g. Dunn et al 1981, Rutter et al 1964, Graham et al 1973, Hertzig 1982).

An alternative approach is to consider each of the many possible temperamental variables separately. This method has been followed by most investigators, at least as the first step in statistical analysis. It has paid off in so far as individual temperamental attributes have proved useful predictors for various sorts of outcome (see the last group of references cited above). On the other hand, in several investigations particular clusters or patterns of characteristics have proved much better predictors than any single characteristic.

This repeated finding has led to a third approach—namely, the development of various composite measures such as the 'temperamental adversity' index (Rutter 1978), the 'difficult child' index (Thomas Chess 1977, Hertzig 1982) and 'temperament risk' scores (Cameron 1978). Again, this approach has proved useful for predicting the development of emotional–behavioural problems. Nevertheless, it would be quite premature to regard any of these measures as having solved the question of how to categorize temperament. In the first place, although most of the composite measures are broadly similar, they differ in certain crucial respects and it remains uncertain which is superior. Secondly, empirical findings show that it is not always the same temperamental features that are crucial. Thus, for example, Schaffer (1966) found that high activity level was protective in a depriving institutional environment; Dunn et al (1981) found mood variables to be the best predictors of children's responses to the birth of a sibling; and Graham et al (1973) found irregularity, lack of malleability and low fastidiousness to be the attributes associated with the development of emotional–behavioural disorder in the children of mentally ill parents. It should *not* be assumed that the categorization of temperament that proves most effective for one purpose or in one situation will be equally effective in others. Nor should it be assumed that composite scores will always be more powerful than single variables (although it is likely that this will often be so). Nevertheless, the strategy of considering the categorization of temperament in terms of the groupings that best predict different sorts of outcome does seem worthwhile.

Implications of temperamental differences

Consistency

The question of consistency, of course, extends far beyond the issue of temperamental attributes in terms of the vigorous clashes over the last dozen years between trait theories and situationism theories. On the one hand, it has been argued that people's behaviour is highly inconsistent over time and place, being largely determined by situational factors (Mischel 1968). On the other, it has been asserted that genetically determined, semi-permanent personality dispositions play a major part in ensuring that people *do* behave consistently (Eysenck 1970). It is now clear that both extremes in these views must be rejected. The importance of personality traits is shown by the great individual variation in people's responses to any one situation, but the need to invoke environmental determinants is equally evident in the extent to which any person's mode of functioning alters from situation to situation (see Bem & Funder 1978, Epstein 1979). However, it is not sufficient to regard both the traits and the situations as important; a further question concerns the extent to which the two interact predictably (see Bem & Funder 1978). It would be misleadingly limiting to regard temperament as the reflection of the degree of similarity in a person's behaviour across all situations. Rather, some of the key aspects of temperament may concern the degree to which a person can adapt or modify his or her behaviour according to different environmental demands, or a person's vulnerability to certain kinds of stressors, or a tendency to respond in an unusual way to specific environments. These various kinds of ordinal and disordinal interaction effects* have been little explored up to now but the knowledge that they may be important in relation to temperamental variables has serious implications for the way in which we both assess temperament and analyse its effects.

Developmental change

The first reports from the New York study (Chess et al 1959) claimed that temperamental patterns were established in the first few months of life and remained stable thereafter. However, these workers' own empirical findings

---

*Ordinal interaction means that one variable (e.g. temperament) influences the *degree* to which a person responds to another variable (e.g. some environmental stressor) without altering the direction or type of response. In contrast, disordinal interaction means that the first variable alters the *direction* of response, so that some people react in one manner whereas others show an opposite response to the same second variable.

(Thomas & Chess 1977), as well as those of others, have been consistent in showing near-zero correlations from the first year of life to age five years onwards. There are various reasons why early infancy measures are likely to show little continuity with measures in later childhood (Rutter 1970). It should be noted especially that temperamental attributes in the first few months of life tend to show less of a genetic component than do the same attributes in later infancy or early childhood (Torgersen & Kringlen 1978, Matheny 1980); and whereas temperamental variables at age three or four years have generally shown significant associations with psychiatric risk, those in the first year of life often have not (see Rutter et al 1964, Cameron 1978). Nevertheless, temperamental attributes, even at age two, three or four years have usually been found to correlate at a very modest level ($r \approx 0.3$) with those assessed in middle childhood. Where does that leave the notion of an enduring temperamental style? Of course, life experiences of various kinds are likely to play their part in shaping temperament and these influences will, necessarily, reduce consistency over time. But the direction and degree of developmental change themselves may be genetically conditioned—as shown by the finding from the Louisville twin study (Matheny & Dolan 1975, Wilson 1977). In addition, as noted already, phenotypic expression may alter its form over the course of development so that the simple correlation of like behaviour with like behaviour may not constitute the most appropriate test for temperamental consistency.

Genetic influences

Up to now, the evidence regarding genetic influences on temperament has stemmed from a small number of twin studies, each based on rather different measures (not all of which have been entirely adequate for the assessment of temperament). However, there are particular problems in the use of twins for temperamental studies if interview or questionnaire measures are used. Because the measures are relative, because many parents like to emphasize the individuality of each twin, and because the other twin tends to constitute the main comparison for ratings, it is unlikely that the degree of difference within twin pairs (monozygotic or dizygotic) will be on the same scale as that between siblings or between unrelated children. There is a great need to utilize other genetic designs in addition to the twin method but, whatever the design, it will be important to examine the possibility that the genetic contribution concerns the overall *pattern* of temperamental functioning as much as the variation on each separate attribute.

Brain damage and mental retardation

Although some published reports suggest that brain damage or mental retardation may be associated with a distinctive pattern of temperamental functioning, there has been little systematic study of the matter (see Thomas & Chess 1977). It is apparent already that both retarded and brain-damaged children exhibit as wide a variety of temperamental characteristics as do normal children, and that few differences are found when individual temperamental features are considered. However, Hertzig's (1982) longitudinal study of low-birthweight infants has shown a significant association between abnormalities on a neurological examination and the 'difficult child' temperamental pattern. It is well established that brain damage and mental retardation carry a markedly increased psychiatric risk, and the possibility that this increased risk is due in part to an effect on the pattern of temperamental functioning warrants further study.

Sex differences

Numerous studies have shown that psychiatric disorder is substantially more common in boys than girls; also it has been found repeatedly that boys are more susceptible than girls to emotional–behavioural problems in association with family discord and disruption (Rutter 1981b). The reasons for this greater vulnerability of boys remain rather obscure but it would seem plausible that sex-linked temperamental differences might play a part. Accordingly, it seems surprising that most investigations have reported few, if any, significant sex differences in temperamental variables. However, the negative findings may be a consequence of looking at each attribute separately rather than examining composite scores associated with psychiatric risk. The question of possible sex differences in overall temperamental pattern requires further study.

Modes of operation of temperament

Perhaps the most fundamental question concerns the manner and mechanisms by which temperamental variables exert their effect. As we have seen, temperamental attributes are important predictors not only of how children respond to 'stress' situations but also of the likelihood that they will develop various types of emotional and behavioural disorder. But what do these statistical associations mean in terms of underlying mechanisms, and why are children with particular temperamental patterns more at risk than those with other temperamental features? Cameron (1978) used the geological metaphor of temperament reflecting 'fault lines' in the emerging personality so that behavioural 'earthquakes' arise in those children with 'fault lines' who experience environmental strains. However, this analogy seems both inapt and unhelpful. Why should particular temperamental patterns be regarded as 'faulty' and in what way do they put the child at risk? Dunn (1980) and Rutter (1977) suggest that children's temperamental differences may influence development through several mechanisms—including effects of these differences on how other people respond to and interact with the child; the shaping of life experiences; the determining of what is an *effective* environment for the child; the reflection of the child's social adaptive capacity i.e. malleability and adaptability in responding to altered environmental circumstances; and the rather imprecise concept of psychological vulnerability. There is a certain amount of empirical support for each of these mechanisms but the issues remain little explored up to now. We do not know, for example, how temperamental variables relate to psychophysiological measures such as autonomic reactivity or to styles of coping with stress situations.

Finally, we have only a limited understanding of the role of temperament in personality development. We use the term 'temperament' in childhood rather than 'personality' and we talk of the importance of temperamental variables in shaping the emerging personality, but just what does that mean? What is the relationship between temperamental attributes such as intensity of emotional expression and personality variables such as extraversion and neuroticism? Do the differences in terminology merely reflect differences in the concepts of the workers who introduced these various terms or are there basic developmental processes and changes that the different terms reflect?

Conclusions

As this brief review has emphasized, the last decade has seen a burgeoning of interest in temperament. There has been an accompanying substantial growth in our knowledge and understanding of the importance of temperamental differences. Temperament constitutes a variable of considerable predictive power in developmental psychopathology, a power with both practical and theoretical implications. But many difficult issues and problems still require resolution.

REFERENCES

Bates JE 1980 The concept of difficult temperament. Merrill-Palmer Q 26:299-319
Bates JE, Freeland CAB, Lounsbury ML 1979 Measurement of infant difficultness. Child Dev 50:794-803

Bem DJ, Funder DC 1978 Predicting more of the people more of the time: assessing the personality of situations. Psychol Rev 81:485-501

Billman J, McDevitt SC 1980 Convergence of parent and observer ratings of temperament with observations of peer interaction in nursery school. Child Dev 51:395-400

Buss AH, Plomin RA 1975 A temperament theory of personality development. Wiley Interscience, New York

Buss DM, Block JH, Block J 1980 Preschool activity level: personality correlates and developmental implications. Child Dev 51:401-408

Cameron JR 1978 Parental treatment, children's temperament, and the risk of childhood behavioral problems. 2: Initial temperament, parental attitudes, and the incidence and form of behavioral problems. Am J Orthopsychiatry 48: 141-147

Chess S, Thomas A, Birch HG 1959 Characteristics of the individual child's behavioral responses to the environment. Am J Orthopsychiatry 29:791-802

Dunn J 1980 Individual differences in temperament. In: Rutter M (ed) Scientific foundations of developmental psychiatry. Heinemann Medical, London, p 101-109

Dunn J, Kendrick C 1980 Studying temperament and parent–child interaction: comparison of interview and direct observation. Dev Med Child Neurol 22:494-496

Dunn J, Kendrick C, MacNamee R 1981 The reaction of first born children to the birth of a sibling: mothers' reports. J Child Psychol Psychiatry Allied Discip 22:1-18

Epstein S 1979 The stability of behaviour. 1: On predicting most of the people much of the time. J Pers Soc Psychol 37:1097-1126

Eysenck HJ 1970 The structure of human personality. Methuen, London

Garside RF, Birch HG, Scott DM, Chambers S, Kolvin I, Tweddle EG, Barber LM 1975 Dimensions of temperament in infant school children. J Child Psychol Psychiatry Allied Discip 16:219-232

Gesell A 1937 Early evidences of individuality in the human infant. Sci Monthly 45:217-225

Goldsmith HH, Gottesman II 1981 Origins of variation in behavioral style: a longitudinal study of temperament in young twins. Child Dev 52:91-103

Graham P, Rutter M, George S 1973 Temperamental characteristics as predictors of behavior disorders in children. Am J Orthopsychiatry 43:328-339

Hertzig ME 1982 Temperament and neurologic status. In: Rutter M (ed) Behavioral syndromes of brain dysfunction in childhood. Guilford Press, New York, in press

Kagan J 1980 Perspectives on continuity. In: Brim OG, Kagan J (eds) Constancy and change in human development. Harvard University Press, Cambridge, Mass., p 26-74

Keogh BK, Pullis ME 1980 Temperament influences on the development of exceptional children. Adv Spec Educ 1:239-276

Matheny AP 1980 Bayley's infant behavior record: behavioral components and twin analyses. Child Dev 51:1157-1167

Matheny AP, Dolan AB 1975 Persons, situations and time: a genetic view of behavioral change in children. J Pers Soc Psychol 32:1106-1110

Mischel W 1969 Personality and assessment. Wiley, London

Mischel W 1979 On the interface of cognition and personality: Beyond the person–situation debate. Am Psychol 34:740-754

Moss HA, Susman EJ 1980 Longitudinal study of personality development. In: Brim OG, Kagan J (eds) Constancy and change in human development. Harvard University Press, Cambridge, Mass., p 530-598

Persson-Blennow I, McNeil TF 1979 A questionnaire for measurement of temperament in six-month old infants: development and standardization. J Child Psychol Psychiatry Allied Discip 20:1-14

Rutter M 1970 Psychological development—predictions from infancy. J Child Psychol Psychiatry Allied Discip 11:49-62

Rutter M 1977 Individual differences. In: Rutter M, Hersov L (eds) Child psychiatry: modern approaches. Blackwell Scientific Publications, Oxford, p 3-21

Rutter M 1978 Family, area and school influences in the genesis of conduct disorder. In: Hersov LA et al (eds) Aggression and anti-social behaviour in childhood and adolescence. Pergamon Press, Oxford, p 95-113

Rutter M 1981a Stress, coping and development: some issues and some questions. J Child Psychol Psychiatry Allied Discip 22:323-356

Rutter M 1981b Epidemiological–longitudinal approaches to the study of development. In: Collins WA (ed) The concept of development. (Proc 15th Minnesota Symp on Child Psychol) Erlbaum, Hillsdale, NJ, in press

Rutter M, Birch H, Thomas A, Chess S 1964 Temperamental characteristics in infancy and the later development of behavioural disorders. Br J Psychiatry 110:651-661

Schaffer HR 1966 Activity level as a constitutional determinant of infantile reaction to deprivation. Child Dev 37:595-602

Thomas A, Chess S 1977 Temperament and development. Brunner/Mazel, New York

Torgersen AM, Kringlen E 1978 Genetic aspects of temperamental differences in infants. J Am Acad Child Psychol 17:433-444

Wilson RS 1977 Mental development in twins. In: Oliverio A (ed) Genetics, environment and intelligence. North-Holland Publishing, Amsterdam, p 305-334

DISCUSSION

Werry: You discussed only briefly the issue of the difference between temperament and personality. While it may be true that the study of children's temperament is relatively recent, that is not true of personality, for which sophisticated methods of analysis have long been available. What do you see as the fundamental difference between temperament and personality? Is temperament simply another name for personality when applied to children?

Rutter: I'm not sure, but it is striking that the two bodies of published work scarcely overlap or cross-reference. Temperament has tended to focus on rather specific aspects of behavioural style, rather than on general concepts such as neuroticism, extraversion and the like. Undoubtedly the two approaches should be brought together.

Werry: Many people believe still that personality is, primarily, constitutionally determined. But even if one eschews the question of aetiology, I think that temperament and personality are the same thing and that we are serving up old wine in new bottles. There is resistance to the concept of personality as a stable thing in children, who are supposed to be malleable, and thus a different term has been coined.

Thomas: One of the problems is what we mean by 'personality'. Although there is some consistency about what temperament means, for every 10

people involved in a discussion about personality one can obtain 15 definitions. There is a wide difference between the constitutional approach to personality and the psychodynamic approach, and that is where the problem lies. We ought to reach a consensus about the meaning of personality so that we can study it in relation to temperament.

Berger: I believe that the issues involved in definitions of personality and of temperament are much more complex than that, as I shall be discussing later in my paper (p 176-190).

Hsu: Cross-cultural studies sometimes give useful clues to answering the issues that Professor Rutter has raised about understanding temperament (see also p 113-119).

Rutter: There are, of course, opportunities to examine cultural differences even within the same country. Jerry Kagan's work on day care (Kagan et al 1978) showed striking temperamental differences between Chinese-American children and white American children. That result is interesting because the measures used in the two groups were the same, and one can be reasonably confident that they meant the same thing. The origins of those differences remain obscure, but I agree that cross-cultural studies are potentially very useful.

Hsu: The validity of studying sufficient numbers of comparable groups of children in different countries, with standardized instruments (i.e. methods of measurement), has already been established by Wolff (1973) as a means of highlighting the constitutional origin of neonates' reactions to alcohol. For instance, by using the same method, we may be able to see the similarities and dissimilarities between Chinese infants born and raised in the United States and in Taiwan.

Thomas: You mentioned, Professor Rutter, that boys surprisingly showed no significant differences in temperament from girls (Thomas & Chess 1977), even though the two sexes differ in rates of behavioural disorder. A reasonable hypothesis to explain this would be that even if the temperaments of boys and girls are similar, the reactions of people in the environment—parents and others—to the same temperamental characteristics in boys and in girls may be very different. This reaction may be crucial in accounting for the difference.

Rutter: Indeed it may. I raised the issue because of the striking disparity between the highly consistent differences between boys and girls, in almost any measure of psychopathology, and the contrasting responses of boys and girls to stress situations. A variety of behavioural measures also highlight striking differences between the sexes. It seems curious that, in most studies, temperamental differences between boys and girls are, on the whole, small. I remain unconvinced, however, that the different responses of people to boys and to girls is wholly a matter of cultural expectations rather than responses 'shaped' by actual differences in the *characteristics* of boys and girls. Some studies (Bell & Carver 1980, Smith & Lloyd 1978) have examined mother's responses to babies, in an attempt to differentiate the effects of cultural expectation and of the impact of sex differences in the babies' behaviour. The ingenious experimental strategy used for this purpose involved getting mothers to play with male and female babies presented in either sex-appropriate or cross-sex clothes and names. In this way it was possible to determine whether the mothers' style of interaction was most influenced by the perceived (but wrong) or the actual (but not perceived) sex of the child. The findings are not wholly consistent but they seem to demonstrate both expectational differences and differences that stem from the actual behaviour of the child. But this field has only just begun to be explored.

Wilson: In opposite-sexed twin-pairs that we have observed, there is a clear difference between the boys and the girls by the age of two years: the boys are generally more physically active, and this cannot be fully explained by parental expectation.

Hsu: In studies that have reported few sex differences, I suspect that the sample size was not large enough. In our study of children aged 3–7 years (Chen 1981) we found that in five of the nine temperamental categories described by Thomas & Chess (1977)—activity, intensity, mood, persistence, and distractibility—there were significant sex differences (see Table 1).

TABLE 1 (Hsu) Sex and temperament scores of young children

Temperament categories	Male children (n = 997)		Female children (n = 934)		
	Mean	SD	Mean	SD	t value
Activity	4.06	0.83	3.74	0.87	8.27**
Rhythmicity	4.47	0.79	4.45	0.78	0.57
Approach/Withdrawal	4.50	0.86	4.44	0.83	1.56
Adaptability	4.84	0.78	4.80	0.76	1.14
Intensity	3.87	0.75	3.78	0.80	2.55*
Mood	4.76	0.62	4.83	0.64	−2.44*
Persistence	3.98	0.62	3.92	0.59	2.18*
Distractibility	4.20	0.71	4.28	0.69	−2.51*
Threshold	3.30	0.77	3.25	0.78	1.42

$**P < 0.01$; $*P < 0.05$; Student's t-test: degrees of freedom, 1930; $t_{0.95} = 1.96$; $t_{0.99} = 2.58$

Rutter: Sample size is certainly one vital feature, and your sample must be one of the largest available. A further issue is whether one is looking at the *relevant* variables.

REFERENCES

Bell NJ, Carver W 1980 A re-evaluation of gender label effects: expectant mothers' responses to infants. Child Dev 51:925-927

Chen YH 1981 (June) A preliminary study of children's temperamental characteristics aged three to seven. Master's thesis, Institute of Public Health, National Taiwan University Medical College

Kagan J, Kearsley RB, Zelazo PR 1978 Infancy: its place in human development. Harvard University Press, Cambridge, Mass

Smith C, Lloyd B 1978 Maternal behavior and perceived sex of infant revisited. Child Dev 49:1263-1265

Thomas A, Chess S 1977 Temperament and development. Brunner/Mazel, New York

Wolff PH 1973 Vasomotor sensitivity to alcohol in diverse Mongoloid populations. Am J Hum Genet 25:193-199

Temperament questionnaires in clinical research

THOMAS F. McNEIL and INGER PERSSON-BLENNOW

Department of Psychiatry, University of Lund, Malmö Allmänna Sjukhus, 214 01 Malmö, Sweden

Abstract Parental questionnaires concerning the nine temperament variables studied in the New York longitudinal study have been developed for the measurement of children's temperament at six, 12 and 24 months of age. Retest reliability for the questionnaires was found to be generally satisfactory and at a level similar to that found in other temperament studies. The temperament characteristics of a large standardization sample, studied longitudinally over the three ages, showed little relation to the children's gender, birth order or social class. Factor analyses of the variables showed that two of the patterns were identical at 12 and 24 months of age: one pattern consisted of *mood, approach, adaptability* and *distractibility*, and the other of *activity, approach* and *intensity*. The standardization sample showed about the same rates of the 'difficult' and the 'slow-to-warm-up' temperament types, as found in early samples. The stability of the subjects' temperament scores over time was low to moderate, and a majority of the subjects changed their temperament type over the 18 months covered by the longitudinal study. The use of temperament questionnaires in clinical research is illustrated in three current studies.

Our research on temperament began in 1971 when we were selecting measures for a longitudinal, multidimensional study of newborn children who were at high risk for the later development of psychopathological conditions (McNeil & Kaij 1982). The ultimate goal of the study was to attempt to identify early-life characteristics of the children and their environments which might predict later disturbance. We were thus looking for measures that would effectively and reliably assess individual characteristics of infants and that might have predictive value for psychopathological conditions.

Our interest in temperament and our approach to its study were formed by two articles which appeared in 1970. Thomas et al (1970) discussed the nine variables in the New York longitudinal study (NYLS), the importance of temperament for parent–child interaction, the temperament types and the

1982 Temperamental differences in infants and young children. Pitman Books Ltd, London (Ciba Foundation symposium 89) p 20-35

apparent predictive value of temperament for behaviour disorders, and this work suggested that the nine NYLS variables should be part of our longitudinal study. About the same time, Carey (1970) first described the practicality, usefulness and advantages of studying the NYLS temperament variables by questionnaire, rather than by parental interview. We were inspired by this article, and began developing temperament questionnaires in Swedish which were appropriate for Swedish child-rearing conditions.

We thus came to develop parental questionnaires relevant for the study of children at six, 12 and 24 months of age, and these questionnaires were used in our longitudinal high-risk project (McNeil & Kaij 1982). Since that time, our study of temperament has branched out beyond this high-risk project. A demographically representative sample of 160 children from Malmö, used for standardizing the questionnaires, also provided the opportunity to study temperament *per se*, e.g. its stability over time, its relation to gender and social class, and the factor structure among the nine variables. Both the standardization sample and the samples in the high-risk project have been followed up on temperament characteristics at about six years of age, using a Swedish translation of the Thomas & Chess (1977) parental questionnaire for 3–7-year-olds.

We have also used both our own and the Thomas & Chess questionnaires in a number of clinical research studies related to psychiatry, paediatrics and obstetrics. In these clinical studies, temperament is used primarily as an aid in evaluating the effect of other influences on children and parents, rather than as a study of temperament *per se*. Throughout these studies, we have retained the nine NYLS variables as defined by Thomas et al (1963).

In this paper we shall first describe the questionnaires we have used, and then summarize our results to date concerning the temperament characteristics of the standardization sample. Thereafter, we shall illustrate the use of these questionnaires in three clinical research projects that are currently in progress.

Characteristics of our three questionnaires

Our own instruments (measurement techniques) consist of parental questionnaires (Persson-Blennow & McNeil 1979, 1980) for the measurement of the nine NYLS temperament variables (*rhythm, activity, mood, approach, adaptability, intensity, threshold, attention-persistence, distractibility*) in children at about six, 12 and 24 months of age.

Our approach to measurement makes no assumptions about the origins of the child's temperament characteristics measured at the time of study. An interactional network of influence and counter-influence between parent and child may well have affected the child's temperament. However, given a choice between measuring the child's own (current) temperament (evidenced by his or her behaviour) and the parent's personal view of the child's temperament, we have intended to *maximize* the measurement of the child's *personal temperament* and to *minimize* the direct influence of *parental attitude* on the measurement. This was done, as suggested by Thomas et al (1963), by formulating the items in the questionnaires in terms of the child's actual behaviour in concrete situations, so as to diminish the possible effect of generalized parental value judgements about the child. When we felt it was important to understand the nature of the parent's attitude towards the child and/or the parent–child interaction, we studied these factors directly, as in clinical research examples I and III below (p 24, 27).

The questionnaires for the three different age-groups consist of 44, 49 and 47 scored items respectively (13, nine and four additional items respectively are included in the questionnaires for contextual reasons but are not scored). The degree of overlap in question content is about 75% between the questionnaires at six and 12 months, and about 70% between those at 12 and 24 months.

The questions are of the multiple-choice type, mostly having three alternative answers, the remainder having five alternatives. The following example is a question about rhythm:

'When does the baby wake up in the morning?
   (a) The time usually varies by more than an hour.
   (b) Quite often at the same time, but sometimes more than half an hour earlier or later (than usual).
   (c) At the same time (within half an hour of the usual time)'.

Each item is scored as 0 (low), 1 or 2 (high) points on the relevant variable. A subject's score for a temperament variable is computed as the mean of the scores for all answered items relevant to that variable. Thus, for each of the nine variables, the child is described by a mean score with a possible range of 0.00 to 2.00.

Parents report that completion of the questionnaire takes about 15 min. Scoring of the questionnaire by overlay templates takes about 5 min and requires little training or special skills.

Retest reliability of the questionnaires (over a 2–4-week period) has been studied on randomly chosen samples. The retest correlations for the variables ranged from +0.50 to +0.92 (mean of +0.70) for the six-month form, +0.16 to +0.90 (mean of +0.63) for the 12-month form, and +0.56 to +0.84 (mean of +0.65) for the 24-month form (Persson-Blennow & McNeil 1982a). These values are similar to those of several other studies.

Temperament findings from the study of the standardization sample

The norms for the questionnaires were developed on a demographically representative sample of 160 children from Swedish-speaking families chosen from Malmö's 29 Well-Baby Clinics (Persson-Blennow & McNeil 1979, 1980). The parents of the children in the sample were contacted in person at the Clinics at six months of age, and were thereafter followed up by *postal* questionnaires at 12 and 24 months, with a 94% follow-up success at 12 months and 93% success at 24 months.

The frequency of unanswered items in the sample's questionnaires was 3.5% at six months, 5.4% at 12 months and 9.2% at 24 months. At all three ages, adaptability was the most difficult variable to represent with items that were applicable to all subjects. The scores on the temperament variables showed a broad range and balanced distributions, providing good discrimination between subjects.

These scores were studied in relation to the subjects' gender, birth order and social class (Persson-Blennow & McNeil 1981). Among the large number of analyses performed, very few significant relationships were found between temperament and these three features. At least in Sweden, these three factors therefore do not appear to play an important role in determining individual differences in temperament at these ages. Further, the three questionnaires should generally be usable without taking the subject's gender, birth order and social class into consideration.

The data for the temperament variables in the standardization sample were factor analysed (principal components, with oblique rotation) separately at each age, in order to study patterns among the variables (Persson-Blennow & McNeil 1982b). No firm, interpretable factor structure was obtained for the six-month data. In contrast, the analyses identified two factors that were identical at 12 and 24 months. One factor included mood, approach, adaptability and distractibility; and the other included activity, approach and intensity. These factors were thus similar but not identical to the NYLS 'easy–difficult child' and 'slow-to-warm-up child' patterns, each having three variables in common. Our results on factor analysis are also similar to the results of other studies (McDevitt 1976, A. Sameroff, personal communication, 1976, Scholom 1975), which group mood, approach and adaptability together on one factor, and activity and intensity together on another factor.

The current sample showed about the same rate of difficult child and slow-to-warm-up types as in the NYLS (when these are defined by 4–5 signs of the type) and a slightly lower rate of the difficult type than Carey (1970, 1972) found on his criteria (I. Persson-Blennow & T. F. McNeil, unpublished results, 1981).

The stability of the individual subjects' temperament scores was studied over the three ages (I. Persson-Blennow & T. F. McNeil, unpublished results, 1981). Stability on the variables (expressed in terms of the product–moment correlation coefficient) was, at most, moderate: the correlations for contiguous ages ranged from $+0.10$ to $+0.50$, with a mean of $+0.31$. The values from six to 24 months ranged from $+0.01$ to $+0.34$, with a mean of $+0.17$. The variables on which the subjects were most stable were rhythm, mood, approach, adaptability and activity. Deviant-scoring children were generally less stable than were middle-scoring children, and over 50% of the children scoring more than 1 SD away from the group mean for a variable at one age scored within 1 SD of the mean on that variable at the next age.

Further, a majority of the subjects changed temperament type over the 18 months covered by the study. Over all age intervals studied, the difficult child type was less stable than the easy child. These findings strongly suggest that more attention should be paid to the age(s) at which children show the types of temperament that might predict other characteristics beyond temperament itself.

Swedish version of the Thomas and Chess questionnaire

Drs A. Thomas and S. Chess kindly granted us permission to use and to translate directly into Swedish their parental questionnaire for children 3–7 years of age (Thomas & Chess 1977). The questionnaire contains 72 questions, with eight questions representing each of the nine NYLS temperament variables. The questions contain a short behavioural/situational statement (e.g. '21. My child likes to try new foods') followed by a seven-point answer scale from 1, representing 'hardly ever', to 7, representing 'almost always'. A child's score for a particular variable is the mean of the scores for the questions answered for that variable.

Temperament in clinical research

Example I: Longitudinal study of children at high psychiatric risk

As described above, temperament questionnaires were selected for use as one of a number of measures in our study of children at high risk for the development of psychopathological conditions (McNeil & Kaij 1982). The samples in this study included the offspring of women with a history of non-organic psychoses, i.e. 'process' schizophrenic, cycloid, affective, psychogenic, *post partum* and other (diverse) diagnostic categories of psychosis, as well as the offspring of demographically matched control parents with no history of hospitalization for psychosis.

The first phase of this longitudinal study covered the period from the mother's pregnancy until the child was two years old. The measures used were: evaluation of the mother's physical and mental health during pregnancy; interviews concerning her experience of and attitude towards both pregnancy and her social situation; observation of the child's birth and delivery regarding both its somatic and its 'psychosocial' aspects (e.g. parental experience, early parent–child interaction); assessment of neonatal neurological and somatic characteristics; and detailed and repeated observation of mother–child interaction from three days *post partum* up to one year of age, at which time attachment to the mother was also studied. Our temperament questionnaires were completed by the parents at six, 12 and 24 months of age; the questionnaires were delivered *in person* to the parents at six and 12 months and sent *by mail* at 24 months.

These samples are currently being followed up at about six years of age. In addition to inclusion of parental interviews concerning the child and the home and family environment, the follow-up includes assessment of the child by the Griffith developmental scale, the *continuous performance test* of attention, the *children's apperception test*, and a scale for motoric development and performance. The parents are also asked to complete the Swedish translation of the Thomas & Chess temperament questionnaire.

This project gives the opportunity not only to test the possibly predictive value of temperament for the development of psychopathological conditions in groups chosen to be at high risk and at normal risk, but also to put temperament characteristics in a longitudinal, developmental and multidimensional perspective in both groups of children.

The temperament results available for this study at present (McNeil & Kaij 1982) can be summarized as follows. The *combined* high-risk and control sample ($n = 158$ at six months, 149 at 12 months and 147 at 24 months) showed very little difference from the standardization sample in the means and SDs for the nine temperament variables and in the frequency of temperament types (difficult child, slow-to-warm-up, etc). The special characteristics of the children in the longitudinal samples, both personally and in terms of their participation in this extensive study, do not appear to have had any substantial effect on the children's temperament scores.

Comparison of the *total* high-risk group versus total control group on the temperament variables showed small and generally non-significant differences (two significant among 27), and similarly little difference in rates for the temperament types.

Comparison of the specific diagnostic groups with their matched controls showed few statistically significant differences in group mean score for the variables, and these differences were inconsistent over the three ages at which measurements were made. In contrast, the comparison of specific diagnostic groups with their controls in terms of the *frequency* of the temperament types appeared to separate the offspring of the schizophrenics and the cycloids from those of the other diagnostic groups. While the offspring of the other diagnostic groups showed no differences, or even a somewhat lower number of difficult and slow-to-warm-up types, as compared with their controls, the offspring of the cycloid and the schizophrenic mothers (as compared with their controls) showed a higher number of the difficult and slow-to-warm-up types (as defined by 4–5 signs; see McNeil & Kaij 1982). The association of these temperament types with the other characteristics of the offspring and their environments is undergoing further analysis.

Example II: Study of the effects on the child of delivery by vacuum extraction

Vacuum extraction (VE) is an instrumental aid that has largely replaced the use of forceps in delivery in Sweden and other parts of Europe (Brody 1970). In typical VE, a suction cup is applied to the leading part of the fetus' head during a somewhat advanced stage of delivery, the vacuum being increased step-wise to a maximum of 0.8 kg cm^{-2}. The fetus is extracted by pull on a rubber tube, attached to the suction cup, synchronously with the mother's contractions.

While mortality after VE is reported to be low, these children have an over-representation of asphyxia, cephalhaematoma and minor scalp lesions, as well as a slightly increased frequency of intracranial bleeding (Brody 1970). Our colleagues from the Department of Paediatrics in Lund (Blennow et al 1977) have systematically studied not only the somatic consequences for the child of delivery by VE but also the later behavioural problems, and these workers thus included our temperament measures in the follow-up of their cases. The questionnaires were mailed to the parents at appropriate ages of the children.

The Lund sample ($n = 46$), while otherwise demonstrating somatic normality, showed cytological signs of haemorrhage in the cerebrospinal fluid in 42% of the infants (as compared with 10% in cases of normal delivery). Further, 25% of the VE cases had shown 'behavioural problems' (i.e. disturbed sleep habits, colics, breath-holding spells, unusual sound sensitivity) at some time prior to the follow-up at 14 months of age. The behavioural disturbances were found mostly when the indication for the VE was 'maternal' rather than 'fetal' (i.e. asphyxia). The analysis of temperament characteristics of children in relation to the indication for the VE should thus be of special interest.

In order to study temperament in a larger VE sample, we contacted *by mail* the parents of all children delivered by VE in Malmö during a 13-month period when the children were at appropriate ages (6–24 months), and we asked the parents to complete our temperament questionnaires (I. Persson-Blennow & T. F. McNeil, unpublished results, 1981). The Malmö VE sample consisted of 99, 151 and 140 children at six, 12 and 24 months respectively. The possible effects of the study on the parental answers to the questionnaire should be minimal in the Malmö sample, as compared with the Lund sample (Blennow et al 1977) because the Malmö sample was not studied extensively in any other way, and the temperament study was not presented to the parent specifically as an evaluation of the possibly negative effects of VE on children's characteristics. We intend to compare temperament scores in the VE sample with those in the standardization sample, and with the different indications for VE.

Example III: Study of the psychological effects of identifying children at high somatic risk

One in every 500 individuals in the Swedish population has a high risk of chronic obstructive lung disease in adulthood as a result of an inherited deficiency of α_1-antitrypsin, a protein found in the blood (Sveger 1978). The risk of chronic lung disease in these individuals is greatly increased by contact with air pollutants, and a considerable preventive effect, which postpones the onset of chronic lung disease, is obtained by protecting the high-risk individual from tobacco smoke and from employment in environments with concentrated air pollution.

A general population screening for antitrypsin deficiency (ATD) may be readily done on newborns, using the same blood sample as that taken for phenylketonuria screening; from somatic and economic viewpoints, general screening for ATD is optimally done in the newborn phase (Sveger 1978). However, serious questions remain about the psychological and psychosocial consequences for the individual and his or her family when the identification of ATD takes place early in life.

From November 1972 to September 1974, all newborns in Sweden (200 000) were screened for ATD in the neonatal period. The degree of deficiency for each newborn identified as having ATD was determined by a new blood test and the parents were informed of the deficiency when the child was about three months of age.

A number of paediatricians who informed the parents about the child's ATD and conducted the medical follow-up of the cases reported that the information about the child's ATD could be highly anxiety-producing for the parents and could have a very negative effect on the parent–child relationship. As a result of these observations, the Swedish general newborn screening program for ATD was discontinued.

The need for a systematic evaluation of the psychological consequences of the neonatal screening was strongly felt. We thus began a follow-up of 61 of the families when the children with ATD were 5–7 years of age (T. F. McNeil, T. Thelin, E. Aspegren-Jansson, T. Sveger, B. Harty, unpublished results, 1981). The primary hypothesis to be tested was that the identification and follow-up of the child's ATD had negatively influenced the parents' view of the child, the parent–child relationship and, possibly, the child's behaviour and personal characteristics, including temperament.

A demographically similar control group ($n = 61$) was also studied, for comparison. As far as we know, there is no inherent biological reason for any systematic differences in temperament characteristics between the ATD and control groups. Any observed differences in the children's temperament reported by the parents should thus reflect the psychological consequences of the ATD-identification and follow-up; these consequences could be seen either (a) in the parent's attitude towards and subjective experience of the child's characteristics and/or (b) in the child's real behavioural style.

The methods used included a detailed interview with each parent and the direct study of mother–child interaction in a structured play situation, both methods being used in the home. The parental interview contained, among other topics, a number of questions regarding the parent's subjective view of the child's temperament characteristics. Each parent was also asked to fill in the Swedish version of the Thomas & Chess parental questionnaire for temperament in 3–7-year-olds.

Our use of temperament in this investigation involved both (a) the straightforward measurement of the child's temperament characteristics, as reported by the parent in the questionnaire and interview, and (b) an indirect strategy mentioned by Carey (1970) for the study of parental attitudes toward the child. In this second approach, the parent's general subjective rating of the child's temperament characteristics is compared with the temperament scores obtained through a behaviourally oriented questionnaire also completed by the parent. The extent and direction of possible discrepancies between the ratings and the questionnaire scores may indicate a tendency by the parent to view the child as generally more positive or negative (e.g. in mood, approach, adaptability) than indicated by the behaviour reported in the questionnaire.

For the interview on temperament we simply asked the parent for his or her view of the child's characteristics: e.g. 'How active do you think the child is?' (activity); 'Would you say he or she is a creature of habit?' (rhythm); 'Does he or she generally like new things?' (approach). All nine NYLS variables except intensity and threshold could be studied in this way in the interview; no adequate general question could be formed in Swedish for intensity, and threshold was changed to 'irritability–touchiness', to be more congruent with the answers received from the parents.

The interview items were scored on carefully defined five-point scales by a trained researcher using a transcript of the interview. All information identifying a transcript as belonging either to an ATD or to a control subject was removed before scoring, which was done blindly also with respect to the subject's group status and other project data. Independent inter-scorer agreement (tested on 20 cases) was found to be high, with a range of inter-scorer coefficients from +0.76 to +0.98 (mean = +0.89) for the seven temperament variables.

We intend to test the hypothesis of a negative effect of ATD-identification. This will involve comparison of the ATD and control groups, both in the temperament scores from the interview and questionnaires and in the extent and direction of discrepancies between the parent's report for the same variable in the interview and questionnaire. These discrepancies will also be related to parental attitudes toward the child, as studied directly in the interview.

While temperament was included in this clinical study for the purpose of evaluating the effect of ATD-identification, such study yields (as usual) opportunities to learn more about temperament *per se* and its relationship to other variables. We intend to analyse e.g. (a) the degree of similarity between the mother's and the father's reports of the temperament characteristics of the same child, (b) the relationship between the child's temperament scores and the mother's and child's behavioural characteristics during their interaction in the structured play situation, and (c) the relationship between temperament and a host of other characteristics of the parent, the child and the family, as studied through the parental interviews, personal observation in the home, medical records and population registers.

Concluding comments on temperament questionnaires, from a constructor's and user's viewpoint

The task of constructing temperament questionnaires is, in reality, very difficult. To satisfy the demands and requirements of parents, clinicians, theoreticians, psychometricians, child development researchers, and perhaps even one's own particular fancies and biasses often feels like an impossible task.

In the first steps of constructing a questionnaire, it seems difficult enough to choose a sufficient number of behaviours, in situations for e.g. a six-month-old child, which represent abstractly defined concepts that are to become variables, and that keep mood separate from approach, activity separate from intensity, attention–persistence separate from distractibility, etc. The items have to be expressed in simple, unambiguous language and be clearly related to the mother's everyday experience with the child, yet they should be (we feel) at least somewhat independent of her management of the child. The choice and development of such items presents no easy task.

The demands then placed on these poor items are that: they should be answerable by all parents and relevant to all children; they should show balanced distributions, and discriminate between high and low scorers on the variable; they should correlate highly with the score for the total variable, and not be thought by blind judges to represent other variables; they should be answered in the same way by the parent who is given the unexpected (and perhaps undesired) opportunity to complete the very same questionnaire twice within a short period of time; they should be answered similarly by the father whose primary experience with the baby often consists of short contacts in the morning and evening; they should reflect a behavioural style which the baby (and mother) will show when a scientist comes to observe them even on only one or two occasions; and, preferably, they should predict something important or abnormal about the child in the future.

It is more than a rhetorical question to ask how many existing research methods of any type and field have even a majority of these desirable characteristics. As users of temperament questionnaires in research, we really wish they did have all of these qualities!

To the user, the most obvious characteristic of temperament questionnaires is the ease in collecting and scoring data. They can be mailed to large samples and over large geographical areas. They can be filled in while the researcher is not waiting or watching. They can generally be scored quickly and reliably by clerical assistants with little training or special skills. They can be made readily available to other researchers for standardized use across studies. They are inexpensive.

In many cases, temperament questionnaires do not tell us everything we want to know about a child's behaviour, the environment in which the behaviour occurs, or the parent's attitude towards the child and experience of the child's characteristics. In such situations, we have—as illustrated above in clinical research examples I and III—also used other methods such as observation and parental interviews to complement the information obtained via the questionnaires. The choice of questionnaires rather than, or in combination with, other research methods should depend on the goals of a particular study and on its practical possibilities for collecting data.

Acknowledgements

Our research has been supported by grants from the Swedish Medical Research Council (Nos. 3793, 5453, 6214), the Bank of Sweden Tercentenary Foundation (No. 71/88), and the National Institutes of Health, USA (No. MH18857).

REFERENCES

Blennow G, Svenningsen NW, Gustafson B, Sundén B, Cronquist S 1977 Neonatal and prospective follow-up study of infants delivered by vacuum extraction (VE). Acta Obstet Gynecol Scand 56:189-194

Brody S 1970 Obstetrik och gynekologi. Almqvist & Wiksell, Stockholm

Carey WB 1970 A simplified method for measuring infant temperament. J Pediatr 77:188-194

Carey W B 1972 Clinical applications of infant temperament measurement. J Pediatr 81:823-828

McDevitt S 1976 A longitudinal assessment of continuity and stability in temperamental characteristics from infancy to early childhood. PhD thesis, Temple University, Pennsylvania (University Microfilms No. 77-13571, Ann Arbor, Michigan)

McNeil TF, Kaij L 1982 Offspring of women with nonorganic psychoses. In: Watt NF et al (eds) Children at risk for schizophrenia: a longitudinal perspective. Cambridge University Press, New York, in press

Persson-Blennow I, McNeil TF 1979 A questionnaire for measurement of temperament in six-month-old infants: development and standardization. J Child Psychol Psychiatry Allied Discip 20:1-13

Persson-Blennow I, McNeil TF 1980 Questionnaires for measurement of temperament in one- and two-year-old children: development and standardization. J Child Psychol Psychiatry Allied Discip 21:37-46

Persson-Blennow I, McNeil TF 1981 Temperament characteristics of children in relation to gender, birth order and social class. Am J Orthopsychiatry 51:710-714

Persson-Blennow I, McNeil TF 1982a Research note: new data on test–retest reliability for three temperament scales. J Child Psychol Psychiatry Allied Discip, in press

Persson-Blennow I, McNeil TF 1982b Factor analysis of temperament characteristics in children at six months, one year and two years of age. Br J Educ Psychol, in press

Scholom A 1975 The relationship of infant and parent temperament to the prediction of child adjustment. PhD thesis, Michigan State University (University Microfilms No. 76-5635, Ann Arbor, Michigan)

Sveger T 1978 α_1-antitrypsin deficiency in early childhood. Pediatrics 62:22-25

Thomas A, Chess S 1977 Temperament and development. Brunner/Mazel, New York

Thomas A, Chess S, Birch HG, Hertzig ME, Korn S 1963 Behavioral individuality in early childhood. New York University Press, New York

Thomas A, Chess S, Birch HG 1970 The origin of personality. Sci Am 223(2):102-109

DISCUSSION

Wolkind: On the question of methodology, you've shown that there are discrepancies about the temperamental categories to which various descriptive items belong, but are you content about the temperamental categories themselves? Do we have enough evidence that there really is, for example, a category of general 'rhythmicity' for a baby or infant, and that all items asking about this are dealing with the same dimensions? I ask this because we found that rhythmicity in feeding and in sleeping went together very well, whereas rhythmicity of bowel motions correlated negatively with those items.

McNeil: Our studies began by simply assuming the theoretical homogeneity of the nine temperamental categories that Thomas et al (1963) first described, in an attempt to confirm their results. Therefore we purposely did not question the homogeneity of each category but, rather, we tended to choose items that would be homogeneous and to remove items that would not. I understand that other workers (Rapoport et al 1977, Bates et al 1979, Rowe & Plomin 1977, Bohlin et al 1979, Wolkind & De Salis, this volume, p 221–239) who have done factor analysis of *items*, rather than factor analysis of *variables*, tend to obtain different constellations of items and variables. The question of how separate these nine variables are is another matter. Most of the judges in the content validity study that I have done (T. F. McNeil, unpublished paper, 1981) said that their job of blindly assigning items to variables was difficult. A few did not feel that anything was wrong with the items themselves, but that the nine variables were not as discrepant from one another as they should be. This is indeed so; the difference between approach and adaptability, for example, is a question of time.

Hinde: I don't think that the question has really been answered: if rhythmicity in bowel movement is not related to rhythmicity in other issues, then what exactly is the status of rhythmicity when one sums all these together?

Torgersen: Indeed that is a relevant question. In my study the items in the category of regularity broadly covered the defined aspects of the category—sleep, bowel movement and eating—and the inter-scorer agreement on each item was exceptionally high; nevertheless the correlation between the different items was low (see p 141).

Thomas: This again raises cross-cultural considerations. Differences in reported regularity in sleep, feeding and bowel movement may reflect different cultural norms. Attitudes of the parents or, indeed, of the raters to different child-care practices, and therefore to different categories, may be more variable within one cultural group than in another.

Rutter: Where do we go from here? Quite apart from the measurement issues that you focused on, Dr McNeil, there is the question of whether we should be dealing with *these* nine variables in the first place and, even if the answer is 'yes', there is the further issue of which behaviours should be included in them.

McNeil: I don't really know how to answer this. How important are these variables as concepts? I presume that they have been useful because they were originally brought out of a clinical context. They were derived largely from very young children, and parents were, presumably, concerned about these aspects of temperament. If one can side-step one of the sacred principles of measurement—namely, that the items for a variable have to intercorrelate highly and the variable be homogeneous—then one can consider what happens when rhythmicity in eating and sleeping and bowel movements are not highly correlated with one another over a whole sample: if the parent nevertheless has a concept, or an understanding, of rhythmicity, then a child who shows rhythmicity in all three items will be seen as more rhythmical than a child who shows it only in two, or one, or none. If the basic variable itself is important—for example, if the variable constitutes something clinically relevant—then it can be useful to measure it even if it is not homogeneous for the entire sample.

Hinde: You used the word 'basic variable', and that is precisely where the assumptions lie: the question I am raising is whether one can say that there is a basic variable.

McNeil: Well, how does one ever find a basic variable? Is it given by God, or by Thomas & Chess, or by a factor analysis? One can assume that something is homogeneous at different levels: the answer to a given *item* may not be homogeneous because, for example, a child may behave in a particular way at one time but not at other times, depending on where the child is, or on who is present. One has to set a starting point somewhere.

Carey: Your study of how the raters dealt with the individual items is fascinating, but one should remember that the questionnaires, as used both clinically and for research, are completed by mothers. The final test of how well they work should, therefore, be not how the questionnaires are judged by experts but how they are completed by mothers. We handled this in our questionnaire construction by running off, in both the pretest and the standardization phases, item–category correlations and by discarding the items that failed to correlate sufficiently with their respective categories. If the items correlated better with another category, we either reassigned them or reworded them, or removed them altogether (Carey & McDevitt 1978, McDevitt & Carey 1978).

McNeil: That approach deals with two different aspects: the question of what *correlates* with what, and the question of what, on a *theoretical* basis, belongs to what. As long as one is supposed to be measuring and representing an abstractly defined and (we hope) homogeneous theoretical concept, it is important that the items do *represent* each particular concept. For example, one may find high correlations between attitudes towards pregnancy and length of breast-feeding, which don't necessarily belong to the same abstract concept. The point is, what name does one give to the phenomenon one is measuring? The mother may view fifteen questions as belonging together very closely, and yet these questions may not represent any previously known variable; at that point one may have to decide whether to put them into another, new category which may be more important than the categories of threshold or attention-persistence.

Keogh: In our work (Keogh et al, unpublished report) we asked fathers, mothers and teachers to rate the same children, and we obtained a somewhat different factor structure for the parental and the teachers' questionnaires. The teachers attach different values to persistence and distractibility in preschool children than do the parents. The expectations about children's performance in school are quite different from what they are at home, at least for four- and five-year-olds. The possible complications are, therefore, not just within the parent scales but in the comparison of teachers' and parents' views of the same youngsters.

Carey: Let me clarify. We started by asking the judges to rate the items and, when we obtained good agreement on that, we went on to see whether the mothers agreed that these items were related to each other in the manner mentioned a moment ago. Thus, item selection was a two-stage process.

Thomas: We used the same two-stage process (Thomas & Chess 1977).

McNeil: Two of these questionnaires have already been put through content validity analysis at construction, i.e. those of McDevitt & Carey (1978) and Thomas & Chess (1977).

Robinson: I would like to ask some questions about the clinical studies that you mentioned. I was not surprised that you found no differences between the groups in the vacuum extraction study because you were dealing with highly heterogeneous conditions in each group. It is very difficult, of course, to separate the effects of the vacuum extraction itself from the effects of the indications for vacuum extraction. Some of the indications for vacuum extraction—for example, difficulty in the mother's ability to push down during labour—will relate not only to organic components but also to the mother's personality. So there are many variables in that clinical context.

McNeil: While temperament is not related to delivery by vacuum extraction *per se*, we are currently looking at the relationship between temperament and the indications for the vacuum extraction in our samples.

Robinson: I have a more fundamental question, about the α_1-antitrypsin work that you have described. Have you discovered what one might call a genetic marker for basic temperament? I don't know whether the chromosome that carries the gene coding for α_1-antitrypsin is known, but if other genetic markers are near it on the same chromosome, then one might, by using cross-linkage observations, begin to define the locus associated with the behavioural variables we are discussing.

McNeil: No-one examining the physiological side of this work, as far as I know, thinks that there should be any correlation between personality and this α_1-antitrypsin defect or other somatic correlates.

Robinson: Your work may help to answer this.

McNeil: The only way to test that, of course, is to study temperament in a group of children who have α_1-antitrypsin deficiency but whose parents do not yet know about the condition. That would be illegal in Sweden.

Chess: I would like to deal with the question of what the different temperamental attributes mean. We came up with nine variables; Mike Rutter and Philip Graham have added a tenth—fastidiousness—which Americans tend not to understand (Graham et al 1973). Within the nine that we've identified, rhythmicity is not the only category with problems about the answers on individual items. This is largely because we are dealing with human beings, who have a terrible tendency not to fit smoothly into niches! For example, some children will have a long attention span with almost any task they start but it is much more common to find selectivity towards different tasks, and the score for attention span will not necessarily indicate this selectivity. In some cases, motivation changes, depending on social scene, or fortuitous events may evoke a persisting interest within the child. In almost every category it is difficult to obtain perfect measurements, because people are people. Some of us, who are clinicians, focus on how these ideas on temperament can be translated for the needs of parents or teachers. Others are more interested in trait versus situational behaviour as theoretical concepts, aside from how they are translated into clinical usage. We may never reach the point of having an absolutely satisfactory measuring technique that will serve everybody's purpose.

Rutter: The implication, then, is that one has to look to a variety of different kinds of prediction from temperament to 'something else' (such as the patterns of interaction or the person's behaviour at some other time or place) in order to justify which temperamental variables are useful.

REFERENCES

Bates JE, Freeland CA, Lounsbury ML 1979 Measurement of infant difficultness. Child Dev 50:794-803

Bohlin G, Hagekull B, Lindhagen K 1979 Early individuality: dimensions in infant behavior. Uppsala University, Sweden (Uppsala Psychological Reports No. 248.)

Carey WB, McDevitt SC 1978 Revision of the infant temperament questionnaire. Pediatrics 61:735-739

Graham P, Rutter M, George S 1973 Temperamental characteristics as predictors of behavior disorders in children. Am J Orthopsychiatry 43:328-339

McDevitt S, Carey WB 1978 The measurement of temperament in 3–7 year old children. J Child Psychol Psychiatry Allied Discip 19:245-253

Rapoport JL, Pandoni C, Renfield M, Lake CR, Ziegler MG 1977 Newborn dopamine-β-hydroxylase, minor physical anomalies, and infant temperament. Am J Psychiatry 134:676-679

Rowe DC, Plomin R 1977 Temperament in early childhood. J Pers Assess 41:150-156

Thomas A, Chess S, Birch HG, Hertzig ME, Korn S 1963 Behavioral individuality in early childhood. New York University Press, New York

Thomas A, Chess S 1977 Temperament and development. Brunner/Mazel, New York

Temperament: a consideration of concepts and methods

JIM STEVENSON and PHILIP GRAHAM*

*Department of Human Biology and Health, University of Surrey, Guildford, Surrey GU2 5XH and *Department of Child Psychiatry, Institute of Child Health, London WC1N 3JH, UK*

Abstract This paper discusses conceptual issues and begins with a consideration of definitions of temperament. It is suggested that the purposes for which temperament has been studied have, to some degree, dictated methods used and inferences drawn. Those psychopathologists interested in the relationship between temperament and psychiatric disorder, or emotional and behavioural disturbance, have tended to use different methods from those more concerned with delineating the structure of personality. Some issues and problems are common to both approaches, e.g. the definition of behaviour reflecting temperament in terms of style rather than content. Other issues, such as the difficulty involved in drawing a clear distinction between temperamental attributes and mental disorders, are restricted to one approach. The relative contribution of genetic and environmental effects is of interest to both psychopathologists (who wish to examine this issue in relation to the development of the individual), and to psychologists (who are usually more concerned with populations or aggregate effects). The application of biometric genetic models might clarify this issue, and various suggestions are made regarding steps that need to be taken if such models are to be successfully applied.

Definition

Definitions of temperament usually treat the concept as a set of behavioural characteristics that can be inferred from the observation of behaviour in a wide variety of forms and in many different contexts. Often, however, discussion of the concept is couched in terms that suggest that temperament could be identified as a type of physiological organization or physiological set, or even as part of the genotype. Work on the heritability of temperamental differences has certainly demonstrated that the processes producing temperamental characteristics must have some representation at the physiological level and in the genome. However, we would suggest that for the present we

1982 Temperamental differences in infants and young children. Pitman Books Ltd, London (Ciba Foundation symposium 89) p 36-50

do not understand these biological processes sufficiently for any fruitful discussion of the concept of temperament in physiological terms or in terms of the action of particular genes.

Temperament is therefore best described as that part of the phenotype of the individual which is a general attribute of behaviour. Like all specific behaviours it will be influenced by cumulative environmental effects. In Fig. 1

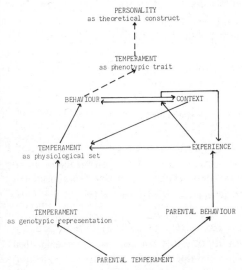

FIG. 1. A schematic representation of the various influences on temperamental characteristics.

we have represented these effects as 'experience'; the current environmental conditions are termed 'context'. This figure is intended to emphasize the location of temperament as an attribute inferred from behaviour despite the biological underpinnings of temperament. It is perhaps necessary to clarify the relationship between temperament and personality, which is similarly inferred from the observation of many specific behaviours. We suggest that temperament represents the part of personality that tends to be manifested in infancy, and which is assumed to have a moderately high degree of stability and to be largely genetically determined. A further feature of the definition of temperament implied in Fig. 1 is that it is a property of the child *per se* rather than, for example, a property of the mother–infant dyad. Parental behaviour will obviously be related to the child's temperament both through common inherited influences and through the parents' impact on experience and in providing the immediate context for the child's behaviour.

We recognize that the evaluation of the extent to which temperament is 'difficult' might well depend on the match between the child's attributes and features of the child's social world. However if, as may be so, it proves impossible to isolate the specific behavioural contribution of the child to these mismatches or poorness of fit, then the concept of temperament, as it is usually defined, is likely to be of little heuristic value.

Purposes of the study of temperament

Two reasonably distinct strands can be discerned in the study of temperament—the psychopathological and the psychological. It is arguable which has the longer history. Although the origin of the medical study of personality is usually accorded to the Greek physician Galen, who lived in the second century AD, it was in fact Hippocrates who first put forward in the fifth century BC the humoral theory of the composition of human beings, and it was Aristotle who proposed four personality types. Galen linked the body humours to personality type. Galen's descendants in modern psychiatry include psychiatrists like Kurt Schneider and Eliot Slater who have tried to relate particular types of personality to characteristic forms of adult mental illness. Thomas & Chess (1977) have applied their work on temperament to an understanding of the development of behaviour and the emotional disorders of childhood. Thus these workers can be seen to be in the same medical tradition.

But issues of personality and temperamental variation have also, since at least classical times, been thought worthy of study for philosophical as well as medical reasons. Thus Lucretius (1952), the Greek poet and disciple of Epicurus, who lived in the early part of the first century BC wrote:

'So it is with men. Though education may apply a similar polish to various individuals, it still leaves [there still remain] fundamental traces of their several temperaments. It must not be supposed that innate vices can be completely eradicated; one man will still incline more readily to outbursts of rage: another will give way a little sooner to fear: a third will accept some conditions too impassively. And in a host of other ways men must differ one from another in temperament and so also in the resultant behaviour. To unfold here the secret causes of these differences is beyond my power. I cannot even find names for the multiplicity of atomic shapes that give rise to this variety of types'.

Lucretius clearly considers temperament in much the same way we do. However he does not appear to think there is much to it. He continues:

'But I am clear that there is one relevant fact that I can affirm: the lingering traces of inborn temperament that cannot be eliminated by philosophy are so slight that there is nothing to prevent men from leading a life worthy of the gods'.

The modern descendants of Lucretius are those who have continued attempts to penetrate 'the secret causes of these differences'. Psychologists such as Gordon Allport and, more recently, Buss & Plomin (1975) can be seen to work in this tradition. The purposes for which psychologists on the one hand and psychopathologists on the other have approached the problem of temperament are different. Those concerned with pathology (and of course these may be psychologists as well as psychiatrists) have been interested to know whether particular personalities are predisposed to certain mental disorders and whether individuals 'at risk' in this way can be prevented from developing disorders or, for example, whether the genetic risk of a disorder is carried in whole or in part by someone who shows the vulnerable personality. From a similarly practical point of view, it may be helpful to establish a person's baseline personality when deciding whether a mental disorder has fully remitted.

The aims of psychologists and philosophers in studying temperament are less easy to pin down. Epicurus thought that man should study his own nature in order to free himself from unnecessary constraints. Allport (1955) a foremost personality theorist of modern times, wrote:

'The goal of psychology is to reduce discord among philosophies of men and to establish a scale of probable truth so that we may feel increasingly certain that one interpretation is truer than another'.

The reasons why child psychologists have recently taken a greater interest in temperament are numerous. There has probably been a decline in enthusiasm for theories of socialization which put sole emphasis on the impact of the environment and, especially, of parental influences on the individual. The seminal work of Bell (1968) prompted much greater interest in the contribution of the child to the interactional processes between parents and children. Later Sameroff & Chandler (1975) and data from the Kuai studies (Werner et al 1971) pointed to the importance of child factors such as reproductive risk and low birthweight interacting with social factors in the determination of intellectual and behaviour differences. Direct observation of very early mother–child interaction has made clear just how much the child stimulates the mother to verbal and non-verbal activity (Stern 1977). Greater awareness of the importance of protective factors in helping to explain why some children live in the most appalling social circumstances, and yet remain relatively unscathed, has promoted interest in the nature of 'vulnerability'—a human personality trait of obvious adaptive value. Finally, and we shall discuss this further below, new techniques have been developed for assessing the genetic contribution to behaviour and temperament. This has made behavioural genetics a more promising subject for study.

The different purposes for which those interested in psychopathology and those concerned with the structure of human personality have studied temperament have probably dictated, to some degree, differences in methods and in interpretation of findings. Both the psychological and the psychiatric approaches to temperament require the development of measures of temperamental characteristics that are reliable and valid. A wide variety of techniques has been developed, including parental diaries, unstructured and semi-structured interviews, ratings by clinicians based on parental reports, direct observation of behaviour in natural and laboratory settings, self- and parent-completed questionnaires, and laboratory-based experimental tasks. Each of the techniques has its own particular strengths and has been developed to meet the varying demands of the particular behaviours being measured (i.e. variation in frequency of the behaviour, its duration, saliency, and so on) as well as the demands of the research question and the economics of the research design.

Psychopathologists have characteristically used diary methods and interviews to obtain information, as well as clinical judgement and clinical information to evaluate and categorize the data obtained. By contrast, psychologists have tended to use self-rating questionnaires or, for children, questionnaires completed by parents. In analysing their results, psychopathologists have tended to place emphasis on 'clustering' techniques, on groups that score at the extremes, and on confirmation of the validity of their methods by consideration of outcome. Thus, Thomas & Chess (1977) have used clustering to analyse their interview data and have shown particular interest in temperamentally distinctive children and in their tendency to develop behaviour disorders. By contrast, psychologists have tended to use factor analysis of large numbers of items of data and, by attempting to identify dimensions along which individuals can vary, to let the factors that emerge speak for themselves rather than to impose any clinical meaning upon them. Finally, psychopathologists tend, in interpreting their findings, to emphasize how their results allow room for plasticity of development, whereas psychologists link their findings to an interpretation which places limits on the possible range of reactions of a child or on the ultimate personality development of an adult.

Rather than to compare the merits of each technique we should like to draw some general conclusions about measurement issues. Emphasis is almost always placed on a high level of test–retest reliability for any particular measure. Given the assumption that temperament represents a stable characteristic of an individual, high test–retest reliabilities are obviously desirable. However, a low reliability might be the product of individual differences in the stability of a particular temperament. Dimensions of temperament that might be excluded as a result of unreliability might represent aspects of behaviour where variability is itself a stable attribute of an individual. More generally, perhaps we should also be investigating those aspects of behavioural style that are consistently variable between individuals. Thus, variability itself could be considered as a temperamental trait likely to have a marked impact on the behaviour of parents and others towards the child. This would add a further dimension to the concept of goodness-of-fit developed by Thomas & Chess (1980). Extreme examples of this dimension might be the restricted variability of behavioural style of the autistic child and the variability shown by some hyperkinetic children.

The validity of measures of temperament has been approached in a variety of ways. The content validity of the Thomas & Chess approach is based on the judgement of experienced professionals concerning the contribution of particular behaviours to different dimensions of temperament. Various difficulties have arisen from this approach. There may be disagreement about the interpretation of any particular behaviour and the temperament it represents. The particular approach taken allows any given behaviour to contribute to the scores on more than one aspect of temperament, and this makes it difficult to interpret the correlations between different categories of temperament. An associated difficulty with this approach is that the predetermined categories of temperament preclude, for example, the exploration of variation in the structure of temperament at different ages. It has yet to be shown whether the nine dimensions of temperament developed by Thomas & Chess (1977) can be consistently replicated by factor analysis i.e. whether these dimensions are independent aspects of temperament. Despite differences in methods and interpretation of findings, a number of issues are common to both psychological and psychopathological approaches and we shall discuss these briefly, in turn.

The manifestation of temperament. There seems general agreement that temperament manifests itself in behavioural style rather than content. For example, the temperamental attribute of bodily activity is thought to be better gauged by considering the way in which the child behaves when walking to school, sitting at the table for meals, and watching television, and whether he or she frequently or rarely undertakes these activities. Such a firm distinction between content and style can, however, be questioned. It is feasible, and some might say probable, that temperamentally physically active children tend to involve themselves more in games requiring physical activity, and less in sedentary occupations such as watching television. Further, when certain types of behaviour are undertaken, they dictate style. One may ask of a child who, when presented with a meal by the mother, throws it on the floor and spits in her face—how did the child go about it? But it would be more sensible to assume that content is a better guide to temperament than style in such an example. Of course, if one insists on defining temperament as that which is manifest by behavioural style there is no more to be said, but such an approach would offend our experience in interviewing mothers on the behaviour of their children. 'What did he do then?' 'He played outside.' 'What was he playing?' 'Well, football is his big love.' '*How* was he playing?' 'Well, he was playing football, wasn't he? Bit different from that great lump of a brother of his who just sits there watching the box.' Do we need to go on asking *how* he plays football? Will we get a sensible answer if we do?

Parental perception versus child behaviour. To anyone with experience of interviewing mothers on the everyday behaviour of their children it is immediately apparent that in order to obtain an unbiased account one must insist on factual descriptions and recent examples. Questionnaire methods of assessing temperament do not allow for this possibility. It is therefore not at all surprising, and Bates (1980) has thoroughly summarized the evidence, that negative maternal perception of a child is related to negative aspects of temperament as assessed by questionnaire. If a mother does not like her child she is likely to describe him as a miserable, irritating wretch. It is not clear whether Bates believes a child who is disliked by his or her mother is not merely likely to be described in this way, but is also likely to *be* a miserable, irritating wretch. It is vitally important to establish the distinction because, of course, the child who is really a wretch will have a very different effect on others outside the family than the child who is only perceived as such by the mother.

Continuity: homotypy and heterotypy. The problems involved in assessing the continuity of temperamental attributes have been summarized by Dunn (1980). The reported correlations in published work are in any case rather low, and it is unclear whether different temperamental attributes are being compared at different ages. This issue has never satisfactorily been resolved. Buss & Plomin (1975) reviewed a number of studies of the longitudinal course of sociability, and they reported reasonably high correlations in some studies but, overall, behavioural stability has not been convincingly established. We shall return to this issue below in more detail.

Behaviour disorder, difficult temperament, or adverse temperamental characteristics? This issue is relevant more to the psychopathological than to the psychological studies. It has been suggested that certain temperamental attributes—especially high intensity, negative mood and low adaptability—predispose towards the development of behaviour disorders (Thomas et al 1968). Is it merely semantic to question whether these two states—temperamental difficulty and behaviour disorder—differ from each other qualitatively? If both are identified behaviourally, if both produce characteristic social disability for the child and if both influence the parental handling that the child receives, how (except quantitatively) do they differ? If they do not differ, is it not misleading to describe one state as presaging a different state, when in fact we are merely observing a mild (or not-so-mild) problem turning into a larger one?

The development of biometric genetic models. Psychological and psychiatric schools of thought put different emphasis on the extent to which genetic and environmental influences on temperament can be separated. On the other hand, such estimates are the very substance of the research programme of Robert Plomin and others. The apparent paradox is that both schools accept a transactional model to explain the process resulting in and consequent upon temperamental differences. This difference probably stems from the emphasis on the development of individuals by Thomas & Chess, and from the population orientation of the behavioural genetics approach. This distinction was clearly formulated by Meehl (1954) when he discussed differences between statistical and clinical prediction. That it is possible to analyse the distinct contributions of genetic and environmental influences does not imply that a mechanistic or deterministic approach to the development of individuals is possible or desirable. Population estimates such as these provide only general insight into processes by which environmental and genetic influences interact, but are invaluable in indicating which parameters need to be considered for different temperaments when models of the transactional process are being studied.

The possibility of reconciling these two approaches has been most clearly demonstrated in the important recent study by Lytton (1980). He investigated interactions between parents and their twin children by using a variety of techniques, but most vividly by direct observation. Amongst other analyses he fitted complex biometric genetic models to his data, thus demonstrating the value of complementary studies of processes at the individual level and the value of estimating genetic and environmental effects on aggregated data.

The next important step in investigation of the genetic and environmental influences on temperament may well be by the fitting of biometric models. This will require a wider range of kinship correlations than is currently available for temperament data. Preliminary studies are necessary to establish structure of temperament at different ages so that instruments can be developed that are applicable both to children of different ages and to adults, thereby making it possible to calculate sibling correlations and correlations between more distant relatives, both biological and adoptive.

Twin data will remain central to this research programme. Consequently it will be necessary to test more systematically whether the assumptions of the twin method are not violated in temperamental data. In particular, it needs to be clarified whether the assumption of an equal share of common environmental influences by monozygotic (MZ) and dizygotic (DZ) twins is correct. For cognitive data it has been shown that the aspects of parental treatment that are more similar in MZ and DZ pairs are not themselves related to individual differences in cognitive development. This same evidence cannot be used in the field of temperament since temperament is likely to be influenced by a wider range of parental behaviours and because we do not yet know which parental behaviours are important. Again, Lytton (1980) provides some crucial data. He was able to show by investigating the time-course of child and parent behaviours that parents of twins do indeed respond more similarly to MZ pairs than to DZ pairs but that this is because MZ pairs exhibit more similar provoking behaviour than DZ pairs. Once a clearer picture emerges of the parental behaviours that are related to temperamental differences, studies like that of Lytton will be required to test the assumptions of the twin method.

Integrated investigation of changes in the structure of temperament, the stability of individual differences and the genetics of behaviour

As already indicated, temperament is usually defined in terms of behavioural style, i.e. as an attribute derived from general properties of behaviour that are shown in a variety of contexts. A second aspect of temperamental characteristics is the assumption of stability of individual differences over time. It is therefore necessary to demonstrate this stability whilst the child's behavioural repertoire is undergoing developmental changes. Consequently, temperamental attributes need to be identified on the basis of general properties of behaviours that are themselves subject to change. A particular behaviour at two different times may be contributing to two different temperaments, or a particular temperament may be indicated by a specific behaviour at an early age and this behaviour may be absent from the child's repertoire at a later age. A third central feature of the concept of temperament is that it is in some sense determined in part by genetic or at least physiological factors. There is evidence that genetic factors are important in temperamental differences at particular ages (e.g. Torgersen & Kringlen 1978, Buss & Plomin 1975). It has yet to be demonstrated that genetic factors are partly responsible for stability in individual differences in temperament over time periods that include major changes in the child's behavioural repertoire.

One possible design for a study to demonstrate such a genetic influence would be a longitudinal twin study such as that reported by Wilson (1982) in this symposium. The measures of particular interest in such a study would not necessarily be the temperament scores at particular ages but rather the scores relating to factors present at more than one age. These scores could be obtained from canonical correlates of behaviours measured at two time points (Fig. 2). The advantage of this multivariate technique is that it identifies

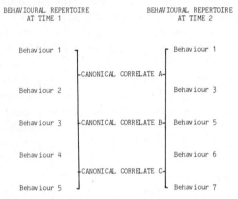

BEHAVIOURAL REPERTOIRE   BEHAVIOURAL REPERTOIRE
       AT TIME 1   AT TIME 2

FIG. 2. Illustration of the derivation of canonical correlates with different behaviours present at two time points.

dimensions that are maximally correlated between two sets of variables. Thus, different behaviours may be measured at two time points, and the canonical correlates would represent the underlying dimensions that explain the variance in both sets of behaviours. In this sense, such dimensions are the temperamental characteristics that are taken to be stable aspects of individual differences over changing behavioural repertoires. Individual scores on each canonical variate could be calculated for each twin, and the data could be subjected to the usual genetic analysis for twin data to demonstrate which environmental and genetic factors are needed to account for the covariance observed for MZ and DZ twin pairs. Such a study would provide a means of obtaining temperament data that showed stability over time and would also give more insight into the genetic control of development and the genetic determination of individual differences. One disadvantage of such a procedure is that the canonical correlation analysis forces the same factor structure onto the two sets of variables. It is plausible that the structure of temperament as well as the behavioural repertoire undergoes developmental changes. Thus additional temperaments may emerge as the child's development progresses, and other dimensions of individual differences may no longer be found. Preliminary factor analyses calculated independently for the two sets of behavioural measures could show whether the canonical correlates adequately reflect the structure of temperament at the two time points.

REFERENCES

Allport GW 1955 Becoming: basic considerations for a study of personality. Yale University Press, New Haven, (see p 17)

Bates JE 1980 The concept of difficult temperament. Merrill-Palmer Q 26:299-319

Bell R 1968 A re-interpretation of the directions of effects in studies of socialisation. Psychol Rev 75:81-95

Buss AH, Plomin R 1975 A temperamental theory of personality development. John Wiley, New York

Dunn J 1980 Individual differences in temperament. In: Rutter M (ed) Scientific foundations of developmental psychiatry. Heinemann, London, p 101-109 (see p 103)

Lucretius 1952 On the nature of the Universe. Penguin, Harmondsworth (see p 105)

Lytton H 1980 Parent–child interaction: the socialisation process observed in twin and singleton families. Plenum Press, New York

Meehl PE 1954 Clinical versus statistical prediction, a theoretical analysis and review of the evidence. University of Minnesota Press, Minneapolis

Sameroff AJ, Chandler MJ 1975 Reproductive risk and the continuum of caretaking casualty. In: Horowitz FD et al (eds) Review of child development research. University of Chicago Press, Chicago, vol 4, p 187-249

Stern D 1977 The first relationship. Infant and mother. Fontana, London

Thomas A, Chess S 1977 Temperament and development. Brunner/Mazel, New York

Thomas A, Chess S 1980 The dynamics of psychological development. Brunner/Mazel, New York

Thomas A, Chess S, Birch HG 1968 Temperament and behavior disorders in children. New York University Press, New York

Torgersen AE, Kringlen E 1978 Genetic aspects of temperamental differences in infants. J Am Acad Child Psychiatry 70:433-449

Werner EE, Bierman JE, French FE 1971 The children of Kuai. University of Hawaii Press, Honolulu

Wilson RS 1982 Intrinsic determinants of temperament. In: Temperamental differences in infants and young children. Pitman Books, London (Ciba Found Symp 89) p 121-140

DISCUSSION

Robinson: Could some of the problems that you raised be tackled by looking at the behaviour characteristics or temperamental attributes of identical twins who were separated at birth?

Chess: I can discuss one such case. Some years ago Rutter et al (1963) obtained finger prints of twins in the New York longitudinal study to identify which pairs were identical. Our sample included one set of identical twins who had been separately adopted and who did not meet until age 16. (The twins themselves first discovered each other by a coincidence, when a classmate of one of them went to a summer camp which the other attended. We had kept our word not to exchange information between them.) There was a remarkable similarity between the separated twins in a number of areas over the many years we studied them. They had similar high/low scores on intelligence tests at different ages. There were also great similarities in their scores in the different temperament categories at each age. The only notable difference is that one of them has consistently handled her life situations badly whereas the other, when she encountered the same kinds of stresses, handled them better. Both girls demonstrated musical and acrobatic talents, gave the same giggle and the same type of blush.

Rutter: Anecdotes can be useful and this case does indeed illustrate Professor Graham's point about the distinction between the '*how*' (or style) of behaviour and the '*what*' (or content) of behaviour. I saw these twins when they were aged about two years, and they were strikingly similar in temperamental style, including marked irregularity in sleep–wake cycles. However, the parents in the two families had responded quite differently, so that the sleep irregularity had led to general behavioural difficulties in only one of the twins. I well remember the second time I went along to interview that family, and the little girl opened the door with the words 'Guess what? I had them all up again last night!'. This illustrates how a particular temperamental style can be modified by the sort of interaction it produces.

Graham: Dr Thomas Bouchard at Minnesota has found extraordinary similarities between the interests and the environmental events at different periods, for identical twins who were brought up apart (see Watson 1981). It is almost as if the twins' genetic make-up is determining the environmental events that happen to them!

Plomin: I'm not so sure that observations on separated twins really do highlight the issues that you were raising. However, some aspects of separated identical twins are particularly interesting. Bouchard's work (Bouchard et al 1981, Eckert et al 1981) at present is primarily anecdotal. Shields (1962) in England had a similar problem: once one tries to attract twins through the public media one never knows what sampling biases are introduced. In Bouchard's study, people are brought into the unit at Minnesota for five days and are asked about everything from how they tie their shoes (literally) to how they button their shirts—producing thousands of pieces of data. With so much information almost any two people could be favourably compared as identical twins! The work might remain anecdotal because the study is unlikely to achieve a sample size that would make it less so. However, anecdotes can be very interesting for hypothesis formation, which is the value of Susan Farber's (1981) new book. She has reviewed all the data on separated twins and has also collected some remarkable anecdotes about similarities in stylistic mannerisms—for example, whether the twins use their hands a lot when they talk, or how they sit. These similarities came across more noticeably than measured aspects of personality, such as extraversion.

I have also worked with adult adoptees in Colorado who attempt to find their biological relatives. When the adoptees have been successful in their search, what impresses them is not similarity in sociability, or even in intelligence, but in stylistic mannerisms. In the few studies of separated twins who have completed personality inventories there is a consistent tendency (although it is not statistically significant, given the sample sizes) for separated twins to be *more* similar than twins reared together. This suggests that for twins reared together there is perhaps a contrast effect (Plomin et al 1976).

Wilson: The work of Dr Bouchard is instructive, particularly in the degree of similarity between the small details of mannerisms and gestures; the expressive component has been closely retained by each of these individuals, who have grown up in quite different circumstances. It is possible that temperamental dimensions feed into these non-verbal communication skills, and this work is a rich source for hypothesis formation, for example, on social interactions and career success.

Robinson: Does Bouchard have a control group?

Plomin: No; he would like to collect them, but it is not easy.

Hinde: Professor Graham, you emphasized the problem of whether temperament was in the eye of the mother or in the child's behaviour, but perhaps you laid insufficient emphasis on whether temperament had to do with a characteristic of the mother–child *relationship*. By labelling temperament as a trait, one is classifying it as a phenotypic characteristic—a characteristic of the child. We should always be aware that what is reported to us may be a product of the *relationship*.

Graham: We are assuming that the child has a contribution to make to parent–child interaction. Interaction is the process which occurs when mother and child bring together their individual characteristics in a particular situation. Temperament is surely more than what is revealed in the mother–child relationship alone, though mothers do, of course, have a great influence on the child's social behaviour in the early few weeks and months.

Hinde: What I wanted to focus on was the first thing that you said—that the child has a contribution of its own to make. One must be aware that the child's contribution depends (for example) on whether it is being put to bed by its mother or by its father—i.e. on the relationship with the particular individual concerned. One must assume that everything the mother reports about the child is a product not just of the child's characteristics, personality or temperament, but of the characteristics or temperament of both of them.

Rutter: Bem & Funder (1978) used the apt phrase 'personality of situations' in the title of their paper expressing a similar argument that there is consistency, not just in the individual or in the situation, but also in the interaction between the two.

Stevenson: Sandra Scarr (unpublished paper, Eastern Psychological Association, New York, April 1981) has put forward a 'genotype–environment correlation theory of development' which supports some of the points that Professor Hinde has made. The theory is based on three types of environment and genetic correlation (Plomin et al 1977), and highlights the difficulties of

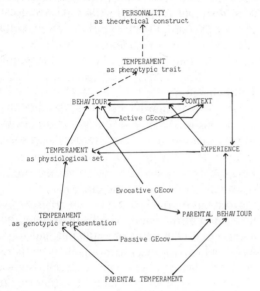

FIG. 1. (*Stevenson*) Genotype-environment correlation (GEcov) as additional influences on temperamental characteristics.

trying to think of the genotypic influence and the environmental influences as being separate and independent. The parental temperament influences the child both genetically and environmentally. Establishing gene–environment correlations throughout the child's developmental history helps us to identify where these joint influences might lie. Scarr's ideas are developmentally oriented: since there is a common genetic inheritance for the parental behaviour and the child's temperament, there will be a passive correlation between the two. This source of gene–environment covariance is the prime one, and is present from an early stage in development. This may explain why temperamental data do not indicate a strong genetic influence until later, because passive correlation will inflate the common environment estimate. As the child's behaviour begins to develop, an evocative gene–environment covariance is found, where the behaviour of the child itself will tend to result in certain modifications of parental behaviour which particularly suit the child's own needs and temperamental characteristics. This emerging pattern is a continuing influence in development. The last developmental component of this theory is an active gene–environment covariance, where the temperamental characteristics of the child itself will result in its actually seeking out and finding particular contexts to suit its own temperamental style (see Fig. 1).

Thomas: The questions Professor Graham has raised are most pertinent. However, we have found it quite possible to distinguish between the symptoms of behaviour disorders in different temperamental types of children, given sufficiently detailed, descriptive and objective data and a clinical evaluation that is done separately. The symptoms of a behaviour disorder that develop in a 'difficult' child—e.g. violent tantrums—are likely to be quite different from those in the 'slow-to-warm-up' child, who exhibits a more passive, inhibitory type of disturbed behaviour.

The question of whether temperament is primarily the perception of the parent or has an objective reality in terms of the model that Philip Graham and Jim Stevenson have presented is fundamental, not only theoretically but practically. If one is considering primarily the perception of the parent, the focus is then on the mother or father, and on why she or he perceives the child in this way. If one considers a difficult temperament, on the other hand, to be an attribute of the child, one begins to focus on the possibility that something in the child, and not just in her perception of the child, is causing difficulties for the mother. From a management, counselling and therapeutic stance, it really makes a fundamental difference which approach is used.

REFERENCES

Bem DJ, Funder DC 1978 Predicting more of the people more of the time: assessing the personality of situations. Psychol Rev 81:485-5-1

Bouchard TJ, Heston L, Eckert E, Keyes M, Resnick S 1981 The Minnesota study of twins reared apart—project description and sample results in the developmental domain. In: Gedda L et al (eds) Twin research 3, Part B: Intelligence, personality, and development (III Int Congr Twin Studies, Jerusalem, June 1980) Alan R Liss, New York (Progr Clin Biol Res 69B), p 277-234

Eckert ED, Heston LL, Bouchard TJ 1981 MZ twins reared apart—preliminary findings of psychiatric disturbances and traits. In: Gedda L et al (eds) Twin research 3, Part B: Intelligence, personality, and development (III Int Congr Twin Studies, Jerusalem, June 1980) Alan R Liss, New York (Progr Clin Biol Res 69B), p 179-188

Farber SL 1981 Identical twins reared apart: a reanalysis. Basic Books, New York

Plomin R, Willerman L, Loehlin JC 1976 Resemblance in appearance and the equal environments assumption in twin studies of personality traits. Behav Genet 6:43-52

Plomin R, DeFries JC, Loehlin JC 1977 Genotype–environment interation and correlation in the analysis of human behavior. Psychol Bull 84:309-322

Rutter M, Korn S, Birch HG 1963 Genetic and environmental factors in the development of primary reaction patterns Br J Soc Clin Psychol 2:161-173

Shields J 1962 Monozygotic twins brought up apart and brought up together. Oxford University Press, London

Watson P 1981 Twins. Hutchinson, London

Temperament and relationships

J. STEVENSON-HINDE and A. E. SIMPSON

MRC Unit on the Development and Integration of Behaviour, University Sub-Department of Animal Behaviour, Madingley, Cambridge CB3 8AA, UK

Abstract Temperamental characteristics of preschool children were related to relationships, mothers' mood, and children's feelings towards family members. Active scores were correlated with some problem behaviour and with negative aspects of interactions with mother and father. *Active* children felt themselves to be independent, while *Timid* children did not. Timid children had relatively more acute illnesses and worries and fears. *Difficult* scores were correlated with problem behaviour and with negative aspects of all the types of interaction assessed: mother–child, mother–father, father–child, and sibling–child. Furthermore, the more Difficult the child, the more Anxious, Outwardly Irritable, and Inwardly Irritable the mother. In turn, Difficult children expressed relatively few positive and dependency feelings towards their mothers, and more negative feelings towards themselves.

The relation between a child's temperamental characteristics and other aspects of a child's life was raised in the initial work of Thomas & Chess (e.g. 1977), who related characteristics to behaviour disorders, school functioning and interpersonal relationships. In this chapter we shall relate characteristics of nursery school children to: (1) reported interactions with family members; (2) mothers' mood; and (3) children's feelings about family members.

The first relation, between characteristics and interactions, has been studied using direct observation of interactions, in the context of both home (Dunn & Kendrick 1980) and nursery school (Billman & McDevitt 1980). Direct observations of the children in our study are related to their characteristics in a paper by Hinde et al (1982, this volume). In this paper, maternal reports provided the basis for assessing interactions. The validity of similar maternal reports has been indicated by Dunn & Kendrick (1980).

The second relation, between children's characteristics and mother's mood, raises the broader issue of how mothers influence, and are influenced by, children's characteristics. With rhesus monkeys, characteristics of mothers

1982 Temperamental differences in infants and young children. Pitman Books Ltd, London (Ciba Foundation symposium 89) p 51-65

and their one-year-olds were significantly correlated, although in different ways according to the sex of the infant. That is, on three dimensions—Confident to Fearful, Excitable to Slow, and Sociable to Solitary—mothers' and daughters' scores were correlated in a one-to-one fashion: Confident mothers had Confident daughters; Excitable mothers had Excitable daughters; and Sociable mothers had Sociable daughters. Although Sociable mothers had Sociable sons, Confident mothers had neither Confident nor Fearful sons, but Excitable mothers had sons who were Fearful (Stevenson-Hinde & Simpson 1981).

With humans, multiparous, extraverted mothers tended to rate their 4–6-month-olds as 'easy' (Bates et al 1979), and maternal unresponsiveness has been related to 'difficult' infants aged three months to two years (reviewed in Bates 1980). High maternal criticism has been related to low fastidiousness in 3–7-year-olds, and this in turn was predictive of later behaviour problems (Graham et al 1973). Finally, Plomin (1976) has correlated questionnaire ratings of temperamental characteristics of parents with ratings of their children. However, of eleven correlations for mother–child and eleven for father–child, the only coefficient above 0.25 was 0.41. This concerned mother and child, on the fear component of Emotionality.

Since the above studies involve rating scales, one must acknowledge the possibility of observer bias. This may take many forms, such as imposing an 'implicit personality theory' (Bruner & Tagiuri 1954) or allowing one's own characteristics to colour the ratings. Lyon & Plomin (1981) explored one form of parental bias—projection—and found that, with the possible exception of the characteristic 'affectionate', neither mothers nor fathers projected their own ratings in a one-to-one fashion onto those of their 2–6-year-old twins.

One way to decrease the possibility of parental bias is to ask parents to describe recent behaviour, and to leave the ratings to the interviewer (Brown & Rutter 1966), who is in a better position than parents to judge deviations from the norm in the sample. As Rutter (1982, this volume) makes clear, rating scales are relative—to the cultural or social group, to the situation, and even to the age of the subjects. Behaviourally based interviews were used in the present study, for assessing both temperamental characteristics and family interactions. Mothers' mood was assessed by a questionnaire (Snaith et al 1978).

Although causal influences cannot be specified in the above studies, and in any case will not be one-way, some direction of effect is suggested by the rhesus monkey study. Both the consistency of the maternal characteristics over the years, regardless of sex of infant, and the different patterns of interactions with daughters and sons suggested an influence of mother's characteristics on those of her developing infant (Stevenson-Hinde & Simpson 1981). Conversely, an effect of infant on mother is suggested by Wolkind

& De Salis (1982, this volume), who found that high Difficult scores of four-month-old infants predicted a high incidence of symptoms of depression and anxiety in mothers when their children were 14 months old.

The third relation is between characteristics and feelings. The Bené-Anthony Family Relations Test allowed the children in our study to express some feelings about family members, including themselves. Perhaps because of the difficulty of assessing feelings of young children, the important question of which sorts of children feel positive to mothers, or indeed to themselves, has not previously been addressed.

Subjects and the temperamental characteristics interview

The subjects were 26 boys and 21 girls, all from families with a mother, father, and one sibling (aged 16 months to seven years, 10 months). No mothers worked full time and all fathers were employed, with a Registrar General's Classification ranging from 1 to 5. The children were assessed at $3\frac{1}{2}$ years of age, and all but six (whose families had moved away) were assessed eight months later. All subjects attended the same playgroup, in a Cambridgeshire village, for several mornings a week.

The temperamental characteristics interview was based on that developed by Garside et al (1975). Each mother was asked to describe her child's behaviour over the past few days in particular settings (e.g. waking, dressing, play, mealtime, bedtime). The interview was semi-structured, with probes continuing until the interviewer felt able to make a rating. Each item was rated on a unipolar, five-point scale, ranging from the characteristic being normal or absent to its being extreme. Because of the skewness inherent in such a scale, we used non-parametric statistics, including Spearman rank-order correlation coefficients.

The characteristics

The characteristics, brief definitions, the number of rated items in each, and correlation coefficients over time are given in Table 1. All correlations were significant. In addition to this rank-order consistency over time, there were no changes with time, in that for no characteristic or summary score (Timid or Difficult) was a Wilcoxon matched-pairs signed-ranks test significant.

For the nine characteristics and the two summary scores (Timid and Difficult), few sex differences emerged. At 42 months, boys were more Dependent and Intense than girls (Mann–Whitney U test $P < 0.05$, two-tailed). At 50 months, neither the nine characteristics nor the two summary

TABLE 1 The characteristics and their consistency from 42 to 50 months

Characteristic	Number of items	Spearman correlation coefficients
Active	5	.73***
always on move		
TIMID[a]	8	.62***
Shy	6	.61***
Approach/withdraw	3	.49***
not Adaptable	3	.60***
Dependent	2	.39**
cling, ask help, cry if left		
DIFFICULT[a]	12	.64***
Moody	6	.50***
inequable, irritable, sulky		
Intense	4	.53***
over-intense expression of feelings		
Unmalleable	2	.44**
refuse to come when asked		
Irregular	3	.36*
time eat, sleep, wake		
Assertive	2	.74***
fights, bullies peers		
Attention span	1	.53***
time at one thing on own		

*$P < 0.05$; **$P < 0.01$; ***$P < 0.001$, two-tailed ($n = 41$). [a]Summary scores—see text.

scores produced a significant difference between boys and girls. This is in keeping with the paucity of sex differences found earlier (e.g. Thomas et al 1963) and more recently with 3–7-year-olds (Garside et al 1975, Graham et al 1973, McDevitt & Carey 1978). However, Graham et al (1973) did support our finding that boys were significantly more Intense than girls.

When a principal component analysis was done on the nine characteristics, two components accounted for 47% of the variance at 42 months and for 56% at 50 months. Following a varimax rotation (Nie et al 1975), Assertive, Unmalleable, Intense, and Active loaded highly (> 0.58) on Component 1 (C1) at both ages, while Dependent, Moody and Poor Attention span loaded highly (> 0.49) on Component 2 (C2) at both ages. Shy went from C1 at 42 months to C2 at 50 months, while Irregular went from C2 to C1. The loadings for all nine characteristics were correlated over time: 0.88 for C1 and 0.77 for C2.

However, in spite of the simple and fairly stable solution, at least two problems remained. (1) On the Spearman matrix which formed the input for the analysis, the highest correlation at 42 months was between Intense and Moody (0.48), and this remained high (0.49) at 50 months. Yet, as suggested above, the two characteristics did not show similar loadings: for Intense the loadings were higher on C1 than on C2, while for Moody they were higher on C2 than on C1, at both ages. (2) When males and females were analysed separately, the solutions differed. That is, C1 for males was correlated with C2 for females (0.77 at 42 months; 0.84 at 50 months) and C2 for males with C1 for females (0.66 and 0.97).

Because of the above problems with the principal component analysis, it was not used for constructing summary scores, which were, instead, based on Thomas & Chess's (1977) work. The first score, similar to Thomas & Chess's 'Slow-to-warm-up' category, was the sum of the mean of the three Approach-withdrawal ratings, plus the mean of the three non-Adaptable ratings, plus the mean of the two Dependent ratings. The second, similar to Thomas & Chess's 'Difficult' category, was the sum of the six Moody ratings, plus the four Intense ratings, plus the two Unmalleable ratings (see Timid and Difficult on Table 1).

Of the four characteristics not included in the two summary scores (see Table 1), Active involved a number of items (five), was highly consistent over time (0.73) and relates to other aspects of development (e.g. Bell & Waldrop 1982, this volume, Buss et al 1980). Active was therefore chosen as a third score for relating to other measures. The intercorrelations were as follows, at 42 and 50 months, respectively:

Active with Timid: .06; −.49
Active with Difficult: .31; .43
Timid with Difficult: .14; .02.

Three other assessments

Relationships Interview

This was a semi-structured interview which focused on past events and mothers' reports of interactions between the child and other family members over the preceding seven days. Items were coded in terms of frequency of occurrence or ratings made by the interviewer. The interview consisted of: 10 items of background information, which involved completely predictable change or no change from 42 to 50 months (e.g. mother's age, father's job); two items about past events (illnesses and stressful events); five kinds of problem behaviour (e.g. night waking and attention seeking); six items about mother–father interactions that were related to the child; seven items about mother–child interactions; five about father–child interactions; and two about sibling–child interactions.

Of these 37 interview items, the only one that overlapped in meaning with the items of temperamental characteristics concerned refusals: the characteristic Unmalleable involved the child's degree of refusal (from coming when asked, to refusing at all costs) in two particular contexts (call to meals, call to bed). The interview about relationships focused on the last time the child refused to do something, without specifying any context. A rating was obtained for what the mother did and what the child then did. The number of occurrences of such refusals in the past week went into the sum of occurrences of tantrums, refusals, and difficult-to-manage behaviour.

The Bené-Anthony Family Relations Test

This test was given to each child (with the exception of one 42-month-old girl who could not manage it) at home. Messages were read out for the child to give to a figure representing either mother, father, sibling, self, or 'nobody'. There were eight Dependency messages (e.g. 'Who should tuck you into bed at night?'), 16 Positive messages (e.g. 'Who is nice?'), and 16 Negative messages (e.g. 'Who gets cross with you?'). The number of messages given to each figure within each of the three categories was then correlated with Active, Timid, and Difficult.

The IDA Scale

At the end of all the interviewing, when the child was 50 months old, and while it was doing the second Family Relations Test, the 41 mothers completed an 18-item questionnaire. This provided a summary rating for Depression, Anxiety, Inward Irritability, and Outward Irritability (Snaith et al 1978).

Active children

Although Active scores were based on descriptions of motor activity as opposed to social behaviour, Active children showed some problem behaviour and negative aspects of interactions with both mother and father (Table 2). At both ages, the more Active the child, the more occurrences of tantrums, refusals and/or difficult-to-manage behaviour. At 42 months, Active children were more attention-seeking, while at 50 months, they gave relatively more Dependency messages to 'nobody' than did less Active children. There were no significant correlations between Active scores and mother–child interactions at 42 months. However by 50 months, the more Active the Child, the less compliant it was to mother. Although the more Active the child the more the father helped the mother with it, father was more harsh (i.e. threatened or punished) when annoyed with the child at 42 months, and did less with the child at 50 months. Finally, sibling's age was negatively correlated with Active. This suggests that firstborns were more Active than secondborns, and this was significantly so at 50 months (Mann-Whitney U test, $P < 0.01$, two-tailed).

TABLE 2 Items from a Relationships Interview (Mother's report), the Bené-Anthony Family Relations Test (Child's feelings), and IDA Scale (Mother's mood) that are significantly correlated with *Active* scores

Family member	Assessment	42 months	50 months
Child	Mother's report	tantrum, refuse, difficult** seek attention**	tantrum, refuse, difficult*
	Child's feelings	—	Dependent on nobody*
Mother	Mother's report	—	−comply to M, post-refuse*
	Mother's mood	not assessed	—
	Child's feelings	—	—
Father	Mother's report	F help M* F harsh**	−joint activities*
	Child's feelings	—	—
Sibling	Mother's report	−age sibling*	−age sibling***
	Child's feelings	—	—

*$P <0.05$; **$P <0.01$; ***$P <0.001$, Spearman rank-order correlations, two-tailed ($n = 47$ at 42 months and 41 at 50 months). M, mother; F, father.

Timid children

The more Timid the child, the higher the incidence of acute illnesses from birth to 42 months (Table 3). At 50 months, Timid children had a relatively high number of worries and fears. As with Active scores, there were no significant correlations at 42 months between Timid scores and mother–child interactions. However, fathers of Timid children were not harsh with them when annoyed, as they had been with Active children. In turn, Timid 42-month-olds gave relatively more Positive feelings to father. These two correlations disappeared later, when, in addition, father helped less and the role of cuddling between both father–child and mother–child was low. This suggests that parental tolerance of Timid children had worn off by 50 months.

By this age they had experienced at least a year of nursery school, and parents may have expected shy children to have 'grown out of it'. Yet they had not, as indicated by the lack of change in Timid scores over time.

Finally, Timid scores were correlated with the child's Dependency feelings to siblings (at 42 months) and not to self (at 50 months). Since Timid scores reflect dependence (see Table 1), these correlations suggest that the child's feelings were in accord with this particular characteristic.

TABLE 3 Items from a Relationships Interview (Mother's report), the Bené-Anthony Family Relations Test (Child's feelings), and IDA Scale (Mother's mood) that are significantly correlated with *Timid* scores

Family member	Assessment	42 months	50 months
Child	Mother's report	past ills*	worries/fears**
	Child's feelings	—	−Dependent on self*
Mother	Mother's report	—	−cuddles*
	Mother's mood	not assessed	—
	Child's feelings	—	—
Father	Mother's report	−F harsh*	−cuddles*
			−F help M*
	Child's feelings	Positive to F*	—
Sibling	Mother's report	—	—
	Child's feelings	Dependent on sibling*	—

*P <0.05; **P <0.01; ***P <0.001; Spearman rank-order correlations, two-tailed (n = 47 at 42 months and 41 at 50 months). M, mother; F, father.

Difficult children

As indicated in Table 1, a high Difficult score reflects a child who is Moody (inequable, irritable, or sulky), Intense (over-intense in expressing feelings), and Unmalleable (refusing to come when asked). With the Relationships Interview, these children had a relatively high incidence of tantrums, refusals, and/or difficult-to-manage behaviour and they were attention-seeking at both ages (Table 4). As with Timid, some insight into their own characteristics is suggested by the correlations emerging from the Bené-Anthony Family Relations Test: the more Difficult the child, the more Negative messages the child gave to itself, and the more Positive messages went to 'nobody'.

Whereas with either Active or Timid scores only one significant correlation involved mother–child interactions, here there were seven. Although Difficult children complied with mother after a tantrum at 42 months, they remained cross for longer at 50 months. At both ages, having refused to do something, they failed to comply when asked again, and by 50 months mothers were relatively harsh when this occurred. At both ages, the more Difficult the child, the less accepting the mothers were of the child's offers of help.

Correlations with the child's feelings suggest some awareness of these tensions: the more Difficult the child, the fewer Dependency and Positive messages went to mother. Eight months later, no significant correlations between Difficult scores and feelings emerged, even though problem behaviour and negative interactions continued. The reason for this is not clear. It was not that correlations for the sexes separately were going different ways. The 24 boys on their own showed no significant correlations, and the 17 girls showed only one: the more Difficult the girl, the more Positive messages went to father.

TABLE 4 Items from a Relationships Interview (Mother's report), the Bené-Anthony Family Relations Test (Child's feelings), and IDA Scale (Mother's mood) that are significantly correlated with *Difficult* scores

Family member	Assessment	42 months	50 months
Child	Mother's report	tantrum, refuse, difficult** seek attention**	tantrum, refuse, difficult** seek attention***
	Child's feelings	Negative to self* Positive to nobody*	—
Mother	Mother's report	comply to M, post-tantrum* −comply to M, post-refuse**	−comply to M, post-tantrum* −comply to M, post-refuse* M harsh, post-refuse*
		−M accept**	−M accept***
	Mother's mood	not assessed	Anxious** Inwardly irritable*** Outwardly irritable**
	Child's feelings	−Dependent on M*** −Positive to M*	—
Father	Mother's report	job class*	F harsher than M* −F aware** −joint activities* annoy F*
	Child's feelings	—	—
Sibling	Mother's report	−age sibling*** −sibling/C enjoy*	−sibling/C enjoy* squabbles*
	Child's feelings	—	—

*P <0.05; **P <0.01; ***P <0.001; Spearman rank-order correlations, two-tailed (n = 47 at 42 months and 41 at 50 months). M, mother; F, father; C, child.

Finally, mothers' mood, which was not significantly correlated with Active or Timid scores, produced three significant correlations out of four with

Difficult. Difficult scores were correlated with Anxious (0.41), Inwardly Irritable (0.50), and Outwardly Irritable (0.46). When the three characteristics which make up Difficult were separately correlated with the mood scores, Unmalleable produced no significant correlations, while Moody and Intense were each significantly correlated with Anxious, Inwardly Irritable and Outwardly Irritable. Thus, it was the two 'mood' characteristics of the child which correlated with mother's mood. Although it is impossible here to specify the direction of any effect, it is worth noting that: (1) significantly more (χ^2, $P < 0.05$, two-tailed) of our mothers (61%) had high Outward Irritability scores than did the students and working women (38%) in the Snaith et al (1978) control group; (2) after completing the IDA questionnaire, many mothers commented on their irritability, saying that they 'did not used to be like this'; and (3) Wolkind & De Salis (1982, this volume) found a correlation between infants' Difficult scores and maternal mood some months later. This implies an influence of child's mood on mother's mood.

With fathers, although those at the top of Registrar General's Classification tended to have more Difficult children, no interactions at 42 months were correlated with Difficult. By 50 months, fathers were reported as being more harsh than mothers, although, as we have seen, mothers themselves were relatively harsh. In addition, the more Difficult the child, the less did the mother feel that the father was aware of her daily life, the less the father did with the child, and the more often the child annoyed father.

Finally, Difficult produced high correlations with the two sibling–child interaction items: mother's description of how the children behaved towards each other (rated by the interviewer on a five-point scale, from mostly aggressive to enjoyment); and the rate of squabbling. Furthermore, it is possible that the sibling made some contribution to Difficult scores at 42 months, since the scores were negatively correlated with the sibling's age. The younger the sibling, the more Difficult the child, especially if the child was a girl ($r_s = -0.71$ and -0.47 for girls at each age). As argued for Active scores, this correlation suggests that firstborns were more Difficult than secondborns, and this was indeed so at 42 months (Mann-Whitney U test, $P < 0.02$, two-tailed). Thus, one of the many effects of a secondborn on a firstborn may be to make at least some of the firstborns more Difficult. Such a view receives support from Dunn & Kendrick (1982), who studied the effect of the arrival of a secondborn on a firstborn and found a marked increase in difficult behaviour of the firstborn.

Conclusions

The focus of this paper has been on correlations, between temperamental characteristics and aspects of family relationships. Thus, we have no direct evidence about the direction of causal influences, whether of characteristics on relationships or vice-versa. In any event, causal influences will not be of a simple, one-way nature. The most appropriate analysis will probably be in terms of feedback mechanisms. Nevertheless, by looking at additional evidence, as we have done with the correlations between Difficult scores and either mothers' mood or siblings' age we were able to infer a possible direction of effect from child to mother or from younger sibling to child.

A general issue arising from the correlations is that characteristics and 'negative' family interactions may become more tightly linked as the child gets older. That is, looking at correlations between mother's report of interactions with mother, father, or sibling and Active (Table 2), Timid (Table 3), and Difficult (Table 4) scores, in six out of nine cases, there were more correlations reflecting negative interactions at 50 months than at 42 months, and there were never fewer at 50 months.

Another general point is that Difficult scores seem to bear on relationships more than do Active or Timid scores. Firstly, correlations involving negative interactions were more prevalent for Difficult scores than for Active or Timid scores. Secondly, Difficult was the only characteristic of the three that involved negative aspects of all the types of interactions assessed, including sibling–child interactions and mother–father interactions, with mothers feeling that fathers were not aware of their day. Thirdly, mothers seemed especially involved with Difficult children. With Active and Timid children, there were more significant correlations involving fathers than mothers (Tables 2 & 3). With Difficult children, there were 12 significant correlations involving mothers, compared with five for fathers (Table 4). Whereas Active and Timid scores were not highly correlated with mother's mood, Difficult scores were correlated with three out of the four mood scales. The more Difficult the child, the more Anxious, Inwardly Irritable, and Outwardly Irritable the mother. Whereas Active and Timid scores were not correlated with child's feelings expressed to mother, the more Difficult the child, the less dependent and the less positive the child felt towards mother. Finally, that the Difficult child itself suffers is suggested by the relatively high number of negative feelings that were self-directed.

REFERENCES

Bates JE 1980 The concept of difficult temperament. Merrill-Palmer Q 26:299-319
Bates JE, Freeland CAB, Lounsbury ML 1979 Measurement of infant difficultness. Child Dev 50:794-803

Bell RQ, Waldrop MF 1982 Temperament and minor physical anomalies. In: Temperamental differences in infants and young children. Pitman Books, London (Ciba Found Symp 89) p 206-220

Billman J, McDevitt SC 1980 Convergence of parent and observer ratings of temperament with observations of peer interaction in nursery school. Child Dev 51:395-400

Brown G, Rutter M 1966 The measurement of family activities and relationships: a methodological study. Hum Relat 19:241-263

Bruner JS, Tagiuri R 1954 The perception of people. In: Lindzey IG (ed) Handbook of Social Psychology. Addison Wesley, Cambridge, Mass, p 601-633

Buss DM, Block JH, Block J 1980 Preschool activity level: personality correlates and developmental implications. Child Dev 51:401-408

Dunn J, Kendrick C 1980 Studying temperament and parent–child interaction: a comparison of information from direct observation and from parental interview. Dev Med Child Neurol 22:484-496

Dunn J, Kendrick C 1982 Siblings: love, envy and understanding. Harvard University Press, Cambridge, Mass

Garside RF, Birch H, Scott DMcI et al 1975 Dimensions of temperament in infant school children. J Child Psychol Psychiatry Allied Discip 16:219-231

Graham P, Rutter M, George S 1973 Temperamental characteristics as predictors of behavior disorders in children. Am J Orthopsychiatry 43:328-339

Hinde RA, Easton DF, Meller RE, Tamplin AM 1982 Temperamental characteristics of 3–4-year-olds and mother–child interaction. In: Temperamental differences in infants and young children. Pitman Books, London (Ciba Found Symp 89) p 66-86

Lyon ME, Plomin R 1981 The measurement of temperament using parental ratings. J Child Psychol Psychiatry Allied Discip 22:47-53

McDevitt SC, Carey WB 1978 The measurement of temperament in 3–7 year old children. J Child Psychol Psychiatry Allied Discip 19:245-253

Nie NH, Hull CH, Jenkins JG, Steinbrenner K, Bént DH 1975 Statistical package for the social sciences, 2nd edn. McGraw-Hill, New York

Plomin R 1976 A twin and family study of personality in young children. J Psychol 94:233-235

Rutter M 1982 Temperament: concepts, issues and problems. In: Temperamental differences in infants and young children. Pitman Books, London (Ciba Found Symp 89) p 1-19

Snaith RP, Constantopoulos AA, Jardine MY, McGuffin P 1978 A clinical scale for the self-assessment of irritability. Br J Psychiatry 132:164-171

Stevenson-Hinde J, Simpson MJA 1981 Mothers' characteristics, interactions, and infants' characteristics. Child Dev 52:1246-1254

Thomas A, Chess S 1977 Temperament and development. Brunner/Mazel, New York

Thomas A, Chess S, Birch HG, Hertzig ME, Korn S 1963 Behavioral individuality in early childhood. New York University Press, New York

Wolkind SN, De Salis W 1982 Infant temperament, maternal mental state and child behavioural problems. In: Temperamental differences in infants and young children. Pitman Books, London (Ciba Found Symp 89) p 221-239

DISCUSSION

Carey: I am interested in the strong correlation that you found between the Difficult child and high activity. McDevitt & I, using slightly different definitions for both, have found similar results (Carey & McDevitt 1978). This is of more than passing theoretical interest. In America, many children are diagnosed as being hyperactive. However, it is probably not the activity itself that the parents and teachers are complaining about but, rather, the associated difficult temperament and, in particular, the low adaptability that makes these children hard to get along with. I am glad that your results replicate ours.

Wolkind: Do you have any explanation, Dr Stevenson-Hinde, for your very interesting finding that the younger the sibling, the more active the child? We should consider whether we are actually talking about *temperament* here. It is terribly difficult to sort out the 'what' and the 'how' of behaviour.

Stevenson-Hinde: I think we are talking primarily about the 'how' of behaviour, since the interview was designed for this, with different questions and ratings for different contexts (e.g. playtime, mealtime, bedtime). If a focal child has a younger sibling, then the household is more chaotic than if the child has a sibling who is at primary school for most of the day. This alone could make the child more Active. However, the effect of a younger sibling is probably more profound than this, as suggested by our finding that the younger the sibling the more Difficult the child, and by Judy Dunn's work (Dunn & Kendrick 1982).

Graham: We should avoid suggesting that there is a one-way traffic here; some studies seem to show that difficult children have an impact on their parents' mood and behaviour. The most convincing are studies of hyperactive children which suggest that the negative interactions between mothers and children diminish if the hyperactivity is controlled (Barkley & Cunningham 1979). We have some evidence that non-disturbed children, whose parents have negative attitudes or are depressed, develop more problems later on (Richman et al 1982). We surely can't expect all the influence to be in one direction.

Rutter: The direction and extent of influence between parent and child may, of course, vary at different ages. Clarke-Stewart (1973) showed that the pattern of relationships changed over the first few years, with more influence from the infant at one age and more influence from the mother at another age.

Chess: We recently reviewed the progress of the Difficult children in our longitudinal study. I re-examined the early interviews, child by child, and was struck by a phenomenon that we had recorded but I had not remembered: although some infants had scored highly in these early interviews in what we term Difficult, the parents (mostly the mothers) gave positive explanations of their infant's behaviour. For example, they described the child as alert. At the 1½ or 2-year-old stage, our interviews included a question at the start and end about the parents' general opinion of the child. These opinions were often contrary to the indications of the child's temperament from the details of the interview. As the children grew older, the mothers gave more overall negative statements, but these were usually qualified by a positive statement. As the children reached three or four years of age these positive statements were less frequent, and the parents' general opinions of the child were more in keeping with the actual description of the child that they themselves had given.

Wilson: Dr Stevenson-Hinde, was there more Activity or more Difficulty in your entire sample at age 50 months than at 42 months? We have seen all our children on annual visits, and have found that 2 years is a truculent age; at age 3 the child is much more adaptable, easy to test and to deal with in the play room; at age 4 the child tends to return to being much more truculent. Your results may reflect normal age changes that tend to be rather wide in terms of your sample, but are perhaps even magnified for the so-called Difficult child.

Stevenson-Hinde: Over our eight months of study, as I mentioned, the correlation coefficients showed that the children tended to be rank-ordered in the same way at 42 months as at 50 months. Furthermore, Wilcoxon matched-pairs tests from 42 to 50 months, for each of the items separately, and for the summary scores, showed no significant changes. Neither did the ranges change, so the correlations are not just an artifact of an increased range at 50 months. Over the eight months we see a rather stable set of characteristics but the correlations with reported interactions become stronger at 50 months.

Graham: Could cross-lag correlations help to sort out the cause and effect issue, i.e. whether irritability in the mother at the two ages was related to activity and difficulty in her child at these times?

Wolkind: We tried to look at that in our study but there is a marked degree of stability about the mothers' mental state. This makes it quite hard to tease out the effects of maternal depression at one stage and child behaviour at a later one.

Rutter: Recently there has been criticism (Kenny 1975) of cross-lag correlations because of distortions created by changing reliabilities and changing ranges. One could, however, look at more than one child in the same family, so that there is one individual (the parent) who remains 'constant' but two children who provide the parent with different stimuli.

Stevenson-Hinde: We could easily have obtained temperamental characteristic data on the other siblings in this study, but did not. Next time we will!

Dunn: But that approach wouldn't really answer the question because the mother's relationship with each of her two children is different, and could be changing differently over time. The simple measure of her irritability wouldn't be appropriate because she could be more irritable with one child than with the other. One cannot treat her as a constant.

Rutter: No, but although the two patterns of interaction may be changing in different directions, the mother is constant in some respects.

Stevenson-Hinde: The ideal study would be to assess the characteristics and the mood of the mother, which one could regard as more constant than her interactions, and to correlate all the information.

Bell: I, and many others, have reached the conclusion that longitudinal studies, although they give the sequences of behavioural changes, seldom if ever sort out causal effects. The Clarke-Stewart (1973) study that Professor Rutter just mentioned did in fact use cross-lag correlations. As statisticians begin to challenge our ability to meet the assumptions which the cross-lag technique requires, we return to where we started. We are unable to sort out causal effects unless the longitudinal study has been designed in some unusual way by, for example, including adoptive families. Nevertheless, the sequences described in longitudinal studies are useful in themselves, especially the interesting changes that you have described between 42 and 50 months.

REFERENCES

Barkley RA, Cunningham CE 1979 The effects of methylphenidate on the mother-child interaction of hyperactive children. Arch Gen Psychiatry 36:201-208

Carey WB, McDevitt SC 1978 Stability and change in individual temperament diagnoses from infancy to early childhood. J Am Acad Child Psychiatry 17:331-337

Clarke-Stewart KA 1973 Interactions between mothers and their young children: characteristics and consequences. Monogr Soc Res Child Dev 38(No 153):1-109

Dunn J, Kendrick C 1982 Siblings: love, envy and understanding. Harvard University Press, Cambridge, Mass

Kenny DA 1975 Cross-lagged panel correlation: a test for spuriousness. Psychol Bull 82:887-903

Richman N, Stevenson J, Graham P 1982 Preschool to school: a behavioural study. Academic Press, London

Temperamental characteristics of 3–4-year-olds and mother–child interaction

R. A. HINDE, D. F. EASTON, R. E. MELLER and A. M. TAMPLIN

MRC Unit on the Development and Integration of Behaviour, University Sub-Department of Animal Behaviour, Madingley, Cambridge CB3 8AA, UK

Abstract Comparisons are presented between the temperamental characteristics of preschool-age children from two-child families and aspects of mother–child interaction observed in the home. The data were collected when the children were 42 months old (*n* = 45) and 50 months old (*n* = 37). Although few behavioural items were directly relevant to temperament, several temperamental characteristics (Moody, Intense, Shy, Assertive) had behavioural correlates of a type that might be expected. Active and Irregular also showed meaningful patterns of correlations. Unmalleable, Dependent and Attention span did not. However, although there were no sex differences in the ratings of temperamental characteristics, the correlations between particular characteristics and behavioural items sometimes differed markedly between boys and girls, and also between firstborns and secondborns. Thus comparisons between temperamental characteristics and the behavioural data involving the whole sample were sometimes less revealing than those concerning each sex or sibling-status group separately.

The nature of the relationship between a mother and her child depends on the characteristics of each of them. At the same time the child's personality (and perhaps that of the mother) may be moulded to some degree by the nature of that relationship. One route towards understanding this dialectic between personality and relationship is to assess how relationships (or their constituent interactions) vary with the characteristics of one or both participants. This paper is concerned with associations between preschool children's temperamental characteristics and the behaviour shown to and by them in interaction with their mothers.

Temperamental characteristics refer to behavioural style—the *how* of behaviour as opposed to *what* an individual does or *why* he or she does it (Cattell 1950, Thomas & Chess 1977). It was assessed by a maternal interview based on one developed by Garside et al (1975). The behavioural data, obtained from observations of the child in interaction with the mother at

1982 Temperamental differences in infants and young children. Pitman Books Ltd, London (Ciba Foundation symposium 89) p 66-86

home, were concerned with the type of behaviour shown, and only to a limited extent with style. Thus, whilst the reliability of parental reports is a proper subject for discussion (Thomas & Chess 1977, Bates 1980, Dunn & Kendrick 1980), it is not the issue here. Rather, the focus is on how temperamental characteristics or their correlates are associated with aspects of mother–child interaction—an issue essential for understanding the significance of temperamental characteristics in the dynamics of development. Any relations between temperament and mother–child interaction must result either from the child's behavioural attributes being correlated with the temperamental characteristic in question, or from aspects of the maternal behaviour or the mother–child relationship constantly found with children of that temperament.

The behavioural attributes that correlate with particular temperamental characteristics are likely to differ between boys and girls, between first- and secondborn children, and with age. Furthermore, mothers of boys differ from mothers of girls in their expectations about their child's behaviour, and the history of relationships with firstborns differs from that with secondborns. Thus this paper is concerned also with the extent to which the relations between temperamental characteristics and behaviour vary with sex, sibling status and age.

Methods

Data were collected on 21 girls (11 firstborn and 10 secondborn) and 24 boys (six firstborn and 18 secondborn) who were 42 months old, and again on 16 of the girls (8 + 8) and 21 of the boys (6 + 15) at 50 months. Further details, and the methods by which the temperamental characteristics were assessed, are given in the preceding paper in this volume by Stevenson-Hinde & Simpson (1982).

Interactions between mother and child were observed in the home, and recorded by spoken commentary onto tape, on two visits at each age. On the first, the mother was asked to engage in any activity that she and the child usually did together (e.g. cooking), and subsequently to carry on with her usual concerns. On the second, she was asked first to introduce the child to some toys provided by the experimenter. Total observation time was about 120 min at each age. The tapes were subsequently coded, usually on the same day, using a modified version of Lytton's (1973) modification of Caldwell's (1969) coding scheme. Details of the behavioural items used and their split-halves reliability are available on request. Temperament assessment and behavioural observations were made by different observers.

The primary data concerned durations of types of behaviour or frequencies of types of interaction, with mother or child as subject. The frequencies were expressed also as proportions of the total interaction of each. Data were reduced to 49 observational items by removal of ones that were rare, unreliable or redundant. They were subjected to a group average cluster analysis on the Spearman rank-order correlations between items (Everitt 1974), clustering being performed to a minimum level of $P < 0.10$ (two-tailed). The items and clusters are given in the Appendix (p 79-80).

The data presented in this paper consist of Spearman rank-order correlation coefficients (two-tailed) between the observational items and each temperamental characteristic. Given the number of observational items, a number of significant correlations might appear by chance. If the observational items were statistically independent of each other, two to three correlations significant at $P < 0.05$ would be expected for each characteristic. However, since the items are variably intercorrelated, it is impossible to give a precise figure for the number of significant correlations that would be expected by chance. This difficulty has been minimized by (a) using the cluster analysis so that the extent to which the items correlating with each characteristic come from different clusters can be assessed by the reader, and (b) focusing on meaningful patterns of correlations rather than on individual items. For most analyses involving all the children, all coefficients significant at $P < 0.05$ have been reported. When boys and girls or firstborns and secondborns were assessed separately this method would have been unnecessarily cumbersome, and only those contributing to a meaningful pattern are presented. The full tables of correlations are available on request.

Correlations involving proportions of interaction types were usually similar to those involving frequencies. If both were significant, the former were used. If only frequency gave a significant correlation, this has been indicated by '(F)'.

Results

The relations between the behavioural data and each temperamental characteristic in turn are summarized here. The nine characteristics are briefly defined in Table 1 (p 54) of the previous paper (Stevenson-Hinde & Simpson 1982).

Active

Children rated as high on this characteristic were restless or 'on the move'. Many of the correlations with the observational data (Table 1) can be seen as

TABLE 1 Active child versus mother–child interaction

Observation	Spearman rank correlation coefficients					
	At 42 months			At 50 months		
	Overall	Girls	Boys	Overall	Girls	Boys
X Expresses pleasure	−.32*			−.33*	−.53*	−.09
M Physical friendly	−.31*(F)	.09	−.59**			
M Verbal friendly				−.38*	−.60*	−.24
M Expresses pleasure	−.34*	−.24	−.42*	−.46**	−.55*	−.42†
M Solicitous	−.35*	−.26	−.44*	−.34*	−.28	−.47*
X Neutral speech		−.45*(F)	−.13(F)	−.43**	−.53*	−.34
X Intellectual speech		.01	−.43*			
X Informational questions				−.41**		
M Neutral speech				−.33*	−.51*	−.19
M Intellectual speech	−.29*(F)	−.47*(F)	−.12(F)			
M Conversational questions				−.43**	−.48†	−.40†
M Informational questions	−.29*(F)			−.42**	−.54*(F)	−.37(F)
X Strong controls				.41*		
X Inhibitory controls				−.34*	−.62**	−.04
X Non-complies					−.10	.53*
M Active hostile	−.31*(F)	.07	−.52**			
X Excitedly		−.11	.43*			
Activity changes	.30*	.23	.41*			

Rank order correlations that were significant overall, or for boys or girls separately, are shown. Overall correlations involved five clusters at 42 months and four at 50 months (see appendix). †$P < 0.10$, *$P < 0.05$, **$P < 0.01$, two-tailed; X, child; M, mother. Where the coefficient for one subgroup was significant, the coefficient for the complementary subgroup is given. (F) indicates that only frequency gave a significant correlation.

correlates of this behavioural style. Although the mothers of Active children interacted only slightly less with them than did the mothers of less boisterous children, the proportions of a variety of interactions were low in Active children. These included physical friendliness and maternal hostility at 42 months and, at both ages, expressing pleasure, a number of measures of neutral speech and maternal solicitude. These negative correlations were countered by a number of mostly non-significant positive ones suggestive of a tense relationship, including strong controls by the child (0.41*).

Mothers responded differently to Active children according to their sex. Correlations concerned with maternal physical friendliness, hostility and solicitude were due primarily to boys, whilst correlations concerned with verbal interactions were nearly all stronger for daughters (see Table 1).

There were also differences between first- and secondborns. At 42 months Active secondborn, but not firstborn, children tended to behave excitedly

*$P < 0.05$.

(0.49** versus −0.13). At 50 months Active secondborn children tended to be non-complying (0.45* versus −0.44) and to show reactive hostility (0.50* versus −0.00); but it was Active firstborns, and not secondborns, who received more maternal disconfirmation (0.53* versus −0.14(F)), strong control (0.57* versus –0.26), gentle control (0.59* versus –0.05(F)), intellectual speech (0.69** versus –0.11) and conversational questions (0.58* versus –0.43*) than non-Active ones.

Shy

This rating was based on a report of behaviour to strange people or in strange places. Not surprisingly, therefore, there were few overall correlations with behaviour at home (Table 2), though the strong tendency for Shy children not to initiate joint activities with the mother at 50 months is noteworthy.

TABLE 2 Shy child versus mother–child interaction

Observation	Spearman rank correlation coefficients					
	42 months			50 months		
	Overall	Girls	Boys	Overall	Girls	Boys
X Physical friendly				.39*	.04	.50*
X Seeks dependence		−.13(F)	.45*(F)			
X Initiates joint activities		−.13	.43*	−.40**	−.67**	−.30
M Solicitous					.53*	−.02
X Intellectual speech	−.32*	−.48*	−.25			
X Conversational questions					.56*	−.43†
X Informational questions				.38*		
M Informational questions				.36*	.62*	.09
X Initiates separate activities		.46*	.29			
X Inhibitory controls					.53*	−.06
X Active hostile					−.33	.50*
X Reactive hostile		−.48*(F)	.06(F)			
M Inhibitory controls					−.54*	.09
X Passive		−.52*	.12		−.54*	.35
M Excitedly					.52*	−.10
Activity changes		−.48*(F)	−.09		−.67**	.40†

Overall correlations in two clusters at 42 months and in four at 50 months are shown. See Table 1 for further details.

However, this was partly because the relation of Shy to mother–child interaction differed with sex. At both ages Shy girls, but not Shy boys, were rarely passive or changed activities, compared with non-Shy children. At 42 months Shy boys showed dependence (seeking help, following their mothers,

**P < 0.01.

seeking approval) and initiated joint activities, whereas Shy girls showed little reactive hostility, and the activities they initiated tended to be separate from those of their mothers. Shy boys were both actively hostile and physically friendly at 50 months. Shy girls, by contrast, showed high levels of conversational questions and inhibitory control to the mother at the older age, yet tended to receive little maternal inhibitory control and much solicitude, compared with non-Shy girls.

In addition, a number of correlations suggested that mothers accommodated to Shy firstborns more than to Shy secondborns. At the 42-month stage, mothers tended to express pleasure and to show verbal friendliness to Shy firstborns more than to non-Shy ones, but this was not true for secondborns (0.61** versus 0.04 and 0.26 versus −0.45*). Furthermore, Shy firstborn girls seldom received maternal disconfirmation (−0.78**); correlations for secondborn girls and for boys were low. At 50 months Shy firstborns, but not secondborns, gave more inhibitory control (0.61* versus −0.23).

Dependent

Although this rating rested in part on the child's behaviour when left by the mother, it also involved questions about clinging and seeking for approval and help. However, there was only one significant overall correlation—with the child's physical friendly responses at 42 months (0.34*).

At 50 months, Dependent firstborns were involved in fewer verbal interactions (−0.70**), a smaller proportion of neutral ones ('child informational questions', −0.58*(F); 'mother intellectual speech', −0.71**; 'mother conversational questions', −0.56*(F)), and received less gentle control (−0.54*(F)), than those who were not Dependent; correlations for secondborns were low or opposite in sign.

Moody

Children rated as Moody tended to be solemn, unhappy or irritable. None of the possibly relevant items, except perhaps maternal reactive hostility, showed significant correlations at 42 months. At 50 months interactions of Moody children involved fewer joint activities and relatively less neutral conversation and verbal friendly interactions, but more of both physical friendly interactions and maternal hostility than those of non-Moody children (Table 3).

At 50 months the relationships of mothers with Moody girls involved a tendency to greater tenseness, which was not present with Moody boys. Thus

TABLE 3 Moody child versus mother–child interaction

Observation	Spearman rank correlation coefficients			
	42 months		*50 months*	
	Overall	*Overall*	*Girl*	*Boy*
X Physical friendly		.38*		
M Physical friendly		.33*		
M Verbal friendly		−.43**(F)	−.57*(F)	−.36(F)
Joint activities		−.32*		
X Neutral speech		−.34*(F)	−.24(F)	−.43†(F)
X Information questions	.33*(F)	−.28†(F)	−.49†(F)	−.19(F)
M Neutral speech		−.42**(F)	−.08	−.46*
M Conversational questions		−.46**(F)	−.00	−.43*
X Disconfirms	−.31*			
X Reactive hostile			.58*	−.17
M Reactive hostile	.37*(F)	.33*	.60*	.18
M Topic changes			.63**	.08

Three clusters are involved at each age. See Table 1 for further details.

Moody girls gave and received more reactive hostility, and had mothers who changed topics and were less friendly, than non-Moody girls; such tendencies were absent or much lower in boys (Table 3).

High ratings were also associated with negative mother–child relationships more in firstborns than in secondborns ('mother negative control', 0.52† versus −0.3; child non-complying, 0.46† versus −0.17; 'mother hostile', 0.46† versus 0.21).

Intense

Children high on the Intense rating could be described as highly strung, screaming when angry, and laughing loudly when amused. As might be expected, they were high on both friendly and (especially at 50 months) hostile interactions with their mothers (Table 4). A strong tendency at 42 months for Intense children to talk about topics not immediately present did not reach significance at 50 months.

The friendly interactions of Intense children involved more physical responses and fewer verbal ones than those of non-Intense children, particularly at 50 months. This was especially true for girls. Indeed a high Intense rating was associated with many more differences in mother–daughter relationships than in mother–son relationships: boys showed no significant correlations at either age, whereas girls showed 13.

†$0.10 > P > 0.05$

TABLE 4 Intense child versus mother–child interaction

Observation	Spearman rank correlation coefficients					
	42 months			50 months		
	Overall	Girls	Boys	Overall	Girls	Boys
X Physical friendly				.33*	.51*	.24
X Verbal friendly	.36*					
M Physical friendly				.34*	.65**	.19
M Verbal friendly				−.32*	−.50*	−.22
M Expresses pleasure		−.44*(F)	.14(F)			
M and X Physical contact	.30*	.40†	.11			
Talks about non-present	.52***	.57**	.39†			
X Total verbal						
X Informational questions	.31*(F)			−.52*		.17
M Neutral speech				−.56*		−.11
M Conversational questions		−.48*(F)	.06			
X Initiates separate activities						
X Disconfirms		−.46*	−.18			
X Strong controls	.39**(F)	.51*(F)	.20(F)		.54*	.08
X Active hostile	.34*(F)			.47**	.73***	.32
M Inhibitory controls	−.35*					
M Reactive hostile	.32*	.52*	.16			

Overall correlations in six clusters at 42 months and in three at 50 months are shown. See Table 1 for further details. ***$P < 0.001$.

A high Intense rating was associated with more difficult mother–child relationships in firstborns but with more friendly interactions in secondborns. Thus, the correlations of Intense with hostility to the mother, and with low maternal solicitude, were stronger in first than in secondborns (50 months, 0.74** versus 0.43* and −0.59* versus −0.05). Conversely, correlations with friendly responses were negative or low in firstborns, but significantly positive in secondborns ('child physical friendly', 42 months, −0.38 versus 0.39*; 'child verbal friendly', 0.14 versus 0.51** and 0.01 versus 0.44*; 'mother physical friendly', 50 months, 0.23 versus 0.41*).

Unmalleable

This rating depends on the ease with which the child complies with the mother's requests. Surprisingly, few correlations with home observational items appeared, though there was a negative correlation with maternal inhibitory control at each age (−0.48*** and −0.30*). Unmalleable children

---

***$P < 0.001$

also received less maternal solicitude at 42 months (−0.31*); at 50 months a similar trend did not quite reach significance.

At 42 months there was some evidence that daughters perceived as unmalleable tended to have a more negative relationship with their mothers than did sons. Thus for daughters, more than for sons, the Unmalleable rating was negatively related to the categories of 'mother verbal friendly' (−0.50* versus 0.36), 'mother express pleasure' (−0.47* versus 0.09), 'mother conversational questions' (−0.47* versus 0.19 (F)) and 'mother solicitous' (–0.44* versus −0.22). Unmalleable girls, but not boys, tended not to comply with maternal controls (0.44* versus 0.08). They were less likely to receive gentle controls than Malleable girls (−0.46*), while for boys there was a non-significant opposite tendency (0.39†). However it was the Unmalleable boys who tended to receive few maternal inhibitory controls (−0.59** versus −0.15).

Irregular

This rating is concerned with consistency in the time at which the child sleeps, wakes and gets hungry, and not surprisingly it bore little relation, overall, to home observations on specific occasions. However, at both ages Irregular children received more strong control from their mothers than children not so rated (Table 5).

TABLE 5 Irregular child versus mother–child interaction

Observation	Spearman rank correlation coefficients					
		42 months			50 months	
	Overall	First-born	Second-born	Overall	First-born	Second-born
X Intellectual conversation					−.27	.46*
X Informational questions					−.10	.42*
M Intellectual speech	−.30*	−.54*	−.13		.00	.43*
M Informational questions		−.33	.42*			
X Disconfirms		−.09	.48**(F)			
M Strong controls	.28†	−.04	.52**	.33*	.35(F)	.42*(F)
M Inhibitory controls					−.18	.44*(F)
M Active hostile					.07	.46*
M Reactive hostile		−.00	.38*(F)			
X Excitedly	−.29*	−.13	−.43*			
Activity changes				.35*	.09	.45*

Correlations in four clusters at 42 months and in three at 50 months are shown. See Table 1 for further details.

At 50 months Irregular girls tended to have a less positive relationship with their mothers than did girls with low ratings. Although they tended to show dependence (0.50*), the correlations with 'child express pleasure', and 'child neutral speech', and with 'maternal neutral speech' and 'maternal informational questions', were all negative (−0.54*, −0.67**, −0.52*, −0.78**). For boys all these correlations were very weak.

At both ages a high rating for Irregular was associated with high levels of neutral conversation and of maternal hostility and control in secondborns, whilst for firstborns the correlations were low or even reversed (Table 5).

Assertive

Assertiveness is rated on bossiness and fighting in interactions with peers, and not with the mother. However, at 42 months the mothers of Assertive children tended both not to comply with their controls and to control them relatively infrequently (Table 6). These correlations were due to girls more than to boys (0.45* versus 0.26 and −0.66*** versus −0.15 respectively). In addition Assertive girls, but not boys, tended to be high on reactive hostility (0.60** versus –0.26).

TABLE 6 Assertive child versus mother–child interaction

Observation	Spearman rank correlation coefficients					
		42 months			50 months	
	Overall	First-born	Second-born	Overall	First-born	Second-born
X Physical friendly		−.49*	.10			
X Initiates joint activities		.28	−.41*	.44**	.02	.65***
M Verbal friendly					−.61*(F)	.04
M Expresses pleasure					−.62*	.21
X Neutral speech		−.63**	.25			
X Intellectual speech					.19	.55**
M Neutral speech				.33*		
M Intellectual speech		−.64**(F)	.14		−.11	.56**
Talks about non-present		−.14	.43*		.14	.49*
X Strong controls				.32*(F)		
X Non-complies		.37	−.38*			
X Active hostile					.56*	.01
M Initiates separate activities				−.33*		
M Strong controls	−.31*					
M Non-complies	.36*					
M Excitedly					−.63*	.16

Overall correlations from two clusters at 42 months and from four at 50 months are shown. See Table 1 for further details. ***P < 0.001.

At 50 months Assertiveness appeared in interactions with the mother as a strong tendency to initiate joint activities and to control her (Table 6). Again, it was related more to mother–daughter than to mother–son interaction. The tendency to initiate joint activities was stronger for girls (0.78*** versus 0.27). Assertive girls, but not boys, tended to show much active hostility (0.52* versus −0.00) and frequent activity changes (0.51* versus 0.11), and tended to receive frequent inhibitory control from the mother (0.51* versus −0.08 (F)). In addition, Assertive girls received little neutral speech (−0.43* versus −0.23) and asked few conversational questions (−0.52* versus −0.12).

As with the Intense rating, Assertiveness was associated with a less positive mother–child relationship more in firstborns than in secondborns (Table 6). Thus, at 42 months firstborns rated as Assertive were involved in less neutral and intellectual conversation, and were less physically friendly, than those who received a low rating, whilst secondborns who were Assertive tended to have conversations about non-present topics and to be complying. At 50 months this trend was still apparent.

Attention span

This was concerned with the duration for which the child engaged in an activity on his or her own. Correlations with changes in activity or topic changes, which might have been expected, did not appear, and there were few significant correlations overall.

Discussion

First, some reservations must be made explicit. Many of the correlations discussed are in the 0.30–0.40 range; the variance accounted for is thus small. Lack of independence between the behavioural items prohibits an overall assessment of the significance of the correlations obtained. And the inappropriateness of parametric statistics for the variably skewed data on temperamental characteristics prevents any useful assessment of the significance of differences between correlations. The data must thus be regarded as tentative. Nevertheless they point to some interesting conclusions.

Few of the behavioural items were directly relevant to temperament. Yet several of the temperamental characteristics had a pattern of correlates of the type that might be expected. Moody children, especially girls, received maternal hostility and more physical but fewer verbal friendly responses. Intense children showed a somewhat similar pattern. Shy boys showed high dependence on their mothers, while the mothers of Shy girls were tolerant and solicitous. At 42 months Assertive children had non-complying mothers and the girls showed high proportions of reactive hostility; at 50 months Assertive children often initiated joint activities and controlled their mothers. The behavioural style of Active children could have contributed to the reduction in many types of interaction with the mothers. Even Irregular children, though rated on behaviour that was quite unrelated to the items recorded in the observations, showed correlates, with Irregular girls tending to have fewer positive relationships with their mothers. However, Unmalleable and Dependent, the two items that might have been expected to show correlations with mother–child interaction, in fact showed few. Of course this could imply that the assessment of these children, though significantly consistent over eight months (see Stevenson-Hinde & Simpson 1982), lacked validity. However, the negative correlations of Unmalleable (and also Intense) with maternal control suggest that the mothers may have adjusted their behaviour to their perceptions of their children and/or to the observer's presence. Similar considerations apply to the Dependent rating.

Some of the similarities in behavioural correlates between temperamental characteristics are undoubtedly due to correlations between those characteristics themselves: for instance, Moody and Intense correlated significantly at both ages. But the precise pattern of correlations between temperamental characteristics differed with age, sex and sibling status—an issue discussed by Stevenson-Hinde & Simpson (1982).

The basis on which the mothers' answers to the questions put in interview are summed to give temperamental characteristics is in part intuitive. Many authors have gone further, summing the scores of these temperamental characteristics into higher-order dimensions (e.g. Thomas & Chess 1977). Thus, Stevenson-Hinde & Simpson (1982) summed Shy (itself a summary score) and Dependent to give Timid; and Moody, Intense and Unmalleable to give Difficult. Such a procedure is justified in part by the correlations between the individual characteristics. Its practical utility no doubt varies with the use to which the summary scores are to be put. If one is considering the impact of the children on their mothers, it may well be that the mothers are more stressed if they have children who are *either* Moody *or* Intense *or* Unmalleable. In the present study correlations between the behavioural items and the summary score were assessed, but no increase in significance was achieved thereby, and some of the richness of the data was lost.

Whilst the overall correlations between the temperamental characteristics and the measures of mother–child interaction were substantial, consideration of the sexes and sibling groups separately was in some cases even more revealing. High ratings on Active and Shy tended to be correlated more with verbal items in girls and physical items in boys. With the 'Difficult' items of Moody, Intense and Unmalleable, and also with Irregular and Assertive, high ratings were associated with difficult mother–child relationships more in girls than in boys. This could of course be due to temperament assessment being in some sense more accurate with girls, but it could also be due to basic differences between mother–daughter and mother–son relationships. In any case it must be emphasized that these sex differences in the relations between temperamental characteristics and behaviour appeared in the near absence of significant sex differences in the temperamental characteristics themselves (Stevenson-Hinde & Simpson 1982). In this respect it echoes earlier data on rhesus monkeys (Stevenson-Hinde & Simpson 1981).

Comparable differences arose between firstborns and secondborns. High ratings on Moody, Intense, Assertive and, possibly, Active were associated with negative interactions more in firstborns than in secondborns, but with Irregular the reverse was true. Since there were more male secondborns than firstborns, sex and sibling group differences were to some extent compounded. However (a) the girls were more evenly divided between the sibling groups; (b) the particular items by which temperamental characteristics were associated with difficult relationships more in firstborns than in secondborns were mostly different from the items responsible for the association with difficult relationships more in girls than in boys; and (c) where the items were the same, correlation coefficients for the lower subgroups (e.g. younger boys versus older boys) were nearly always in harmony with the generalizations given in this paper though often not reaching significance because of the lower numbers involved.

In summary, these data demonstrate that temperamental characteristics assessed from maternal interview show strong associations with aspects of mother–child interaction. But, although the differences between correlations could not be established as significant, the pattern and direction of differences strongly suggest that the importance of temperamental characteristics in the development of personality may be greatly enhanced if girls and boys, and if first and later-borns, are considered separately.

Of course, the value of the assessment of temperamental characteristics would be even greater if they predicted behaviour outside the home. Two studies have shown that temperamental characteristics assessed by preschool teachers can provide low to moderate correlations with assessments by mothers (Billman & McDevitt 1980, D. A. Corsini & K. Doyle 1979, cited in Bates 1980). In addition, the former authors reported correlations between six temperament variables and other aspects of preschool behaviour. Our own data (R. A. Hinde, R. E. Meller, J. Stevenson-Hinde & A. M. Tamplin, unpublished work) confirm these findings: the subjects of the present study were observed also in preschool, and patterns of correlations between temperamental characteristics and behaviour even richer than those found at home emerged. In several cases the preschool correlations were in accord with those found at home. For example Moody children, who tended to receive both physical friendly interactions and hostility from their mothers at home, tended (at school) to receive friendly responses from adults at 42 months and to be involved in controlling and in hostile interactions at both ages. Furthermore, differences comparable to those found at home occurred also in preschool between boys and girls, and between firstborns and secondborns, in the relations of temperamental characteristics to behaviour. To the extent that temperamental characteristics are related to behaviour outside the home as well as in interaction with the mother, and to the extent that they show similar relations to behaviour in different situations, they are more likely to represent enduring characteristics of behaviour that are important in the development of personality.

Acknowledgements

This work was supported by the Medical Research Council, The Royal Society and the Grant Foundation. We are indebted to the Managers of the preschool for permission to work in the school, to the head teacher Mrs Head and her colleagues for all the support they gave us, and to the mothers for their time and cooperation. We are grateful to Judy Dunn and Joan Stevenson-Hinde for comments on the manuscript.

Appendix

Home variables

X Physical friendly (2,2); X Verbal friendly (2,1); X Expresses pleasure (1,1); X Initiates joint activities (4,4); M Physical friendly (2,2); M Verbal friendly (5,1); M Expresses pleasure (1,1); M solicitous (6,6); M Initiates joint activities (4,4); X and M Physical contact (2,8); Joint activities (1,7); X Total verbal (10,1); X Neutral speech (1,1); X Intellectual speech (8,1); X Conversational questions (1,6); X Informational questions (12,1); M Total verbal (10,1); M Neutral speech (1,1); M Intellectual speech (1,1); M Conversational questions (1,1); M Informational questions (1,1); Talk about non-present (11,1); X Initiates separate activities (9,9); X Seeks dependence (3,5); X Gentle controls (13,7); X Strong controls (7,3); X Inhibitory controls (14,10); X Disconfirms (6,4); X Non-complies to gentle control (3,3); X Non-complies to strong control (3,3); X Non-complies to all control (3,3); X Active hostile (8,11); X Reactive hostile (3,3); M initiates separate activities (2,5); M Gentle controls (11,7); M Strong controls (5,5); M Inhibitory controls (6,7); M Disconfirms (8,5); M Non-complies to all control (7,7); M

Active hostile (8,7); M Reactive hostile (7,7); X Passive (9,7); X Auto-manipulates (15,1); X Play-noises (11,1); X Excitedly (7,1); X Topic changes (10,7); M Excitedly (11,1); M Topic changes (10,7); Activity changes (9,7).

The numbers after each item are arbitrary labels for the clusters at age 42 months and 50 months. Clusters 1 to 6 at 42 months correspond approximately to clusters 1 to 6 at 50 months. Clusters 7 to 10 at 42 months are all related to Cluster 7 at 50 months. X, child; M, mother.

REFERENCES

Bates JE 1980 The concept of difficult temperament. Merrill-Palmer Q 26:299-319
Billman J, McDevitt SC 1980 Convergence of parent and observer ratings of temperament with observations of peer interaction in nursery school. Child Dev 51:395-400
Caldwell BM 1969 A new "APPROACH" to behavioral ecology. In: Hill IP (ed) Minnesota symposia on child psychology, vol 2. University of Minnesota Press, Minneapolis
Cattell RB 1950 Personality: a systematic and factual study. McGraw-Hill, New York
Dunn J, Kendrick C 1980 Studying temperament and parent–child interaction: a comparison of information from direct observation, and from parental interview. Dev Med Child Neurol 22:484-496
Everitt B 1974 Cluster analysis. Heinemann Educational Books Ltd, London
Garside RF, Birch H, Scott DMcI et al 1975 Dimensions of temperament in infant school children. J Child Psychol Psychiatry Allied Discip 16:219-231
Lytton H 1973 Three approaches to the study of parent–child interaction: ethological, interview and experimental. J Child Psychol Psychiatry Allied Discip 14:1-17
Stevenson-Hinde J, Simpson MJA 1981 Mothers' characteristics, interactions, and infants' characteristics. Child Dev 52:1246-1254
Stevenson-Hinde J, Simpson AE 1982 Temperament and relationships. In: Temperamental differences in infants and young children. Pitman Books, London (Ciba Found Symp 89) p 51-65
Thomas A, Chess S 1977 Temperament and development. Brunner/Mazel, New York

DISCUSSION

Rutter: Could you speculate on the reason for the sex differences you observed? It is striking that you see few sex differences in the behavioural measures and yet marked differences in the pattern of correlation. Do the data throw any light on this?

Hinde: No. That is our next task. One possibility is that the mothers or the teachers simply respond to, or make allowances for, boys differently from girls, or firstborns differently from secondborns. It is also possible that the temperamental characteristics we assess are correlated with different *other* characteristics in boys and in girls, or in firstborns and in secondborns.

Stevenson-Hinde: With rhesus monkeys we have also found few sex differences in terms of the actual male and female scores, but we have found striking sex differences in patterns of correlations. For example, at one year of age there were no sex differences in scores along a Confident to Fearful, Excitable to Slow, or Sociable to Solitary dimension. However, the scores of mothers showed one pattern of correlations with their one-year-old daughters' scores and a different pattern with their sons' scores (Stevenson-Hinde & Simpson 1981).

Rutter: What mechanisms could explain how these patterns arose?

Stevenson-Hinde: These are correlational data. We found, for example, that daughters tended to be ranked in a similar way to their mothers, so that Confident mothers had Confident daughters ($r_s = 0.79$), but the correlation between Confident scores of mothers versus sons was effectively zero (0.07). By looking at behavioural interactions from eight weeks onwards, we could see that Confident mothers were behaving in a way with daughters, but not sons, that in the Mary Ainsworth sense would maximize their security (Ainsworth et al 1978). In this way, a high Confident score could arise for a daughter (Stevenson-Hinde & Simpson 1981).

Rutter: Could this occur as a result of rhesus monkey mothers having different expectations of their male and female offspring?

Hinde: In this species of monkey the daughters stay with their mothers and form permanent extended family groups, while the sons leave the group in due course. The relations between mothers and sons and between mothers and daughters are very different for that reason (Stevenson-Hinde & Simpson 1981).

Berger: What I detect in these studies so far is the failure to monitor closely the variety of relevant *parental* characteristics that have been observed. The interaction between parental and child characteristics is likely to be quite important.

Thomas: One reason for this gap is that satisfactory methods for assessing parental temperament have not been available. We have now had some success in this area (see also p 168-175). There is not necessarily any correlation between parental temperament and child temperament; we have seen all kinds of combinations. In our earlier work (Thomas et al 1968) we observed that there was likely to be a poor outcome if both the child and the parent had intense reactions and intense temperaments.

Kohnstamm: It is surprising, Professor Hinde, that the behaviour of the child in school correlated more with the child's temperamental characteristics than did the child's behaviour at home. In addition, I believe your recent work has shown a greater correlation between the child's temperamental characteristics and *outdoor* play at school than with *indoor* play at school. Could it be that the behaviour of a child of a certain temperamental type in the British home situation, whether or not an observer is present, is more controlled than in the preschool, especially when the child's behaviour is difficult or active? It would then be less easy to see the child's temperamental features at home. Is the modern British preschool environment such that any child may behave as his or her own temperament dictates, and without much control? Even so, the best chance to see the child's real temperament would be in outdoor activities at school, where the control is least severe.

Hinde: Yet another issue is the extent to which the mother, as opposed to the child, is controlling her behaviour at home. We had the impression that we had good relations with these mothers and that they were relaxed and not put off by the observer in the home. They were already used to the observer's presence when the behavioural observations were taken. But when we found that the mothers of Unmalleable boys tended especially *not* to show inhibitory controls, we wondered if they were controlling their own behaviour so as not to appear to the observer to be too inflexible with their Unmalleable children!

Stevenson-Hinde: This might be a case where an interview can show more than the observations. It was relatively easy for me to get the mothers to talk about difficult scenes with their children, whereas it might be harder for them to act it out in front of the observer.

Dunn: You interpreted fewer correlations at 42 months than at 50 months in terms of a 'floor'-effect at the school. If that's so you might expect it to be evident in the distributions of the scores.

Hinde: We haven't looked at that yet.

Dunn: I was a bit surprised by it because the temperament interview that we have used focuses on children's reactions either to new situations or to slightly stressful situations (Dunn & Kendrick 1980). One might have expected that with the arrival of the child in school the temperamental differences, and their association with the children's observed behaviour, would become *more* apparent, rather than *less*.

Thomas: I would agree that the first experiences at school are perhaps more revealing for certain characteristics than the period when there has been habituation. Overall, we think that some temperamental characteristics come out more clearly in new situations and certain others in a habituated situation.

Chess: How long had the children been at school during the 42-month observations?

Hinde: It varied with their birthdays, but all were in either the second half of their first term or in their second term. None had been at school for only a few days.

Stevenson-Hinde: Therefore these studies were not catching the child in the initial stress of starting preschool. They normally started preschool at three years of age and we observed them at 3½ years.

Hinde: Children judged as Shy on the basis of the maternal interview interacted less with peers and were more withdrawn than children not so rated at 42 months. But at 50 months these Shy children had turned into outgoing, peer-oriented children.

Thomas: That may not be surprising, because these would be 'slow-to-warm-up' children, who become outgoing once they have had sufficient time to adapt positively.

Kolvin: Your comments on Shy children seem to coincide with some of the Birmingham work (Brown & Lloyd 1975) on children who do not talk when they first go to school but who, within a short time, are making relationships and talking to the other children and the staff. But these must be distinguished from elective mute children (Kolvin & Fundudis 1981).

Hinde: The precise length of time they had been at school may be important here. At 50 months, although they interacted a lot with other children, the interactions involved significantly less often the qualifying adjective 'boastfully'.

Chess: In our group of slow-to-warm up children many of the mothers and teachers described the children at the start of each new school year in the autumn as timid or anxious. Yet we found consistently that by Thanksgiving time (mid-November) the children's new teachers would tell each mother that the teacher had succeeded in bringing the child out of its shell. The child was thus 'brought out of its shell' year after year, at about the same time! By calling this sort of child slow-to-warm-up, we were beginning to assume that we would see a characteristic behaviour of the child in any new situation and that, by the time the child had warmed up, there would be a characteristic familiarized behaviour of the child, given continuity of the situation.

Hinde: It is an open issue whether we would have done better to have standardized the children with respect to their first going to school. In practice we standardized them with respect to age.

Graham: Does this slow-to-warm up phenomenon occur in rhesus monkeys to the same degree as in children? Going to school, and going into the class of a different teacher every year, is something that we impose on children, but not on rhesus monkeys! Is there any similar identifiable phenomenon in the monkeys?

Stevenson-Hinde: Yes; when each monkey was 1-year-old and 2½-years-old, it was removed from its group to a 'strange situation', which could provide a slow-to-warm-up score. While living there for a few weeks, young monkeys received brief tests with novel objects, such as a ball, novel food, and slides of other monkeys. At each age, individual differences were consistent (Stevenson-Hinde et al 1980a). Initial responses to test objects could therefore provide an index of Approach/Withdrawal, while changes over time could provide an index of Adaptability. In addition, at one year the presence of mothers could allow for a Dependency index, based on measures such as time spent off the mother and frequency of leaving the mother (Stevenson-Hinde et al 1980b). With our children, ratings for Approach/ Withdrawal, Adaptability, and Dependency provided a 'Timid' summary score, comparable to Thomas and Chess's 'slow-to-warm up' (Stevenson-Hinde & Simpson, this volume, Table 1, p 54). However, with the monkeys, such a summary score would have been misleading since the measures did not correlate with each other in any simple way, and no neat principal component analysis emerged (Stevenson-Hinde et al 1980a,b). That is not to say that summary measures were never used with monkeys, for in the context of the 'home' situation, sums of observers' ratings have provided convenient 'anchors' for relating to behavioural interactions (Stevenson-Hinde & Simpson 1981).

Keogh: We have measures of adaptability (or flexibility), as rated by different teachers, on children over a two-year period. The Pearson correlation was 0.49 between the teachers' ratings of the same children in year one (age 4) and in year two (age 5). It is interesting that the correlations were higher for girls than for boys.

Hinde: One of our notable observations is that girls rated as Difficult tend to *be* more difficult, in terms of the behavioural data both at home and at school, than boys are. Perhaps the mothers are more tolerant of difficult little boys than of difficult little girls.

Chess: We have commonly heard mothers use the phrase 'Oh, he's a boy' to explain away a great deal of difficult behaviour, even in supposedly egalitarian families! But I don't remember ever hearing that phrase applied to a girl's behaviour.

Wolkind: There might be quite different mechanisms at work in boys and girls. In a study of children in long-term residential care this certainly seemed to be true (Wolkind 1974). It is interesting that in the residential settings the quality of disturbance amongst girls appears to be far more difficult for staff to cope with.

Thomas: The boy in our study who scored as one of the most 'difficult' all through early childhood never actually became a behaviour problem in later childhood (Thomas et al 1982). His father always characterized him as a 'lusty boy', but if he had been a girl it might had been a different story!

Hsu: Coming back to the kindergarten behaviours and children's temperamental characteristics, I would like to emphasize the desirability of international studies (see p 113-120). In different countries, or even within the same country, the sizes of kindergartens are different and the teachers are different. For example, in Taiwan, in one class of kindergarten there may be

40 or 50 children with a highly structured environment and curriculum, and very little time for outdoor activities. In the UK there may be only 10 or 15 children with one or two teachers. Cross-cultural studies would be invaluable here.

Hinde: We deliberately designed this study around a constant element—one school—because we wanted to be able to relate the different home environments to the children's behaviour in the one school.

Rutter: Your data on home–school correlations, then, are not directly comparable with studies in which the children were scattered across many schools.

Bates: Did you test the significance of the differences between the correlations within the different sub-samples?

Hinde: No; one cannot because these are non-parametric items. The temperamental characteristics are rated on a skewed scale from zero to five so one cannot use parametric statistics and cannot assess the relations between the rank-order correlations.

Rutter: Could you, at a rough and ready level, get some notion of the stability of the differences between correlations by splitting the sample in half and seeing to what extent the pattern of differences was similar in the two halves?

Hinde: I would attach much more significance to the pattern of the correlations than to any *P* value showing the significance of the difference between them.

Bates: But the meaning of the pattern differences is not yet clear to me. There are so many published instances of differences between girls and boys, in correlations with certain variables, which turn out to be simply fluctuations due to small-sample correlations.

Hinde: In our data on Intensity versus the mother—child interaction at home, girls showed a total of 13 significant correlations and boys showed none. These 13 significant correlations formed a suggestive pattern. The cluster analysis that we did of the behavioural items showed us the extent to which a correlation in one item necessarily involved a correlation in another item.

Thomas: Did you evaluate the interviews with the teachers in comparison with the teachers' own observations?

Hinde: We have also used a questionnaire on the teachers of these children, and this overlapped partly with the behavioural observations (R. Hinde et al, unpublished results). Of the items that overlapped, at 42 months there were reasonable correlations between the teachers' ratings and the behavioural data; at 50 months those correlations were smaller. We think we know the reason for the falls at least in some cases. For Aggressiveness, there was quite a high correlation at 42 months, but it dropped to about 0.3 at 50 months.

However the *rated* aggressiveness of the children at 50 months correlated most highly with teacher hostility towards children. We believe that the teachers may 'label' the children at 42 months, and continue to assess them and behave towards them in accordance with those labels.

REFERENCES

Ainsworth MDS, Blehar MC, Waters E, Wall S 1978 Patterns of attachment. Erlbaum, New Jersey

Brown JB, Lloyd H 1975 A controlled study of children not speaking at school. J Work Mal Child 3:49-63

Dunn J, Kendrick C 1980 Studying temperament and parent–child interaction: a comparison of information from direct observation and from parental interview. Dev Med Child Neurol 22:484-496

Kolvin I, Fundudis T 1981 Elective mute children: psychological development and background factors. J Child Psychol Psychiatry Allied Discip 22:219-232

Stevenson-Hinde J, Simpson MJA 1981 Mothers' characteristics, interactions, and infants' characteristics. Child Dev 52:1246-1254

Stevenson-Hinde J, Stillwell-Barnes R, Zunz M 1980a Individual differences in young rhesus monkeys: consistency and change. Primates 21:498-509

Stevenson-Hinde J, Zunz M, Stillwell-Barnes R 1980b Behaviour of one-year-old rhesus monkeys in a strange situation. Anim Behav 28:266-277

Thomas A, Chess S, Birch HG 1968 Temperament and behavior disorders in children. New York University Press, New York

Thomas A, Chess S, Korn S 1982 The reality of difficult temperament. Merrill-Palmer Q, in press

Wolkind SN 1974 Sex differences in the aetiology of antisocial disorders in children in long term residential care. Br J Psychiatry 125:125-130

Temperamental differences, family relationships, and young children's response to change within the family

JUDY DUNN and CAROL KENDRICK

MRC Unit on the Development and Integration of Behaviour, University Sub-Department of Animal Behaviour, Madingley, Cambridge, CB3 8AA, UK

Abstract In a longitudinal study of 40 firstborn children, temperamental differences between the children were found to be linked to the emergence and persistence of anxious and unhappy behaviour over the year following the birth of a sibling. Direct observation showed that these temperamental differences were also associated with differences in the children's interactions with their mothers, and with differences in their behaviour towards their mothers when mother and sibling were interacting. In contrast, the wide range of individual differences in the behaviour of the firstborn children to their siblings was not associated with temperamental differences between the children. There was some evidence for continuity in temperamental differences between the assessments before and after the sibling birth, but in many children the behavioural changes were marked. These findings underline the clinical significance of temperamental differences in children's vulnerability to changes in family life; they also indicate that 'temperament' should be considered not as a characteristic of the child independent of his or her particular family relationships but, on the contrary, as closely linked to his or her relationship with the mother, and as susceptible to the effects of marked change in the family environment.

Clinicians have for many years been interested in the notion that temperamental differences in early childhood are linked to the later development of behavioural disorders and to differences in children's vulnerability to stress. There is now some evidence for such a view. Results from the New York longitudinal study did show an association between temperamental differences and later rates of referral for psychiatric help (Rutter et al 1964). In a very different sample of families Graham et al (1973) found a similar association between temperamental differences and later disorder, and Carey (1970) reported that temperamental differences were linked to the frequency

1982 Temperamental differences in infants and young children. Pitman Books Ltd, London (Ciba Foundation symposium 89) p 87-105

of accidents that required suturation during the first two years of life. In a study of 40 families followed over the period when a second child was born we found that the pattern of the firstborn children's reactions to the constellation of events surrounding the birth was related to temperamental differences between the firstborn children assessed before the sibling birth. Children who scored above the median on an assessment of the temperamental trait 'negative mood' before the sibling birth were more likely to increase in withdrawal and in sleeping problems immediately after the birth than the rest of the sample, while those who scored above the median on the traits of 'intensity of emotional expression' and negative mood were more likely to show an increase in clinging. Those who scored above the median on withdrawal before the sibling birth were less likely to show positive interest in the new baby than did the other children in the sample (Dunn et al 1981).

These findings on the relationship between temperament and the immediate reaction of children to the arrival of a sibling raise both *general* questions, about the nature of the association between temperamental differences and the development of behavioural problems, and more specific questions about the long-term significance of the response to the change in family life—do the behavioural changes persist over the following months, and are temperamental differences between the children linked to the persistence or disappearance of problems over the next year?

On the general issue of the association between temperament and the development of behavioural difficulties the sibling study provides an opportunity for examining a central question about the nature of temperamental differences: how far should differences in temperament be regarded as differences between *children*, or as differences in their relationships with their mothers? In any attempt to gain a clearer understanding of the relationship between early temperament and later behavioural problems this is of course a key issue. Interpreting the pattern of association between temperamental differences assessed in maternal interview and later behaviour difficulties presents two particular problems. The first is a measurement issue. The description of a child's behaviour by the mother reflects her perception of the child: if a child with a 'difficult' temperament is later reported to have particular behaviour problems this could reflect a consistently biased perception of the child by a critical and hostile mother. The second problem is that even where direct observation by an 'outsider' confirms the mothers' description, it is clearly possible that what underlies both the 'difficult' temperament and the development of behaviour problems is in fact the hostile and tense relationship between mother and child. The issue here is whether individual differences in children's temperament in fact reflect differences in their relationships with their mothers, rather than 'constitutional' differences between the children.

In the sibling study we addressed the measurement issue by comparing the assessment of children's temperament by maternal interview with the assessment on the same interview questions by an observer, and with direct measures of the children's behaviour. The results (reported in Dunn & Kendrick 1980b) showed that there was good agreement between mother and observer on the description of all temperament traits except activity, and that there was support for the mothers' descriptions of the children's temperament ratings from direct observations. The direct observations also showed, however, that before the sibling birth, the mothers behaved differently with children of different temperament. In families where the children were described as 'unmalleable' or 'negative in mood', mother and child spent less time jointly attending to the same common focus of interest, and the mothers helped and showed things to their children less frequently. While such a finding tells us nothing about the origins of differences in temperament, it does highlight the point that differences in temperament are likely to be associated with differences in the quality of family relationships. But is it only differences in the *mother*–child relationship that are associated with temperamental differences? How far are differences in the *sibling*–child relationship linked to the first child's temperament?

In this paper we consider first the questions of how far the emergence and persistence of behavioural problems during the year following the sibling birth are related to temperamental differences in the firstborn children. Second, we examine the issue of how far temperamental differences are associated with differences in the quality of the relationship between child and mother, and between child and sibling. Finally, the issue is examined of continuity in temperamental differences between the assessment carried out before the birth of the sibling and that carried out when the baby sibling was eight months old.

The study

Full details of the study, the sample, the methods of observation and of interview, and the reliabilities and stabilities of the measures are given in Dunn & Kendrick (1982).

In brief: the families were, in terms of father's occupation, largely lower middle-class and working-class. There were 19 firstborn girls, 21 firstborn boys, 19 secondborn girls, 21 secondborn boys. There were 8 girl–girl pairs, 11 girl–boy pairs, 10 boy–boy pairs and 11 boy–girl pairs. The firstborn children were aged 18–43 months at the birth of the sibling (median 24 months).

All observations and interviews were done in the homes. The families were visited at four time points: during the mother's pregnancy with the second child, 2–3 weeks after the second baby's birth, then eight months and 14 months later. At each time point two one-hour-long observations were made and the mothers were interviewed. The observations were unstructured: precoded categories of behaviour were recorded on a 10 s time base. Only one observer was present at the observations. Verbal interaction during the observations was tape recorded, and transcribed afterwards by the observer.

The observation measures showed good stability from week to week, and the agreement between the observation measures and interview items was considerable (Dunn & Kendrick 1982).

Interviews

At each time point the mothers were interviewed: this interview included questions on the children's feeding, sleeping and toilet habits, on attention-seeking behaviour, independence and dependence, fears, worries, ritualistic behaviour, miserable moods, use of comfort objects, and so on. The answers to each question were coded on three-point or four-point scales. Changes in each child's behaviour from one time point to another were assessed in terms of changes in their scores on these questions.

Interview to assess temperamental characteristics

An assessment of temperamental characteristics of the firstborn child was made at the pregnancy visits, and when the baby was eight months old. This interview was developed by Sturge from other temperament assessments (e.g. Carey 1970, Graham et al 1973) based on Thomas et al 1968.

In the interview the mother is asked for detailed descriptions of how the child has behaved in specific situations in the previous day or so. The situations are all common daily (or weekly) events in the life of preschool children: for example, being dressed and washed, being asked to stop playing and come to a meal, being expected to sit still and eat during the meal, and being reprimanded. The interview also covers issues such as how the child behaves when ill, when faced by a change in routine, or when another child takes his or her toys. Many of the questions focus on how the child behaves in situations where the child's behaviour is being controlled, when the child's routine is altered, or when the child is faced by mildly stressful but routine events. The answer to each question is rated on a three-point scale, and the completed interview gives a total of 37 questions concerned with seven dimensions: intensity, negative mood, activity, malleability, approach–withdrawal, persistence and assertiveness.

This procedure of adding scores on separate questions to form a score on each trait involves two assumptions: that the answers to each question are on equal interval scales, and that each question is equally important in contributing to the dimension. It is a standard procedure to make these assumptions in most interview ratings of temperament and behaviour; however, these assumptions may be unwarranted. Our reservations about using the temperament rating scales as equal interval scales were particularly strong because of the nature of the behavioural differences with which the temperament assessment is concerned. In view of this, we decided to use the assessment simply to dichotomize the sample for each dimension into one group of children who scored towards one extreme and one group that included the rest of the sample. When the distribution of scores was inspected for each trait, it was found that a high proportion of the children scored on or within 0.1 of the median. Since we were interested in the children who were relatively extreme in their ratings, we accordingly divided the sample for each trait into those children who scored on, below, or within 0.1 above the median, versus the rest. This accounts for the discrepancy in the size of the two groups compared for each trait. The extreme groups, namely those scoring above the median, were: high activity, highly intense mood, high negative mood, highly unmalleable, extremely withdrawing, highly assertive and highly persistent. The temperament assessment was carried out as a separate interview from the main maternal interview, and there was little overlap in the details of behaviour about which the mother was asked in the two interviews, with the exception of the items included in the assessment of the frequency of *miserable moods*: the description of unhappy behaviour elicited by these questions overlapped with the descriptions of the child's behaviour that were categorized as showing 'negative mood' on the temperament assessment (see below p 94).

The reliability and stability of the temperament assessment are reported in Dunn & Kendrick 1980b.

Tests of significance. All significance levels reported are based on two-tailed tests.

Results

Temperamental differences, and the emergence and persistence of problems

Over the course of the 14 months following the birth of the sibling, many of the behavioural problems that had shown a marked increase at the arrival of the baby disappeared (Fig. 1a). When the answers to interview questions at

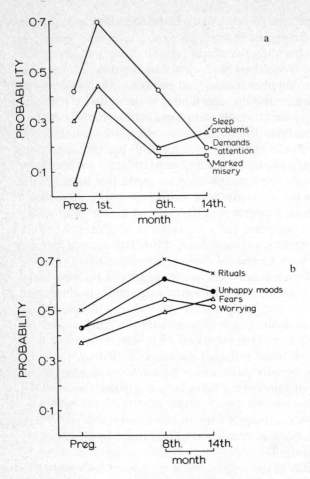

FIG. 1. Changes in problems between the visits during pregnancy and the visits when the secondborn child was 14 months old.

each of the four time points of the study were compared, the results showed that the marked increase in demanding behaviour immediately after the birth declined over the next months, so that by the 14-month visit only six children were described by their mothers as continually demanding attention. Toilet training, which had broken down at the birth of the baby in about half the children previously trained, had by the eight-month interview been re-established in most children, and the sleeping problems that had increased sharply after the sibling birth declined. Several children had shown an increase in *marked misery* (a category defined as the child being frequently miserable on most days, or unhappy for long periods on more than three days per week) at the sibling birth, and this marked misery, too, decreased sharply over the eight months following the birth.

In sharp contrast with these 'improvements' the number of children who were reported to have marked specific *fears* had increased (Fig. 1b). Thirty-eight per cent of the children *increased* in marked fears, and only 7% decreased. Marked *ritualistic* behaviour also tended to increase, between the first interview and the eight-month visits. Bedtime, bathtime and mealtime rituals were particularly strong, as were rituals for saying goodbye to parents: 35% of the sample increased in *ritualistic* behaviour of this kind, and only 8% decreased. There was also no decrease in the numbers of children who were described as frequently worrying. The mothers had been asked 'Is X a worrier? . . . Does he [or she] get anxious about something that might happen, about plans, changes in routine . . . things being changed? . . . if he [or she] loses something? Does he [or she] brood over things . . . like accidents or monsters?' The number of children who were described by their mothers as having miserable or grumpy moods on most days for short periods (less than an hour), or for long periods once or twice a week, had *increased* between the first interview and the interview at eight months from 43% to 62% of the sample.

Such a pattern of change could of course reflect developmental change, rather than a response to the arrival of the sibling. Without a control group of children of this age range who had not experienced the birth of a sibling we cannot ascertain how far the sibling birth contributed to this increase in anxious or unhappy behaviour. There was, in fact, no relation between the age of the children and the incidence of these aspects of the children's behaviour: the older children were not more likely to be described as moody, or as having marked fears or as worrying. But we should be cautious about coming to any general conclusions about the lack of significance of age in connection with these features of behaviour, since in their large-scale epidemiological study, MacFarlane and her colleagues (MacFarlane et al 1954) did find an increase in fears between $1\frac{1}{2}$ and 4 years of age, with a peak at age 3 for girls and at age $3\frac{1}{2}$ for boys. It is clearly possible that the patterns shown in Fig. 1b reflect developmental changes unrelated to the arrival of the sibling. But, whatever the origins of the patterns, it is important that we should understand more clearly the individual differences in the persistence of such anxious or unhappy behaviour. (We do know from the large-scale study of N. Richman, P. J. Graham and J. Stevenson that neurotic behaviour, and particularly fearful behaviour, in three-year-old children is associated with a pattern of persisting difficulties over the next five years; Richman et al 1982.) How far was the increase or persistence of fears, worries, or unhappy moods related to temperamental differences between the children, to the quality of the parent–child relationship, or to sex differences?

TABLE 1 Increase in behavioural problems and temperament: significant differences between those children scoring above the median on particular temperament traits and the rest of the sample

Behavioural problem	Temperament trait	Extreme group greater or less than rest of sample	P level (Fisher exact probability)
Increase in rituals	Negative mood + intensity	greater	0.05
Increase in fears	Intensity	greater	0.0001
	Intensity + unmalleability	greater	0.04
Increase in worry	Negative mood + intensity	greater	0.06
Increase in tantrums	Withdrawal	less	0.08

Individual differences in the increase of fears, worrying, unhappy moods and ritualistic behaviour following the sibling birth were examined in relation to temperament, age and sex. At the first interview, the reported frequency of marked fears, worrying, ritualistic behaviour and use of comfort objects was not related to the children's scores on the temperament assessment (though unhappy moods were reported to occur more frequently in children who on the temperament assessment were rated as extreme in 'negative mood': $\chi^2 \pm 4.25$; 1 degree of freedom; $P < 0.05$). However, the analysis of *changes* in fearful, worrying, ritualistic and unhappy behaviour showed that the children whose scores on these items of behaviour had increased between the pregnancy interview and the eight-month interview were indeed different in temperament from those children who showed no increase in such behaviour (Table 1). For instance, children rated as extreme in intensity of emotional reaction and in negative mood before the sibling birth were significantly more likely than the other children to have increased in rituals and worrying by the time that the baby was eight months old. The increase in marked fears was significantly more common among children who had been rated as intense in emotional reaction and as unmalleable before the sibling birth.

This relationship, between the *increase* in fears, rituals and worrying and the temperament of the children, meant that by the time the baby was eight months old the incidence of marked fears, frequent worrying, marked rituals, constant use of comfort objects, and frequent unhappy moods were all associated with temperamental differences between the children assessed before the sibling's birth (Table 2). The only association between temperamental differences and these aspects of behaviour *had been* that unhappy moods were reported more frequently in children who on the temperament assessment were rated as extreme in negative mood. Age and sex were not

TABLE 2 Behaviour at eight-month interview and temperament: significant differences between those children scoring above the median on particular temperament traits and the rest of the sample

Behaviour	Temperament trait	Extreme group greater or less than rest of sample	P level (Fisher exact probability)
Constant use of comfort object	Intensity	greater	0.04
Marked fears	Intensity	greater	0.001
Frequent worry	Intensity	greater	0.04
Marked rituals	Intensity	greater	0.001
Frequent miserable moods	Intensity	greater	0.04
Feeding problems	Intensity + unmalleability	greater	0.04
Sleeping problems	Negative mood	greater	0.01
Tantrums	Withdrawal	less	0.001
Marked affection for mother	Intensity	greater	0.02
Marked affection for father	Intensity	greater	0.02

found to be associated with the increase in these aspects of behaviour, nor in their incidence at the eight- or 14-month interviews.

These results show that differences between children on the temperament assessment were related not only to the first children's reactions to the birth, but also to the increase in the first children's unhappy or anxious behaviour over the next year. But how far did these differences in temperament, and in the incidence of unhappy or anxious behaviour, reflect differences in the *relationship* between mother and child? Whatever the origin of temperamental differences between children, we might well expect mothers to behave differently with children of different temperament.

When we examined the patterns of interaction between mother and child at the 14-month observations we found that there were some consistent differences associated with the temperaments of the children as assessed before the sibling birth. Table 3 shows that children of 'intense emotional reaction', and those predominantly 'negative in mood' spent less time in joint attention with their mothers, and less frequently showed or gave objects to their mothers; in addition, those of intense emotional reaction spent more time sitting without playing. The 'unmalleable' children spent more time wandering aimlessly and less time in joint attention with their mothers; (seven comparisons out of the 36 done were significant at $P<0.05$). So in families in which the children had

TABLE 3 Comparison of frequency of measures of observed behaviour at 14-month visits in families with children of differing temperament (Mann-Whitney U test)

		Observation measures (median 10s units/1000)		
Temperament trait		Children above median on temperament trait	Children on or below median on temperament trait	P level
Intensity	Joint attention	3	16	0.05
	Child gives/ shows object	3	6	0.05
	Child sits without playing	13	4	0.05
Negative mood	Joint attention	4	15	0.05
	Child gives/ shows object	4	7	0.05
Unmalleability	Joint attention	3	16	0.05
	Child wander	8	2	0.05

been reported to have 'difficult' temperaments, they were, 14 months later, not only showing more frequent, fearful, ritualistic or worrying behaviour, but were also receiving less attention from their mothers. This pattern of association suggests that the differences in the joint attention of mother and child may have contributed to the increase in the anxious behaviour. Indeed,

TABLE 4 Spearman rank correlations between pregnancy, first month and 14-month observations

14-month observations	Correlations with:	
	Pregnancy	First month
Joint attention	0.29	0.45*
Joint play	0.32*	0.41*
M shows	0.36*	0.42*
M (suggests highlights)	0.50*	0.53*
M affectionate tactile contact	0.32*	0.14
M prohibits	0.45*	0.57*
M initiates verbal interaction with prohibition	0.36*	0.37*
Confrontation	0.36*	0.43*

*$P<0.05$; M, mother.

it could be argued that the differences in the mother–child interaction, rather than the differences in the children's temperament, were of paramount importance in the aetiology of the anxious and unhappy behaviour. There are, however, three lines of evidence against such a view: there was no significant association between the differences in mother–child interaction and (1) the incidence of marked fears, worries, ritualistic behaviour or unhappy moods at the first interview, (2) the increase in such anxious behaviour over the year following the sibling birth, or (3) the incidence of anxious behaviour at the 14-month interview. Individual differences in the measures of mother–firstborn interaction were relatively consistent over the period of the study (Table 4), and at no time were they related to the incidence of fears, worries, or ritualistic or unhappy behaviour. It is of course possible that aspects of the mother–firstborn relationship other than those which we measured were related to the incidence of these problems.

Temperament differences, and interaction with mother and with sibling

These results thus suggest that differences in the mother–child interaction should not be considered to contribute in an exclusive way to the appearance of problems in the year following the sibling birth. However, it is important to note that the differences in temperament, as assessed in the pregnancy interviews, *were* associated with differences in the observed interaction between mother and child over the following year. The association between temperamental differences and the child's behaviour with the mother was further exposed when we examined the first child's behaviour when the mother played with or cared for the sibling at the 14-month visits. It was evident that many children 'monitored' the interactions between their mothers and siblings very closely. They either protested at, or attempted to join, an extremely high proportion of the mother–second child interaction bouts—in some families as many as 78% of such bouts.

The first child's responses to mother–baby interaction bouts were categorized as follows:

(a) *Joins positive:* during the course of a mother–baby interaction bout the firstborn child approaches or vocalizes in a positive way, gives toys, helps, affectionately contacts either the mother or the baby, joins in an ongoing 'game' or joint physical play between the mother and the baby.

(b) *Protests:* during a mother–baby interaction bout the firstborn child makes verbal protests, or demands objects, help, attention, food, or hits or pinches the mother.

(c) *Joins negative to the baby:* during a mother–baby interaction bout the firstborn child hits, pinches or screams at the baby, takes away toys, or prohibits or restrains the baby.

(d) *Watch:* during a mother–baby interaction bout the first child watches but makes no attempt to approach or join in.

(e) *Ignores:* during a mother–baby interaction bout the first child continues his or her ongoing behaviour and makes no attempt either to join, to disrupt or to watch the mother-baby interaction.

The first three categories (a, b & c) were not mutually exclusive, i.e. it was possible for the first child to join positively and to protest within the same interaction bout. However, the extent of this overlap was small: only 4% of interaction bouts included more than one response. Categories d & e, by definition, could not overlap with any of the others.

The individual differences between the firstborn children, in the way they behaved when mother and sibling interacted, varied greatly. While some children frequently protested, others almost always joined the mother–baby interaction in a friendly fashion. Temperamental differences assessed before the sibling birth were associated with the differences in this behaviour towards mother-and-baby.

Those children who scored above the median on the traits of unmalleability and intensity protested at a larger proportion of the mother–baby interactions than the children who scored on or below the median: the group above the median on these traits protested at 32% (median) of interactions; the group on or below the median protested at 18% (median); Mann-Whitney U test, $P<0.05$. These 'unmalleable and intense' children were also less likely to *ignore* an interaction between their mothers and baby siblings: the group above the median on these traits ignored 51% (median) of interactions; the group on or below the median ignored 64% (median); Mann-Whitney U test, $P<0.05$. Children scoring above the median on the 'intensity of emotional expression trait' *watched* a higher proportion of the mother–baby interaction bouts than the rest of the sample: the group scoring above the median on this trait watched 20% (median); the group scoring on or below the median watched 12% (median); Mann-Whitney U test, $P<0.05$.

In marked contrast, temperamental differences were not important in accounting for the dramatically wide differences in the quality of interaction between the siblings. Here, the important variables were the quality of the relationship between the mother and firstborn, the way in which the mother had discussed the baby as a person with wants and feelings, and the sex constellation of the sibling pair. Such a contrast between the significance of temperamental differences in the first children's behaviour with their *mothers* and the unimportance of these differences in relation to behaviour directed towards the sibling reinforces the point that temperamental differences must be viewed as closely bound up with differences in children's relationships with their mothers.

Continuity in temperamental differences

The issue of continuity in temperamental differences is considered in depth in a number of other papers at this symposium. In view of the comparatively small size of our sample we clearly need to be extremely cautious in drawing any general conclusions about the issue. But since all the children in the study did experience a major upheaval in their family lives between the two temperament assessments, the degree of consistency in temperament between the two time points is of obvious interest. If temperament is considered as a characteristic of a child's personality which is comparatively unsusceptible to environmental change, then we might expect considerable continuity between the two assessments. There was, in fact, rather little consistency in the composition of the 'extreme' groups between the two time points. The exceptions to this lack of consistency are shown in Table 5. Children who

TABLE 5 Consistency in scores on temperamental traits between pregnancy assessment and eight-month assessment

Temperament trait	Probability that the child scores above median at pregnancy and at eight-month assessments	Probability that the child scores above median at pregnancy and on or below median at eight-month assessment	χ^2	P level
Negative mood and intensity	0.77	0.22	5.88	0.02
Withdrawal	0.66	0.33	3.33	0.10

scored above the median on negative mood and on intensity of emotional expression before the sibling birth were more likely to score above the median at the eight-month assessment than to score on or below the median, and children who scored above the median on the trait of withdrawal at the first assessment tended to do so also at the eight-month assessment. (Such a finding tells us, of course, nothing about the *basis* for the continuity in individual differences: continuity in patterns of interaction with parents probably contributes in an important way to the persistence of individual differences, and we have already noted the relative consistency in some aspects of the mothers' behaviour towards their first children.) The lack of consistency in the children's scores for the other traits draws attention to the marked changes in many of the children's behavioural traits after the sibling birth, and suggests that some aspects of temperament are, in children of this age, very susceptible to the effects of changes in the family.

Conclusion

Temperamental differences between firstborn children were not only associated with the pattern of children's reactions to the constellation of events surrounding the birth of the sibling but were also linked to the persistence of anxious, worrying and fearful behaviour over the next year. The results suggest that in any attempt to understand individual differences in children's vulnerability to other potentially stressful events—a matter of considerable concern to clinicians—it is important to consider those aspects of a child's personality which the temperament assessment reveals. Temperament differences were also associated with differences in children's interaction with their mothers, and in their behaviour when mother and sibling were interacting. In contrast, the wide range of individual differences in behaviour towards the sibling was not associated with temperamental differences between the children. This last finding underlines the importance of considering temperament not as a characteristic of the child independent of his or her particular family relationships but, on the contrary, as closely linked to his or her relationship with the mother. The findings also indicate that temperament is potentially susceptible to the effects of marked changes in the family environment.

Acknowledgements

This work was supported by the Medical Research Council. We are very grateful to the families in the study for their generous help, and to Robert Hinde for his helpful comments on the manuscript.

REFERENCES

Carey WB 1970 A simplified method for measuring infant temperament. J Pediatr 77:188-194

Dunn J, Kendrick C 1980a The arrival of a sibling: changes in patterns of interaction between mother and first-born child. J Child Psychol Psychiatry Allied Discip 21:119-132

Dunn J, Kendrick C 1980b Studying temperament and parent–child interaction: a comparison of information from direct observation and from parental interview. Dev Med Child Neurol 22:484-496

Dunn J, Kendrick C 1982 Siblings: love, envy and understanding. Harvard University Press, Cambridge, Mass

Dunn J, Kendrick C, MacNamee R 1981 The reaction of first-born children to the birth of a sibling: mother's reports. J Child Psychol Psychiatry Allied Discip 22:1-18

Graham P, Rutter M, George S 1973 Temperamental characteristics as predictors of behavioral disorders in children. Am J Orthopsychiatry 43:328-339

MacFarlane J, Allen L, Honzik M 1954 A developmental study of behavior problems of normal children between 21 months and 14 years. University of California Press, Berkeley

Richman N, Stevenson J, Graham P 1982 Pre-school to school: a behavioural study. Academic
    Press, London
Rutter M, Birch H, Thomas A, Chess S 1964 Temperamental characteristics in infancy and the
    later development of behaviour disorders. Br J Psychiatry 110:651-661
Thomas A, Chess S, Birch HG 1968 Temperament and behavior disorders in children. New York
    University Press, New York

DISCUSSION

Rutter: What explanation do you have for the lack of consistency of temperament over time? Do you have any measures of the children or of their family environments that will predict which children will change in their temperamental characteristics?

Dunn: None of the measures of family interaction that we have looked at predicted the changes in temperament; however we do have data that will predict changes in other aspects of the children's observed behaviour. It is a complicated picture, but a number of things stand out: first, the quality of the relationship with the mother; secondly, the sex constellation of the children in the family; thirdly, the relationship with the father, and so on (Dunn et al 1981).

Graham: Without a comparable sample of children who didn't experience the birth of a sibling one can't say even that the behaviour was inconsistent in relation to a sibling birth; it may be inconsistent in relation to the ordinary everyday progression of a child's life. Did the temperament around the time of the birth relate to the presence of unusual and perhaps handicapping behaviour, such as rituals?

Dunn: In only two cases were the rituals extreme enough to be described as handicapping. At the first interview, the temperament assessment was not related to the incidence of fears, worrying or anxious behaviour, contemporaneously. The temperament assessment was, however, related to the increase between that first assessment and the eight-month one, where the birth of the sibling had intervened. This evidence therefore suggests that the birth of the sibling had contributed to the increase in anxious behaviour.

Graham: You've said that there was not a substantial degree of consistency in the temperament of the first child at the two ages. Have you examined, from the predictive points of view, whether there was a consistency in pathological behaviour, e.g. in fearfulness or rituals, at the two ages?

Dunn: Yes. A child showing fearfulness and ritualistic behaviour at the first interview is likely to show them also at the second interview (probabilities of 0.70 and 0.69, respectively). However, this initial incidence of fearful or ritualistic behaviour is not a significantly better predictor of the child's behaviour at the 14-month interview than is the temperament assessment.

Berger: What we are considering is a series of cumulative stresses on the child, culminating in the birth of a sibling, plus a fairly stressed parent; as the parents begin to adapt to the arrival of the new baby, and to the new complex of interactions, one would expect other changes. It is difficult to talk about the stability of temperamental characteristics when the human potentiality to react to stress is present in any case, and when fundamental changes in life style are taking place. Somehow, these effects have to be distinguished.

Dunn: Well, that is exactly why we were looking at it. If there was this big change in the children's lives, would we find any consistency? You are assuming that there is a predictable and common change in the stress in the family over this period. But this did not happen: for some families, the end of pregnancy seemed to be the most stressful time; for other families, it was the first month; for yet others it was the time the baby was crawling, and so on. So there was no simple equation between the arrival of the sibling and the timing of stress for either child or mother.

Berger: You commented on the lack of stability in the temperamental characteristics. Perhaps the most appropriate way to look for stability would be to take measures before pregnancy and some months after the second sibling birth.

Dunn: That is so; however if it is assumed (as it has been) that temperament is 'constitutional', then one might expect that there would be consistency in temperamental characteristics in spite of a major change in the family.

Berger: I don't think anybody claims that for temperament.

Hinde: To come back to this tedious question of how much temperament is a property of the relationship and how much a property of the child: we have agreed that the more relationships in which a given characteristic of behaviour turns up, the more likely it is to be a characteristic of the individual and not of the relationship *per se*. I now wonder how much the converse of that is true. If temperamental characteristics predict aspects of mother–child interaction but don't predict aspects of sibling–sibling interaction, that could be because other issues are more important. One cannot therefore conclude that temperament is a characteristic of the mother–child relationship.

Dunn: That's fair enough. One could also say that perhaps a 14-month old is not as sensitive to differences in the other child's behaviour as a mother is, and that is why differences in sibling behaviour are not closely linked to differences in the other child's behaviour. It is, however, striking that the individual differences in how the siblings get along with each other are dramatically wide. The differences are even more extreme than the differences in how the mothers and children are getting on.

Rutter: In order to sort the problem out, one must know whether sibling–sibling interaction is predicted by something else.

Dunn: Yes. We have already addressed that question: the variables which we found to be important in relation to the sibling–sibling interaction are described in Dunn & Kendrick (1982). They were the sex constellation of the sibling pair, the quality of the relationship with the mother and father before the baby was born, the way in which the mother had talked to the first child about the baby and, of course, the behaviour of each child towards the other.

Carey: I am not sure why you found such a low stability—whether it was due to the crisis in the child's life or to a measurement problem. Another possible explanation is that temperament is not so stable at that early age as it is later. I would contrast with your findings some that R.L. Hegvik, S.C. McDevitt and I presented at a recent meeting (International Society for the Study of Behavioural Development, Toronto, Canada, August 1981). We measured the temperaments of 187 children in my paediatric practice at around 3–7 years and again at 8–12 years (mean interval, 4.4 years). For eight of the nine New York longitudinal study characteristics we found significant correlation coefficients from 0.40 to 0.59. The only characteristic with a lower correlation (0.21) was Rhythmicity, which had ceased to be a viable scale after seven years and was replaced by Predictability in the 8–12-year-old group. Yet, even that correlation was significant. This contrasts with your results and with our own data for infants (McDevitt & Carey 1981). Could it be that temperament becomes more stable as children get older?

Thomas: In the early years differences in the sequences of development levels may be such that they influence consistency or inconsistency over time in the first few years but not in later years, which is intriguing (Dunn 1980).

Robinson: Is there a message for the clinician in this? We are familiar with the idea that before a child is born one can tell from the family what is the chance of that child being battered, and one can delineate a high-risk group. Does the information that you are providing on temperament provide any similar indications of families at high risk?

Dunn: Others here (Wolkind & De Salis, this volume p 221-239; Rutter, this volume, p 1-19) have looked at samples that are much more appropriate than ours for answering that question. But I must stress that, in many of these families, life was very hard for the mothers. These children were difficult to live with, and the mothers were under a considerable stress. I have noticed that a lot of attention gets paid to primiparous mothers, especially in the early period after the baby is born. But for mothers who have both a difficult toddler and a small baby, and interrupted nights for several weeks, there tends to be very little routine support from social services or doctors. The financial situation of the families did not extend to the provision of paid help, and often the fathers were unable to help because they were working overtime. I would hope that the findings do have relevance for clinicians, not necessarily for predictions about child battering, but for alerting clinicians to the quality of life for mothers and small children, and for the people who need particular attention.

Wolkind: Your study suggests a follow-up point to Professor Graham's comments earlier about the relationship between temperament and behavioural problems. Before the birth of the baby you obtained information, at the same interview, about temperamental characteristics and behavioural problems and found that they didn't relate. If one considers fears or worries or mood as behavioural problems, how did those differ from the same information that you analysed on temperament?

Dunn: The only item that directly overlapped was unhappy mood in the behaviour assessment and the trait of negative mood on the temperament assessment. Although the specific questions in this case were different, and we were asking the mothers about particular behavioural situations that were different in the two interviews, there was some overlap and, unsurprisingly, the scores were closely related on the interview and on the temperament assessment. But the questions on fears, worries and ritualistic behaviour didn't relate to any of the temperament dimensions.

Wilson: Your approach would provide an ideal design for studying the extent to which the mother's behaviours have been pushed to an extreme, or at least pushed away from what they might have been, by the birth and caretaking of a difficult child. You have data on older siblings who are not difficult and on younger siblings who become difficult; you also have data on how the mothers behaved without a difficult child and then when faced with one.

Dunn: Yes. Unfortunately we didn't assess the temperament of the second child systematically. In the interviews the mothers talked at length about comparing the two children, and this data showed that one of my initial preconceptions was wrong—namely, that second children are considered easier than first children. In practice, about half the mothers felt that the first one had been much easier than the second, and half felt the second had been easier. There were some consistencies in the differences they described: second children were more likely to be described as inquisitive, assertive and independent than the firstborns, who were often described as being more malleable.

Wilson: You mentioned the problems that the mothers had in caretaking of a younger infant when the older one was difficult. An analysis of the mother's behaviour with the younger one would come up with a different picture than it might have done if she had not, at that point, had a difficult child to deal with.

Dunn: We've looked in detail at how the mother's handling of the baby relates to her handling of her older child. Not surprisingly, confrontation between the mother and the first child increases when she does certain things with the baby. Less surprisingly, many positive interactions between the mother and the first child also increase when she's doing something with the baby; the second child joins in with play, and there is more joint attention between mother and first child at those times (Kendrick & Dunn 1980).

Berger: Do you know how many of the second pregnancies were planned, or how many of the children were wanted?

Dunn: By the time we saw the mothers, I think all except two were quite pleased to be having the baby.

Berger: There is an interesting compound effect here. I have come across several cases clinically where the mother has said that, given the difficulties of the first child, she would never have chosen to have a second child. So in two-child families there may be a biasing effect in that parents with difficult children may decide not to have other children.

Dunn: Many of the mothers in the sample did little about family planning until after the second child, when they couldn't bear the thought of having a third child.

Thomas: We noticed that the middle-class rather than the working-class mother with a difficult child tended to feel most guilty and anxious about whether the child's temperament was her fault (Thomas et al 1974). So when she had a second child that she initially dreaded but who turned out to be easy temperamentally, her guilt was lifted. This factor further complicates the picture of a mother's differential response to a second child.

REFERENCES

Dunn J 1980 Individual differences in temperament. In: Rutter M (ed) Scientific foundations of developmental psychiatry. Heinemann, London. p 101-109

Dunn J, Kendrick C 1982 Siblings: love, envy and understanding. Harvard University Press, Cambridge, Mass

Dunn J, Kendrick C, MacNamee R 1981 The reaction of first-born children to the birth of a sibling: mothers' reports. J Child Psychol Psychiatry Allied Discip 22:1-18

Kendrick C, Dunn J 1980 Caring for a second child: effects on the interaction between mother and firstborn. Dev Psychol 16:303-311

McDevitt SC, Carey WB 1981 Stability of ratings vs. perceptions of temperament from early infancy to 1-3 years. Am J Orthopsychiatry 51:342-345

Thomas A, Chess S, Sillen J, Mendez O 1974 Cross-cultural study of behaviour in children with special vulnerabilities to stress. In: Ricks D et al (eds) Life history research in psychopathology. Univ Minn Press, Minneapolis, vol 3:53-67

General discussion I

Methods of assessment of temperament

Rutter: We have now heard about studies using questionnaire measures, interview measures and observation measures. Both Philip Graham and I have posed questions about the most satisfactory of the available ways of measuring temperament. Perhaps we should now consider this in a little more detail.

Bell: I should like to discuss a point that is easily overlooked in ratings made by observers. In most cases a floating measurement system is used, so that changes in subjective norms, or changes in how the observer reports an individual's temperament can occur over time even though there are no true changes. But in studies such as Joan Stevenson-Hinde's (p 51-65), where the number of behaviours is counted, the system is anchored. This system made it possible to assess how these behaviours increased between 42 and 50 months of age. This assessment would have been impossible by means of the other type of data. So, for a definable variable, it is desirable to specify the measures and to count the incidence of various behaviours.

Thomas: In some instances, one item (measured by observation or report) is so special that it should merit more than a single count, even though in our system of item-counting it could not (Thomas et al 1968). For example, we know of one child who, at 18 months, learned to tie his shoelaces and spent hours at a time doing this. That was scored as one item of persistence, and yet it was a highly significant item; the temperamental attribute of persistence turned out to be functionally highly important in the child's later development and in the sequences of interaction between himself and his teacher and peers. So, besides the item count there is the problem of how to deal with the special instance.

Bell: It would not be useful to devise a measurement system for all items based only on rare and infrequent items. A rare but highly significant item could be handled in whatever way is possible but one should not fail to count the ones that *can* be counted. Generally speaking, we forget that in the social and behavioural sciences we too often have unanchored systems, which produce great problems for us longitudinally.

Werry: We, like others, have spent a lot of time and effort on observational measures, and have reluctantly come in the end to using questionnaires (e.g. Conners 1969, 1970, Quay 1977, Werry 1978). Gerald Patterson has made many observations in families and developed a complicated system of observations but even he was ultimately forced to use it only as a validating tool for his rating scales (see Werry 1978). There are both advantages and disadvantages to observational systems and to ratings. In the observation type of measurement there is a problem of high variance, unless one uses long runs of behaviour, which are, themselves, expensive and intrusive. But, as Dr Bell said, observational systems have the enormous advantage of being *anchored*. Another point of disadvantage that is not generally recognized relates to the reliability of behavioural measures. One does obtain very good rater/re-rater correlations at the beginning but as D. O'Leary (see Werry 1978) points out, reliability drift occurs as a function of time. This is because observers, being human, and needing to use their cognitive processes, begin unwittingly to modify the observational procedure. On the other hand, the big advantage of the rating scales is that they are generally averages of enormous runs of behaviour across time and across situations. In addition the effect of the initial rater standard can be eliminated to some extent by using the same rater in repeated measure designs. But one must be aware that there tends to be, on many of these rating scales, a 'practice' effect between the initial observation and the second one (which others call a regression to the mean). This effect should be minimized because otherwise these changes are interpreted as being due to other factors, such as a given treatment which happens to be under investigation.

Bell: Douglas et al (1968) have used a diary system to obtain reports from the mothers on the day's activities. This method might provide a means of exploiting the tremendous observational advantage the mother has, while insulating the results a little better from her proclivities to interpret what *we* want by the way we approach her with our questions. The mother doesn't need to know what one is trying to study. Data from the diary system did show correlations with direct observations on the same day, and so Douglas et al were able to validate this system.

Hsu: But to assess a child's temperamental characteristics thoroughly, surely this kind of diary made by the mother for only two or three days would not be enough?

Rutter: Other investigators have used daily diaries over much longer periods and found that the families could maintain that system for a reasonable period of time.

Dunn: In a study that I did with Martin Richards, we used diaries for the first ten days after the baby was born (Richards & Bernal 1972, Bernal 1972, 1973). But one can't discuss the relative advantage of one method over another without considering what question one is trying to answer.

Stevenson-Hinde: I agree. In general, observations are probably more sensitive to moment-to-moment changes but, if a global view is sought, then ratings are better. Ratings give the observer flexibility—to filter, weight and integrate information (Block 1977). However, interviews and questionnaires are, in the present context, attempts to get at the same thing—temperamental characteristics. If questionnaires are as good as interviews, then we should all use them, because questionnaires are so much quicker and preclude any effects of an interviewer on responses.

Rutter: It is surprising that there haven't been systematic comparisons between questionnaires on temperamental characteristics and interviews.

Carey: I did four comparisons between interviews and questionnaires (Carey 1970), but did not continue because I realized that the questionnaire was not identical to the interview and therefore there was no reason why the results by the two methods should be the same, although they were in practice rather similar. There are differences in scoring technique. For example, any crying detected during the interview, such as after an injection, was scored as negative mood, but it was not scored on the questionnaire since I didn't see any justification for giving a negative mood score in such circumstances. Also, while the questionnaire is fixed as to subjects covered, the content of the interview is more flexible and may emphasize some experiences more than others.

Rutter: One must not consider only whether the interview and the questionnaire results intercorrelate, which they're bound to do, but also whether one is more influenced by biases or distortions than the other, and whether one predicts better than the other. In some of our work (not with temperament) we have two examples of good predictions over time from interview measures but not from questionnaires supposed to measure the same variables. In an early study (Rutter 1963) on peptic ulcer, an interview measure of anxiety predicted the course of the ulcer over the next six months, whereas a questionnaire measure did not, although they intercorrelated reasonably well. And in the *Isle of Wight* longitudinal study (M. Rutter et al, unpublished data) of children's behaviour at age 10 and 15 years, the interview measures were better predictors than questionnaires. Whether that applies to temperament remains to be seen.

Thomas: We have some data on that, from the early adult follow-up in our longitudinal study (A. Thomas & S. Chess, unpublished work). We made temperament ratings from the long interview with the subject, and we also developed a self-rating questionnaire, which we gave to the subject after the interview. We compared the two methods of assessment and calculated the correlations between them. These correlations were moderately good, and the predictive power on issues like adaptive scores and clinical diagnosis was better with the interview than with the questionnaire.

Torgersen: I preferred the interview for some of the reasons already mentioned by Dr Stevenson-Hinde. To compare the two methods, I also used a translation of the questionnaire for 3–7-year-olds published by Thomas & Chess (1977). On the whole, the data from the questionnaire and from the interview did not correlate well. One reason for this seemed to be that the items which could be reliably measured by one method often differed from the items reliably measured by the other method. So it was not surprising that they measured different aspects of temperament. What I *did* detect was that the definition of a category is highly dependent on the particular items in it.

Wolkind: When considering mothers' reports, one sees a sharp distinction, as Dr Stevenson-Hinde's work brought out, between allowing the mother to act as the judge, i.e. to use her own norms, and allowing the person asking the questions to develop his or her norm. I feel unhappy about letting the mother produce her own norm. This relates to the work of Vaughn et al (1980) which, rather worryingly, suggests that one can predict the baby's temperament on the basis of the mother's attitudes in pregnancy.

Carey: Vaughn et al (1980) claim to have demonstrated that maternal prenatal attitudes correlated better with observed temperament than did the temperament questionnaire. However, the correlations between attitudes and temperament were few and weak, and no data were presented on the behaviours observed. A later report from the same group (Vaughn et al 1981) describes two factors derived from brief observations but still does not identify the exact behaviours observed. A personal communication (B. Vaughn 1981) revealed that some of the observed behaviours (such as coordination and muscle tone) were not temperament items at all, and that these investigators did not consider it necessary to match the behaviour rated on the questionnaire with what was observed. I believe they did not prove their point (Carey 1982).

Bates: We have made some comparisons of observations and questionnaires, to look for the effects of perceptual distortion, but we have found no evidence for this. We could not confirm the findings of Vaughn et al (1981) about the relationship between personality and temperament perceptions. We found some slight correlations in one study (Bates et al 1979) but could not replicate them (Bates et al 1982). Some aspects of personality may determine how a child is perceived (see Bates 1980), but our observational studies show that the way the mother perceives the child in the questionnaire is to some extent confirmed by the way an observer perceives the child. However, about 90% of the variance in how the mother perceives the child, or in how the child actually behaves according to an observer's data, is unexplained.

Stevenson: Are you suggesting that you had an R^2 of only about 0.1 between direct observational and questionnaire measures of temperament?

Bates: Yes (see Bates et al 1979).

Stevenson: And was that true across all the dimensions, or were some better than others?

Bates: I am mostly interested in the concept of 'difficult' temperament, so I'm looking for the kinds of child behaviour that relate to the mother's perception of the child as difficult. I am looking at a whole variety of different child behaviours, and the clearest correlates with the parents' perception of the child as difficult at 6–13 months are the amounts of fussing and crying by the child (Bates et al 1979, 1982, G.S. Pettit & J.E. Bates, unpublished results). This is true whether one is using my questionnaire, which homes in on the quality of difficult, or Dr Carey's questionnaire, from which a difficult score can be derived. The observer–parent correlations range from about 0.20 to about 0.40, and are replicable, although small.

Carey: You were correlating observed crying with a rating of difficult, but crying is only one of five components of difficult temperament.

Bates: Yes, but one can look at other variables too. For example, we have not found correlations between infant activity, social, and soothing-responsiveness indexes and perceived difficultness (Bates et al 1979, 1982).

Stevenson: Presumably you are entering many variables at the same time to improve the prediction?

Bates: Yes.

Carey: Would it not be more meaningful to compare observed crying with maternally rated crying or mood?

Bates: Yes, and if one does that, one sees about the same. We found that Carey's mood scale correlated at 0.22 ($P<0.05$) with amount of fussing and crying in 6-month-olds (Bates et al 1979).·

Thomas: When one tries to categorize temperament in children, no matter what scheme one uses, the parental report is an invaluable source of information which observations may supplement but can't really duplicate. Future research should be directed towards: (1) how to make maternal reports more precise and accurate; and (2) how to identify distortions and their significance in a systematic way.

Berger: We have really been talking about issues of validation and we must admit that there is no ultimate criterion for validation in this work. We are therefore discussing independent measures that are producing different information and the choice of measures is fairly arbitrary. When we contrast indirect measures, e.g. interview questionnaires, with direct observations of behaviour, we should remember the finding (from clinical studies on the effects of behaviour therapy) that there is a desynchrony between cognitions and behaviour (Rachman & Hodgson 1974). Thus, even though one may obtain a picture of the child from the mother at time (a), the child's behaviour may well have changed, possibly dramatically, by the time the mother is interviewed at time (b). So the actual behaviour may have changed, but the mother's cognitions have not caught up with the behavioural changes. How one should cope with such an effect is an interesting question.

Categorizing temperament (See also p 289)

Rutter: Another broad issue that has been touched on already is how to categorize temperament. In the Cambridge studies (Hinde et al, p 66-86; Stevenson-Hinde & Simpson, p 51-65; Dunn & Kendrick, p 87-105; this volume) some items have been put together, and some have been kept separate, for very good reasons, but where do we go from here? Is there a way of deciding which is the right way of combining items, and if so, how?

Plomin: You mentioned (e.g. p 9) that you didn't think factor analysis of items was a reasonable strategy.

Rutter: I was not making a general attack on factor analysis, but rather I was arguing that the fact that items intercorrelate doesn't necessarily indicate which grouping of items is going to be most useful for prediction purposes.

Plomin: I would also consider the reverse problem—that is, the definition of a dimension when, in fact, there is no real indication for it. For example, infant temperament questionnaires frequently contain several items involving reactions to food which are meant to tap different temperamental dimensions such as rhythmicity, approach–withdrawal, adaptability, intensity of reaction, and threshold of responsiveness. However, these reaction-to-food items correlate more highly with each other than with items on their putative temperamental dimension. Thus, a situation-specific factor such as reaction-to-food can emerge when one had thought that general dimensions of temperament were being measured (Rowe & Plomin 1977). The maxim that 'you only get out of factor analysis what you put in' tends to be swept away in a swirl of statistical sophistry but I believe it should be remembered in any discussion of factor analysis. For this reason, I do not favour the use of factor analysis as a tool for discovering the structure of temperament. However, I do subscribe to the view of Guilford (e.g. Guilford & Zimmerman 1956), who advocates factor analysis as a tool for verifying the coherence of logically derived dimensions. In this sense, I find it difficult to accept the existence of a temperamental dimension in the absence of factor analytic verification.

Rutter: Let me give a specific example. Probably one would find in the UK that playing soccer and playing rugby football don't factor together, because if a boy plays one game he doesn't play the other—that is the way the sports system in this country is organized. Yet, on a conceptual basis, playing each of these games is a measure of an interest in group sport. That is, there may be *alternative* ways of showing a particular behavioural style. It is not difficult to think of examples where behaviours hang together conceptually although they don't actually intercorrelate when studied in the usual way.

Bell: If that is so, and one tests the constructs for cross-time stability, by adding together the items that are logically but not actually related, the longitudinal relationship might be attenuated simply because one has added together items that don't increase the quantitative power of the construct. The effect is particularly devastating if one is *adding* together items that are negatively correlated: in other words, the quantitative values for these items ought to be *subtracted* from each other. It might be possible to conduct all analyses with single items, but single items usually have very low reliability. In other words, when we take on the task of demonstrating cross-time stability, we have some problems. We cannot achieve reliability at the level of individual items, and if we put a hodgepodge together as a construct, we shall not obtain any summarizing power. Measurement considerations therefore place limits on our longitudinal relations if we don't have a stable composite.

Rutter: I was not arguing *against* putting things together. One has to do that. The nine temperamental dimensions that Alex Thomas, Stella Chess and their colleagues (1963) put together have proved to be a useful way of grouping a variety of individual items. Whether they should be further grouped or differently grouped is a separate issue. My point was simply that, although intercorrelations between items constitute one useful way of deriving groupings, this is not the only way. Of course, one's own concepts and prejudices are never sufficient either; they require empirical justification of some kind.

Bates: We haven't talked much about the really fundamental temperamental variables. Having a more basic theory might be another way to proceed. For example, Rothbart & Derryberry (1982) define temperament as individual differences in reactivity and self-regulation and try to relate those concepts to some basic physiological and constitutional variables. Once one has a relatively simple theoretical construct, one can then graft other, phenotypic variables (e.g. irritability and activity level) onto that more basic system.

Stevenson: I would like to extend the discussion about creating composites, and to consider the implications that has for detecting stability. We discussed in our paper (p 36) what happens when one is trying to determine stability while the behavioural repertoire of the child is changing. One could use canonical correlations between items obtained at time 1 and time 2; and the scores on these canonical correlates can be used as the basic temperament measures. This method integrates the single time-factor analytical procedures with the criteria for demonstrating stability over time. The optimum time scale would probably be a nine-month to one-year period between the two time points.

Hinde: We must concern ourselves with concrete issues and not with generalities. It may be more economical, and just as productive, to sum items into more global variables like Timid when looking for correlations with interview material. But when the two items—Shy and Dependent—were put together to form Timid, there were fewer than half the number of correlations with the school data, i.e. fewer predictions of how the child would behave in school, than one would obtain with the two items separately (R. A. Hinde et al, unpublished). This is an empirical matter; the fact that the two items correlate may or may not mean they have more predictive power for the future.

Bell: The only trouble is that when one computes correlations between shyness and timidity, on the one hand, and several other criterion measures on the other, there is no defensible way of estimating how many of those correlations should be significant by chance. However, there is much to be gained from longitudinal correlating measures that are relatively independent within each time period, because the correlations expected by chance can then be estimated. So in the case Professor Hinde just mentioned, it would probably be best to put the composites together first and then, if they yield more correlations between two time periods than one would expect by chance, it would be defensible to analyse longitudinal relations between the individual items.

Thomas: This discussion of correlations and factor analysis reflects the problems of using quantitative methods of analysis which, like qualitative and clinical methods, have inherent limitations. Our statistical consultant, Jacob Cohen, has always recommended that, no matter what sophisticated quantitative methods are available, one should always take into account qualitative clinical analysis. Dr Herbert Birch used to emphasize the importance of combining quantitative and qualitative measures. Professor Rutter has also emphasized that of all the various schemes and techniques available now for categorizing temperament, each is valuable only if it has functional relevance, for example in genetic terms or behavioural terms. The reason that our basic nine temperamental categories remain in use is that they have functional significance for the developmental process. Any alternative scheme must also satisfy that criterion. But sometimes a single item can be highly significant, and therefore the issue of single versus multiple items should also be considered qualitatively as well as quantitatively (see also p 106).

Rutter: Our discussion seems to have revealed that the different ways of grouping items together may be appropriate for different purposes.

Cross-cultural studies (see also p 16-19)

Hsu: My interest in temperament emerged for several reasons. First, dissatisfaction with psychoanalytic theory convinced me that psychoanalytic interpretations, to date, had not been helpful for most of the psychiatric problems I had encountered during the past 30 years as a child psychiatrist.

Secondly, as a consultant to paediatricians in general hospitals and in schools, after I had interviewed the children, parents and teachers concerned, I found that most of the feeding, sleeping, learning, as well as the behavioural problems of the children, could be understood in terms of the ignorance of the parents and teachers about the 'difficult' temperamental clustering in the children and the dissonance of the environment with their temperamental characteristics. Clarification of the issues and guidance of parents and teachers in providing situations and attitudes consonant to the child in question have usually solved the problems and relieved the anxiety, anger, and even the feelings of inadequacy experienced by the parents and teachers.

Thirdly, having had the opportunity to study both in western countries and in Japan, I have been deeply impressed by the consistent racial differences in styles of behaviour, or racial characters, though there are, of course, extreme individual differences within the same race. The results of many studies, as measured by questionnaires, have indicated racial differences, so I feel that we need to establish our own normal data for clinical use with infants and young children. In order to compare our data with the data from other cultures, instead of developing our own questionnaire, we translated verbatim the Carey–McDevitt and the New York longitudinal study questionnaires, revising only a few of the contents to make them applicable to our culture.

In our study of temperamental characteristics of Chinese children we included samples from the well-baby clinics of five general hospitals in Taipei City. We had 349 normal infants (182 males, 167 females) ranging in age from about four to eight months (mean, 179 days). The test–retest reliabilities of the revised Carey and McDevitt questionnaire were measured after a two-week interval and ranged from 0.74 for 'intensity' to 0.86 for 'approach'. Table 1 shows that we found significant differences for eight of the nine categories, with 'persistence' not significantly different. What these differences mean clinically, I don't know. Table 2 shows the sub-classification of temperament into five groups. There were fewer Chinese babies in the 'slow-to-warm-up' group.

We studied the mother's overall ratings of her child. Only 15.8% of the mothers classified their children as easier than average (see Table 3), while 38.3% classified their children as more difficult than average. In the second stage of our study we studied all the normal 3 to 7-year-olds living in a rural village (Taishen) as well as randomly selected normal children from an urban population (from the Chung-shan district of Taipei City). The total number of children studied was almost 2000. The age, sex and geographical data are summarized in Table 4. The correlations for re-rating reliabilities after a two-week interval for each temperamental category are shown in Table 5, and

TABLE 1 (*Hsu*) **Comparison of infant temperament scores for Chinese norms and Carey-McDevitt norms**

Category	Meaning of scale			Chinese norms (n = 349)		Carey-McDevitt norms (n = 203)		t value
	1	*to*	*6*	Mean	SD	Mean	SD	
Activity	low		high	3.96	0.64	4.40	0.56	−8.15*
Rhythmicity	regular		irregular	3.09	0.63	2.36	0.68	12.75*
Approach/Withdrawal	approach		withdrawal	2.91	0.83	2.27	0.78	8.94*
Adaptability	adaptive		non-adaptive	2.56	0.65	2.02	0.59	9.74*
Intensity	mild		intense	3.78	0.72	3.42	0.71	5.97*
Mood	positive		negative	3.44	0.64	2.81	0.68	10.90*
Persistence	persistent		non-persistent	3.00	0.85	3.03	0.82	−0.41
Distractibility	distractible		non-distractible	2.73	0.64	2.23	0.63	9.06*
Threshold	high		low	4.13	0.71	3.79	0.76	5.29*

* *P*<0.01

TABLE 2 (*Hsu*) Comparison of subgroup classifications of temperament for Chinese study and Carey-McDevitt study

Subgroup	Chinese study (n = 349) Percentages; numbers in parentheses	Carey-McDevitt study (n= 203) Percentages; numbers in parentheses
Difficult	8.3 (29)	9.4 (19)
Slow-to-warm up	2.9 (10)	5.9 (12)
Intermediate high	15.5 (54)	11.3 (23)
Intermediate low	21.5 (75)	31.0 (63)
Easy	51.9 (181)	42.4 (86)

$\chi^2 = 11.80$; degrees of freedom = 4; $P<0.02$.

TABLE 3 (*Hsu*) Relations between mother's overall ratings and subgroup classification

Subgroup[a]	Mother's overall ratings[b] Easier than average	Average	More difficult than average	Total (100%)
Difficult	4 (13.7)	9 (31.0)	16 (55.1)	29
Slow-to-warm-up	2 (20)	25 (15.8) (n = 86)	4 (40)	28 (22.8) (n = 86)	4 (40)	33 (38.3) (n = 86)	10	86
Intermediate high	19 (40.4)	15 (31.9)	13 (27.6)	47
Intermediate low	35 (49.4)	29 (40.8)	7 (9.8)	71
Easy	98 (58.3)	66 (39.3)	4 (2.3)	168
Total	158 (48.6)	123 (38.1)	44 (13.5)	325

[a] Subgroups as defined from questionnaire results. [b] Percentages in parentheses throughout.

the scores of the urban group and the rural group on each of the nine temperamental categories are shown in Table 6. We found no appreciable sex difference between the subgroups shown in Table 7.

These results can serve as a starting point for discussion about the necessity for and the methodological issues related to cross-cultural studies on such an important issue as temperament—its interactions with the environment and its role in the development, socialization and learning of children, as well as in the psychopathology of these children and their families.

TABLE 4 (*Hsu*) **Age, sex and geographical location of Chinese children aged 3 to 7 years**

Age	Male		Female		Totals		
	Urban	Rural	Urban	Rural	Total Urban	Total Rural	Overall Total
3	83	102	79	81	162	183	345
4	124	122	100	116	224	238	462
5	82	70	102	76	184	146	330
6	119	92	109	84	228	176	404
7	94	109	61	126	155	235	390
Total	502	495	451	483	953	978	1931

TABLE 5 (*Hsu*) **Rating–re-rating reliabilities for different temperamental categories at two-week intervals**

Temperamental category[a]	r[b]
Activity	0.70
Rhythmicity	0.44
Approach/Withdrawal	0.63
Adaptability	0.64
Intensity	0.75
Mood	0.52
Persistence	0.38
Distractibility	0.60
Threshold	0.42

[a] From the Chinese version of the New York longitudinal study questionnaire. [b]$n = 32$.

TABLE 6 (*Hsu*) **Comparison of temperament scores for urban and rural Chinese young children**

Temperamental category	Urban scores (n = 953)		Rural scores (n = 978)		t value[a]
	Mean	SD	Mean	SD	
Activity	3.90	0.87	3.92	0.86	−0.51
Rhythmicity	4.47	0.79	4.46	0.78	0.28
Approach/Withdrawal	4.51	0.84	4.43	0.85	2.08*
Adaptability	4.84	0.79	4.80	0.74	1.15
Intensity	3.86	0.80	3.80	0.76	1.69
Mood	4.80	0.63	4.79	0.63	0.35
Persistence	3.97	0.61	3.94	0.61	1.08
Distractibility	4.24	0.71	4.23	0.69	0.31
Threshold	3.22	0.77	3.33	0.77	−3.14**

[a] Student's t test; degrees of freedom = 1930; *$P<0.05$; **$P<0.01$.

TABLE 7 *(Hsu)* **Sex and temperamental subgroups**

Subgroup	Male[a]			Female[a]			Total[a]	
Difficult	63	(6.3)		40	(4.3)		103	(5.3)
Slow-to-warm-up	7	(0.7)	294	10	(1.1)	257	17	(0.9)
Intermediate high	224	(22.5)	(29.6)	207	(22.1)	(27.3)	431	(22.4)
Intermediate low	373	(37.4)		371	(39.7)		744	(38.5)
Easy	330	(33.1)		306	(32.8)		636	(32.9)
Total	997			934			1931	

$\chi^2 = 5.299$; degrees of freedom = 4; $P > 0.05$. [a] Percentages in parentheses throughout.

Rutter: I am struck by the similarities in temperamental characteristics between the urban and rural populations in your study. Were there any differences in the rates of disorder, for example in psychiatric problems, delinquency or any other indexes of psychosocial difficulties?

Hsu: I cannot yet answer that. So far, in urban populations we have used a Chinese version of screening tools for the children. So we do have data regarding the rates for the urban school children but not yet for the rural population.

Wolkind: Westerners who have visited China tend to report that Chinese children are much less active and more controlled than children in the western world. The differences that you found were not as marked as I would have expected. Is this a problem of allowing the parents to do the rating—do they have an image in their own minds of a range of 'normal'? The next step ought to be for detached observers to study different cultures, after establishing a consensus of what qualifies as a particular rating.

Hsu: This would certainly be worthwhile, and I have been exploring the possibilities of setting up an international training centre or institute where such observers might be trained before going into different cultures. By measuring the mother's perceptions, we may, indeed, be measuring aspects of the mother's temperament rather than the child's temperament.

Torgersen: Dr Hsu's results are very interesting. Even if we find an objective, measurable difference between cultures in 'activity', for example, we still face the problem of the experiential notion of what constitutes high activity and what constitutes the difficult temperament in different cultures.

Wolkind: If one had a reliable measure one could learn much, for example, by comparing the Chinese population in the United States and in China. This would allow an exploration of the origins of temperament.

Rutter: As long as we are confined to using adverbs and adjectives we are very unlikely to find valid differences. If one were measuring height by asking people to rate children as taller than average or smaller than average, one would almost certainly end up with all ethnic groups being evaluated as having the same height! Even within one's own culture, comparisons of behavioural ratings between special schools and ordinary schools produce some very peculiar results because teachers in special schools are using a different norm. The issue is a difficult one to deal with in the absence of objective measurements.

Carey: We tried to get around this problem in the design of our questionnaires by asking about specific behaviours in specific situations—yet there is room for improvement. Some evidence suggests that some items are not specific enough. For example, I compared ratings by fathers and mothers and found that they tended to agree far more on some characteristics than on others (Carey 1981). They agreed least about 'intensity', for example, but rather well about 'mood', where it is fairly easy to assess what is positive and what is negative. This is the kind of problem that must be solved in the next generation of questionnaires.

Berger: In cross-cultural studies, the linguistic equivalence of words is very important. Even within a culture, it is difficult in personality research to find out what people mean by different words. The translation from English to Chinese may confuse the sense in some ways and create a (superficial) impression of comparability.

Hsu: In the entire study we were very lucky. Dr Harold Stevenson of the University of Michigan sent one of his co-workers, who spoke excellent Chinese, to help us translate the Chinese version, and Dr Carey reminded us that one should not even change the order of the wording. We have just started an international study of children's reading in collaboration with the University of Michigan, Tohoku Fukushi University in Japan and the National Taiwan University.

REFERENCES

Bates JE 1980 The concept of difficult temperament. Merrill-Palmer Q 26:299-319
Bates JE, Freeland CB, Lounsbury ML 1979 Measurement of infant difficultness. Child Dev 50:794-803
Bates JE, Olson SL, Pettit GS, Bayles K 1982 Dimensions of individuality in the mother–infant relationship at six months of age. Child Dev, in press (April issue)
Bernal JF 1972 Crying during the first 10 days of life, and maternal responses. Dev Med Child Neurol 14:362-372
Bernal JF 1973 Nightwaking in the first 14 months. Dev Med Child Neurol 15:760-769
Block J 1977 Advancing the psychology of personality: paradigmatic shift or improving the quality of research. In: Magnusson N, Endler NS (eds) Personality at the crossroads. Wiley, New York
Carey WB 1970 A simplified method for measuring infant temperament. J Pediatr 77:188-194
Carey WB 1981 The importance of temperament–environment interaction for child health and development. In: Lewis M, Rosenblum L (eds) The uncommon child. Plenum Press, New York

Carey WB 1982 The validity of parental assessments of development and behavior. Am J Dis Child, in press

Conners CK 1969 A teacher rating scale for use in drug studies with children. Am J Psychiatry 126:152-156

Conners CK 1970 Symptom patterns in hyperkinetic, neurotic, and normal children. Child Dev 41:667-682

Douglas JWB, Lawson A, Cooper JE, Cooper E 1968 Family interaction and the activities of young children. J Child Psychol Psychiatry Allied Discip 9:157-171

Guilford JP, Zimmerman WS 1956 Fourteen dimensions of temperament. Psychol Monogr (Gen Appl) 70:(No 417)

Quay HC 1977 Measuring dimensions of deviant behavior: the behavior problem checklist. J Abnorm Child Psychol 5:277-288

Rachman S, Hodgson R 1974 Synchrony and desynchrony in fear and avoidance. Behav Res Ther 6:159-165

Richards MPM, Bernal JF 1972 An observational study of mother–infant interaction. In: Blurton-Jones N (ed) Ethological studies of child behaviour. Cambridge University Press, London

Rothbart MK, Derryberry D 1982 Development of individual differences in temperament. In: Lamb ME, Brown AL (eds) Advances in developmental psychology. Erlbaum, Hillsdale, NJ, vol 1

Rowe DC, Plomin R 1977 Temperament in early childhood. J Pers Assess 41:150-156

Rutter M 1963 Psychosocial factors in the short-term prognosis of physical disease. I: Peptic ulcer. J Psychosom Res 7:45-60

Thomas A, Chess C 1977 Temperament and development. Brunner/Mazel, New York

Thomas A, Chess S, Birch HG, Hertzig ME, Korn S 1963 Behavioral individuality in early childhood. New York University Press, New York

Thomas A, Chess S, Birch HG 1968 Temperament and behavior disorders in children. New York University Press, New York

Vaughn B, Deinard A, Egeland B 1980 Measuring temperament in pediatric practice. J Pediatr 96:510-514

Vaughn B, Taraldson B, Crichton L, Egeland B 1981 The assessment of infant temperament. A critique of the Carey infant temperament questionnaire. Infant Behav Dev 40:1-17

Werry JS 1978 Measures in pediatric psychopharmacology. In: Werry JS (ed) Pediatric psychopharmacology—the use of behavior-modifying drugs in children. Brunner/Mazel, New York, p 29-78

Intrinsic determinants of temperament

RONALD S. WILSON

Department of Pediatrics, Child Development Unit, Health Sciences Center, University of Louisville, Louisville, Kentucky 40292, USA

Abstract Infant twins have been recruited to participate in a longitudinal assessment of temperament, beginning at three months of age. The twins are brought into a structured laboratory setting and are videotaped as they interact with the mother, with staff personnel, and with each other. The infant's temperament is rated from the videotapes, and additional data are obtained by having the parents fill out the Infant/Toddler Temperament Questionnaire at each visit. A neonatal assessment has also been done for most twins to obtain initial measures of irritability, reactivity and soothability. Monozygotic twins showed high concordance for irritability as neonates, and for ratings of emotional tone at 12 months. Monozygotic twins also tended to show synchronized patterns of change between ages. The questionnaire ratings correlated significantly with the laboratory ratings at six and 12 months, and this convergent linkage between two sources argues for a core temperament profile that manifests itself with some consistency.

History

The Louisville Twin Study was instituted in 1959 as one of the international studies of child development. Its original emphasis was on the longitudinal study of twins as a first step in determining the contribution of genetic and environmental factors to physical growth and mental development. While these studies are continuing, the research programme was reorganized in 1976 to focus on an assessment of temperament in infant twins.

The transition was based on three major factors: (a) a resurgence of interest in the intrinsic response characteristics of the infant, and the influence of these characteristics on the caretaker of the infant (Bell 1974, Lewis & Rosenblum 1974); (b) in our twin sample, an appreciation of the central role played by the twins' temperament in shaping the parent's initial reaction, especially where differences in temperament were evident; and (c) a

1982 Temperamental differences in infants and young children. Pitman Books Ltd, London (Ciba Foundation symposium 89) p 121-140

detailed and provocative body of research on temperament from the New York longitudinal study (Thomas et al 1963, Thomas & Chess 1977).

In the New York longitudinal study, the infant's behaviour (as reported by the mother) was rated on nine attributes (e.g. adaptability, approach–withdrawal, intensity of reaction); and for many infants, individualized patterns of reaction were evident in the earliest months. The effect of these individual differences in reactivity was particularly well illustrated by two sets of twins who displayed marked differences from birth onwards. As Thomas et al (1963) described, the mother in each family started with the same general attitude towards both infants, but then developed increasingly different affective bonds, largely in response to these initial differences in reactivity.

The early appearance of these rudimentary temperament patterns raises the basic issues of origins—what role is played by genetic and constitutional factors—and of the extent to which there is stability or continuity in the expression of temperament from infancy onwards. These are the core issues from a developmental standpoint, and some related evidence is briefly reviewed below.

The role of genetic influence was highlighted in a twin study by Torgersen & Kringlen (1978), who used the interview schedules from the New York longitudinal study and found significantly greater concordance for monozygotic (MZ) twins on all rated attributes of temperament at nine months of age. Thomas & Chess (1977) also reported a provocative case of MZ twins adopted at birth into separate families and raised apart, both of whom showed strikingly similar temperamental traits in the preschool years.

To the same point are the preliminary findings of T. Bouchard on MZ twins who have been raised separately and reunited as adults—the similarities in temperament traits and personality are often striking (see Holden 1980). Such findings suggest that there may be genetic determinants that exert an enduring influence on temperament.

Continuity

Turning to the issue of stability and continuity in temperament, the general expectation is that if temperament is rooted in constitutional and genetic variables, there must be some continuity in its expression over the developmental history of the child.

But as Carey (1980) notes, a variety of normal phenomena may confound efforts to demonstrate stability of temperament, not the least of which are varying rates of maturation for the underlying central nervous system structures, and for age-linked behavioural competencies that may alter the mode of expression for a given temperamental style. The problem (and the challenge) is one of determining when dissimilar behaviours over time may reflect the same characteristics of temperament. The behavioural criteria would therefore be age-specific, and the thread of continuity would be educed from a coherent patterning of behaviours during childhood.

Related background studies in Louisville

Our work in this area began with the mother's interviews, in which she reported whether the twins were concordant or discordant for various aspects of behaviour (Wilson et al 1971). Many pairs were discordant for a cluster of behaviours relating to temperament (i.e. temper frequency and intensity, crying, irritability, and demanding attention), and the mothers were often sharply aware of these differences in the first six months of life. When one twin displayed these behaviours in greater degree, the other twin would typically be described as having a longer attention span and remaining absorbed in an activity for a longer period. A recent follow-up of data obtained since 1971 replicated these two basic clusters, and further demonstrated that individual differences in temperament remained reasonably stable across ages (Matheny et al 1981).

In addition, as part of the previous mental testing programme, we had routinely kept one twin in the playroom with our staff while the other twin was being tested, while accompanied by the mother. This had given us extensive experience with the specific care-taking problems and aspects of temperament that arose at each age, and the effective diversionary activities to deal with them.

Therefore, we began to construct an extensive series of play episodes and interactions with the infant, which could be implemented in a standardized manner. In essence, the infant would be confronted with a battery of play opportunities and challenges, the latter including instances of separation from the mother and the other twin. The staff would then employ a graded series of soothing techniques and diversionary play activities, as required. The sessions would be videotaped, and the staff would ultimately rate the infant's behaviour from the videotapes.

Outline for each visit

The pretesting evolved a basic outline for the temperament assessment at each age, as follows. After the twins arrive there is a brief 'warm up' period including both twins, the mother, and the two staff members serving as interactionists. The mother leaves subsequently for an interview and the twins remain together with the interactionists, who engage in specific activities vis-à-vis the twins. The mother returns briefly and then leaves with one twin for testing.

The second twin remains alone with the staff members until the mother comes back for a brief reunion; then the second twin goes with the mother for testing and the first twin remains alone with the staff. In these solo episodes, the staff engage each twin in a prescribed set of activities, or vignettes, for a fixed period of time, so that there will be uniformity of treatment across all participants. The schedule is carefully organized to yield one hour of videotaping for each pair, and in a format that is exactly duplicated for all twins.*

Behavioural rating scales

These nine-point scales have been designed for ratings of emotional tone; attention; activity; orientation to staff, parent and co-twin; initial reaction to separation and reunion; interest in toys and play activity; and, at appropriate ages, mouthing, vocalization, and locomotion. The rating categories and representative descriptors for two of the scales are illustrated below; the complete set may be found in Matheny & Wilson (1981).

(a) *Emotional tone.* Refers to principal emotional state manifested during the rating period: for example (1 point) extremely upset, crying vigorously; (3) upset, but can be soothed; (5) bland, no apparent reaction; (7) contented, happy; (9) excited or animated.

(b) *Attention.* This category refers to the degree to which an infant is alert and maintains attention to objects and events: for example (1 point) unoccupied, non-focused, vacant staring; (3) minimal or fleeting attention, easily distractible; (5) moderate attention—generally attentive but may shift; (7) focused and sustained attention; (9) continued and persistent attention to the point of being 'glued' to object or event.

After the visit is completed, the raters work from the videotapes and make the appropriate scale ratings for each successive two-minute period of the visit. No rater scores the episodes for which she was the principal inter-actionist with the twin. Inter-rater reliability was satisfactory (81% to 96% agreement), and has been reported in detail elsewhere (Wilson & Matheny

---

* A complete description of all vignettes and how they are employed may be found in Matheny & Wilson (1981).

1982). After the ratings are completed, they are condensed into composite summary scores for each scale. The summary scores are computed separately for each twin, and the scores furnish the basic data for constructing each infant's behavioural profile as displayed in the laboratory.

Physical measures

When the laboratory assessment is completed, the twins are taken to an adjacent room for physical measurements, which includes weight, length and head circumference. The infants are undressed for the measurements—a procedure that is upsetting for some infants—and the length measurement requires that the infant be stretched out in a supine position and held stationary while the bootboard is brought into contact with the heels.

The necessary restraint often evokes expressions of temperament, and ratings are made by observers of the infant's emotional tone, cooperativeness, and activity during each measurement. Inter-rater agreement for results on these scales has been 87%, 75% and 65%, respectively. The composite temperament ratings made during physical measurements have been combined with the summary scores for the laboratory assessment, and together they have furnished a composite behavioural profile for each infant.

Neonatal assessment

In addition, to get at the earliest expression of temperament in these infants, a comprehensive neonatal assessment was performed at the hospital for many of the twins. The assessment was designed to measure rudimentary aspects of temperament in the form of irritability, reactivity, resistance to soothing, activity, and reinforcement value of the infant's behaviour to the examiner. The neonates were tested as soon as they were stable enough to permit the necessary handling, and the assessment for each twin was conducted during the entire interval from one feeding period to the next (3–4 h). The procedure and the results from a large standardization sample of twins have been described by Riese (1982a,b).

Composite scores from the neonatal examination were obtained for each of the categories named above, and these scores furnished the earliest behavioural profile for each infant. The principal questions concerned how this profile related to such intrinsic factors as genotype and prenatal growth, and how the profile related to the later measures of temperament obtained in the laboratory.

Sample

The twins recruited for this study were drawn from the entire twin-birth registry in the Louisville area, with a special effort made to enrol and retain families of low socio-economic status. The twins make their first visit to the research centre at three months of age; they return for quarterly visits throughout the first year and then semi-annual visits up to 30 months of age.

Twins are still being recruited, and at present 42 pairs have completed the visits through 12 months. Of this sample, 24 pairs have been tentatively diagnosed as monozygotic as a result of unanimous concurrence among staff members. For technical and psychological reasons, the twins are not blood-typed until they are three years old, so the final diagnosis of zygosity is not yet available; but past comparison of staff judgments about zygosity with blood-typing results has shown very high agreement.

Since the principal point of this paper is to examine the prospective role of intrinsic determinants of temperament, the data analysis has been confined to these 24 MZ pairs. The results therefore constitute a preliminary report of findings that will be subject to revision as further cases are added and as dizygotic pairs are included. Similarly, the analyses of the laboratory ratings are limited to the data obtained at six and 12 months, since the data are virtually complete at these ages. The principal interest is in the temperament profiles generated by the ratings—i.e. in whether individual differences were evident, whether there was continuity over age, and whether there was concordance in the patterning of temperament variables for MZ twins.

Results

The scores for the neonatal assessment were analysed first, and the intercorrelations between the categories are shown in Table 1, which is based on the complete standardization sample ($n = 280$). Also shown are the correlations between birthweight and the scores in each category and, in the final column, the first-factor loadings for four of the categories, as obtained from a principal-components factor analysis. The entries in brackets are the MZ within-pair correlations for each variable, and are based on only 13 pairs; the remaining pairs in this MZ sample had been recruited before the neonatal programme began.

As shown by the correlations and the factor loadings in Table 1, a strong cluster emerged linking high irritability, marked resistance to soothing, activity while awake, and low reinforcement value to the examiner. Notably, birthweight was moderately related to irritability and soothing, with heavier infants being more irritable and more resistant to soothing. Conversely, the

TABLE 1 Analysis of neonatal assessment scores

Variables	Irritability	Resistance to soothing	Activity awake	Activity asleep	Reactivity	Reinforcement value	Birthweight	First-factor loadings
Irritability	(0.69)							0.86
Resistance to soothing	0.70	(0.21)						0.84
Activity awake	0.36	0.49	(0.21)					0.64
Activity asleep	0.04	0.04	0.12	(0.21)				—
Reactivity	-0.26	-0.18	-0.09	-0.13	(0.08)			—
Reinforcement value	-0.66	-0.54	-0.38	0.03	0.37	(0.36)		-0.82
Birth-weight	0.47	0.56	0.23	0.06	-0.07	-0.15	(0.81)	—
First-factor scores								(0.38)

Correlations are Pearson r values except for entries in brackets which are monozygotic within-pair correlations. Dashes indicate small factor loadings (<0.35), omitted from table.

TABLE 2 Analysis of six-month temperament scores

Variables	Emotional tone	Activity	Attention	Physical measurements				First-factor loadings
				Emotional tone	Activity	Cooperation	Birthweight	
Emotional tone	(0.16)			0.18	0.04	0.08	0.08	—
Activity	0.06	(0.56)		-0.16	-0.05	-0.15	0.06	—
Attention	0.46	-0.12	(0.00)	0.64	0.49	0.57	-0.19	0.87
Physical measurements:								
Emotional tone				(0.24)	0.33	0.82	-0.48	0.86
Activity					(0.12)	0.26	0.10	0.56
Cooperation						(0.26)	-0.53	0.80
First-factor scores							a	(0.15)

Correlations are Pearson *r* values except for entries in brackets which are monozygotic within-pair correlations (24 pairs). [a] Correlation not computed. Dashes indicate small factor loadings (<0.35), omitted from table.

low-birthweight babies were less irritable and easier to soothe, but birth-weight itself had no significant bearing on the examiner's rating of reinforce-ment value. The MZ twins showed high concordance for the ratings of irritability, but relatively low concordance for the other categories, and moderate concordance for the first-factor scores.

The results from the laboratory assessment at six months are summarized in Table 2. The correlations showed a cluster of relationships between attention, and emotional tone and cooperation as rated in physical measurements. In fact, at this age the challenges of physical measurement more effectively provoked expressions of temperament and revealed individual differences than did the structured vignettes of the laboratory assessment. Separation from the mother was not particularly upsetting at this age, and many of the infants were relatively calm during the session, or easily soothed if upset.

Physical measurements triggered off a stronger display of temperament, however, and it may be noted that the higher birthweight babies were the more distressed and uncooperative in the physical measurements. They were also more irritable and resistant to soothing in the neonatal assessment. By contrast, birthweight showed no relation to emotional-tone ratings in the laboratory assessment.

The entries in brackets in Table 2 show that MZ twin concordance was quite modest for all variables except activity (in the laboratory), including the composite first-factor scores. Whatever genetic influences there were on temperament at six months, they were not sharply apparent from a single laboratory assessment at this age. Data to be reported later, however, showed a much higher concordance for MZ twins when based on the cumulative observations and ratings made by the parents.

What linkage was there between the neonatal ratings and the six-month temperament ratings? The correlations between variables are shown in Table 3. Resistance to soothing was significantly related to emotional tone and to cooperation in physical measurements; and, to a lesser degree, activity while awake and irritability showed the same relationships. Those neonates rated as more irritable, active and resistant to soothing were also more distressed and uncooperative when being measured at six months.

Interestingly, a neonate who was more active during the hospital assess-ment was more likely to be upset and to have a short attention span in the six-month laboratory assessment. In conjunction, the two sets of behavioural ratings showed a significant degree of continuity between birth and six months for variables expressive of temperament.

At 12 months, the full range of play vignettes could be employed for the first time, and the results are summarized in Table 4. The clustering of variables became considerably more organized at this age, and the laboratory variables

TABLE 3 Intercorrelations between neonatal assessment scores and six-month temperament scores

Neonatal categories	Six-month temperament categories			Physical measurements		
	Emotional tone	Activity	Attention	Emotional tone	Activity	Coopera- tion
Irritability	—	−0.29	—	−0.28	—	—
Resistance to soothing	—	−0.40	—	−0.45	—	−0.36
Activity awake	−0.44	—	−0.45	−0.34	—	—
Activity asleep	—	—	—	—	—	—
Reactivity	0.31	—	0.33	0.29	—	—
Reinforcement value	—	0.36	—	—	—	—

Dashes indicate correlations smaller than 0.25. $n = 29$.

were more closely interrelated, as were the ratings for the physical measurements. There was, however, only a moderate relationship between these two clusters. Evidently the physical measurements induced crying and distress in some infants who had handled the laboratory experiences with equanimity.

The laboratory cluster sketched the picture of an infant who was positive in mood, attentive and receptive to the staff; or, conversely, of an infant who was distressed, had fleeting attention and was not easily comforted. Birthweight dropped out entirely as a significant factor, so the initial linkage between birthweight and distressed emotional tone vanished as development proceeded.

MZ twins were more concordant on nearly all variables at 12 months than at six months, particularly for emotional tone and the first-factor scores. In view of the high MZ correlation for irritability in the neonatal assessment, it would appear that some basic dimension of irritability and distress versus positive mood was shared by MZ twins, and might be expressive of a genetic contribution to this dimension.

Correlations between ages

In the relationship between the six-month ratings and the 12-month ratings, there were virtually no significant correlations between ages, even for scales ostensibly measuring the same characteristics. Further, the correlation between the first-factor scores at six and 12 months was $r = -0.04$. The only evidence of linkage was between emotional tone for physical measurements

TABLE 4 Analysis of 12-month temperament scores

Variables	Emotional tone	Activity	Attention	Orientation to staff	Physical measurements			Birth-weight	First-factor loadings
					Emotional tone	Activity	Cooperation		
Emotional tone	(0.51)	0.63	0.81	0.62	0.29	0.03	0.27	−0.03	0.86
Activity		(0.34)	0.55	0.21	0.15	0.10	0.08	0.14	0.60
Attention			(0.25)	0.48	0.29	−0.03	0.24	0.05	0.82
Orientation to staff				(0.30)	0.20	−0.05	0.21	0.07	0.65
Physical measurements:									
Emotional tone					(0.23)	−0.48	0.79	0.03	0.59
Activity						(0.20)	−0.67	−0.21	—
Cooperation							(0.31)	0.08	0.58
First-factor scores								a	(0.49)

Correlations are Pearson r values except for entries in brackets which are monozygotic within-pair correlations (24 pairs). Dashes indicate small factor loadings (<0.35), omitted from table. [a]Correlation not computed.

at six months and laboratory ratings at 12 months for emotional tone
($r = -0.24$) and activity (-0.31).

These are very modest relationships, and the conclusion has to be that
there was negligible continuity in the rated aspects of temperament from six
to 12 months, as measured in the laboratory for this sample. This may partly
reflect a reorganization due to birthweight dropping out as a significant
variable. In the main, however, the maturational changes during this period
and the quantum jump in neuromuscular capabilities exerted a major
influence on the manner in which temperament could be expressed, and this
was probably responsible for the apparent discontinuity. There was greater
consistency between newborn status and temperament ratings at six months,
but by the same token the temperament profile was more loosely organized
than at 12 months.

Synchronized change. It may be recalled that the MZ within-pair correlations
for the variables were somewhat higher than the age-to-age correlations, and
this was also true for the factor scores. It would appear that while each infant
may have changed position in the ratings from age to age, there was still
demonstrable concordance for the MZ pairs at each age. The question was
whether the changes between ages occurred in parallel for these MZ twins.

There were sufficient pairs to allow for the test of changes only between six
and 12 months, and each infant's temperament profile was condensed into a
single first-factor score at each age. A within-pair correlation was then
computed for concordance of change in first-factor scores between six and 12
months, and the resultant correlation was $r_{MZ} = 0.38$ ($P < 0.05$).

So for the laboratory measures of temperament, which on an individual
basis were uncorrelated between six and 12 months, there was nevertheless a
significant degree of concordance in the pattern of change for MZ twins. The
nominal discontinuity was qualified by the fact that the changes tended to be
synchronized for MZ pairs. In fact, this correlation, reflecting synchronized
change in the factor scores, was very close to the corresponding MZ
correlation for change in mental-test scores over the same period (Wilson
1978).

Temperament questionnaires

The laboratory assessments are one-slice observations of behaviour obtained
in a structured, standardized setting. How do the twins compare with each
other as seen from the perspective of the parents, who have daily exposure to
their behaviour? Further, how do the parents' reports of temperament
compare with the ratings from the laboratory?

The questionnaires designed by Carey and his colleagues have been used with these twins, and were completed at home by the parents after each visit. At six months, the appropriate version was the revised Infant Temperament Questionnaire (Carey & McDevitt 1978); at 12 months, the Toddler Temperament Questionnaire (W. Fullard, S. C. McDevitt & W. B. Carey, unpublished test, 1980). Due to varying dates of availability, there were questionnaires for only 12 MZ pairs at six months and for 14 MZ pairs at 12 months; and even fewer with questionnaires at both ages. However, the factor analyses (mentioned below) were done on the data for all available twins ($n = 84$) before the factor scores were obtained for the MZ pairs.

The questionnaire included about 100 items that were grouped into nine categories or scales. The scales are listed in Table 5, along with the major

TABLE 5 First-factor loadings for temperament questionnaires

	First-factor loadings	
Scales	Six months	Twelve months
Activity	−0.70	—
Rhythmicity	0.63	—
Approach/withdrawal	0.79	0.74
Adaptation	0.60	0.84
Intensity	—	—
Mood	0.63	0.73
Persistence and Attention span	—	0.80
Distractibility	0.61	0.65
Threshold of response	—	—

Dashes indicate small factor loadings (<0.35), omitted from table.

first-factor loadings at each age. The results showed that approach–withdrawal, adaptation, mood, and distractibility appeared in the first factor at both ages, and persistence–attention span was added as a strong contributor at 12 months. This cluster of variables represented the major constellation of behaviours that parents perceived as expressive of temperament.

How did these ratings by the parents compare with the laboratory assessment? For the available MZ pairs, each infant was represented by his or her first-factor score for the temperament questionnaire (TQ I) and the laboratory ratings (Lab I), and a correlation was computed between the factor scores. At six months, the correlation between TQ I and Lab I was $r = 0.41$ and, at 12 months, $r = 0.52$.

Thus, there was a considerable degree of convergence in the ratings of temperament from two entirely different sources. Despite differences in observers, in rating scales, and in periods of observation, there was significant consistency in how each infant's temperament profile was rated.

Each source furnished an overlapping perspective on the foundation elements of temperament, and while some aspects were necessarily unique to each source, there was a gratifying degree of coherence in the temperament profile from two complementary sources.

As a final analysis, the within-pair correlations were computed for these MZ pairs for the first-factor scores on the temperament questionnaire. At six months, the MZ within-pair correlation for TQ I was $r_{MZ} = 0.74$, and at 12 months it was $r_{MZ} = 0.80$. Clearly, there was a high degree of concordance in these MZ pairs for the parent-rated aspects of temperament.

The concordance for the questionnaire ratings was considerably higher than for the laboratory scores, and this may reflect a distilling of essential attributes for both twins through repeated observations of their behaviour. Conversely, it may reflect a tendency for parents to rate both twins alike. Ultimately we shall have enough DZ pairs to address these questions in terms of differential concordance, but at this point it is reassuring to find significant MZ concordance for both sources of ratings, and a significant convergent linkage between sources.

DISCUSSION

These results constitute a first report of directly observed temperament ratings made in the newborn period and throughout the first year of life. The continuity of ratings was stronger from birth to six months than from six to 12 months, but the measures of twin concordance showed that some of the changes were occurring in parallel for MZ twins. Each infant's temperament profile seemed to become more fully organized by 12 months, and the concordance for MZ twins also increased.

A fuller interpretation of results, especially in relation to genetic influences, must await the addition to the study of dizygotic twins. It does seem, however, that some of the nominal discontinuities may reflect organized pathways of change, which in turn have their roots in the genetic programming. It may be anticipated that as the sample size is enlarged and other ages are added, the intrinsic determinants of temperament will be more sharply detected.

Acknowledgements

This research was supported in part by PHS grant 90-C-922, from the Office of Child Development. I am indebted to Dr Adam Matheny and Dr Marilyn Riese for major contributions to the programme, and to K. Adkins, R. Arbegust, D. Batres, D. Brawner, P. Gefert, M.

Hinkle, P. Kameen, P. Litwin and S. Nuss for dedicated assistance in data collection and analysis.

REFERENCES

Bell RQ 1974 Contributions of human infants to caregiving and social interaction. In: Lewis M, Rosenblum LA (eds) The effect of the infant on its caregiver. Wiley, New York

Carey WB 1980 The importance of temperament–environment interaction for child health and development. In: Lewis M, Rosenblum LA (eds) The uncommon child. Plenum, New York, p 31-55

Carey WB, McDevitt SC 1978 Revision of the infant temperament questionnaire. Pediatrics 61:735-739

Holden C 1980 Identical twins reared apart. Science (Wash DC) 207:1323-1329

Lewis M, Rosenblum LA (eds) 1974 The effect of the infant on its caregiver. Wiley, New York

Matheny AP, Wilson RS 1981 Developmental tasks and rating scales for the laboratory assessment of infant temperament. J Suppl Abstr Serv Cat Sel Doc Psychol 11:81

Matheny AP, Wilson RS, Dolan AB, Krantz JZ 1981 Behavioral contrasts in twinships: stability and patterns of differences in childhood. Child Dev 52:579-588

Riese ML 1982a Assessment of behavioral patterns in neonates. Infant Behav Dev, submitted

Reise ML 1982b Procedures and norms for assessing behavioral patterns in full-term and pre-term neonates. J Suppl Abstr Serv Cat Sel Doc Psychol 12:10

Thomas A, Chess S, Birch S, Birch HG, Hertzig ME, Korn S 1963 Behavioral individuality in early childhood. New York University Press, New York

Thomas A, Chess S 1977 Temperament and development. Brunner/Mazel, New York

Torgersen AM, Kringlen E 1978 Genetic aspects of temperamental differences in twins. J Am Acad Child Psychiatry 17:433-444

Wilson RS 1978 Synchronies in mental development: an epigenetic perspective. Science (Wash DC) 202:939-948

Wilson RS, Brown AM, Matheny AP 1971 Emergence and persistence of behavioral differences in twins. Child Dev 42:1381-1398

Wilson RS, Matheny AP 1982 Assessment of temperament in infant twins. Dev Psychol, in press

DISCUSSION

Robinson: How did you handle the gestational age variability between the 24 monozygotic pairs of twins? I believe some were born at about 32–33 weeks of gestation and some were born at term. Could the variations in gestational age account for some of the lack of congruity at six months and at 12 months?

Kolvin: A further point that I would like to add to that is the problem arising from the differences in birthweight within a particular monozygotic twin pair. The likelihood of substantial differences in birthweight is greater in monozygotic pairs then in dizygotic pairs. This is the result of an imbalance of placental circulation in the two-thirds of monozygotic pairs who are monochorial. Thus, any differences in intrauterine circulation, and consequent differences in birthweight, may themselves lead to apparent differences in temperament simply because the monozygotic twins may have different physical environments and experiences. They begin their lives in rather different conditions and become more similar only as they grow older. I think this picture would stabilize only at about 12 months of age, and this may explain the lack of continuity in neonatal and six-month assessments.

Wilson: The neonatal assessment is done at the hospital when the twins reach a point at which they are medically stable. The very young twins are therefore not assessed at birth, but at the time when they are ready to go home. In no case was there a marked disparity in gestational age within the pair, but there are obviously some differences between the pairs. Both gestational age and birthweight tend to be highly correlated with early mental development. If only one measure is used, it accounts for most of the variation that the other would give. We have not corrected our temperament data for gestational age but, in our work on mental development, gestational age was a significant factor in mental status at three and six months but was negligible after one or two years of age. We have therefore preferred to develop norms for *twins* in our mental development study, and not attempted to correct for gestational age; any initial lag disappears progressively over the first two years. As with gestational age, no pair of twins in this group I have described had a large difference in birthweight—the within-pair correlation was 0.81. There was a moderate association of irritability, and resistance to soothing, with birthweight, both in the neonatal period and at six months. The larger twin tended to be, in an 'emotional tone' sense, the more distressed one during the physical measurements at six months. But at 12 months these correlations had disappeared, and the birthweight factors had regressed, or been overcome.

Rutter: The low correlation on temperamental variables between the monozygotic twins in the early months is therefore even more striking, because to some extent the temperamental intercorrelations must reflect the high correlation between the twins on birthweight. Because birthweight itself is related to the temperamental characteristics, the true monozygotic pair intercorrelation (having taken account of the similarities in birthweight) must be very low indeed.

Wilson: The interesting thing is that while birthweight relates both to irritability ($r = 0.47$) and to resistance to soothing ($r = 0.56$) at about the same level, the monozygotic correlation for those two variables was quite different: for irritability, $r = 0.69$; for resistance to soothing, $r = 0.21$. This occurred even though birthweight had an equivalent relationship to both variables and even though they tended to be intercorrelated with one another.

Carey: The 12-month first factor derived from the examination had more or less the same components as the first factor derived from the temperament questionnaire—i.e. they were conceptually somewhat similar. Was that true also at six months?

Wilson: The factor structure at six months was less clearly consolidated for the temperament scale than it was at 12 months. Four of the categories appeared in the first factor at both ages—approach/withdrawal, mood, adaptation, and distractibility.

Rutter: How far was the developmental discontinuity that you observed between six and 12 months due to the different meaning of the test situation for the child at these ages? The separation of the mother and child plays a prominent part in your analysis, but in most children this event has a quite different meaning at six months than at 12 months. That, in itself, may produce a discontinuity related more to situational variables than to anything about the child's temperament.

Wilson: That is probably true, but we hope that when we have enough of these children followed up to 24 months of age, we shall be able to work back and anchor, at each age, the predominant response mode. This will enable us to see how patterns emerge in the infant across the 24 months. We have not yet gone over the data to look at the child's response to specific interactions within the total complex. I expect that some of these results will be more revealing, in a developmental sense, than dealing with the total composite score.

Bates: Do you also have data on the three–six month and six–nine month periods?

Wilson: I did not report the three-month data because many of the infants dozed during part of the laboratory visit, and we have not yet reached a workable formula for deciding which segments of the visit to score and to incorporate into the child's composite score in order to make any valid comparisons. Even at the six-month visit some of the children snoozed. We have now moved the feeding vignette to the end of the visit at six months, because once the child is fed, it falls asleep!

Stevenson: You mentioned your method of scoring as one of taking ratings at two-minute intervals. Do you create, by this method, any sub-scores that might override some of the problems about the separation episode? Do you have separate scores of temperament for when the mothers are present and when they are absent?

Wilson: The results are broken down in that way. The entire visit is structured so that the mother either leaves or returns at the beginning of a two-minute interval. She doesn't appear in the midst of any scoring period.

All major transitions—for example, the use of new vignettes—are introduced at the beginning of two-minute intervals. We can then analyse the intervals that deal specifically with the situations of mother present, mother leaving and mother absent.

Stevenson: Do you know yet whether there is a differential stability between those different settings?

Wilson: No. We did the initial breakdown of the data at 12 months of age, because the data were more stable then. We looked initially at four variations within the whole package—the original orientation, the periods where the twins were together but the mother was absent, the periods in which each twin was alone, and a final reunion episode. Each of the episodes correlated with one another, but not at the $r = 0.90$ level. We ultimately decided to use a single score summed across all of those episodes. Thus, in an extreme case, when a highly irritable infant cried throughout most of the visit, that was detected no matter what happened in relation to the mother being present or attempting to sooth the infant etc. We shall be looking in more detail at those patterns during each of the four episodes that I just mentioned.

Hsu: We have some clinical evidence suggesting that children react differently to the mother in the laboratory and at home. From what you have observed, can you tell whether the children will behave similarly at home?

Wilson: Most of our studies are done in the standardized (laboratory) setting, but we do include home visits by a social worker at seven and at 33 months. We shall eventualy have information available from her about the relationship between the mother and the twins at home. Even in the home, we may not see a spontaneous view of the twins' reactions when the mother leaves, of course. However, our impression, which is confirmed by the mothers, is that the behaviour of the children at 24 months in response to the mother leaving the room will be the same when a baby sitter comes in. The mothers have commonly reported that the children throw tantrums when the baby sitter takes charge of them.

Keogh: Do you have any index of the stability of the home, and the response of the parents to the impact of having twins?

Wilson: Eventually we shall have this information. That is one reason for including the seven-month visit and then the follow-up at 33 months.

Keogh: I believe that the stability of the home in relation to the impact of twins is an important influence on how quickly the children's temperamental pattern becomes stabilized. We find enormous differences among families in their responses, for example, to the birth of a handicapped child (Keogh, Bernheimer & Young, unpublished paper, 1981 Bienn Meet Soc Res Child Dev, Boston, Mass). When there is a lot of chaos in the home there is more variability in the child's response.

Fulker: Do you also have detailed information on *dizygotic* twins that would enable you to separate genetic and environmental effects?

Wilson: Some of our data are in the preliminary stage, and we do not yet have enough dizygotic twins for valid comparisons to be made. I am not entirely happy with only a visual diagnosis of zygosis; eventually, when the twins reach three years they will all be blood-typed, and we shall then have a more definitive diagnosis of monozygosis and dizygosis. We are fairly confident about the preliminary diagnosis in the 24 pairs that I have discussed, but we must await the blood-typing for both groups.

Rutter: Presumably it follows, though, that effects of changes in genetic contribution as the children grow older can't really be judged from the change in correlations for the monozygotic twins without a knowledge also of what is happening with the dizygotic twins.

Wilson: That is correct.

Bell: Did you assess short-term stability in the neonatal period, or were the children examined only once?

Wilson: There was only one examination, but the observer was with each infant for roughly three hours during a single day. Given the time spent by the babies in the hospital, it frequently becomes something of a rush to do the full data assessment before the family goes home. We now have a graduate student working with us and being trained to do the assessment. Thus, we shall eventually build up a repertoire of comparable tests, done by two observers, to indicate the reliability. It would be less easy to test for stability in terms of what happens at the hospital and then at home. We shall obviously have to look further at the linkages between the neonatal assessment and what we see at three months and at six months during the standard visits.

Bell: Kenneth Kaye (1978) has reported that it would take five repetitions of the best clusters from the Brazelton neonatal assessment to establish sufficient stability for cross-time comparisons.

Wilson: One reason why we are not using the Brazelton test and are using an extensive neonatal assessment is to try to assess what appears recurrently and stably in the infant's behaviour on that particular day. The observer does not simply sit and watch the infant, but does a whole series of adapted tests—some from the Einstein Neonatal Neurobehavioural scale, some from the Graham-Rosenblith scale, a few things modified from the Brazelton scale, and some from the observer's own design (Riese 1982).

Bell: When we used neonatal assessments other than the Brazelton, repeated after one day, only 11 out of 31 measures showed stability across the two days (Bell et al 1971).

Wilson: The acid test for the neonatal assessment is whether it tells you anything about later behaviour. We are concerned most with whether the one-day assessment has some bearing on the expression of temperament later, as seen in the laboratory and in the home. The initial assessment was related to the temperament observations at six months; the irritability and resistance to soothing in the hospital were related to the child's response to the physical measurements at the later age.

Berger: You said that the irritability index was a composite score. What went to make up the irritability index? Did you have separate components?

Wilson: Yes. Irritability was a composite of many of the test procedures, and we attempted to include the child's reactions not only to relatively innocuous visual and auditory stimuli, but also to a Moro reflex, a pinprick and a cold disc on the thigh, and so on.

REFERENCES

Bell RQ, Weller GM, Waldrop MF 1971 Newborn and preschooler: organization of behavior and relations between periods. Monogr Soc Res Child Dev 36(Nos 1–2):1-145

Kaye K 1978 V. Discriminating among normal infants by multivariate analysis of Brazelton scores: lumping and smoothing. In: Sameroff AJ (ed) Organization and stability of newborn behavior: a commentary on the Brazelton neonatal behavior assessment scale. Monogr Soc Res Child Dev 43(Nos 5–6): 60-80

Riese ML 1982 Procedures and norms for assessing behavioral patterns in full-term and pre-term neonates. J Suppl Abstr Serv Cat Sel Doc Psychol 12:10

Influence of genetic factors on temperament development in early childhood

ANNE MARI TORGERSEN

Department of Child Psychiatry, avd. 18, Ullevål Hospital, Oslo 1, Norway

Abstract The temperamental development of 53 same-sexed twin pairs was studied when the twins were aged two months, nine months and six years. The results showed that hereditary factors seem to influence the development of temperament at all three age-levels studied, but that they influenced different temperamental traits to a varying degree. This paper emphasizes that some of the temperamental traits of the 'difficult child' are mainly influenced by environmental factors. The clinical implications of this relationship are discussed.

There are two opposite attitudes to the relationship between genetic factors and temperament. One claims that temperament is by definition the stable, genetically determined core of personality. This view is in accordance with an old idea in psychiatry. Others prefer not to use the concept 'temperament' at all, simply because of the old constitutional associations with this label. The 'behavioural tendencies' that these people prefer to describe, however, are also concerned with the special part of the personality that can be observed from infancy onwards and they are thought to have a stable influence on personality development throughout life.

It seems attractive to be able to measure purely genetic temperamental variables, which may be the core of personality. Methodologically, however, even with the best factor-analysis programme, and with the largest sample, this is unrealistic. In reality, the emerging factors are highly dependent on the items used, and vary a lot from study to study as the items vary. Even if this approach were possible, such purely genetic variables would, at best, be of theoretical interest, since genetic and environmental factors interact.

1982 Temperamental differences in infants and young children. Pitman Books Ltd, London (Ciba Foundation symposium 89) p 141-154

I believe, however, from the results of my own research and those of others (Plomin & Rowe 1977, Cohen et al 1977, Wilson 1974, Matheny 1980) that genetic factors do influence personality development, and that some of the temperament variables that we are studying are closely related to these factors. However, there is a real danger in this 'genetic' view, which might explain why many research and clinical workers are reluctant to relate to it. The danger lies not in the belief in genetic factors themselves but in the conclusions one is apt to draw from them about the possibilities of predetermined personality, and the heritability of psychiatric illness and behavioural problems.

It is easy to misunderstand or to misuse the results from genetic studies. In modern genetic research it does not make much sense to ask a general question about how much temperament is due to genetic and how much to environmental influences. For any individual, one cannot answer such a question because genetic and environmental factors are inseparable. Among a population, however, it is possible to estimate the extent to which the observed variations of a trait rely on genetic and on environmental factors. One can determine the heritability of a trait—that is, the proportion of the variance of the trait that is due to the genetic variation among individuals.

The question in the study reported here was not to find genetically determined temperamental categories, but to investigate the degree to which the variation within the nine temperamental categories defined in the New York longitudinal study (NYLS) (Thomas et al 1963, Thomas & Chess 1977) depends on genetic factors.

To study the genetic influence on temperamental development the twin method was used. Twins provide an opportunity for estimating the relative contributions of innate and experiential factors, in that identical twins (monozygotic) share similar genes, while same-sexed fraternal twins (dizygotic) vary in their genetic similarity around an average of 50%. For the follow-up study that I have done on a group of twins in infancy and at six years, methodological details and results can be found in other publications (Torgersen & Kringlen 1978, Torgersen 1981). Here I shall briefly refer to some of these data.

Materials and methods

The group of twins consists of 53 same-sexed pairs. On the basis of questionnaires and blood and serum typing, 34 pairs were classified as monozygotic (MZ) and 16 as dizygotic (DZ) while three pairs had an uncertain zygosity diagnosis. In the follow-up study two of the MZ pairs were not included, giving 32 MZ and 16 DZ.

The group contained approximately equal numbers of pairs from lower and from higher social classes, and at six years the group included 22 pairs of boys and 26 pairs of girls.

The nine temperament categories from the NYLS were evaluated at three ages: two and nine months (in infancy) and again when the twins were $6\frac{1}{2}$ years of age. At all the three ages, on a home visit lasting 3–5 hours, I gave an open-ended semi-structured interview to the mothers. The questions were similar to those used in the NYLS. The mothers were always asked how the child behaved in different daily routine situations and the goal was to get as objective and as detailed a description as possible of the child's behaviour. The interviews were tape-recorded and all the information relating to temperament was scored.

In the infant study the clustering of items in the temperamental categories relied mainly, for conceptual coherency, on the traits proposed in the NYLS (Thomas et al 1963). I did all the scoring myself while at that time being blind to the twins' zygosity.

With the exception of 'persistence' at two months, it was possible to differentiate the children within all the NYLS temperamental categories at both ages.

In the study at six years of age, the same definitions of temperament were used in the item construction and scoring. The scoring was this time done by someone who was not familiar either with the twins or with their zygosity. I then re-scored the interview protocols of 20 children (10 pairs), and items with inter-scorer consensus lower than 80% within one scale-point were excluded, as well as items not scorable for more than 70% of all the children in the total sample.

In the study of six-year-olds, a principal-components factor analysis of all the items within each of the nine temperamental categories was done. Items with factorial loadings lower than 0.30 were excluded.

Distractibility was excluded after this procedure because of few reliable items and low inner consistency among the items. After the elimination of all items with low reliability, the number of items left in the other temperamental categories varied from 4 to 10. The inner consistency within the categories was satisfying, with the exception of the 'regularity' category. The four items in this category that were reliable also covered the same behavioural area as in the NYLS concept, but these items seemed not to constitute a unitary category because their inner consistency was low.

Results

At all three ages the MZ twins were more like each other, within the twin pair, than were the DZ twins in all the temperamental categories studied. To find out whether these differences were statistically significant, F-ratios were calculated to give the relationship between the intra-pair variances within the two zygosity groups. These results are presented graphically in Fig. 1. The calculation used for the F-ratios was as proposed by Vandenberg (1966), but some of the F-ratios needed to be recalculated according to critical comments on the statistical procedure given by Christian et al (1974). These F-values, shown by F' on Fig. 1, do not alter the tendency significantly.

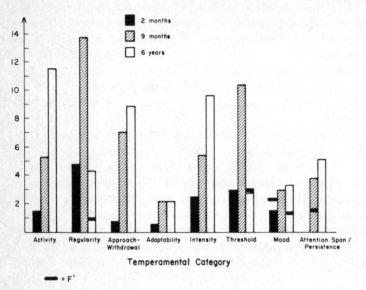

FIG. 1. F-values (ordinate) of the twin variances in temperamental dimensions at two months, nine months and six years.

The results showed that at two months the differences between the two MZ and DZ groups were statistically significant for regularity, threshold, intensity and mood. At nine months, distractibility and persistency were the only categories that were not statistically significant; and, at six years of age, mood and regularity were not statistically significant.

Fig. 1 also suggests environmental influences on some of the temperamental categories. *Regularity* can be seen to be highly genetically dominated at nine months, while at six years the differences between the two zygosity groups are no longer statistically significant. This result shows that stability must not be confused with heritability. Even if heritability is high at nine months, this trait can easily be modified by environmental factors.

Mood and *adaptability* each have low F-ratios at all ages, which may mean that they are heavily influenced by environmental factors. It is of interest to look closer at the differences within the twin pairs in these two temperamental categories. A low F-ratio is caused either by great dissimilarity within the MZ twin pairs, or by great similarity within the DZ pairs, or by both. The intra-class correlations within each temperamental category can tell us which of these explanations is most appropriate. The intra-class correlations (see Table 1) show how much alike are the twins within a pair. Table 1 shows that

TABLE 1 The intra-class correlations of the twin variances in temperament at six years

Temperamental category	Intra-class correlation Monozygotic	Dizygotic
Activity	0.93	0.14
Regularity	0.81	0.47
Approach/withdrawal	0.94	0.45
Adaptability	0.81	0.68
Intensity	0.95	0.54
Threshold	0.85	0.23
Mood	0.37	−0.06
Attention span/Persistence	0.73	−0.27

in the mood category the differences within the twin pair are high in both groups of twins. This could mean that mood is affected by environmental factors that influence differently the individuals within the same family. The opposite is true for adaptability; the twins in a pair are very alike, irrespective of whether they are DZ or MZ. This could mean that environmental factors within the family encourage the twins to develop the same adaptability trait.

Even if the sex differences in temperament are few, there are signs to suggest that the environment, rather than inherited sex differences, influences some of the temperamental categories. For example, there is no difference between the sexes in activity in infancy, but boys are more active than girls at six years of age, as shown in Table 2.

TABLE 2 Sex differences in activity at two months, nine months and six years

Age	Sex	Mean	Standard deviation	t value
Two months	girls	0.97	0.29	1.13
	boys	1.05	0.39	
Nine months	girls	1.03	0.42	0.14
	boys	1.02	0.48	
Six years	girls	3.45	1.07	2.81**
	boys	2.85	0.96	

** $P < 0.01$

Discussion

The results from this study strikingly support the view that genetic factors influence some aspects of the development of temperament, and it is difficult to reject this conclusion in spite of methodological uncertainty connected with the twin method. Cohen et al (1977) held the same view in their comparable twin study on some of these special methodological problems.

However, it is impossible from the results to draw the more general conclusion that 'temperament is inherited'. It is, for example, impossible to claim from the results that the observed temperamental behaviour in any individual is inherited. Even if activity is found to be highly dominated by genetic factors, the actual activity observed in one child can be entirely dominated by the situation that the child is experiencing at the time. The results also show that some of the temperament categories studied seem to be minimally or not at all influenced by genetic factors.

It is primarily in clinical work that general conclusions about genetic factors represent a threat. It is here that they can lead to attitudes that influence the treatment of the child. Because the temperamental categories referred to in this study have special clinical relevance, it is especially important to bear in mind the limitations of conclusions that may be drawn from the results about any genetic influences.

The main hypothesis from the New York longitudinal study (Thomas et al 1963, Thomas & Chess 1977) was that the child's emotional problems, as well as the child's observed temperamental behaviour, are the result of the child's basic temperamental style in interaction with environmental influences. Even if this view does not support a theory of a purely inherited constitution, the fact remains that a child with a 'difficult' temperament will be more likely to develop problems. This indicates that genetically determined temperamental structures in personality are of great importance in determining a child's chances of developing problems later.

This conclusion makes it important to look closer at the temperamental aspects that constitute the 'difficult child' syndrome. This cluster of traits has been found to be clinically relevant. A further question is whether the temperamental categories that form the cluster are heavily loaded with genetic factors or not.

The 'difficult child' is characterized in the NYLS (Thomas et al 1968) by irregularity, high intensity, negative mood, withdrawal and slow adaptation. Persson-Blennow & McNeil (1982) suggest that the 'difficult child' concept can be reduced to the three categories: mood, approach and adaptability. This is because these are the only three categories that have been found to be linked in several studies. A closer look at the Persson-Blennow & McNeil study shows that these three categories in particular are highly intercorrelated at all three ages (six months, one and two years), and that mood, which is highly correlated both to approach and to adaptability, might be the most relevant trait in the 'difficult child' concept.

From other research results it seems to be established that mood is a significant variable in the development of emotional problems in children (Thomas et al 1968, Graham et al 1973, Matheny 1980, Jullen 1981). It is therefore of special interest to note that mood was the temperament category that showed no statistically significant differences in similarity between the zygosity groups (low F-ratio) in my study at six years, and consequently that this category was dominated mainly by environmental and not genetic factors. This seems also to be confirmed by the results of Matheny (1981), who reported a low genetic influence on 'emotional tone', in contrast to other temperamental categories such as activity and attentiveness. Besides mood, adaptability was one of the other two temperamental categories in the 'difficult child' concept that have been found to constitute a factorial unit in several studies. This category is also related to the development of emotional problems in children (Thomas et al 1968, Graham et al 1973, Jullen 1981). In my study adaptability was dominated by environmental influences.

One may conclude that there is strong evidence that genetic factors influence the development of the temperamental aspects of personality. However, while this can be of theoretical interest, it is of only minor relevance in clinical settings. This is owing to at least two factors: (1) Because genetic and environmental factors interact, it is impossible to know which part of the observed temperamental behaviour of a single child is 'basic' to the child's character, and which part is developed mainly as defence against environmentally difficult situations; (2) For a difficult child having emotional problems it seems not to be primarily the basic temperamental variation, but other, non-genetic parts of the temperament, that are most relevant to the development of problems.

The main contribution of these results to clinical work is that they emphasize that not all variation in personality is environmentally determined. If one looks for genetic trends in temperamental development these can generally be found. On the other hand, if one looks for environmental factors that influence temperament these can also be found. The results depend on the particular methods used and on the hypotheses to be examined in any given study.

Acknowledgements

This study was supported by grants from the Norwegian Research Council for Science and the Humanities.

REFERENCES

Christian JC, Kang KW, Norton JA Jr 1974 Choice of an estimate of genetic variance from twin data. Am J Hum Genet 26:154-161

Cohen DJ, Dibble E, Grawe JM 1977 Parental style. Mother's and father's perceptions of their relations with twin children. Arch Gen Psychiatry 34:445-451

Graham P, Rutter M, George S 1973 Temperamental characteristics as predictors of behavior disorders in children. Am J Orthopsychiatry 43:328-339

Matheny AP 1981 Assessment of temperament in twin children: a reconciliation between structured and naturalistic observations. In: Gedda L et al (eds) Twin research 3, Part B: Intelligence, personality and development (III Int Congr Twin Studies, Jerusalem, June 1980) Alan R Liss, New York (Progr Clin Biol Res 96B), p 279-282

Persson-Blennow I, McNeil TF 1982 Factor analysis of temperament characteristics in children at six months, one year and two years of age. Br J Educ Psychol, in press

Plomin R, Rowe DC 1977 A twin study of temperament in young children. J Psychol 97:107-113

Thomas A, Chess S 1977 Temperament and development. Brunner/Mazel, New York

Thomas A, Chess S, Birch HG, Hertzig ME, Korn S 1963 Behavioral individuality in early childhood. New York University Press, New York

Thomas A, Chess S, Birch H 1968 Temperament and behavior disorders in children. New York University Press, New York

Torgersen AM 1981 Genetic factors in temperamental individuality: a longitudinal study of same-sexed twins from two months to six years of age. J Am Acad Child Psychiatry 20(4): in press

Torgersen AM, Kringlen E 1978 Genetic aspects of temperamental differences in infants: a study of same-sexed twins. J Am Acad Child Psychiatry 17:433-444

Vandenberg SG 1966 Contributions of twin research to psychology. In: Manosevitz M et al (eds) Behavioral genetics. Appleton-Century-Croft, New York, p 145-164

Wilson RS 1974 Twins. Mental development in the preschool years. Dev Psychol 10:580-588

DISCUSSION

Hsu: In your information gathered from home visits do you have data about which twin will be fed or bathed or soothed first, and does this reflect a better attachment to that baby by the parents?

Torgersen: I did not rate those observations in each case but I observed that for some twins the parents were in the habit of dealing with one twin first; that particular twin usually started to cry half an hour before the other one. However, such situational aspects, although interesting in themselves, had nothing to do with the genetic conclusions because the feature was similar for the monozygotic and the dizygotic twins.

Carey: Somehow we need to separate the environmental influences, and to distinguish those that are prenatal from those that are postnatal. Both types of influence can occur. Identical twins could be different at birth due to intrauterine factors. I am not sure how to investigate this, but one way might be to compare a group of monozygotic twins having widely different birthweights with a group of monozygotic twins having similar birthweights. This might tease out the possible intrauterine effect of less than optimal nutrition, and might indicate whether some of the environmental differences have their origin there. Clinically it is important to know to what extent neonatal behaviour is environmentally induced.

Torgersen: Seven of the monozygotic pairs in my study had a birthweight difference greater than 500 g. Typical for all these pairs was a higher intrapair difference in temperamental scores at two months; these enlarged differences were, however, significantly lower at nine months. This illustrates the problem that present methods of measuring temperamental differences are poor for the youngest age groups because the degree of general development, rather than the temperament, is sometimes what is measured.

When it comes to genetic questions, I should emphasize that the overall variability of birthweight *differences* between the pairs of monozygotic twins was even greater than the variability of birthweight differences for the group of dizygotic twins. So the differences in birthweight do not interfere with the genetic conclusions.

Wolkind: The concept of the prenatal environment and its influence is interesting. Several published reports associate emotional stress during pregnancy with a certain temperamental pattern in the baby (see Wolkind 1981). The evidence is largely anecdotal, but these reports from different parts of the world make quite a consistent story. One of the problems is that it is difficult to disentangle the social environment during a pregnancy with the same environment *afterwards*.

Huttunen: I am especially interested in your finding that mood and the other aspects of temperament related to the 'difficult child' seem to have a low heritability. I have been studying the effects of prenatal stress on the neuronal functions of rat offspring (Huttunen 1971). In general, the timing of the stress during pregnancy seems to be related to the subsequent behavioural changes in the animals (Joffe 1969). It is conceivable that the prenatal stress may produce in the young animals something similar to the difficult child syndrome of human children. In Finland, we have also conducted a retrospective epidemiological study of the children whose fathers had died *before* their births. We compared the incidence of any later psychiatric disorders of these children with the incidence in the group of children whose fathers had died during the first year of the child's life. We found that where the fathers had died before their children were born there was a statistically higher incidence of psychiatric disorders in the offspring (Huttunen & Niskanen 1978). There was also an indication that the timing of the fathers' death during the pregnancy was important. The results suggest that the third to the fifth months of pregnancy may be particularly important for the effects of prenatal stress. This time coincides with the appearance of the hypothalamic nuclei in the central nervous system of the fetus (Dörner & Staudt 1972). Thus, the behavioural styles that are involved in the difficult child syndrome may be produced by environmental stress at a specific time during the pregnancy. If this is true, it would certainly have implications for practical preventive measures.

Hinde: In some other animal studies, stress during pregnancy has affected mother–infant interaction after birth and the effects you mention could be mediated by that interaction.

Fulker: But the stresses used in animal studies are often quite severe and may not compare with the mild psychological stresses that the majority of human mothers experience.

Huttunen: In my opinion, it is probably the *timing* of any strong on–off stressful signal rather than the nature of the stress that is crucial for the effects of prenatal maternal stress on differentiation of the fetal brain.

Rutter: Did you look, Dr Torgersen, at the consistency over time of these temperament variables and, if you did, how does that relate to monozygotic and dizygotic differences?

Torgersen: I looked at the continuity, which was quite good between two and nine months of age for most of the categories, irrespective of the zygosity of the twins. From infancy to six years of age the correlations were very low, but one category—threshold—had a slightly significant statistical correlation ($P < 0.05$) both between two months and six years and between nine months and six years. In the New York longitudinal study, threshold was also the only category that showed a statistically significant correlation between the longest age-span measured: one to five years. The correlation was on the same low level (Thomas & Chess 1977).

Rutter: It would be interesting to look at the concordance within pairs for changes over time. Some data (Wilson 1977) suggest that the changes in developmental course may themselves be genetically determined. Did you analyse monozygotic and dizygotic differences in relation to the difficult child pattern?

Torgersen: No.

Rutter: It would be interesting to do so because it doesn't necessarily follow that the heritability for the *pattern* will be the same as the heritability of the elements that make up the pattern. Margaret Hertzig (1982), for example, found no relationship between neurological findings and any of the separate temperamental dimensions in her study of premature babies. Nevertheless, there was a significant association between neurological abnormality and the difficult child pattern.

Torgersen: One reason I didn't do this is that to combine the study of the difficult child concept with a genetic study can be a sensitive issue. The difficult child concept can give rise to a child being labelled as such in a clinical setting. The concept can be exploited and misinterpreted in potentially damaging ways if one links it to heritability. The hyperactive concept also falls into this problem area.

Carey: I agree that labelling children difficult is to be avoided, but the possible dangers of acknowledging the phenomenon clinically can be offset by letting parents know that most difficult infants get easier as the next few years go by (Carey & McDevitt 1978).

Stevenson: If one is trying to use the twin method to talk about the difficult child syndrome, with a prevalence rate running at about 10%, and with only 32 dizygotic individuals, one will not get a very good estimate of the concordance rate within the dizygotic pairs.

Rutter: There are two separate issues here—the question of looking at extremes and that of looking at patterns. The difficult child concept was translated into a score, rather than into categorical terms, by Margaret Hertzig (1982). Although I entirely accept that negative labels such as the difficult child may be misused, I am struck by the fact that Dr Torgersen found least heritability with the variables that predict best. Thus, on its own or as part of some composite, mood has appeared a good predictor in Judy Dunn's material (p 87), in the New York study (Thomas et al 1968) and in the study that Philip Graham and I did (Graham et al 1973).

Kolvin: Aren't you producing a composite by adding together variables to produce a dimension?

Rutter: Yes. Several genetic studies suggest that when one produces composites, one obtains a higher genetic component. It is a separate issue whether that genetic component is related to what predicts best for stress situations or for development of deviance.

Fulker: Could I make a general remark about the usefulness of twin studies in studying the causes of individual differences? Most investigators regard twin studies primarily as a means of detecting the presence of genetic effects. However, another way of looking at twin studies is to view them as a research design that can control for genetic effects, should they be important, and enable us to better assess the effects of the environment. This approach is increasingly used in behavioural genetics. For example, in the models that I and others build, there are often many more environmental parameters than genetic ones. These provide estimates of environmental effects unbiased by genetic influences.

Torgersen: Thinking back on my data, that is what I have also found to be most interesting. For example, when one dizygotic pair of girls was two months old their mother claimed that one of them was more like a boy—she was the bigger one. When I saw these twins again at six years, this girl was very attached to her paternal grandfather and was playing like a boy, whereas the other one was engaged in more traditionally female activities—she was sitting in the house and sewing. The differences were striking.

Thomas: You mentioned that Inger Persson-Blennow's factor analysis suggests that for the difficult child the emphasis should be mood, adaptability and approach. But from the clinical, qualitative point of view, intensity is also of great importance, and rhythmicity may be, too, depending on the age. A tendency towards negative mood, slow adaptability and withdrawal, combined with low intensity, gives the characteristics of what we have described as the 'slow-to-warm-up' child, and not the difficult child (Thomas et al 1968). That distinction is important in terms of the reactions of the parents to the child or what constitutes stress situations for these two temperamentally different patterns.

McNeil: This relates to what we were discussing earlier about how to make up composites of temperamental characteristics. Thomas & Chess's approach is clinical and Professor Carey's is a more empirical approach. In the long run we are going to create a totally confusing picture: there are already at least six different constellations of characteristics that have been suggested to constitute the difficult child concept (Thomas et al 1968, Carey 1970, Wolkind & De Salis, this volume, p 221-239, Cameron 1978, Campbell 1979). When shall we be able to achieve convergence across different studies if everyone has different versions?

Thomas: The ultimate decisive criterion, as I mentioned earlier, is whether a particular formulation has functional significance.

Bell: Progress in the field results not only from work at the cutting edge but also from the degree to which results from different studies can be combined, to reveal patterns that indicate the direction of results. If everyone uses a separate system, even though it seems to them to have functional significance, there will be nothing to combine. Hertz & I (Bell & Hertz 1976) summarized results from reviews of socialization research covering a period of 40 years. These reviewers could cite very few commonly agreed conclusions. Yet it would have been fairly simple, in retrospect, for most investigators to have included a marker variable that would have helped in comparisons between studies. In our paper we report how such marker variables have been recommended by various conferences. We also mention that the United States government financed many 'Head-Start' projects, but that results from only a few could be used to evaluate the effectiveness of the programme, because of the lack of consistency of measurement between the various projects.

McNeil: Different factor analysis procedures can obviously influence the way in which the variables are loaded on factors. Factor analysis may be a good way to decide which variables should be grouped together but, here again, personal preferences for different methods can confuse the picture. Numerous variables can operate: the different constellations of temperamental variables; the different samples; the different countries; the different times; the different ages. Some constancy is necessary.

Rutter: The immediate solution, presumably, is not to come to some decision about which is the best method—the evidence to allow that is not available—but, rather, to test which approach works. This would involve comparisons between several of the available models. One of the models or composites may turn out to be generally much more useful than all the others. Alternatively, different models may be useful for different purposes.

Bates: What we are discussing could be subsumed under the heading construct validation; we need anchoring points for forming a net of relationships between variables. Unlike Dr McNeil, I see quite a bit of similarity and convergence in the various factor analysis results. For example, the cluster of the characteristics of mood, adaptability and approach seems to be replicated over and over again, with intensity and rhythmicity generally being left out.

Thomas: I agree, but in certain clinical situations even though the factor analysis does not produce certain clusters, the inclusion of intensity may be useful for other reasons.

Bates: Yes. I think that's an independent point.

REFERENCES

Bell RQ, Hertz TW 1976 Toward more comparability and generalizability of developmental research. Child Dev 47:6-13

Cameron JR 1978 Parental treatment, children's temperament, and the risk of childhood behavioral problems. 2: Initial temperament, parental attitudes, and the incidence and form of behavioral problems. Am J Orthopsychiatry 48:140-147

Campbell SB 1979 Mother–infant interaction as a function of maternal ratings of temperament. Child Psychiatry Hum Dev 10:67-76

Carey WB 1970 A simplified method for measuring infant temperament. J Pediatr 77:188-194

Carey WB, McDevitt SC 1978 Stability and change in individual temperament diagnoses from infancy to early childhood. J Am Acad Child Psychiatry 17:331-337

Dörner G, Staudt J 1972 Vergleichende morphologische Untersuchungen der Hypothalamus—differenzierung bei Ratte und Mensch. Endokrinologie 59:152-155

Graham P, Rutter M, George S 1973 Temperamental characteristics as predictors of behavior disorders in children. Am J Orthopsychiatry 43:328-339

Hertzig ME 1982 Temperament and neurological status. In: Rutter M (ed) Behavioral syndromes of brain dysfunction in childhood. Guilford Press, New York, in press

Huttunen MO 1971 Persistent alteration of turnover of brain noradrenaline in the offspring of rats subjected to stress during pregnancy. Nature (Lond) 230:53-55

Huttunen MO, Niskanen P 1978 Prenatal loss of father and psychiatric disorders. Arch Gen
    Psychiatry 35:429-431
Joffe JM 1969 Prenatal determinant of behaviour. Pergamon Press Ltd, London
Thomas A, Chess C 1977 Temperament and development. Brunner/Mazel, New York
Thomas A, Chess S, Birch HG 1968 Temperament and behavior disorders in children. New York
    University Press, New York
Wilson RS 1977 Mental development in twins. In: Oliverio A (ed) Genetics, environment and
    intelligence. North-Holland, Amsterdam
Wolkind SN 1981 Prenatal emotional stress—effects on the foetus. In: Wolkind SN, Zajicek E
    (eds) Pregnancy: a psychological and social study. Academic Press, London

Behavioural genetics and temperament

ROBERT PLOMIN

Institute for Behavioral Genetics, University of Colorado, Campus Box 447, Boulder, Colorado 80309, USA

Abstract Three recent developments in behavioural genetics are relevant to temperament research. First, the search for genetic influences on temperament has been frustrated by the finding that twin studies using self-report and parental rating instruments detect a genetic influence for all personality traits whereas twin studies using objective assessments rarely find a genetic influence. Secondly, environmental influences salient to temperament appear to operate in such a way as to make members of a family (siblings, for example) as different from one another as are individuals in different families. The importance of such 'E$_1$', or non-shared, environmental influences suggests the need for studies of more than one child per family. Thirdly, adoption studies are needed to complement the extensive research on temperament in twins. In addition to its usefulness in isolating genetic influences, the adoption design can study environmental influences devoid of the confounding effects of hereditary influences; it can also isolate interactions between genotypes and environments. Preliminary results from the Colorado Adoption Project show little relationship between the temperaments of adopted and non-adopted one-year-olds and the personality characteristics of their parents. Measures of the home and family environment did not relate to infant temperament, and no genotype–environment interaction was detected.

Behavioural genetics is relevant to the study of temperament regardless of the importance that one attaches to genetic influences on temperamental characteristics. Three examples of the relevance of behavioural genetics are described in this paper. The first issue is most closely tied to the definition and identification of temperament: it concerns the use of behavioural genetic methods to select a few highly heritable dimensions of behavioural style from the myriad of personality dimensions. Research has not yet settled this issue but has led to an interesting result of major importance to the study of temperament: although the environment is critically important in the aetiology of behavioural style, behavioural genetic data suggest that the way in which the environment influences behavioural style is radically different from its widely assumed mode of action. The second section of the paper discusses

1982 Temperamental differences in infants and young children. Pitman Books Ltd, London (Ciba Foundation symposium 89) p 155-167

E_1, or non-shared, environmental influence and its relevance to temperament research. Finally, the usefulness of adoption studies to complement twin studies in the search for genetic influence, and to augment twin studies by isolating environmental influences and genotype–environment interaction, is the topic of the third section. Preliminary results on temperament are briefly mentioned for a large sample of adopted and non-adopted one-year-old infants in the Colorado Adoption Project.

Selecting highly heritable components of behavioural style

As a behavioural geneticist, I became interested in temperament because I wanted to use behavioural genetic methods as a sieve to winnow the diverse aspects of personality down to a few traits that displayed substantial genetic influence. A genetic or constitutional foundation used to be the hallmark of temperament, as distinguished from the rest of personality, although in recent years there has been a tendency among temperament theorists to play down this criterion. One popular recourse is to state that behaviour is influenced by the interaction between genes and environment and that their separate effects cannot be disentangled. I have called this mistaken view *interactionism* (Plomin et al 1977). If interactionism were taken seriously, it would mean that we cannot study the influence of the environment because environmental effects are irretrievably lost in the web of gene–environment interaction. However, we can study the relationship between experiential differences and behavioural variability; in the same way, we can study the relationship between the genetic differences and the behavioural differences between individuals (Plomin et al 1980).

Thus, the goal of selecting highly heritable components of behavioural style is reasonable. However, research along these lines has met with surprising roadblocks that may have implications for all temperament research. When Arnold Buss and I proposed the EASI temperament theory of personality in 1973, we suggested that Emotionality, Activity, Sociability and Impulsivity be considered as candidates for further temperament research because of the evidence for their heritability (Buss et al 1973). However, it turns out that we could have picked any personality dimensions and found evidence for heritability. In 1976, Loehlin & Nichols reported that twin studies using self-report personality questionnaires invariably find moderate heritability, with identical-twin correlation coefficients of about 0.50 and fraternal-twin correlation coefficients of about 0.30, although Fulker (1981) recently reported that extraversion is a possible exception. The lack of differential heritability has mischievous implications for studies that purport to show significant heritability for yet another set of personality dimensions and for small twin studies that are interpreted as showing that some traits are significantly heritable and others are not (Plomin 1981).

It is interesting in itself that any personality questions asked of twins will yield correlations for identical twins that are greater than correlations for fraternal twins. However, it is difficult to believe that all personality traits are subject to the same moderate genetic influence. I had hoped that parental ratings of young twins might side-step this problem. Several twin studies later (e.g. Plomin & Rowe 1977), the data began to suggest that parental ratings yielded the same lack of differential heritability. Identical twin correlations were generally about 0.50 and fraternal twin correlations were near zero or even negative, thus yielding heritability estimates greater than 1.0. These data violate the twin model because fraternal twins share half of their segregating genes and thus should be about half as similar to each other as identical twins. The disappointing lack of evidence for differential heritability also appears in twin studies in which global ratings are made by observers, and for specific 'molecular' rating items as well as for global 'molar' items used in most personality questionnaires (Plomin 1981). It is too soon to tell whether twin studies using interview data will conform to the general pattern. Although one might blame the twin method for the lack of differential heritability, results of two recent adoption studies also failed to show differential heritability for self-report measures of personality (Loehlin et al 1981, Scarr et al 1981). It should be noted that these problems have implications beyond behavioural genetics: they may signal a general problem with the use of self-report and parental rating instruments in the study of temperament. Rather than accepting the conclusion that heredity affects all personality traits to the same moderate extent, I realized that the peculiar results might be caused by the use of rating instruments, either self-report or parental report. I decided to try objective observations in semi-standardized situations and conducted a study of one- and two-year-old children in their homes using 24 observational measures of social responsiveness. Unknown to me, Lytton (Lytton et al 1977) was working on a study similar to mine (Plomin & Rowe 1979). The studies yielded similar results which were strikingly different from those of studies using ratings: although a few traits showed significant heritability, most measures were uninfluenced by heredity. I have also conducted a study of objectively assessed activity, impulsivity and aggressiveness in five- to 10-year-old twins which yielded similar results when test–retest reliability was taken into account (Plomin & Foch 1980, Plomin et al 1981). Similar results are also emerging from a study of emotional development in infancy (H. H. Goldsmith et al, unpublished paper, 1981 Bienn Meet Soc Res Child Dev, Boston, Mass.).

Thus, although relevant data on objective assessments of behavioural style are limited, we can tentatively conclude that objective assessments, unlike self-reports or parental ratings, do not show ubiquitous heritability. On the contrary, twin studies using objective assessments yield the opposite problem, which is nearly as severe when one is seeking evidence for differential heritability of components of behavioural style: nothing much seems to be heritable.

The temperament research of the Louisville twin study discussed by Ronald Wilson in this volume (Wilson 1982) will make an important contribution to this area. However, the problem is not likely to be resolved quickly because quantitative genetic designs require large samples, which are difficult enough to obtain when one uses paper-and-pencil measures sent through the post but which become nearly overwhelming in their demand on time and energy when objective assessments are used. Another strategy to aid understanding of the lack of differential heritability is to use quantitative genetic designs other than the twin method. The last section of this paper presents preliminary temperament results from the first adoption study of temperament in infancy.

In summary, what appeared to be a simple and straightforward question nearly a decade ago—which aspects of personality are most heritable?—has turned out to be neither simple nor straightforward. Nonetheless, we have learned some interesting things along the way, one of which is the topic of the next section.

Importance of non-shared (E_1) environmental influences

Behavioural genetic research may be as important in elucidating environmental influences as genetic ones. A critical example for temperament research is that while environmental variance accounts for most of the observed variation in behavioural style, the salient environmental influences have a most peculiar feature: whatever they are, they are not shared by members of the same family. The most striking example of this comes from adoption studies of psychopathology (DeFries & Plomin 1978). The incidence of schizophrenia or alcoholism is just as great for individuals adopted away from their affected biological relative as it is for individuals reared with their affected relative. Sharing the family environment makes little difference.

Another major conclusion of the important work by Loehlin & Nichols (1976) is that shared family environment makes little difference to personality. Their conclusion is supported by more recent work (Fulker 1981). The distinction is between environmental variance shared by members of a family and environmental variance that is not shared by members of a family. This decomposition of environmental variance into two parts was first called E_2 and E_1 respectively by Jinks & Fulker in 1970. The E_1, or non-shared, environmental influences which make family members different from one another appear to account for the bulk of environmental variance salient to behavioural style (Fulker 1981).

This conclusion has far-reaching implications for the study of temperament. Research has nearly always operated on the assumption that a child in one family is different from a child in another family because the family environments differ. However, we now know that the environmental factors that have an important influence on behavioural style are just as likely to make two children in the same family different from one another. This should be a key to unlock the secret of environmental influences salient to the development of personality. David Rowe and I (1981) recently reviewed the relevant published work and attempted to provide a conceptual framework for thinking about non-shared environmental influences. I have come to realize that any E_2, or shared, environmental factor can be reconsidered as an E_1 factor. For example, the well-known child-rearing dimensions of love and control are nearly always thought of as E_2 influences but they can be considered as E_1 influences to the extent that parents love and control one child more than another. We have also suggested some methods to help identify E_1 influences. Identical twins may be particularly useful because their genetic identicalness ensures that differences between members of a pair are due solely to environmental influences of the E_1 variety.

Although we are shooting in the dark in suggesting approaches to studying non-shared environmental influences, one thing is clear: we shall not begin to understand this important class of environmental influences until we study more than one child per family and seek the causes and correlates of differences between children in the same family. Work by Judy Dunn reported in this volume (Dunn & Kendrick 1982) represents a valuable first step in this direction.

An adoption study of temperament

Adoption studies are needed to complement the extensive research on temperament in twins, and to augment this research by study of genetic influences independently of family environment, E_2 familial environmental influences independently of heredity, and genotype–environment interaction. In non-adoptive families, parents share both heredity and environment with their children, and in these circumstances any relationship between parental behaviour and children's temperament could be explained genetically as well as environmentally. The adoption design separates these influences. For example, biological parents share heredity but not family environment with their children, and adoptive parents share family environment but not heredity with their adopted children (Plomin et al 1980).

One of the considerable benefits of the adoption design is therefore that it permits an examination of environmental relationships devoid of the possibly confounding effect of heredity. When an environmental measure relates to children's temperament in adoptive homes, we can be sure that the relationship is not mediated genetically. Another advantage of the adoption design is that it permits tests of genotype–environment interaction—that is, the possibility that individuals of different genotypes may respond differently to environmental treatments (Plomin et al 1977). Even in the absence of 'main effects' for genotype or for environment, genotype–environment interaction may prove to be important.

In 1975, John DeFries, Steven Vandenberg and I began a longitudinal, prospective adoption study called the Colorado Adoption Project. Our goal is to collect extensive behavioural and environmental data for 300 adopted and 300 matched non-adopted children yearly from their first birthday. The oldest children are now five years of age, and we have tested over 200 adopted and 150 non-adopted one-year-olds. The biological and adoptive parents of the adopted children and the parents of the non-adopted children have been tested on a three-hour battery of behavioural measures which includes the EASI Temperament Inventory (self-report as well as mate rating) of Buss & Plomin (1975) and Cattell's 16 PF personality questionnaire (Cattell et al 1970). Our yearly visit to the adoptive and non-adoptive homes includes diverse behavioural and environmental measures. Both parents complete the Colorado Childhood Temperament Inventory (CCTI, Rowe & Plomin 1977), which is an amalgamation of items from the New York longitudinal study (Thomas & Chess 1977) and from the EASI Temperament Inventory. Bayley's Infant Behaviour Record (IBR) is completed by the test examiner after the administration of the Bayley Scales of Infant Development (Bayley, 1969). Time-sampled videotaped observations are also collected, although we are not far enough advanced in the time-consuming business of rating videotapes to present these data at present. Environmental measures collected during the home visit include Caldwell's HOME Inventory (Caldwell & Bradley 1978) and the Family Environment Scale of Moos (1974).

So far we have found no differences between adopted and non-adopted children's temperaments, between adoptive and non-adoptive parents' personalities, or between the adoptive and non-adoptive home environments. However, the basic results are somewhat disappointing and can be described simply: individual differences in temperament at one year of age appear to be unpredictable in terms of parental temperament and home environment. Neither the test examiners' IBR ratings of the infants nor the parents' CCTI ratings relate to parental personality (as measured by the EASI self-report or mate rating, or by Cattell's 16 PF) or to the home environment (as indexed by the HOME Inventory or Family Environment Scale).

Although some significant parent–offspring relationships emerged, none was consistent across the three types of parent–offspring relationship or across sex. For example, if adoptive parents are similar to their adopted children for a particular character, then non-adoptive parents should also be similar to their children because both types of parent–offspring relationship share family environment. One fairly consistent pattern of results was observed for boys alone. Parent–offspring correlations between EASI emotionality of the parents and CCTI emotionality of the boys are generally significant for biological, adoptive, and non-adoptive parent–offspring relationships, which suggests that both genetic and family environmental influences are operating. However, because the pattern was not seen for girls, and because many correlations have been examined with a consequent danger of accepting chance patterns, it is best to treat these results as suggestive only.

When we assessed genotype–environment interaction by using the method described by Plomin et al (1977), no evidence for such interaction emerged from analyses of personality variables for the adopted children and their adoptive and biological mothers. More detailed analyses including other environmental measures are in progress.

In summary, the parent–offspring design of the Colorado Adoption Project has yielded no evidence for genetic influence or for E_2 influences shared by parents and their one-year-old children. Family and home environment measures showed no relationship to one-year-old temperament, and no evidence was found for genotype–environment interaction. These results may be viewed as congruent with poor stability of temperament measures in infancy.

Conclusion

Behavioural genetics has much to offer the study of temperament. Even if the criterion of heritability is to be excluded from one's definition of temperament, it is nonetheless a reasonable first step in understanding behavioural individuality to ask about the extent to which genetic variability among children can account for observed variability in temperament. However, the most important and immediate application of behavioural genetics may be in elucidating the role of the environment as seen in these examples of the importance of E_1 influences, in studying environmental relationships in adoptive families (in which family members share family environment but not heredity), and in analysing genotype–environment interaction.

Acknowledgements

This work was supported in part by grants from the National Institute of Child Health and Human Development (HD-10333) and the National Science Foundation (BNS-7826204). This paper was written while the author was supported by a Research Scientist Development Award (AA-00041).

REFERENCES

Bayley N 1969 Manual for the Bayley Scales of Infant Development. Psychological Corporation, New York

Buss AH, Plomin R 1975 A temperament theory of personality development. Wiley Interscience, New York

Buss AH, Plomin R, Willerman L 1973 The inheritance of temperaments. J Pers 41:513-524

Caldwell BM, Bradley RH 1978 Home observation for the measurement of the environment. University of Arkansas, Little Rock

Cattell RB, Eber HW, Tatsuoka MM 1970 Handbook for the sixteen Personality Factor questionnaire (16 PF). Institute for Personality and Ability Testing, Champaign, Illinois

DeFries JC, Plomin R 1978 Behavioral genetics. Annu Rev Psychol 29:473-515

Dunn J, Kendrick C 1982 Temperamental differences, family relationships, and young children's response to change within the family. In: Temperamental differences in infants and young children. Pitman, London (Ciba Found Symp 89) p 87-105

Fulker DW 1981 Biometrical genetics and individual differences. Br Med Bull 37:115-120

Jinks JJ, Fulker DW 1970 Comparison of the biometrical genetical, MAVA, and classical approaches to the analysis of human behavior. Psychol Bull 73:311-349

Loehlin JC, Nichols RC 1976 Heredity, environment and personality: a study of 850 twins. University of Texas Press, Austin

Loehlin JC, Horn JM, Willerman L 1981 Personality resemblance in adoptive families. Behav Genet 11:309-330

Lytton H, Martin NG, Eaves L 1977 Environmental and genetical causes of variation in ethological aspects of behavior in two-year-old boys. Soc Biol 24: 200-211

Moos RH 1974 Preliminary manual for family environment scale, work environment scale, and group environment scale. Consulting Psychologists Press, Palo Alto, California

Plomin R 1981 Heredity and temperament: a comparison of twin data for self-report questionnaires, parental ratings, and objectively assessed behavior. In: Gedda L et al (eds) Twin research 3, part B: Intelligence, personality, and development (Proc III Int Congr Twin Studies, Jerusalem, June 1980) AR Liss, New York (Prog Clin Biol Res 69B), p 269-278

Plomin R, Foch TT 1980 A twin study of objectively assessed personality in childhood. J Pers Soc Psychol 39:680-688

Plomin R, Rowe DC 1977 A twin study of temperament in young children. J Psychol 97:107-113

Plomin R, Rowe DC 1979 Genetic and environmental etiology of social behavior in infancy. Dev Psychol 15:62-72

Plomin R, DeFries JC, Loehlin JC 1977 Genotype-environment interaction and correlation in the analysis of human behavior. Psychol Bull 84:309-322

Plomin R, DeFries JC, McClearn GE 1980 Behavioral genetics: a primer. WH Freeman, San Francisco

Plomin R, Foch TT, Rowe DC 1981 Bobo clown aggression in childhood: environment, not genes. J Res Pers 15:331-342

Rowe DC, Plomin R 1977 Temperament in early childhood. J Pers Assess 41:150-156
Rowe DC, Plomin R 1981 The importance of nonshared (E_1) environmental influences in
  behavioral development. Dev Psychol 17:517-531
Scarr S, Webber PL, Weinberg RA, Wittig MA 1981 Personality resemblance among adolescents
  and their parents in biologically related and adoptive families. In: Gedda L et al (eds) Twin
  research 3, part B: Intelligence, personality, and development (Proc III Int Congr Twin
  Studies, Jerusalem, June 1980) AR Liss, New York (Prog Clin Biol Res 69B), p 99-120
Thomas A, Chess S 1977 Temperament and development. Brunner/Mazel, New York
Wilson RS 1982 Intrinsic determinants of temperament. In: Temperamental differences in infants
  and young children. Pitman, London (Ciba Found Symp 89) p 121-140

DISCUSSION

Bell: To what extent is the unshared environmental variance within one family (E_1) attributable to the differential conditioning of parents *by children* or to differences in socialization due to the presence of siblings? For instance, sexual development is certainly influenced by sibling and peers. The children themselves could be responsible for differential reinforcement of different parental techniques, assuming that the parents have a diversified repertoire of behaviours that they can use with children. Each child in the family could thus select out different environmental effects.

Plomin: Adoption designs are indeed useful for studying genotype–environment *correlation* rather than *interaction* (Plomin et al 1977). The parents can react differentially to their children as a function of the children's genotypes. We have done some analysis along those lines and found some evidence that supports your suggestion: parental techniques seem to differ as a function of the genotype of these adopted children, as estimated by the phenotypes (personalities) of the child's biological parents. It is difficult, of course, to untangle these directional influences, and our analysis is only in the preliminary stage.

Hinde: Another issue could be operating here. If one child selects certain responses from the parent, another child could select different responses not only because its nature is different but also because the first child has already pre-empted one set of behaviours from the parent. One can observe, in a purely qualitative way, that the parents of monkey twins treat the twins more and more differently as they grow up, as a consequence of their initial divergence (Spencer-Booth 1968). It is almost a positive feedback.

Fulker: Some behavioural genetic evidence, from studies of extraversion (Fulker 1981) and sexual attitudes (Martin 1978) in twins, supports that idea. The results suggest that the siblings, especially monozygotic twins, react negatively against each other. If a child has a sibling who is highly extravert, the effect is to make the child less extravert than he or she would otherwise have been. Sexual attitudes also seem subject to this kind of influence. Dick Rose and I have evidence from studies of fears and phobias (see Fulker 1982) suggesting that fearful parents attempt to minimize the same fears in their children. The Texas Adoption Study (Horn et al 1982) produced some interesting similar results concerning parent–child interactions in families where two children were adopted into the same home. The children were rated according to their biological mothers' mental stability, using the Minnesota Multiphasic Personality Inventory, and then rated according to their own emotional stability and similar measures. It was found that the child with the less stable biological mother was more stable than the child with the more stable biological mother, suggesting that the adoptive parents are sensitive to the child's needs, and react appropriately to provide a supportive environment. Studies in this area are therefore suggesting that the specific environment (E_1) effect involves peer and inter-personal relationships.

Wilson: In your data at one year of age, Professor Plomin, there was an apparent absence of relationships with the parents—biological or adoptive. I am not too surprised by this; by the time the children reach two or three years these relationships between parent and offspring usually begin to consolidate, in terms of the appearance of significant correlations between them. This raises the interesting question of what is *really* doing the consolidating—is it a genetic effect or a cumulative environmental effect? In our data, mental test scores at one year of age were unrelated to socioeconomic status, parental education etc., but were strongly related at two years of age. You described the within-family dispersion between siblings or twins (E_1), but there is obviously a dispersion in the genetic sense within the family as well. How, in your design, would one separate the expected genetic variation within the family members from the environmental influences?

Plomin: We are hoping to study adolescent pairs of unrelated adoptees and biological siblings. Adoptees magnify E_1 effects, as compared to non-adopted siblings such as twins, because adoptees are unrelated genetically. However, as you point out, differential treatment of members of adopted or non-adopted pairs might reflect genetic differences between them rather than causing a behavioural difference between them. My test of this possibility is as follows. If genetic factors underlie an E_1 effect, then the association between the E_1 factor and behavioural differences within pairs will be greater for adoptee pairs (who are not correlated genetically) than for biological sibling pairs (who are correlated at 0.50 genetically). Hypotheses gained from this study of adolescent sibling pairs will be tested prospectively for the sibling pairs in the Colorado Adoption Project.

Wilson: How many adoptive families have had a baby subsequently?

Plomin: There are many myths about adoption, including those describing the 'typical' social class of both the natural and the adoptive parents, but these myths are not supported by the wide cross-section of people in our study. The national figure for the number of adoptive families who subsequently have a baby of their own has been estimated at 10% (Mech 1973), but this is likely to fall to 0% because the regulations governing adoption in the United States now require medical evidence for infertility.

Dunn: I was delighted to hear your discussion of the E_1 variance, which emphasized the point that I made earlier (p 64) about not treating the mother's mood as a constant factor for each child during the development of firstborn and secondborn children. Little systematic work has been done on the mother's behaviour with two children within a family. We have studied this and found relatively little consistency, although some aspects do show some stability. To specify the sources of E_1 variation will be a very complicated job, but it is clear that the lack of mutuality in the sibling relationship is potentially important. The sibling relationship can be very uneven; one child may be extremely warm and friendly to its sibling, while the sibling remains hostile and negative in that relationship. The experience of each child within the family is therefore very different. Further complexity is introduced because of the mutual influences over time.

Bell: The Genain quadruplets (Schaefer 1963) provide a good example of the range possible within identical schizophrenic quadruplets. The mother was uniformly extreme in restrictiveness with her daughters, but not uniform in affection.

Stevenson: We have already discussed the potential for sibling competitiveness in terms of mother–child interaction and Sandra Scarr's work on gene–environment correlation (p 49). The Birmingham group (Eaves 1976) have created models of sibling competitiveness and cooperation. What are the design implications of these particular models? What sorts of genetic and kinship correlations are necessary to help identify some of these cooperative and competitive effects using those models?

Fulker: To detect sibling effects in many cases one simply needs monozygotic and dizygotic twins and, optionally, some additional siblings (Fulker 1981). In order to detect gene–environment covariance (GE_{cov}) emanating from parental pressures one needs, as a minimum, one set of twins and their parents (Fulker 1982). Because these designs are 'minimal' they cannot be properly tested, and one would want to seek additional information, either from more complex family studies or from independent observational studies. Some leverage on the problem can nevertheless be obtained by using relatively simple designs.

Huttunen: Professor Plomin, isn't it inaccurate to say that the unrelated adopted siblings do not share the same genes? Most of the genes regulating our behaviour are common to all people and this is certainly important when we consider the probable multigenic aetiology of temperament.

Plomin: Yes. It is important to emphasize that we are talking about genetic *differences* that may affect temperament. Within all species—humans, mice and fruit flies—at least half of all loci are polymorphic, as shown by population genetic studies, electrophoretic techniques and amino acid sequencing studies (Plomin et al 1980). Thus, although we may share exactly similar sequences of DNA at many non-segregating loci, we are talking here about genetic differences as they relate to observed differences in temperament. Similarly, we all share substantial elements of our environment and, again, it is the differences that count.

Carey: As an adoptive parent myself, I think your design is excellent for untangling some of these variables. Yet, one factor that doesn't appear in your model is: what do the adoptive parents *know* about the biological parents? From my own experience, and that of others, I believe that what one knows about the biological family does affect, to some degree, how one reacts to the child. One should surely consider that as part of the interaction.

Plomin: The large-scale Texas Adoption Study that Dr Fulker mentioned has recently reported data directly relevant to this issue (Horn et al 1982). There were over 300 cases in which the adoptive parents claimed some knowledge of the mother's intelligence or education. The correlation for IQ between the adopted children of these parents and the children's own biological mothers was 0.30. For about 50 cases where adoptive parents were given no information about the biological mother's intelligence or education, the correlation was 0.34. Thus, the authors concluded that knowledge of the biological parents' intellectual abilities is not an important source of the IQ correlation between adoptees and their biological parents. Although the results for temperament might differ from the results for IQ, they are unlikely to do so because adoptive parents are given even less information—both in terms of quantity and quality—concerning the biological parents' personality.

Fulker: The finding that I mentioned from the work of Horn et al (1982) suggests that the parents may react either to what they *know* or to what they *suspect*; the children who were biologically disadvantaged, on a series of counts, seemed to have been provided with a compensatory environment in the adoptive home; they exceeded the low-risk child on several emotional-stability ratings. I don't know if this effect was due to information that the parents had about the background of these children, or whether it was simply that they inferred from the child's behaviour that he or she needed special help.

Graham: Most current clinical therapy for children and families is based on the notion that non-shared environmental variance (E_1) is of paramount importance. The assumption behind such concepts as enmeshment and alliances, and so on, is that there are important differences in the ways that parents treat their children and children treat their parents within families. It is not easy to investigate this aspect of families for all sorts of reasons. Those global concepts have been so far very poorly investigated from a scientific point of view. Adequate methods to investigate the problem at that level do not exist, although Rutter & Brown (1966), in their family illness study, have demonstrated that it is possible to measure differential criticism, hostility, warmth and other such factors. However, the degree to which those factors have been elicited by the children's behavioural problems remains uncertain.

REFERENCES

Eaves LJ 1976 A model for sibling effects in man. Heredity 36:205-215

Fulker DW 1981 Biometrical genetics and individual differences. Br Med Bull 37:115-120

Fulker DW 1982 Extensions of the classical twin method. Sixth Int Congr Hum Genet. Alan R Liss, New York

Horn JM, Loehlin JC, Willerman L 1982 Aspects of the inheritance of intellectual abilities. Behav Genet, in press

Martin NG 1978 Genetics of sexual and social attitudes. In: Nance WE (ed) Twin research (2nd edn) Part A: Psychology and methodology. Alan R Liss, New York (Progr Clin Biol Res 24A)

Mech EV 1973 Adoption: a policy perspective. In: Caldwell BM, Ricciuti HN (eds) Review of child development research. Vol 3 Child Development and social policy. University of Chicago Press, Chicago

Plomin R, DeFries JC, Loehlin JC 1977 Genotype–environment interaction and correlation in the analysis of human behavior. Psychol Bull 84:309-322

Plomin R, DeFries JC, McClearn GE 1980 Behavioral genetics: a primer. WH Freeman, San Francisco

Rutter M, Brown GW 1966 The reliability and validity of measures of family life and relationships in families containing a psychiatric patient. Soc Psychiatry 1:38-53

Schaefer E 1963 Parent–child interactional patterns and parental attitudes. In: Rosenthal D (ed) The Genain quadruplets. Basic Books, New York

Spencer-Booth Y 1968 The behaviour of twin rhesus monkeys and comparisons with the behaviour of single infants. Primates 9:75-84

Temperament and follow-up to adulthood*

ALEXANDER THOMAS and STELLA CHESS

Millhauser Laboratories, Department of Psychiatry, New York University Medical Center, School of Medicine, 550 First Avenue, New York, NY 10016, USA

Abstract A follow-up of the New York longitudinal study at the 18–22-year period has been completed. Only one of the 133 subjects was not interviewed and evaluated. A temperament questionnaire for this age period has also been developed and given to 70 of the subjects. From the interview, ratings of temperament, adjustment and clinical psychiatric status were made. Statistical correlations showed significant relationships between 'difficult–easy' temperament at three and five years of age and early adult 'difficult–easy' temperament, adjustment, and presence or absence of a clinical psychiatric diagnosis. The importance of qualitative analyses of idiosyncratic developmental factors in individual cases is emphasized.

We have just completed a follow-up of our New York longitudinal study (Thomas & Chess 1977), at the 18–22-year period (which reflects the age-spread of the original group). We have 133 subjects in the group (and not 136 as suggested in some of our reports as a result of a tabulation error). We have followed up and interviewed 132 of these subjects, the missing one being away at sea with the United States Navy. (We have data from this man's mother, but he is not included in our analyses.) We have also seen all the parents except one mother who has been seriously ill.

We have from the beginning been interested in the functional significance of temperament for normal and deviant development. Our data collection and our methods of analysis have therefore covered a variety of issues, such as the ontogenesis of behavioural disorders, the influence of parental attitudes and practices, the effects of divorce, parental death, the mother's return to work, the patterns of defence mechanisms, self-image and self-esteem, and levels of adaptation and functioning in childhood and adoles-

1982 Temperamental differences in infants and young children. Pitman Books Ltd, London (Ciba Foundation symposium 89) p 168-175

*Our first use of the term 'temperament' in the early 1960s to replace the term 'primary reaction pattern' was in response to a specific suggestion from our Chairman at this symposium, Professor Michael Rutter.

cence. We have so far not attempted to characterize our subjects in terms of so-called personality traits, because this is a difficult area which we shall, no doubt, have to explore in the next few years. The analyses have permitted us to look at various issues apart from temperament, but here we shall concentrate on the data dealing with temperament, and attempt to cover three aspects: (1) the development of a questionnaire for early adult temperament; (2) the relationship between early childhood and early adult temperament; and (3) the influence of childhood temperament on early adult functioning. We shall also comment briefly on the consistency of temperament over time.

Questionnaire

We had previously deferred the issue of tackling a questionnaire for early adult life because the rating of temperament in the adult is complicated by a markedly increased individual variability in daily activities that form the basis of questionnaire items. Social life, school curriculum, work experience, athletic activities, hobbies and other special interests all become diversified in their form, content and prominence in the individual's life as he or she grows up. For example, many questions on temperament can be covered by items relating to what happens during car driving or cooking; but not everyone drives a car or cooks. However, we pursued the idea of a questionnaire and listed a very large number of items that were descriptive. For the first draft, we retained only those items that were scored by all three of our raters independently within the same temperament category. We used a seven-point scale for each item, through 'always' and 'almost always', to 'hardly ever' and 'never'. The draft version of 341 questions was given to 490 young adult college students and the appropriate statistical manoeuvres were done to determine the items that correlated most highly with the mean scores for their specific temperamental attributes and most lowly with eight other categories. This identified the reliable items and reduced the number of items. The final questionnaire has 132 questions, with 12 items for the 'quality of mood' category, and 16 items for the categories of 'activity level', 'rhythmicity', 'approach/withdrawal', 'adaptability', 'sensory threshold', 'intensity', 'distractibility', and 'persistence/attention span'.

We gave the questionnaire to 70 of our subjects in the New York longitudinal study. This incomplete sample is explained by the fact that the questionnaire was finished only when 52 subjects had already been seen and interviewed: although they were cooperative in the interview, these subjects were reluctant to return questionnaires by mail, so we did not pursue them. The questionnaire is also in use in several other studies of young adults.

Interviews

We also had temperament ratings for all 132 subjects from the interviews, which covered a wide range of issues, such as functioning in different areas—in the family, in sexual areas, at work, at school, and so on. We also included questions on temperament. In about 50% of cases a second interviewer was present throughout, and in about two-thirds of cases we tape-recorded the interviews, which were later scored by a third person who had not met the subjects. The reliabilities among the three interviewers were moderate. The worst reliability for an individual item was, unexpectedly, for intensity. It turned out that one experienced interviewer had had long experience as a psychotherapist, and she automatically made interpretations about the subject's underlying feelings rather than recording the subject's overt expressions of feelings. She was thus making judgements that, for our purposes, were not only unusually unreliable but were also unrelated to the objective evidence about intensity. The third person, who did the ratings from the tapes, found that the item of intensity was particularly difficult because of the absence of visual cues.

Results

We pooled the final interview ratings and self-report questionnaire results for each subject and found the correlations between the two ranged from low (0.32) for intensity and (0.33) for distractibility (which is a particularly difficult category to rate), to moderate (0.40, 0.50) and to fairly high (0.65) for activity level.

Our first analysis at the functional level dealt with the constellations of items that make up the 'easy' and 'difficult' types. We shifted the ratings to a continuous scale by taking an arithmetical average of the scores for each subject in the five categories of rhythmicity, approach/withdrawal, adaptability, intensity and quality of mood. This provided a continuous score from the most extremely easy temperament to the most extremely difficult temperament. This method has proved more satisfactory, both conceptually and for quantitative analysis, than the previous ratings that we used of the number of signs for the difficult type.

We also developed a number of outcome measures. For example, we scored a child for 'home adjustment', which is a composite of various subscores for feeding, discipline, sleep, peer relations, sibling relations, and so on, at three and five years of age. We also used a 'school adjustment' score at five years of age, and an 'early adult adaptation' score which started as a global score by the raters (with high inter-rater reliability) and was then converted by the 'bootstrap' statistical procedure (Goldberg 1970) into a score that also took into account the scores on the subcategories of self-evaluation, relationship with family, school functioning, sexual functioning, social functioning, goals, implementation of goals, patterns of coping, routines of daily life, communication and emotional expressiveness.

We also rated the presence or absence of a clinical psychiatric diagnosis, for which the inter-rater reliability has been very high. Table 1 summarizes all

TABLE 1 Correlations between difficult–easy temperament scores in the first five years and adjustment ratings in childhood and early adult life

Year	Correlation between difficult–easy temperament in each year and: Child global adjustment			Adult adjustment	
	Home: Year 3 (111–127)[a]	Home: Year 5 (113–117)[a]	School: Year 5 (82–84)[a]	Bootstrap score[b] (115–131)[a]	Clinical diagnosis in adult interview (116–132)[a]
1 (0–12 months)	0.03	−0.03	−0.02	0.08	0.03
2 (12–24 months)	0.14	0.02	−0.06	−0.09	−0.03
3 (24–36 months)	0.38*	0.21*	−0.02	−0.21*	0.05
4 (36–48 months)	0.55*	0.36*	0.30*	−0.32*	0.24*
5 (48–60 months)	0.24*	0.58*	0.11	−0.23*	0.19*

[a] Numbers in brackets indicate range of number of subjects (complete data were not available on all the children at each age).
[b] Bootstrap is overall adjustment (see text). *$P < 0.05$. A high correlation with the child global adjustment scores (first three columns) indicates less adjustment (negative values: more adjustment). A high correlation with the adult adjustment scores (last two columns) indicates more adjustment (negative values: less adjustment).

these results, and shows the pooled correlations for each full year up to five years of age. We found, as shown, no significant correlations between the various adjustment ratings and the difficult–easy score for the first or second years of life. For the third year (age 2–3) we found significant correlations with difficult–easy score and the contemporaneous adjustment at home, the five-year adjustment and the adult adjustment. The best correlations were at age 3–4 years, and 4–5 years was almost as good. We do not have enough data beyond age 5 to carry this analysis forward.

These correlations (Table 1) between early temperament and later outcome were confirmed by a series of both multiple regressions and set correlation analyses. The latter is a new method developed by Cohen (1982), involving a set of dependent and independent variables; this is not a canonical correlation. The set of independent variables included: the adjustment scores at three and five years at home and at five years at school; the difficult–easy temperament at three years and five years; parental conflict at three years (which other analyses had revealed to be the most significant correlate with adult outcome, out of all the parental function measures that we had obtained independently when the children were aged three); separation, divorce or death of the parents; and the presence of clinical diagnoses at <6 years or at 6 to 12 years. The set of dependent variables included: the adult adaptation ('bootstrap') score (Goldberg 1970); and the difficult–easy temperament at 18–22 years from the pooled interview data on 132 subjects, from the questionnaire data on the 70 subjects, and from the presence or absence of a clinical psychiatric diagnosis in adult life.

From the multiple regression and set correlation analyses that were relevant to temperament, the difficult–easy temperament scores at three and five years were significantly related both to the adult score for difficult–easy temperament derived by the interview raters and to the adult adjustment score. However, the multiple regression correlations for individual temperament categories in childhood (when the effects of other variables were partialled out) did not show an independently significant effect on adult adjustment. The questionnaire ratings of difficult–easy for early adult life were also significantly correlated with difficult–easy temperament at three years of age.

Our initial hypothesis had been that the highest risk for the difficult child for development of behavioural disorders would be primarily in the early years of life when demands for socialization and adaptation come in rapid sequence and at many levels. We had supposed that in later childhood and early adult life the risk would be lower. However, the results of the correlational and multiple regression analyses show, to our surprise, that the risks remain high in these later years as well.

The findings of the set correlation analyses indicate that the predictive power of the childhood variables for the adult variables accounts for 34% of the variance. This is indeed high considering the age-span involved and the methodological problems. The remaining variance is not, in our opinion, accounted for primarily by the methodological problems but by idiosyncratic factors (in the child or in the environment) that influence the child's developmental course significantly. We are currently attempting to characterize these factors, which form one of the major issues for our research efforts.

REFERENCES

Cohen J 1982 Set correlation as a multivariate data-analytic method. Multivar Behav Res, in press

Goldberg LR 1970 Man versus model of man: a rationale, plus evidence for a method of improving on clinical inferences. Psychol Bull 73:422-432
Thomas A, Chess S 1977 Temperament and development. Brunner/Mazel, New York

DISCUSSION

Bell: Did any of the interviewers who assessed the 'difficult–easy' scores from the interviews with the mothers in the child's infancy contribute data to the global home appraisal at age three years?

Thomas: Yes. The global home appraisal was done from the same protocol, even though the protocol was originally set up to gather data on temperament. We were always concerned with the child's detailed behaviour, and when we re-examined the protocols they contained a great deal of information on behavioural adjustment. The school data were collected independently by another interviewer.

Huttunen: In the clinical diagnoses of the adults, did you see any meaningful clustering of the cases? For example, in terms of the American Psychiatric Association (1980) diagnostic categories (DSM-III) of the character disorders, were the psychiatric cases more fearful, more impulsive or more withdrawn in character?

Thomas: In childhood most of the clinical cases were relatively mild reactive disorders and most of the patients recovered. The remainder tended to get worse rather than stay the same. The new cases that arose in adolescence and early adulthood tended to have a more severe diagnosis. We have seen two cases of severe primary depression, but not schizophrenia as yet. The more severe cases correspond to the American Psychiatric Association (1980) diagnostic categories (DSM III) of either conduct disorder or neurotic depression.

Rutter: Were these mainly long-standing disorders?

Thomas: They were variable. Some disorders that arose in adolescence were better by adulthood and others were not. Those that did not get better in childhood tended to be long-standing at the adult stage.

Rutter: Although, as you say, the correlations are low in absolute terms, nevertheless they are surprisingly high when one bears in mind the time span that you are considering. The correlations from early childhood to adulthood and those to later childhood are remarkably similar. That raises the question of how far the correlations with adult functioning are explicable in terms of your childhood measures; how far are you dealing with continuities in behaviour already manifest in childhood, and how far are you seeing continuities that were not evident in childhood?

Thomas: We haven't looked at that as such, but my impression is that in most cases we are dealing with continuities from childhood. For example, there is a positive correlation between the adjustment scores at three years and at five years of age and the early adult adjustment score.

Stevenson: I was interested in the highlighting of the age of three years as the time when these predictions to adulthood start to emerge, particularly because of the results of our study of behaviour problems from three to eight years (Richman et al 1982). These behaviour problems are probably in part reflecting a similar characteristic to the 'difficult–easy' dimension. One striking feature from our five-year follow-up was that the relationship between the three-year-old measure and the eight-year-old measure was far higher for boys than for girls. Did you do separate correlations for the sexes, and were they higher for males than for females?

Thomas: We have done all the ratings and correlations for males and females and they really do not show any dramatic differences in temperament or in level of function in the early or the late periods. The correlations were about the same for boys and girls, but there were a few scattered differences. Considering the large number of correlations done, these differences were small.

Kolvin: There seems to be a marginal overlap between the 'what' and the 'how' of behaviour, particularly in relation to activity. This must be a problem that you have been thinking about, over the years.

Thomas: This overlap has been a problem, as has the one between the 'how' of behaviour (i.e. temperament) and the 'why' of behaviour (motivation). Just as lung function is inextricably linked to heart and kidney function, these behavioural factors are linked, but they must be separated for the purposes of study. We have tended to be concerned only with the 'how' of behaviour, but now we must return to the interaction and the areas of overlap. Sigmund Freud made the penetrating observation that if one looks back at the life-history of an individual after a disturbance has occurred one can understand and explain the sequence of events that led up to it. But if one starts out ahead of time, before the end result is known, one is at a loss to predict any inevitable sequence of events (Freud 1950).

Keogh: I was struck by the fact that you were able to contact 132 of the 133 subjects, given the problems of following up subjects. Has your involvement with the subjects in your longitudinal study over the years increased or decreased the likelihood of particular relationships developing between early characteristics and late characteristics?

Thomas: When a child developed evidence of a behavioural disorder we were always faced with the problem of whether we should treat the child ourselves or suggest intervention by another physician. The overwhelming conclusion was always to intervene ourselves, despite possible effects on our longitudinal study results. If we had not done this, the first effect would have been that we would have lost our subjects; the parents would have felt that we were not interested in them or their children. Furthermore, if we intervened, at least we would then know what the parents had been told, and what advice they were following. It remains possible that if a mother was told that she had a temperamentally difficult child, which was not her fault, this knowledge might have increased the stability of this temperament constellation over time. I don't know how we could test this out from our own data.

REFERENCES

American Psychiatric Association 1980 Diagnostic and statistical manual of mental disorders, 3rd edn. Task force on nomenclature and statistics. American Psychiatric Association, Washington DC

Freud S 1950 Collected papers, 2nd edn. Hogarth Press, London, p 226

Richman N, Stevenson J, Graham P 1982 Preschool to school: a behavioural study. Academic Press, London

Personality development and temperament

M. BERGER

Department of Child Psychiatry, St George's Hospital, Blackshaw Road, London SW17 0QT, and Department of Psychology, St George's Hospital Medical School, University of London, UK

Abstract This paper identifies a number of problems that emerge in our attempts to trace a developmental linkage between early-appearing individual differences in temperament and later personality. It is suggested that the major problem is that of inadequate theory, from which it follows that there will be problems of definition and methodology. Attention is also drawn to difficulties associated with the concept of 'development'.

Certain early-appearing individual differences are identified, for which there is accumulating evidence of a genetic or constitutional basis. Further, these appear to show some stability and are accorded an important role in a number of theories, especially that of Eysenck. It is suggested that his approach, despite its many limitations, is worth further exploration.

There have, without doubt, been major conceptual and theoretical as well as methodological and technical advances in the study of personality. Despite these, personality research is in a state of some chaos and confusion. In the study of temperament in infancy and childhood there are, already, obvious signs of similar chaos and confusion, to be expected perhaps because of the similarities at various levels between such study and the study of personality in adults. Any attempt to examine the developmental relationship between temperament and personality is further complicated by the existing confusion within each field of enquiry and by several other fundamental problems. These are: our limited understanding of what we mean by development; how we go about studying development; the poorly articulated theoretical and conceptual links between early temperament and personality; and the methodological and other problems associated with the study of continuity and change.

Even a cursory glance at the published work would reveal an increasing interest in the study of early temperament. Much of this research concentrates on empirical and technological matters—such as constructing tests,

1982 Temperamental differences in infants and young children. Pitman Books Ltd, London (Ciba Foundation symposium 89) p 176-190

testing for associations, genetic influences, stability—and on the moderating effect of temperament in normal and behaviourally difficult children. No doubt such research does emanate from a theoretical framework, but this is usually vague and implicit. No doubt, too, the reported findings have a potential theoretical import. But what the framework is, and what theoretical implications emerge, are more often than not difficult to ascertain. Harré & Secord (1972) have said that much of contemporary psychological research suffers from an overemphasis on 'empiricism at the expense of conceptualization, or fact at the expense of ideas'. With some exceptions research on temperament is little different.

The clinical usefulness of the conceptual frameworks associated with research on temperament cannot be denied: but which of these is currently selected seems to be a matter of personal rather than rational choice. Similarly, the empirical relationships identified in research can be clinically helpful even though the choice of those to which attention is paid seems to be a function of individual differences among clinicians and not a consequence of a coherent rationale. Nevertheless, a knowledge both of conceptual frameworks and of empirical relationships gives different and helpful insights into clinical problems. It would therefore be a disservice to ignore them in clinical practice, despite the difficulties encountered in the study of personality and temperament.

If we wish to discover something about the development of personality, we need to have a clear idea of what is meant by the term and what, if anything, can be concluded from personality research. There are, however, fundamental problems in virtually every aspect of personality study, as is emphatically documented by a number of writers (Block 1977, Fiske 1978, Moss & Susman 1980, Jackson & Paunonen 1980). Block (1977) goes as far as to say of the published research that 'perhaps 90% of the studies are methodologically inadequate, without conceptual implication and even foolish'. Fiske (1978), in a similar vein but more pessimistic, notes the absence of, or at least poor consensus on, the fundamental constructs and definitions, the links between constructs and what is to be observed, and the absence of what is to constitute the basic observations of the discipline. All of these, among other things, lead him to conclude that current research on personality is, and is likely to remain, pre-scientific.

At the level of theory there is still a substantial number of fundamentally different positions (Hall & Lindzey 1978). In the realm of personality assessment there are, at the most recent count, 220 tests of personality to choose from (Buros 1978) and an untold number developed for particular projects which have yet to reach the catalogues. Over ten years ago Buros (1970) pointed out that many of the tests then in use (and now as well) were developed 20–40 or more years previously.

Methodologically and technically, contemporary research has been described as showing 'chaotic diversity' (Jackson & Paunonen 1980), despite the availability of many advances in test theory, measurement and data analysis. The theory of generalizability, for instance, was published in 1963 by Cronbach and his colleagues (see Cronbach et al 1972), but has had little impact either conceptually or in terms of its application to research problems.

The chronic unresolved questions in the study of personality occasionally give rise to significant eruptions. Mischel's (1973) monograph, *Personality and assessment*, is a recent instance. He attempted to demonstrate that situational influences are so substantial that the role of personality variables in behaviour can be ignored. This view, expressed here in an oversimplified form, was not a new one, in terms either of its particular features, or of the more general underlying position which argues for nurture, as opposed to nature, in influencing behaviour. The general form has been with us a long time; the specific arguments had been raised in the 1940's and before (see Jackson & Paunonen 1980). This example of one of several crises has again led to a compromise—the interactionist position—as described, for instance, by Magnusson & Endler (1977).

Crises in psychology do not lead to scientific revolutions, despite the frequency with which Thomas Kuhn (1970) is quoted in our literature. They lead instead to somewhat clearer thinking, usually in the form of clarification of concepts and the introduction of sometimes important conceptual distinctions, which in turn have implications for the way research is conducted and the consequent data analysed and interpreted. These points are clearly exemplified in the article by Magnusson & Endler (1977) on interactional psychology. My choice of the 'situationism crisis' is of course deliberate, because it has had an appreciable impact on the study of temperament (e.g. Thomas & Chess 1980). The real challenge is whether or not research on temperament can begin to respond in a non-trivial way to the intricate theoretical and conceptual analyses that interactional psychology has developed.

The term temperament is used in two contexts. The first is in relation to adult personality, with which it has a longstanding intimate relationship and, secondly, in the study of the behaviour of infants and young children, where there appears to be a reluctance to use the term personality, especially when referring to infancy. Like many concepts in child psychology, the term temperament seems to have been borrowed from the adult field, perhaps without too much thought about the implications of so doing, and in the process has been slightly transformed. Both usages—in relation to adults and to infants and children—need to be considered.

From an admittedly small but probably representative sample of definitions, the following characteristics can be identified.

(1) The terms personality and temperament have been used interchangeably (Allport 1961).

(2) Personality is commonly used as a more general term than is temperament, the latter being seen as a component of personality (Allport 1937, 1961, Vernon 1953, Eysenck 1953, Cattell 1965).

(3) Definitions also present temperament as one of the sources of personality, the 'raw material' (Allport 1961, Vernon 1953) from which personality is fashioned or derived.

(4) Temperament has been and still is seen either as the emotional side or component of personality (Eysenck 1953, Allport 1961, Dienstbier 1979) or as the stylistic aspect (Cattell 1965), or both.

(5) The definitions emphasize the constitutional ('genetic') origins of temperament (Allport 1961, Vernon 1953, Eysenck 1953) from which it almost inevitably follows that temperamental characteristics are presented as fairly stable or enduring (Allport 1961, Eysenck 1953), usually from infancy onwards (Vernon 1953).

What remains uncertain from these definitions is the nature of the relationship between personality and temperament: do the early characteristics remain discernible throughout life; do they become so intermingled with later characteristics that their identify is lost through gradual diffusion; or, do they undergo some radical transformation in the process of development? None of these or related issues is considered in any depth in published work, probably because those concerned with adult personality have little interest in the question of development.

Recent interest in temperament has led to a new crop of definitions and, as would be predicted, a variety of differences (see Goldsmith & Gottesman 1981), some minor and others major. Again, the sample that I give here is representative rather than exhaustive.

Thomas & Chess (1980) use temperament in two related but potentially confusing senses. Firstly, they present temperament as a general term referring to the 'how' of behaviour and then try to neutralize it by identifying it as a categorical term, without implications about its aetiology or its immutability. But they then go on to propose that temperament should be used to designate stylistic characteristics in infancy, and behavioural style to be the equivalent for later childhood. In effect they confine temperament to the initial segment of the life-span, presumably for non-neutral, theoretical reasons.

Buss & Plomin (1975), in addition to proposing a different organizational framework for temperamental characteristics, are more conventional in their definition, emphasizing the genetic or constitutional component. This, they maintain, enables the retention of a distinction between personality and temperament.

Two recent examples contribute further to the not insubstantial individual differences in the conceptualization of temperament. Rothbart (1981) defines temperament as 'individual differences in reactivity and self-regulation' and assumes a constitutional basis with a degree of immutability. Willerman (1979) sees temperament as having a role in the production of later personality. In the view of Goldsmith & Gottesman (1981) 'temperament encompasses a broad array of behavioural styles', some of which have 'indicators which may be discernible at birth', while others will not become apparent until later. They suggest that all the dimensions of temperament should be considered as developmental phenomena with varying degrees of genetic and environmental influences being possible. They anticipate that these dimensions will be 'relatively stable over specified developmental periods and that they may predict later individual differences in personality'.

It is also worth restating at this point that different writers identify different components of temperament (Thomas et al 1968, Graham et al 1973, Rothbart 1981, Goldsmith & Gottesman 1981, Buss & Plomin 1975) and that these are then indexed by a variety of indicators at the behavioural level by means of a variety of techniques (interviews, rating measures, direct observations in varied settings, etc).

In brief, therefore, the current picture of temperament appears as one of diversity heading for chaos which, bearing in mind its kinship with personality study, is not surprising.

Good scientists, we have been taught, always define their concepts and, wanting to be good scientists, we struggle to define personality and temperament. I believe that if we try to seek too much clarity at this point we will be disappointed. The main reason why we do not have good definitions is because we do not have good theories. Clarity of definition will begin to emerge only as we begin to achieve clarity in our theories. The two processes are interdependent. This applies irrespective of the type of definition (Miles 1957) with which we are concerned.

There are at least three options, not necessarily mutually exclusive, open to us. One is to accept that we have to improve our theories. The second is to follow the example of the intelligence test movement and simply assert that 'temperament (or personality) is what temperament (or personality) tests measure' (Miles 1957), a solution not unfamiliar to students of intelligence. The third option is to recognize that many of our concepts are essentially what Waddington (1977) calls 'fuzzy entities'—that is, terms with a soft core and an indefinite boundary. These fuzzy entities function well enough to delineate, for particular purposes, an area of interest isolated from the complex of human behaviour and experience. At least if we do this, we can be reassured by Waddington's observation that there is beginning to emerge a mathematics of fuzzy entities and computer programming systems which deal with notions that cannot be precisely defined. Fuzziness is not a problem inherent in psychology alone.

Our common sense, our implicit and explicit theories as well as our attempts at definition all suggest that there must be some links between early characteristics that we call temperament and the emerging 'personality'. How these are identified and studied is very much a function of how we understand development and of how this understanding is translated into research at the levels of problem specification, methodology, design and analysis.

Given the existing problems in the study of temperament and personality, the task becomes one of linking one 'fuzzy entity' with another. In our attempts to do so, however, it is soon discovered that the link itself is yet another 'fuzzy entity'. That is, there is no clear understanding of what is meant by development and of how to use this understanding to guide research.

Published work on child development clearly indicates that the implied issues are being taken seriously by contemporary researchers (Sroufe 1979b, Lewis & Starr 1979, Bronfenbrenner 1977, McCall 1977). Yet there are, equally, many unresolved questions of a fundamental nature—theoretical, conceptual and methodological. McCall (1977) has argued recently that we do not yet have 'a substantial science of naturalistic developmental processes' and proceeds to outline what steps he feels will be needed to remedy this. Life-span developmental psychologists have also indicated that the conceptual framework and methodologies of present-day child development research are too limited, with respect to meeting the requirements of an adequate psychology of development (Baltes et al 1980). This lack of clarity has not prevented the identification of certain features of the complex notion of development and the undertaking of research on some of them.

The central preoccupation of developmentally orientated research has undoubtedly been the identification of the continuity of behaviour (Bloom 1964, Kagan & Moss 1962, Sroufe 1979a,b, Moss & Susman 1980). As Sroufe (1979a) puts it 'the idea that the child is a coherent person, that despite changes he or she remains in important ways the same individual, has been a powerful force in developmental psychology'. But, as he goes on to note, it is not until recently that 'continuity in individual development proved empirically demonstrable'.

The identification of 'continuities' is much more complex than early students of development supposed. There was, for instance, a failure to take into account the important distinction, emphasized by Wohlwill (1973) and reiterated by McCall (1977, 1979), between the continuity/discontinuity of developmental functions and the stability/instability of individual differences.

The conceptual framework for identifying stabilities, continuities, or both has only recently begun to be better articulated (Kagan 1971, Lewis & Starr

1979). What is beginning to emerge is not only the diverse ways of isolating the basic behavioural data, and of indexing their various dimensions (e.g. frequency, duration, etc.), but also the different forms of abstraction from these data, which have differential implications for the detection of continuities or stability. Sroufe (1978, 1979a), for example, has studied what he calls patterns of individual adaptation. These patterns focus on the organization of behaviour, are complemented by temperamental characteristics, but are broader than the temperament dimensions and are designed to be independent of them. There are, for instance, probably good grounds for differentiating between Sroufe's qualitative analyses and those used by Thomas & Chess (1980), for example, in abstracting what they term the 'how' aspect from more specific behavioural events. But both types of analysis are needed, according to Sroufe (1978).

Even when stabilities are uncovered, as for instance in Block's (1971) research (see also review by Moss & Susman 1980), how these are to be understood is by no means clear. As Moss & Susman (1980) point out, 'Much of the stability that is observed is probably a function of the individual living in a stable environment or maintaining psychological equilibrium'.

There is a further important problem in trying to understand the development of personality from infancy onwards. Again, as Moss & Susman (1980) point out, the 'greatest disparity in definitions of personality occurs for definitions of infant and adult personality'.

One final point on stability needs to be noted. It is only in recent years that many important issues in the methodology of longitudinal research and the analysis of repeated measures have been identified, and although there have been innovations in design and techniques of data analysis, consensus on some of the significant questions is still somewhat limited (McCall 1977, Nesselroade & Baltes 1979).

The idea of development also encompasses notions of change (McCall 1977, 1979). Whereas we have a fairly good idea of what to look for in research on stability, the study of change does not have explicit theoretical guidelines as to what is being predicted by such study. There are, for instance, three 'somewhat independent approaches to the study of change' (Moss & Susman 1980).

There are several other features of development and yet other ideas about how it should be studied, even within the framework of conventional developmental psychology (McCall 1977, Sroufe 1979b). Several other major frameworks are beginning to exert an increasing influence on the study of child development. Life-span developmental psychology (Baltes et al 1980) is put forward as an orientation rather than as a theory, but it does have its own conceptual and methodological framework which encompasses early development. Indeed, its proponents argue that, despite protestations to the contrary, early development with its features of rapid change and increasing diversity is nevertheless intimately bound up with other phases of the life span (Thomae 1979). Specifically, Baltes et al (1980) have suggested that child development students could profitably borrow a number of ideas from the life-span approach, such as an emphasis on a 'changing ecology', 'a search for organizers other than chronological age' and 'the understanding that the study of parent–child and other family relations involves multiple developing individuals'. The importance of cohort (secular) effects in longitudinal research and of recent advances in multivariate and sequential analysis procedures has already been acknowledged by researchers in child development (see McCall 1977, for example). Both these influences stem more or less directly from the life-span developmentalists and no doubt their work will have a further impact on our understanding of development.

Other ideas about development are beginning to emerge: in particular, Bronfenbrenner's (1977) attempt to formulate an experimental ecology of human development; and the increasingly influential work of Waddington (1963, 1977), who has formulated an approach to development and gene–environment interaction which needs further serious examination. The latter model, which proposes canalized, genetically based, developmental pathways (*creodes*), has the special attraction of relocating the study of development in a framework that has always been concerned with development, namely the study of progressive biological systems which in turn has its roots in the basic science of development—embryology. Wilson (1978) has, for instance, drawn extensively on the work of Waddington in his research on the development of intelligence.

In summary, any attempt to link early temperament to personality is hampered by prevailing problems in the study of both personality and temperament and, further, the bridge between them—development—is itself a notion, the nature of which is still to be clearly specified. Nevertheless, certain trends can be identified, albeit speculatively, and these are considered next.

At the level of our everyday experience, and when we undertake systematic study, we find differences between people in almost every attribute on which we focus. Among the mass of individual differences can be differentiated, for analytical purposes, at least five dimensions: physique; activity; sociability; emotionality; and cognition. The characteristics and their precursors can be detected very early in life, and there is some evidence of heritability and stability. Recent attempts have been made to study their mutual interactions and interactions with the environment (Sroufe 1979b).

'Activity' has been of particular interest for some time. Although it features as a dimension in a number of temperament schemes (for example, Thomas et al 1968, Buss & Plomin 1975), it is, as Buss et al (1980) point out, not necessarily confined to one or other aspect of human functioning, and it cuts across several domains, conceptual and behavioural. Further, activity has conceptual continuity with the clinical notion of hyperactivity, even though the clinical phenomenon and the normal variate may be qualitatively different. Two important features of activity are that it is usually observable in the behaviour of all children and that it is incorporated as a feature in a number of systems of personality. We can measure it prenatally, and Korner et al (1981) have reported the development of interesting techniques for monitoring frequency and amplitude of activity in babies in the first few days of life. Some of their data show fairly high day-to-day stability. Buss et al (1980), using a composite index of activity derived from actometer measures and activity items of the California Children's Q Set, were able to demonstrate fairly consistent levels of activity from three to seven years of age.

Activity also features prominently in the extraversion *(E)* dimension of certain personality theories and systems, for example that of Eysenck & Eysenck (1969), who describe the high *E* scorer as someone who among other things 'prefers to keep moving and doing things'. Finally, we need to note the accumulating evidence for a genetic component in activity (e.g. Goldsmith & Gottesman 1981).

There are, of course, many problems in trying to develop a well argued case for activity as a feature that expresses itself from genetics and gestation to geriatrics. But the theme occurs with sufficient prominence to indicate that its developmental course is something worth studying.

A second theme that occurs in published work with greater than chance frequency is 'sociability'. Schaffer (1979) has commented that 'the more one learns about the growth of sociability in the early months of life, the more difficult it becomes to escape the conclusion that the infant is pre-adapted for social interchange'. To this can be added the accumulating evidence for a genetic basis to sociability/extraversion (e.g. Scarr 1969, Matheny et al 1981, Goldsmith & Gottesman 1981) and the regularity with which longitudinal studies refer to sociability/extraversion (e.g. Moss & Susman 1980) as a dimension with some stability.

The two strands, activity and sociability, come together in the broader personality dimension of extraversion, as described by Eysenck (Eysenck & Eysenck 1969, for example) and also form two of the four temperament dimensions in the Buss & Plomin (1975) scheme. Schaefer & Bailey (1960) have reported that early activity predicts extraversion in adolescence. In addition, the recent paper by Buss et al (1980) identifies fairly strong associations between activity measures and ratings of interpersonal functioning which are consistent with the associations that would be predicted from the Eysenckian description of extraversion.

The second major dimension in Eysenck's schema is emotionality, for which individual differences can be observed early in life (Bridger & Birns 1968, for example) and there is evidence for a genetic basis. Evidence for stability is more difficult to identify because of the great diversity of concepts used (see Goldsmith & Gottesman 1981). Buss & Plomin (1975) include emotionality as a major component in their scheme.

It is still too early to know how best to organize research on personality development, and to know what sorts of theoretical guidance we should seek in order to do so effectively. My speculative attempt to force-fit a few admittedly selected ideas of temperament and personality development into the Eysenckian conceptual framework has obvious limitations. So too does the Eysenck theory. It was, for instance, never really orientated either towards children or to development and there may be alternative structural models to those proposed. His theory, despite some of its limitations does, nevertheless, attempt to be both comprehensive and multi-level, and there is a programme of research which attempts to examine the empirical status of predictions derived from the theory. If we follow Brody's (1972) careful and detailed assessment of the theory and associated research, there seem to be good grounds, at least within the framework of conventional psychology, for adopting 'a pro-Eysenck position'. At the very least, it should be given serious attention in relation to the study of personality and its development.

Despite the many problems in studies of temperament and personality and of their developmental relationship, there are sufficient grounds for optimism. A convergence is indicated, both theoretically and empirically, between studies of certain temperamental attributes and studies of personality. Conceptual and methodological advances have been made, and the availability of computers and multivariate and other procedures for data analysis will enable a greater deal of complexity in research, a degree of complexity that at last is beginning to do justice to the complexity of 'personality'.

REFERENCES

Allport GW 1937 Personality: a psychological interpretation. Holt, New York
Allport GW 1961 Pattern and growth in personality. Holt, Rinehart & Winston, New York
Baltes PB, Reese HW, Lipsitt LP 1980 Life-span developmental psychology. Annu Rev Psychol 31:65-110
Bloom B 1964 Stability and change in human characteristics. Wiley, New York
Block J 1971 Lives through time. Bancroft Books, Berkeley
Block J 1977 Advancing the psychology of personality: paradigmatic shift or improving the quality of research. In: Magnusson D, Endler NS (eds) Personality at the crossroads. LEA, Hillsdale, New Jersey, p 37-63
Bridger WK, Birns B 1968 Early experience and temperament in human neonates. In: Newton R, Levine S (eds) Early experience and behavior. Thomas, Springfield, Illinois

Brody N 1972 Personality research and theory. Academic Press, New York

Bronfenbrenner U 1977 Toward an experimental ecology of human development. Am Psychol 32:513-531

Buros OK (ed) 1970 Personality tests and reviews I. Gryphon, Highland Park, New Jersey

Buros OK (ed) 1978 The eighth mental measurements year book. Gryphon, Highland Park, New Jersey

Buss AH, Plomin R 1975 A temperament theory of personality development. Wiley Interscience, New York

Buss DM, Block JH, Block J 1980 Preschool activity level: personality correlates and developmental implications. Child Dev 51:401-408

Cattell RB 1965 The scientific analysis of personality. Penguin Books, Harmondsworth, Middlesex

Cronbach LJ, Gleser GC, Nanda H, Rajaratnam N 1972 The dependability of behavioral measurements. Wiley, New York

Dienstbier RA 1979 Emotion-attribution theory: establishing roots and exploring future perspectives. In: Dienstbier RA (ed) Nebraska symposium on motivation. University of Nebraska Press, Lincoln, USA

Eysenck HJ 1953 The structure of human personality. Methuen, London

Eysenck HJ, Eysenck SBG 1969 Personality structure and measurement. Routledge & Kegan Paul, London

Fiske DW 1978 Strategies for personality research. Jossey-Bass, San Francisco

Goldsmith HH, Gottesman II 1981 Origins of variation in behavioral style: a longitudinal study of temperament in young twins. Child Dev 52:91-103

Graham P, Rutter M, George S 1973 Temperamental characteristics as predictors of behavior disorders in children. Am J Orthopsychiatry 43:328-339

Hall CS, Lindzey G 1978 Theories of personality (3rd edn). Wiley, New York

Harré R, Secord PF 1972 The explanation of social behaviour. Blackwell, Oxford

Jackson DN, Paunonen SV 1980 Personality structure and assessment. Annu Rev Psychol 31:503-551

Kagan J 1971 Change and continuity in infancy. Wiley, New York

Kagan J, Moss HA 1962 Birth to maturity. Wiley, New York

Korner AF, Hutchinson CA, Koperski JA, Kraemer HC, Schneider PA 1981 Stability of individual differences in neonatal motor and crying patterns. Child Dev 52:83-90

Kuhn TS 1970 The structure of scientific revolutions. University of Chicago Press, Chicago

Lewis M, Starr MD 1979 Developmental continuity. In: Osofsky JD (ed) Handbook of infant development. Wiley, New York, p 653-670

Magnusson D, Endler NS 1977 Interactional psychology: present status and future prospects. In: Magnusson D, Endler NS (eds) Personality at the crossroads. LEA, Hillsdale, New Jersey, p 3-31

Matheny AP, Wilson RS, Dolan AB, Krantz J 1981 Behavioral contrasts in twinships: stability and patterns of differences in childhood. Child Dev 52:579-588

McCall RB 1977 Challenges to a science of developmental psychology. Child Dev 48:333-344

McCall RB 1979 Qualitative transitions in behavioral development in the first two years of life. In: Bornstein MM, Kessen W (eds) Psychological development from infancy. LEA, Hillsdale, New Jersey, p 183-224

Miles TR 1957 Contributions to intelligence testing and the theory of intelligence. Br J Educ Psychol 27:153-165

Mischel W 1973 Personality and assessment. Wiley, New York.

Moss HA, Susman EJ 1980 Longitudinal study of personality development. In: Brim OG, Kagan J (eds) Constancy and change in human development. Harvard University Press, Cambridge, Mass, p 530-595

Nesselroade JR, Baltes PB 1979 Longitudinal research in the study of behavior and development. Academic Press, New York

Rothbart MK 1981 Measurement of temperament in infancy. Child Dev 52:569-578

Scarr S 1969 Social introversion–extraversion as a heritable response. Child Dev 40:823-832

Schaefer ES, Bailey N 1960 Maternal behavior, child behavior and their intercorrelations from infancy through adolescence. Monogr Soc Res Child Dev 37:389-396

Schaffer HR 1979 Acquiring the concept of dialogue. In: Bornstein MH, Kessen W (eds) Psychological development from infancy. LEA, Hillsdale, New Jersey, p 274-306

Sroufe LA 1978 Enduring patterns of individual adaptation. In: Wilson RS, Matheny AP (eds) Conference on temperamental research: abstracts of presentations. University of Louisville School of Medicine

Sroufe LA 1979a The coherence of individual development. Am Psychol 34:834-841

Sroufe LA 1979b Socioemotional development. In: Osofsky JD (ed) Handbook of infant development. Wiley, New York, p 462-516

Thomae H 1979 The concept of development and life-span developmental psychology. In: Baltes PB, Brim OG (eds) Life-span development and behavior. Academic Press, New York, Vol 2, p 281-312

Thomas A, Chess S 1980 The dynamics of psychological development. Brunner/Mazel, New York

Thomas A, Chess S, Birch HG 1968 Temperament and behavior disorders in children. New York University Press, New York

Vernon PE 1953 Personality tests and assessments. Methuen, London

Waddington CH 1963 The nature of life. Unwin Books, London

Waddington CH 1977 Tools for thought, Paladin Books, St Albans

Willerman L 1979 The psychology of individual and group differences. WH Freeman, San Francisco

Wilson RS 1978 Synchronies in mental development: an epigenetic perspective. Science (Wash DC) 202:939-948

Wohlwill JF 1973 The study of behavioral development. Academic Press, New York

DISCUSSION

Wilson: The concepts used by Waddington (1962), which emphasize an unfolding of developmental processes, will become a crucial addition to developmental psychology and to the understanding of the whole course of child development, including temperament and mental development. As we understand gene–environment interactions better and, particularly, switchable gene systems that control the rate of maturational processes, we shall begin to see a closer coordination between some of the apparent discontinuities of human behaviour and underlying biological processes.

Dunn: Do you think that the concepts of 'life-span' psychologists are precise enough to add to the way development in early childhood is thought about?

Berger: One can give specific instances. Mothers, fathers and siblings are all developing. Therefore developmental research based on temperamental interactions ought to take into account the changes and stabilities in each member of the group. Another important aspect of the life-span developmental approach is the emphasis placed on forms of theory. It is currently popular to talk about the dialectics of development, and these ideas first emanated, in part, from theoreticians who were writing within the framework of life-span developmental psychology.

Rutter: You commented that studies on personality and temperament have, on the whole, omitted developmental issues. How do you think development should be brought more into the picture?

Berger: This is difficult to answer briefly. Alan Sroufe (1979), in discussing socioemotional development in infants, puts forward a framework of development and then tries to relate both social and emotional development to that framework. Much the same approach could now begin to be applied to personality and temperament.

Stevenson: I would also add a note of scepticism about the usefulness of Waddington's epigenetic landscape (Waddington 1957). This may not have been a useful or productive theory even in embryology. It strikes me simply as a redescription of phenomena and one which does not facilitate the drawing up of testable predictions about the nature of those phenomena.

Hinde: Waddington's ideas seem to have drawn attention to the concept of regulation, which was rather left out of developmental theories for a long time, so in that sense his work is useful.

Berger: Waddington identifies what he calls 'a set of tools to help our thinking'. His model is just a conceptual tool, and is not put forward as *the* explanation of development. Developmental psychologists are finding the idea of different degrees of canalization very helpful in thinking about influences on developmental processes unfolding at particular times.

Hinde: I have reservations about your quotation from Harré & Secord (1972), which implies that we needed more conceptual framework and less empirical work. The Harré & Secord ethnomethodology is solid conceptual framework with rather little empirical data!

Berger: Their critique of contemporary psychology and their solution to its problems are different. One can accept the critique without accepting the solution.

Huttunen: In principle, it is certainly important to distinguish between the 'ideal' development of human behaviour and the numerous negative effects of environment on development. Some noxious environmental effects may be so common that they become aetiological factors of the statistically normal forms of personality. Theoretically one must clearly differentiate between the ideal human development and the imposed noxious effects of life stresses, of prenatal viral infections, and of nutritional factors during pregnancy or early development.

Kohnstamm: The Dutch psychologist, G. Heymans (1857–1930), working in Groningen early this century (Heymans 1908, Vandenberg 1967), created a conceptual framework that consisted of three personality dimensions, which he derived from all the personality theories that he had seen, from centuries before. These dimensions were activity, emotionality and primary or secondary functioning of thought processes. He was later accused of having too much conceptual framework and too little empirical support. He was accused of finding in this empirical data what his conceptual framework predicted he would find. In 1905 he sent 3000 questionnaires by mail to all Dutch doctors and had them rate, for those three variables, a family in their practice, on the basis of all his questions. I am struck by the similarity between at least two of those three variables and the ones that seem to remain in general use today.

Wolkind: One problem about producing a theory of temperament or any other aspect of human development is that our work tends not to allow for the incredible importance of quite small random events in the lives of individuals and families. A child referred to our clinic had a marked neurotic school phobia. He was the youngest of six siblings and all the others were out-and-out delinquents. His mother said to me, 'He has always been different'. When the boy was a tiny baby he had had a severe viral infection that had produced in the mother a feeling that this child was her 'special one'. This quite random small event seemed to have set up a chain of interactions which would have been terribly difficult to detect by any research project. It can therefore be difficult to fit our findings into a general theory unless we have various theories which include the concept of uncertainty.

Berger: A propos of your comment, and our earlier discussion about life-span psychology, people working in the latter field have a specific 'slot' for just that sort of event—the unexpected crisis.

Thomas: One needs a basis for judging when such an unexpected crisis will have a long-term or a transient effect, and for judging what kind of effect it will have.

Bell: Other family factors might be pin-pointed as a trigger for the unexpected event. The usual assessment of a family would normally encompass the factors that fuse together to make up a particular mother's treatment of her infant. For example, the marital relationship might develop in such a way that the mother begins to reach out in other directions for contact and intimacy. There might then be a problem in the way she relates to her infant. Both problems would be detected by the usual assessment. Similarly, Dr Wolkind mentioned the viral infection that acted as a trigger, and led the mother to see her infant as in need of protection. This may well have brought together, or focused, all the temperament and behavioural data that had already been recorded. Yet no one could have predicted that the trigger itself would be activated.

Wolkind: An interesting variable that we don't know about is whether, had this child been extremely active, with a negative mood, he would have *allowed* his mother to accept him in that way.

REFERENCES

Harré R, Secord PF 1972 The explanation of social behaviour. Blackwell, Oxford

Heymans G 1908 Ueber einige psychischen Korrelationen. Z Angew Psychol psychol Sammelforschung 1:313-381

Sroufe LA 1979 Socioemotional development. In: Osofsky JD (ed) Handbook of infant development. Wiley, New York, p 462-516

Vandenberg SG 1967 Hereditary factors in normal personality traits (as measured by inventories). In: Wortis J (ed) Recent advances in biological psychiatry, vol 9. Plenum Press, New York, p 65-104

Waddington CH 1957 The strategy of the genes. Allen & Unwin, London

Waddington CH 1962 New patterns in genetics and development. Columbia University Press, New York

Clinical use of temperament data in paediatrics

WILLIAM B. CAREY

319 West Front Street, Media, Pennsylvania 19063, USA

Abstract Temperament data can aid the clinician in fostering parent–child relationships on three levels. First, general educational discussions about temperament between the clinician and parents provide background information, which increases parents' awareness and understanding of individual differences. Second, identification of the temperament profile of the particular child provides the parents with a more organized picture of the child's behavioural style and of possible distortions in their perceptions of it. This is primarily useful to the clinician when the child is rather difficult or when, for example the mother's perception of the child makes the child seem more difficult than her own ratings suggest. This clarification process may provide parents with enough insight for them to make their own shifts in interaction patterns. Third, the clinician may attempt to influence the temperament–environment interaction, when its dissonance is leading to reactive symptoms, by suggesting alternative methods of parental management. If this is successful, the stress of the interaction should diminish and the reactive symptoms disappear. At the same time parents and teachers must learn to live in a more tolerant and flexible manner with the child's relatively less changeable temperament.

As the only full-time, primary-care physician at this symposium, I consider it my responsibility to supply a clinical perspective derived from my 21 years as a practising paediatrician. I shall share with you my experience of the ways I have found temperament data useful. I hope that I can impress upon academic researchers and others that temperament is not just an interesting concept worthy of research and learned discussion. Individual differences are real, they do matter in everyday life, and we researchers and clinicians should be working together to learn more about them and about how to help parents deal with them.

This paper discusses three ways in which temperament data can aid the clinician in fostering parent–child interaction. First, general educational discussions about temperament between the clinician and parents help to

1982 Temperamental differences in infants and young children. Pitman Books Ltd, London (Ciba Foundation symposium 89) p 191-205

provide a background of information, which increases parents' awareness and understanding of individual differences. Second, the identification of the temperament profile of the particular child provides parents with a more organized picture of the child's behaviour pattern and of possible distortions in their perceptions of it. Third, the clinician may attempt to influence the temperament–environment interaction, when its dissonance is leading to reactive symptoms, by suggesting alternative methods of parental management. The alert clinician may use each of these three levels of involvement at different points or at the same time. For the sake of clarity the three should be discussed separately (Carey 1981b, 1982a).

General educational discussions

The most superficial level of involvement using temperament data is educational discussion between the clinician and parent. In this process the concept of normal individual differences is presented in general terms or in relation to instructions about feeding, sleeping, crying, elimination, etc. These discussions can take place at almost any time from before delivery to adolescence.

By this means parents should develop a greater awareness and understanding of normal individual differences in behaviour. Many parents have been previously exposed only to a behaviourist view of child development. They can now appreciate that some behavioural predispositions are present in children at birth, and that disagreeable behaviour is not all directly attributable to faulty parental care or to brain malfunction. Parents need to know that simple rules for child rearing cannot be applied to all children with equal success even in the first few months.

Some illustrations should clarify this process. A parent may find it helpful to know that an infant's slow approach to foods or people may be a temperamental characteristic and not a sign of parental inadequacy. Equally, a highly active preschool child is more likely to be normal than to be overstimulated or to have a malfunctioning brain.

Nevertheless, the benefits to the parents of such general discussions may not be enough to meet the parents' needs. Before the advent of refined interview and questionnaire techniques this was as far as the clinician could go, and such discussion of generalities is probably as far as most go even now. One need not stop at this point.

Identification of the specific profile of the child

It is now possible to identify simply and somewhat accurately the specific temperamental profile of a particular child. Current questionnaire techniques such as the Infant Temperament Questionnaire (Carey & McDevitt 1978a) provide, with 20–30 min of the parent's time and 10–15 min for scoring, a detailed picture of the individual child's reaction pattern and of the mother's general perceptions of it. Further interviewing and observations are necessary to obtain a fuller appreciation of the interaction. Just when this should be done routinely is a matter of personal opinion. My present plan is to ask parents to complete the Infant Temperament Questionnaire when the infant is about six months old; additional forms at later ages are used only when indicated by problems in the child or in the interaction. The more organized, objective view of the child provided by these scales can be valuable in two principal ways:

(1) Identification of difficult and slow-to-warm-up children

Most parents of 'difficult' infants do not need to be told that their childen are a challenge but they are often only dimly aware of the nature of the problem. To know that the difficult characteristics are probably inborn, but usually changeable, takes a great load of guilt off their shoulders and allows them to respond to their infants with less anger and apprehension (Thomas & Chess 1977). Even so, parents of difficult children must exercise great patience and flexibility. Parents have also often blamed themselves unjustly for the timidity seen in the 'slow-to-warm-up' child. Sometimes the clinician has to correct mistaken diagnoses from fellow professionals. For example, the parents of a five-year-old boy were recently told by a psychologist that the child's low adaptability in nursery school was attributable to his allergies and to their treatment, but the psychologist did not know that the child had been rated similarly at six months, before the allergies began.

Even without any specific advice on management from the clinician, this process of identifying the child's characteristics may provide the parents with enough insight for them to make healthy shifts in interaction patterns. For example, one mother wisely realized that her infant's intensity was just part of a flamboyant style and that she did not need to continue to respond to every yell. When she stopped over-reacting, the relationship became much more agreeable for both.

The available longitudinal data make it reasonable for clinicians to express a cautious optimism about the outlook for difficult infants. Although a significant number of difficult infants become difficult children during the following few years, most become less difficult (Carey & McDevitt 1978b). How difficulty decreases is far from clear but there are clues that it is more likely in the presence of certain infant and certain parental characteristics (Cameron

1977). At the same time some easy infants may become more difficult and the mechanisms of this change are poorly understood at present. Some assume that all changes are due to environmental effects, but it is possible that congenital factors are involved too.

We must remember that this definition of 'difficult' was based on the clinical experience of the New York longitudinal study with white middle-class New Yorkers in the first few years of life (Thomas & Chess 1977). Other cultures may have different tolerance of these characteristics, as the same workers showed with their Puerto Rican sample in New York. Different ages make various traits more or less troublesome. In the toddler age group (1–3 years) mothers agreed almost completely that these traits (low approach and adaptability, intensity and negative mood) were the behaviours they found most difficult (McDevitt & Carey 1981). In 4–8-month-old infants, however, mothers were more bothered by low distractibility (soothability) and high activity as well as negative mood (Carey & McDevitt 1978a). In early school-age children (ages 3–7 years) a group of teachers was most troubled by children who were low in adaptability, low in persistence (or attention span) and high in activity (Carey et al 1979). Parents of 8–12-year-old children complained most about low adaptability, negative mood and low persistence (or attention span) (R. L. Hegvik, S. C. McDevitt & W. B. Carey, unpublished paper, 1981 Bienn Meet Soc Res Child Dev, Boston, Mass.).

(2) Identification of major discrepancies between ratings and perceptions of temperament

This is the other principal clinical value in determining the child's specific profile. Before developing this idea it is necessary to clarify the difference between ratings and perceptions. Much of the published work in the behavioural sciences distinguishes only between 'perceptions' of behaviour by mothers—generally regarded as inferior sorts of reports—and 'observations' by outside professional persons—invariably considered to be reporting scientific data of a higher order regardless of how brief and unrepresentative the data may be. McDevitt and I (1981) have rejected this perjorative and inaccurate dichotomy. We use the term 'ratings' to mean multiple-scored judgements as to the frequency of various reactions, and 'perceptions' to indicate hasty or superficial general impressions of the child. Both parents and professionals can produce ratings and perceptions. To the clinician, parental ratings and parental perceptions of temperament are each of interest.

Since a comprehensive, standardized professional rating technique is not yet available, the clinician is compelled to rely on parental ratings. Observations are possible in the clinical setting, but experienced clinicians realize that these observations are too brief and unrepresentative to be of much value. Fortunately, evidence is accumulating that parental ratings of temperament are largely valid (Carey 1982b), if we accept as an adequate measure of parental validity an agreement with the brief professional ratings (or are they perceptions?) of the child that have generally been used so far. If behavioural scientists wish to be useful to their clinical colleagues, they should abandon their traditional deprecations of parental reports and help us to find ways of improving these reports since they are the best tools now available to us.

Let me resume discussion of the other principal value in determining the child's specific profile—the identification of major discrepancies between ratings and perceptions of temperament. Although general impressions or perceptions of temperament tend to agree with the ratings, they may be substantially different (Carey & McDevitt 1978a). Of particular concern to the clinician should be the *perception* of a child as being difficult when the same person has just *rated* the same child as easy. One should be wary of psychosocial problems or inappropriate interaction when this happens. This is illustrated by a mother who, because of her personal problems, viewed her boy as generally more difficult than average, although she rated him as quite easy on the questionnaire.

On the other hand, when children are rated as difficult but perceived as generally average or easy, as happens commonly, the course is not so clear. Certainly one should not insist on applying an unappealing label to an infant whose mother is pleased with him or her. It seems wiser to retain the findings for possible future use. The reasons why such a mother does not complain may be various: inexperience, denial or effective coping. For example, when I learned to my surprise that a seven-month-old infant was rated as difficult and perceived as easy, I asked his experienced mother at our next meeting how things were going with him. She replied with a smile, 'He's hysterical! He screams a lot but we just laugh at him and he stops'.

The clinician who identifies temperamental profiles of patients must be aware of some problems and some pitfalls. First, the clinician must understand that a difficult temperament profile does not necessarily indicate a stressful parent–child interaction. Diverse parental expectations and coping capacities strongly affect the environment with which the child interacts. Therefore, intervention programmes, intended to prevent emotional problems by early screening for difficult temperament alone, are destined to failure.

Furthermore, the use of labels should be avoided. It is better to give parents questionnaire results (when these are requested) in terms of descriptions of characteristics such as 'rather intense' or 'fairly regular' rather than as diagnostic labels, the meaning and prognostic implications of which may be misunderstood.

If parents do not ask for the results of a routinely performed temperament profile and if the interaction and development seem normal, I do not feel any obligation to discuss test findings. Some parents rightly think they can learn little new from the results; others assume that the clinician will bring up anything that is of concern.

However, the principal problem with only identifying the child's individual behavioural style may be that this is insufficient to meet the parents' needs. They may need advice about what they should do.

Influencing the temperament–environment interaction

When there is a developmental or behavioural problem from a temperament–environment interaction and the clinician knows enough about these matters in general, and about the specific situation in particular, it may be possible for the clinician to influence the interaction favourably by suggesting alternative patterns of parental handling. If this is successful, the stress in the interaction should diminish and the reactive symptoms should disappear. The other part of the therapeutic process is that the parents, teachers or other caretakers must learn to live in a more tolerant and flexible manner with the child's behavioural style, which is evidently less changeable and not abnormal in itself. This might be done, for example, by providing an active child with more space. Here the clinician is supplying both diagnostic insight and therapeutic help.

It may be possible to alter a child's temperament pharmacologically. Cerebral stimulants, such as amphetamines and methylphenidate, are observed to decrease activity and to increase attention. These effects are thought by some to be the result of treatment of a cerebral malfunction, yet that may not be so since the same alterations have been noted also in normal children (Rapoport et al 1978). This complicated issue can only be mentioned here; its resolution awaits clarification by future research (Carey & McDevitt 1980).

The two areas in which the process of influencing the interaction has been most helpful so far are behavioural problems at home and scholastic adjustment difficulties:

(1) *Role of temperament factors in behavioural problems.* The demonstration of the role of temperament factors, such as the 'difficult child' syndrome, in behaviour problems was the major achievement of the New York longitudinal study of A. Thomas, S. Chess and associates (Thomas & Chess 1977). Several subsequent studies, although smaller and less elegant, have supported their conclusions (Graham et al 1973, McInerny & Chamberlin 1978, Terestman 1980).

The implementation of this point of view has not been without pitfalls. First, some clinicians have trouble in distinguishing between difficult temperament and behavioural problems. Temperament is a matter of style; behavioural maladjustment means substantial disturbance of social relationships, autonomy or task performance. A volatile temper is behavioural style; social alienation due to the temper is a behavioural maladjustment.

Difficult temperament may continue from infancy into childhood, and perhaps beyond, in spite of psychotherapy (Carey & McDevitt 1978b). This should not be interpreted automatically as evidence of poor parental care or inadequate therapy. It may simply mean that some characteristics are relatively resistant to environmental manipulations.

A third problem in the clinical application of this theory of the origins of behavioural problems is that many psychotherapists seem not to believe it. When one has a longstanding grasp of temperamental factors in a troubled interaction, it is frustrating to have the therapist to whom the child has been referred revise the diagnostic formulation and blame all the problems on parental attitudes, family dynamics, diet or minimal brain dysfunction. Similarly, most child-rearing advice published by professional therapists ignores individual differences in the reaction characteristics of children. For example, 'Parent effectiveness training' (Gordon 1975) seems designed for adaptable children but does not work well for difficult children.

An illustration of influencing the interaction in a behavioural problem is provided by the story of a two-year-old difficult boy. His mother had managed fairly successfully for the first two years of his life. At that point the second child was born and the father's business kept him away from home much more than usual. The boy was upset by the sibling competition and became aggressive and destructive. The mother over-reacted and became impatient and punitive. The boy emptied jars of food on the floor and smeared cosmetics on the walls. The mother finally asked for help. Since the ingredients of the troubled situation were clear, advice on altered management could be given in the first session. The dynamics were discussed, the mother was to spend more time alone with the jealous child, and the unacceptable behaviour was to be extinguished by some simple behavioural modification techniques. His behaviour improved rapidly and no psychiatric referral was needed. Knowledge of his difficult temperament helped in two ways: it explained why he reacted so extremely to a relatively ordinary situation, and it set limits on expectations of the outcome of the intervention. He has remained a difficult child but the behavioural problem is gone. Subsequently he endured the arrival of another sibling uneventfully.

(2) *Problems of scholastic adjustment* are a second area in which the clinician can fruitfully influence the temperament–environment interaction. Several

studies have established that scholastic adjustment is affected not only by cognitive skills, emotional and physical health but also by temperament. In particular, the characteristic of adaptability has been shown in four independent studies to be related to teachers' judgements of children's intelligence in nursery school (Gordon & Thomas 1967), scores on academic achievement tests (Chess et al 1976), teachers' assessments of school adjustment in kindergarten and first grade (Carey et al 1977), and referral to a paediatric neurologist for problems in behaviour and learning (Carey et al 1979).

Teachers seem to be beginning to think more consciously in terms of the once unfashionable concept of temperament. In the coming years we shall probably see an upsurge of interest in this phenomenon as it affects students. In the meanwhile, some misunderstandings are evident in reports from school. Difficult children are often spoken of as 'immature' because of such behaviour as temper outbursts and inflexibility. Slow-to-warm-up children are frequently described as 'insecure'. They may be reluctant to begin new tasks but, once through the initial phases, they are just as sure of themselves as are their peers.

Perhaps the major scholastic area of misinterpretation at present is with children who are low in adaptability and attention span, and high in activity. These characteristics tend to cluster together, being found in 22.3% of the 3–7-year-old children in the standardization sample of the Behavioural Style Questionnaire (only 12.5% expected by chance $P < 0.001$; McDevitt & Carey 1978). These were the main traits of the population that was referred to a paediatric neurologist (Carey et al 1979). Such children are apparently the ones being given the label of 'hyperkinetic' or 'minimal brain dysfunction' (and now 'attention deficit disorder') by teachers, psychologists and physicians. However, for the most part, there is no evidence that these children have anything wrong with their brains or that they are in any way benefited by being given these labels (Carey & McDevitt 1980).

I shall review briefly the story of a seven-year-old girl to illustrate intervention in a school adjustment problem. This rather difficult child had some trouble settling down at the beginning of her kindergarten and first-grade years, but resourceful experienced teachers patiently allowed her to get used to the novelty, and her educational progress was unimpaired. However, in second grade, her rigid young teacher could not tolerate deviations from her highly structured programme, and consequently the child was frustrated, had frequent temper tantrums, was threatened with expulsion from class and deteriorated in her scholastic achievement. Her hard-working, highly-achieving parents were unable to understand how a child of theirs could fall into such a state. The mother felt guilty that her full-time employment was responsible for the turmoil. In this case, intervention strategy consisted (1) of giving the parents a better perspective on the child's low adaptability and how to deal with the adaptability at home and (2) of relieving the mother of her guilt feelings. The situation at home improved greatly but due to the teacher's continuing inflexibility the rest of the school year went only a little better. In the following year with another mature, understanding teacher the child flourished and joined the programme for academically talented students. Once again the knowledge of the child's temperament aided the diagnostic process by explaining the magnitude and direction of her behavioural reactions and it guided management plans and expectations.

(3) Several additional areas of clinical concern have been shown to be influenced by temperamental factors but grounds for clinical intervention are less clear so far. Outstanding among these is the influence of temperament on the incidence, manifestations and management of *physical illness*. Two studies in paediatric populations (Matheny et al 1971, Carey 1972) have shown a higher rate of *accidents* in more difficult children. A recent study of physicians from Johns Hopkins (Betz & Thomas 1979) reported significantly more major health problems and early death in those who as medical students had been of Gesell's γ temperament type (uneven and irregular) rather than the α (slow and solid) or the β (rapid and facile) types.

Clinical experience suggests that children who complain a great deal are more likely to be taken for medical care and to have more procedures done to them, but this phenomenon needs much study. Furthermore, the concept of parental compliance with medical care must be expanded to consider the child's contribution to, or interference with, the management.

Temperament appears to interact with and to affect to a minor degree the *rate of psychomotor maturation* (Carey 1972, 1981a). Temperament seems to participate in the physiological disturbances of *colic* (Carey 1972) and *night waking* (Carey 1974). The role of intervention should be explored here.

In several other areas of clinical concern attention is beginning to be focused on possible temperament–environment conflicts: *child abuse, failure to thrive, obesity*, and other *psychosomatic problems* (Carey 1981a). These may be promising fields for intervention in the future. In children with various handicaps there is no strong evidence of any characteristic profiles of temperament, but there is a clinical impression that such traits as adaptability and persistence may affect the outcome of treatment.

Conclusions

A different set of conclusions seems appropriate, depending on whether I am addressing fellow clinicians or fellow researchers.

To fellow clinicians my advice is:

(1) We should learn about temperamental differences and should actively educate parents about them. Parents gain, thereby, a background knowledge of individual variations against which to understand their own child better.

(2) We should acquaint ourselves with the available measurement techniques and consider their routine use. This process would help to sharpen parents' views of the individual reaction patterns of their children and would sometimes aid them in perceiving and interacting with their children in a healthier way.

(3) Using this general knowledge about temperament, and specific information about the particular child, we should attempt to influence disharmonious interactions when secondary symptoms have arisen or are likely to arise. Although changing the temperament characteristics themselves, other than pharmacologically, may be beyond our reach now, alterations in interaction patterns may bring about better behavioural adjustment.

To fellow researchers, my suggestions cover the same ground, but in a different way:

(1) We should continue to develop our knowledge of temperament: its most significant variables, their origins and stability. All this is interesting but is not enough.

(2) Researchers should be finding ways to improve parental and professional rating techniques. We need to know more about the strengths and weaknesses of currently available parental questionnaires. We should find out which parents distort the truth, and in what ways; and what sorts of behaviour are most and least subject to errors in rating. Clinicians *must* rely heavily on parental reports of behaviour. It is up to us to provide them with the best possible tools. Temperament research would be enhanced considerably by a comprehensive, standardized professional rating technique, which would probably be of little direct value to the clinician because of the great length and detail necessary. However, it might be possible to develop from it an abbreviated version that would be truly representative of the child's full repertoire of reactions and therefore would be appropriate for validity testing of parental ratings and for meaningful clinical observations.

(3) There should be a major effort to investigate the many ways in which temperament appears to be clinically significant and intervention helpful. Here lies the ultimate social value of our efforts.

Information on obtaining temperament questionnaires

The addresses from which our four temperament questionnaires may be obtained are listed below. Since these instruments were developed with minimal financial support, please send a prepaid contribution of $5.00 for each scale to help us cover expenses. The form you receive may be photocopied as much as you wish.

(1) Infant Temperament Questionnaire (4–8-month-old infants), revised 1977 by W. B. Carey and S. C. McDevitt. *From:* William B. Carey, MD, 319 West Front Street, Media, Pennsylvania 19063, USA (*Telephone:* (215) 566-6641.) *Reference:* Carey & McDevitt (1978a).

(2) Toddler Temperament Scale (1–3-year-old children), developed in 1978 by W. Fullard, S. C. McDevitt and W. B. Carey. *From:* William Fullard, PhD, Department of Educational Psychology, Temple University, Philadelphia, Pennsylvania 19122, USA. (*Telephone:* (215) 787-6102.) *Reference:* in preparation.

(3) Behavioral Style Questionnaire (3–7-year-old children), developed in 1975 by S. C. McDevitt and W. B. Carey. *From:* Sean C. McDevitt, PhD, Devereux Center, 6436 East Sweetwater, Scottsdale, Arizona 85254, USA. (*Telephone:* (602) 948-5857.) *Reference:* McDevitt & Carey (1978).

(4) Middle Childhood Temperament Questionnaire (8–12-year-old children), developed in 1979–80 by R. L. Hegvik, S. C. McDevitt and W. B. Carey. *From:* Ms Robin L. Hegvik, 307 North Wayne Avenue, Wayne, Pennsylvania 19087, USA. (*Telephone:* (215) 687-6058.) *Reference:* in preparation.

All four scales assess the New York longitudinal study temperament characteristics by eliciting parental responses to about 97 behavioural descriptions. Total internal consistency was 0.83, 0.85 and 0.84, respectively, for the first three scales; one-month retest reliability was 0.86, 0.88 and 0.89. For the MCT Questionnaire the median-category internal consistency was 0.82, and the $2\frac{1}{2}$-month retest reliability was 0.87. Some external validity data are available.

REFERENCES

Betz BJ, Thomas CB 1979 Individual temperament as a predictor of health or premature disease. Johns Hopkins Med J 144:81-89

Cameron JR 1977 Parental treatment, children's temperament and the risk of childhood behavioral problems. Am J Orthopsychiatry 47:568-576

Carey WB 1972 Clinical applications of infant temperament measurements. J Pediatr 81:823-828

Carey WB 1974 Night waking and temperament in infancy. J Pediatr 84:756-758

Carey WB 1981a The importance of temperament–environment interaction for child health and development. In: Lewis M, Rosenblum L (eds) The uncommon child. Plenum Press, New York

Carey WB 1981b Intervention strategies using temperament data. In: Brown CC (ed) Infants at risk. Johnson & Johnson, Piscataway, NJ [abbreviated version] 96-106

Carey WB 1982a Intervention strategies using temperament data. In: Brazelton TB, Lester BM (eds) Infants at risk: toward plasticity and intervention. Elsevier/North-Holland, Amsterdam [full text]

Carey WB 1982b The validity of temperament assessments. In: Brazelton TB, Als H (eds) Behavioral assessment of newborns and young infants. Erlbaum Associates, Hillsdale, NJ

Carey WB, McDevitt SC 1978a Revision of the Infant Temperament Questionnaire. Pediatrics 61:735-739

Carey WB, McDevitt SC 1978b Stability and change in individual temperament diagnoses from infancy to early childhood. J Am Acad Child Psychiatry 17:331-337

Carey WB, McDevitt SC 1980 Minimal brain dysfunction and hyperkinesis. A clinical viewpoint, Am J Dis Child 134:926-929

Carey WB, Fox M, McDevitt SC 1977 Temperament as a factor in early school adjustment. Pediatrics 60(Suppl):621-624

Carey WB, McDevitt SC, Baker D 1979 Differentiating minimal brain dysfunction and temperament. Dev Med Child Neurol 21:765-772

Chess S, Thomas A, Cameron M 1976 Temperament: its significance for school adjustment and academic achievement. NY Univ Educ Rev 7:24-29

Gordon EM, Thomas A 1967 Children's behavioral style and the teacher's appraisal of their intelligence. J Sch Psychol 5:292-300

Gordon T 1975 Parent effectiveness training: the tested new way to raise responsible children. Plume, New American Library, New York

Graham P, Rutter M, George S 1973 Temperament characteristics as predictors of behavior disorders in children. Am J Orthopsychiatry 43:328-339

Matheny AP Jr, Brown AM, Wilson RS 1971 Behavioral antecedents of accidental injuries in early childhood: A study of twins. J Pediatr 79:122-124

McDevitt SC, Carey WB 1978 The measurement of temperament in 3–7 year old children. J Child Psychol Psychiatry Allied Discip 19:245-253

McDevitt SC, Carey WB 1981 Stability of ratings vs perceptions of temperament from early infancy to 1–3 years. Am J Orthopsychiatry 51:342-345

McInerny TK, Chamberlin RW 1978 Is it feasible to identify infants who are at risk for later behavior problems? Clin Pediatr 17:233-238

Rapoport JL, Buchsbaum MS, Zahn TP, Weingortner H, Ludlow C, Mikkelsen EJ 1978 Dextro-amphetamine: cognitive and behavioral effects on normal prepubertal boys. Science (Wash DC) 199:560-563

Terestman N 1980 Mood quality and intensity in nursery school children as predictors of behavior disorder. Am J Orthopsychiatry 50:125-138

Thomas A, Chess S 1977 Temperament and development. Brunner/Mazel, New York

DISCUSSION

Torgersen: In a clinical setting it is extremely important to remember that a behaviour problem observed in one child can be entirely caused by family dynamics or the social situation of the child. To give parents advice on how to handle the child one therefore needs a very good method for measuring basic temperament. The advice might differ a great deal, depending on the reason for the behaviour problem.

Carey: I agree that one has to make that distinction. In the cases I was speaking of, I had the advantage of knowing the families already for some time. I could be fairly sure that the behaviour problem was not due primarily to the family dynamics.

Torgersen: But if temperamental questionnaires are to be commonly in use as a screening method for detecting difficult children, it is necessary to bear this point in mind.

Carey: If one sees the child for the first time when the behaviour problem is already established, then it becomes harder to disentangle the aetiological factors. The child's regular physician should be in an advantageous position for diagnosis.

McNeil: I don't intend to suggest that you should do anything differently, because you have a responsibility towards the parents, but does the degree of involvement that you have with these people, as their physician, have any effect on the stability of the temperament characteristics? After all, you give the parents feedback about their children and, naturally, you intervene to try to help them improve their interactions. I can think of ways that would increase and ways that would decrease stability as a result of the changes that you intentionally institute. It would not be sufficient to compare your patient sample with a sample in which you didn't intervene, because some of the possible effects would balance each other out, and the total level of stability wouldn't necessarily be higher or lower in your patients than in another sample.

Carey: That is a good question but I really don't know how to solve it.

Hsu: I work in a somewhat different setting from you, Dr Carey, as a consultant psychiatrist in a general hospital. About five years ago we started routinely to ask the mothers to fill out a questionnaire. We explain to each mother that this is just one of the many sets of information that the paediatrician would like about her child. We say nothing about temperament, or about any likely problems. Afterwards, however, if the child comes back with a problem, we do exactly what Dr Carey has described. For instance, a mother attempting to wean a child with 'withdrawal' and low 'adaptability' may have difficulty in introducing the child to new food. In such cases we tell the mother how to cope. So in a general hospital setting it is extremely useful to have the information routinely available in case it is needed.

Wolkind: It is difficult in clinical practice to know the relative weight to give to temperament and to other factors. I see a certain danger in obtaining questionnaire data routinely. Rejection of a child by a parent is not uncommon and, therefore, if one uses this simple screening method, which depends so much on the parent, it is easy to gloss over certain issues unless one also has a good knowledge of the family.

Carey: I agree that the questionnaire by itself is not enough for clinical management. It must be accompanied by appropriate interviewing and observations.

Thomas: The work of a clinician is often described as the work of a detective unravelling a puzzle and putting the clues together. This means that the important clues must be distinguished from the red herrings. One can identify when the parent's approach is wrong for a particular child, and one can explain the correct approach but, if the parent doesn't follow the advice, this already gives a clue about the family dynamics. For example, the mother of one highly distractible boy felt that he was out to provoke her because he always forgot to do what she wanted him to do. But we pointed out to her, from her own information given to us, that he also forgot to do things that he himself wanted to do, because he was distracted easily. This therefore had nothing to do with her. Despite our advice, the mother persisted in her attitude towards the boy, which helped us to identify that she herself had psychological problems of control and domination. This approach, rather than obscuring the issues of family dynamics, helps to clarify them.

Werry: I would like to raise the theoretical question of whether giving methylphenidate to children would or does alter their temperament. One could argue that if temperament is considered to be partly genetic or constitutional in origin, there is an implicit assumption that it has something to do with a level of physical organization. There should be potential here, particularly in view of recent developments in neurotransmitter physiology and psychopharmacology, to try to modify temperament clinically and also to explore some of the research directions suggested by Dr Berger (p 176).

Torgersen: Research on medicaments for modifying temperament is a very tricky area. I would say that the use of drugs to modify temperament is an example of misuse of the knowledge of temperamental individuality. We do not have methods for measuring any physiological correlates to a temperament trait. Even if genetic factors that influence temperamental behaviour can be detected, it is the social and situational influences that are obviously most important in clinical settings, and these aspects have to be studied when changes in behaviour are being looked for.

Werry: Exploratory studies of this type do not, of course, need to be done on human beings but can be done on animals, and initially the work could be concerned with neurotransmitters rather than genes.

Rutter: We need to distinguish between the use of stimulants, to treat a *disorder* that involves overactivity, and using them to treat a temperamental characteristic that is not part of a current disorder but is correlated with a *risk* of disorder later.

Werry: If temperamental characteristics are normally distributed, then at the extreme end of the distribution there could, in theory, be a form of temperamental deviation that is so extreme that it, *of itself*, constitutes a disorder. There is, after all, a rather nice distinction between temperament in children and the sort of behavioural and emotional problems that we are actually confronted with at the clinical level.

Graham: Our discussion about the use of drugs highlights the difficult problem in deciding where difficult temperament ends and pathological behaviour begins. Thus, attempts to alter 'temperament' with drugs may be regarded as unethical, but if the same problem is termed a 'behaviour disorder', there is less objection! If the problem is a semantic one, as I believe it often is in relation to the difficult child, then for the clinician who has a wider vocabulary there is really no ethical problem.

Carey: If a problem is called a disease, it seems ethical to treat it with medication but, if it is called an extreme of normal, such action is generally no longer viewed as ethical. But if poor attention is responsible for a significant learning handicap and can be modified by medication, without a major compromise being made, one could make a case for that being ethical.

Thomas: One can always make an ethical case for doing something that is beneficial. One would need drugs that are potent therapeutically and have minimal side-effects. Labelling a child as having a behaviour disorder carries, in itself, all kinds of unknown consequences. The problem of when extreme temperament becomes a behaviour disorder is analogous to the problem of dealing with high blood pressure, and is not really a semantic issue. In a clear-cut case of high blood pressure there is no question about the theapeutic approach, but at the extreme of the normal distribution curve, should one call it normal or hypertension? The same is true of the definition of mental retardation.

Carey: I might mention here that when I refer a child and a family to a child psychiatrist, I always tell him or her my diagnostic formulation. The problem is that this view is often turned around completely, and on the basis of less information than I have. (I refer patients in this way when the magnitude of the symptom or the interaction problem has reached a point where it is no longer appropriate for a paediatrician to act alone.)

Graham: I think we have run into a problem of the construction of shared frameworks of understanding. Dr Carey, as a primary care paediatrician, is involved at the beginning and he therefore helps to construct the framework of expectations that enables parents to understand their children's behaviour. He will sometimes be a potent influence, but sometimes he will have less influence, e.g. with parents who believe that they themselves produce their child's temperament. If he then refers to another physician who has a different framework both he and the parent are going to be disappointed. One cannot help somebody to understand a problem if they use a totally different framework from oneself. If I believe that a child's temperament is important in a given problem and I talk to parents who don't believe this, they are not convinced immediately. To influence someone else's framework of understanding one must form a relationship over quite a long period of time. So I am not surprised that referral can be a problem.

Carey: I should explain that Philadelphia is a major centre of family therapy, and many of the child psychiatrists are staunch advocates of family therapy and believe that practically all behavioural problems are due to family dynamics. It is sometimes difficult to find a child psychiatrist who thinks otherwise.

Temperament and minor physical anomalies

RICHARD Q. BELL and MARY F. WALDROP*

*Department of Psychology, University of Virginia, Charlottesville, Virginia 22901 and *Laboratory of Developmental Psychology, National Institute of Mental Health, National Institutes of Health, Bethesda, Maryland 20014, USA*

Abstract Minor physical anomalies (MPAs) are an index of deviant embryological development due to genetic defects or insults to the fetus. A brief 10-minute examination on an individual makes it possible to establish a count that shows highly stable individual differences from the newborn period up to age seven years, the latest age studied longitudinally. For males, high MPA counts in the newborn period have shown strong predictive relationships to preschool temperament factors such as short attention span, high activity level, and aggressive–impulsive behaviour. For females, high anomaly scores showed relationships to short attention span and to inhibition. Such findings are in contrast with inconsistent results from genetic studies and with infrequent, weak relationships of neonatal variables to later behaviour. These results from the Bethesda longitudinal study have been confirmed in most cases by several cross-sectional studies. Sex differences in behaviour, usually considered to result from differential sex-role training, disappear in preschool samples from which high MPA individuals have been removed, but are much more pronounced than usual in samples with high MPAs.

For the purpose of this paper temperament is defined as behaviour involving regulation of arousal, and its expression through qualities of emotion, that shows cross-time and situational predictability. This definition distinguishes the phenomenon from the larger field of personality, while retaining the key elements that appear in both older and current theories. Most current theories assume a basis in the biological nature of the individual, and this paper will present evidence for one such contribution, although such evidence is not considered essential. Experience could conceivably produce mechanisms of arousal and emotional expression that would yield predictability. Note that only *predictability* of behaviour, and not *consistency*, is postulated. A search for consistency assumes a mechanical, robot-like organism that does not differentiate between situations. Female preschoolers

1982 Temperamental differences in infants and young children. Pitman Books Ltd, London (Ciba Foundation symposium 89) p 206-220

change activity level between play settings more than males (C. Halverson, personal communication, 1973). The activity of females is transformed more than that of males but the transformation itself is predictable.

One further qualification is in order. A biological contributor to temperament is no longer seen as a cause of unchanging, unmodifiable behaviour. The biological contributor will produce different manifestations of behaviour at different times, but these manifestations will be products of how the biological factor interacts with environmental factors.

Reports from the Kauai studies (Werner et al 1971, Werner & Smith 1977) indicate that a biological factor (severe complications of pregnancy and delivery) interacted with socio-economic level to depress behaviour–development quotients at age two years, effects that vanished in favour of predominant socio-economic factors by age 10 years. Later, the biological factor returned to interact with environmental factors in affecting social adjustment during adolescence. Furthermore, our informal experience with preschoolers whose hyperactive behaviour showed a relationship to a biological contributor, as we shall discuss later, suggests that the behaviour manifestation is modifiable.

Problems of establishing a biological substrate

Goldsmith & Campos (1981) have reviewed genetic studies of early manifestations of temperament and they report finding inconsistent results, even when consideration is limited to studies using the same measurement system and the same behaviour. Order may emerge as genetic studies adjust to the likelihood of changes in longitudinal relations. At least heritability has repeatedly been found.

In contrast, few findings, most of which are not strong, arise from efforts to establish innate contributors to later behaviours by searching for characteristics shown by an infant before any substantial extrauterine behavioural interaction with family members has taken place. Our own efforts, and those of many others, show that links between neonatal behaviour and characteristics of later infancy or early childhood seem unlikely, unless investigators are willing to repeat their assessments of neonates may times in order to build up psychometric stability. Sameroff & Chandler (1975) have reviewed the published work indicating lack of stability of individual differences and sparsity of longitudinal results from a large number of studies that have used one of our most promising measurement systems, the Brazelton system.

The problems are not specific to this measurement system, as our monograph (Bell et al 1971) from the Bethesda longitudinal study has reported. We found very few longitudinal relations from the neonatal period in a variety of measurement approaches used in several other studies, and very few weak longitudinal relationships in our own data from the neonatal period to age $2\frac{1}{2}$ years. Only one of these findings has been replicated in later work or in other laboratories; this is related to temperament and was reported in a previous Ciba Foundation symposium (Bell 1975). Up to the first month, a slow low-magnitude reaction of the newborn to interruption of sucking is associated with a later low rate of smiling (when smiling is primarily under the control of sleep processes) but, beyond the third month, when the social smile is emerging, and at least up to the preschool period, there is an inversion, and the association is consistently found with various manifestations of positive emotional expression. The finding is enigmatic and did not appear in all efforts at replication, but emerged in four studies cited in the report. From the weak relationship it appears likely that many repetitions of the neonatal test over a period of several days would be needed to establish a strong and dependable relationship.

If it is so difficult to establish neonatal associations with temperament, why not wait until a little later in infancy, such as the third month, to assess innate factors? Unfortunately, there is now considerable evidence that the infant is modifiable by the third month. Continuities from the third month onwards may merely indicate continuity of child-rearing techniques, especially if our only means of assessing temperament is by parental report.

Indexing deviant embryological development

Fortunately, there is another approach to establishing congenital contributors. This consists in indexing effects of disorders in embryological development by counting minor physical anomalies. Here, however, we are indexing a possible congenital contributor, not an unchanging, unmodifiable behaviour.

Nature and origins of minor physical anomalies

Description of anomalies. There are 18 anomalies of head, hands and feet associated as a set with Down's syndrome. These are: head circumference beyond normal range; more than one hair whorl; fine electrostatically charged hair; epicanthus; hypertelorism; malformed ears; low-set ears; asymmetrical ears; soft pliable ears; no ear lobes; high-steepled palate; furrowed tongue; geographic (smooth–rough spotted) tongue; curved fifth finger; single palmar crease; wide gap between first and second toes; partial syndactylia of toes; and third toe longer than second. Most of the behavioural associations of those anomalies relevant to temperament were first established in data from the Bethesda longitudinal study (Waldrop et al 1968) though this work, and that of many others stimulated by it, has gone far beyond into other samples and into a wider age range.

Origins of anomalies. Most researchers in this area assume that the associations of minor physical anomalies (MPAs) with behaviour are due to some genetic defect or to a teratogenic factor that mimicks the defect phenotypically, which affects both the physical characteristics that are developing rapidly during early pregnancy and the central nervous processes that control arousal and self-regulation. There is evidence both for genetic defects and for insults during pregnancy which mimic these defects, but the evidence does not clearly rule out one or the other, and the definitive studies remain to be done. First of all, the association with Down's syndrome certainly indicates the likelihood of genetic defects, and the relationships between anomalies in parents and children (Firestone et al 1978, Oettinger et al 1979, Rapoport et al 1974) point in the same direction but do not rule out continuities in environmental factors. Similarly, the observations that MPAs are associated with maternal history of complications in pregnancy (Rapoport et al 1974), and that the number of MPAs is high in children whose mothers had rubella in pregnancy (Waldrop & Halverson 1971), point towards teratogenic factors. von Hilsheimer & Kurko (1979) cite the extensive work of W. A. Price indicating that MPAs are associated with a diet based on highly processed and preserved foods since, in island-living populations, long-term shifts between this and a more primitive diet were associated with changes in frequencies of anomalies in offspring. On the other hand, using a list of 87 anomalies, and not analysing separately for the set employed in most studies, one report (C. Blackard, K. Tennes, unpublished paper, 1981 Bienn Meet Soc Res Child Dev, Boston, Mass.) found no evidence that use of nicotine, marijuana, caffeine or alchol, within the ranges found in normal mothers, was associated with later MPAs in offspring. MPAs were associated with fetal distress during labour, frequency of caesarian sections, and with lower birthweight.

Whatever their origins, a hypothesis has been advanced of how MPAs operate to produce behavioural effects (C. Halverson, unpublished paper, 1981 Bienn Meet Soc Res Child Dev, Boston, Mass.) Halverson postulates that the factors which produce MPAs interact, in males, with fetal androgen, because fetal androgen present during prenatal development is considered to masculinize the nervous system of males; the behavioural derivatives of this masculinization—activity, aggressivity and impulsivity—are those behaviours that maximally differentiate males from females. Later in this paper we shall report some findings relevant to this hypothesis.

Technical data. Waldrop et al (1978) reviewed a number of facts of technical importance in the study of behavioural correlates of MPAs, while also reporting results from a longitudinal study on males. First of all, from the newborn period onwards, an MPA count can be established with a simple 10-minute examination, for which a manual is available. The training requires examining at least 50 normal individuals or 25 showing high counts (such as rubella cases) in order to become familiar with the appearance and range of some low-frequency anomalies. Although not as difficult, this training is similar to learning to do a neurological examination on infants. The average individual has three anomalies. An incidence of five or more (shown by 12% of the population) is usually associated statistically with an increase in frequency or intensity of related behaviour, and counts of 0 to 1 are associated with low frequency or intensity. Although individual MPAs change in nature with development, the count shows high stability of individual differences from the newborn period through ages one, two and three years and onwards up to seven years ($r > 0.80$). No racial differences between blacks and whites are found in frequency of any anomaly except for fine 'electric' hair and hypertelorism. The relationships of MPAs to behaviour are found within samples that are relatively homogenous with respect to social class, but children from lower-class homes have more MPAs then those from middle- or upper-class homes. MPAs are not associated with attractiveness. Associations are still present when behaviour is assessed completely independently of the MPAs. Most importantly, the number of MPAs is higher in a wide range of childhood behaviour disorders ranging from autism through learning disability to hyperactivity. Thus, a high number of MPAs is not specific to any one disorder, even though it is strongly associated with hyperactivity in males.

Relations of MPAs to temperament

Attention

In Rothbart & Derryberry's (1981) theory of temperament, the channelling or maintenance of attention is an aspect of self-regulation, along with alerting, orientation and detection. Thomas & Chess's (1977) list of behaviour dimensions also includes distractibility and attention span.

All relevant data to be summarized below come from the Bethesda longitudinal study. Results for males have been published (Waldrop et al 1978), but results for females have been reported previously only at a scientific meeting (M. F. Waldrop, unpublished paper, 1981 Ontario Conf Assoc Child Learn Disabil, Toronto), as a part of a general summary of current research on MPAs. Findings reported here on females are limited to those most relevant to temperament. The sample consisted of 23 males and 25 females examined by one of us for MPAs in the newborn period, and then followed up until age three years, when the children became part of a larger sample of 59 males and 60 females studied for four weeks when they attended a research nursery school in mixed-sex groups of five. Measures of play and social behaviour were based on time-sampling observation in three settings: indoor play, rest and outdoor play. In addition, behaviour measures were available from experimental settings that were designed to indicate competence and ability to cope with physical problems, and from teachers' ratings based on all three settings. The data were gathered in keeping with Epstein's (1980) call for more adequate behaviour aggregation, since the unusual sustained period of observation permitted attainment of not only high levels of observer agreement, but also selection of behaviours that showed stability over the course of the four weeks' attendance. Factors were analysed out of behaviours that showed similar loadings on two samples, thus providing measures of high summarizing power from factors that were very unlikely to be artifactual.

A factor summarizing 23 free-play observations that reflected different aspects of attention span (e.g. n play bouts; n different play categories; time spent in gross motor activity; time spent exploring for less than 10 s) correlated ($r = 0.57$) with the number of MPAs for males and ($r = 0.35$) for females, the direction of the relation indicating an association of short attention span with a high number of MPAs. The direction of this relationship has been confirmed in several cross-sectional samples, as well as on the larger samples of the present study that included preschoolers who were not studied at the newborn period. Furthermore, the magnitude of the relationship for males is noteworthy; it is rare for any measure of newborn characteristics to correlate significantly with later preschool behaviour, let alone above the $r = 0.30$ level (Bell et al 1971).

Activity

This dimension appears in conceptualizations of temperament by Thomas & Chess (1977) and Buss & Plomin (1975) and is relevant to the concept of reactivity in the formulations of Strelau (1975) concerning self-regulation. The latter formulations were an important source of the theory articulated by Rothbart & Derryberry (1981). Within the preschool period there is empirical support for a concept of general activity, in that it accounted for 48% of the variance in a representative set of all the measures (C. Halverson, unpublished paper, 1981 Bienn Meet Soc Res Child Dev, Boston, Mass.). However, three components appear to be much more meaningful: an aggressive–impulsive factor, representing poorly controlled behaviour; and two others representing much better modulated, but high-energy, behaviours—positive social interaction and assertive–busy play.

Another approach to activity is to take it literally as indicating physical activity, measure it mechanically (with small wrist-watches attached to various parts of the body and set to record movements rather than time), and then to determine the observation, rating and experimental measures to which it is related. The resulting list of correlates is similar to the aggressive–impulsive factor resulting from factor analysis of a representative set of all the preschool measures: counts of negative peer interaction in a rest-period room in which there were no toys, and in the playroom; instigation of peer conflict in all settings; ratings of negative peer interaction; induction of intervention; frenetic and impulsive behaviour; assertiveness; and nomadic play. Apparently, high levels of sheer physical activity are linked with the component of the general activity factor that subsumes poorly controlled rather than adequately modulated behaviour with peers. Since several previous cross-sectional studies indicated that the aggressive–impulsive factor based on mechanically recorded activity was associated with MPAs, it was justifiable to select this factor for a longitudinal test. Newborn MPAs correlated ($r = 0.51$) with the factor score for males, implying that aggressive–impulsive (and highly active) males in the preschool period manifested a high count of MPAs in the newborn period.

Prediction of combined attention and aggressive–impulsive scores

Since the attention and aggressive–impulsive factors are each components of clinical hyperactivity, and even on non-clinical cross-sectional samples have shown strong relations to MPAs, scores were computed to represent both factors and were correlated with MPAs assessed in the newborn period. The correlation coefficient was 0.67 for males. The relationship was neither significant nor appreciable for females. Even though the male sample studied at both the newborn and preschool period is small, it is of considerable interest that there was only one false positive in predicting preschool behaviour (standardized scores) from newborn characterization (also standardized scores).

(This false positive was only half a standard deviation from the average for the two preschool factors.) There were five false negatives. The findings mean that hyperactive boys may have had low newborn anomaly scores, but boys with high newborn anomaly scores were almost always seen as hyperactive at age 3. *Hyperactive*, in this non-clinical sample, means behaviours that would be seen as clinically hyperactive if they were more extreme.

Emotionality

One correlate of MPAs that is unique to females involves a longitudinal relationship that is only marginally significant, although cross-sectional studies confirm the association at a significant level. The preschool factor involved was based primarily on teachers' ratings. This factor, labelled 'inhibition', consisted in measures of unfriendliness, withdrawn behaviour, lack of involvement with peers, lack of excitability or expressiveness, low movement in space, low vigour, and low interest in shaking bells in an experimental procedure. This factor contains many elements that are clearly related to the mood dimension described in the work of Thomas & Chess (1977), the emotionality dimension in Buss & Plomin (1975), and to Rothbart & Derryberry's (1981) concept of emotion as one channel through which the dynamics of reactivity and self-regulation are expressed. On the small sample of 25 females followed from the newborn period, a high number of MPAs was associated with high inhibition ($r = 0.25$, $P < 0.10$) (M. E. Waldrop, unpublished paper, 1981 Ontario Conf Assoc Child Learn Disabil, Toronto).

Negative results

Are MPAs a touchstone for research studies, or a fountain-head of psychopathy? While the effort to index deviations in embryological development has borne fruit in a very large number of studies, there is no insurance that aspects of temperament, no matter how measured, will always show strong and consistent relations to MPAs. The relationships reported for the Bethesda longitudinal study in this paper were based on dependent variables involving four weeks of assessment. Epstein (1980) has documented the importance of repeating measurements over time and in the same settings, in order to overcome the problem of low replicability and low generalizability experienced in the social and behavioural sciences. Some of the few negative results that have been reported for MPAs involved brief half-day assessments of behaviour at ages one and two years, and teachers' single ratings on children from 69 different nursery schools at age three years. Sparse and weak relationships of newborn MPAs with later behaviour were found, though it was reported that mothers of one-year-olds with high MPAs rated the infants higher on irritability than did mothers of one-year-olds with low MPAs (Quinn et al 1977). Data from parental interviews indicated that children with high MPAs were seen as temperamentally difficult, a finding confirmed by direct observation (Burg et al 1978).

Sex differences and MPAs

C. Halverson's hypothesized relationship (unpublished paper, 1981 Bienn Meet Soc Res Child Dev, Boston, Mass.) between fetal androgen in males and factors producing MPAs in pregnancy has been mentioned already. The finding that led to this hypothesis came from the same longitudinal study of MPAs and preschool behaviour that we have discussed. Halverson found that sex differences in the general activity factor, as well as in its three components— aggressive–impulsive behaviour, positive peer interaction, and assertive busy-play behaviour—were striking in a subsample with high MPA counts, whereas these differences disappeared in the subsample with low MPAs. It is surprising that an index of deviant embryological development due to chromosome breakdown or to teratological insults to the fetus is so strongly associated with behaviours that are commonly ascribed to differential sex-role training. Halverson sees a need for studies of heritability of MPAs in monozygotic and dizygotic twins, and a contrast of heritability in males and females, in addition to controls for the effects of complications of pregnancy.

Precursors of short attention span

One of the most important aspects of self-regulation is span of attention, and we have already reported above that the higher the MPAs the shorter the attention span in both males and females. How does this aspect of temperament emerge in development, and how early? For several years our staff in the Bethesda longitudinal study have searched with little success for infant behavioural precursors of the preschool behaviours associated with MPAs. Without such precursors it is not possible to study the developmental course of behaviour from which these temperamental characteristics emerge. Aside from the few leads mentioned under the section on negative results (p 213), only an actuarial relationship exists between MPAs and behaviour prior to the early preschool period. Without a knowledge of developmental course, one cannot determine the optimal timing and the mode of intervention in children at risk of more extreme forms of behaviour, such as clinical hyperactivity. It is gratifying to report that in collaboration with Jerome Kagan, we obtained a lead from data on his longitudinal study in Boston (see Schexnider et al 1981). No data exist yet for the earliest period of infancy, but by age one year, males high in MPAs show a loss of attention (i.e. they habituate), more quickly than those with low MPAs, to the repeated presentation of visual stimuli (human and geometric forms) when the infants have been given prior tasks of a highly demanding nature. These infants also show deficits in short-term memory. When infants with high MPAs start afresh on such a task, they attend for a more sustained period (e.g. they habituate more slowly) than those with low MPAs.

REFERENCES

Bell RQ 1975 A congenital contribution to emotional response in early infancy and the preschool period. In: Parent–infant interaction. ASP (Elsevier/Excerpta Medica Amsterdam (Ciba Found Symp 33) p 201-212

Bell RQ, Weller GM, Waldrop MF 1971 Newborn and preschooler: organization of behavior and relations between periods. Monogr Soc Res Child Dev 36: Nos 1-2

Burg C, Hart D, Quinn P, Rapoport J 1978 Newborn minor physical anomalies and prediction of infant behavior. J Autism Child Schizophr 8:427-429

Buss AH, Plomin R 1975 A temperament theory of personality development. Wiley, New York

Epstein S 1980 The stability of behavior. II: Implications for psychological research. Am Psychol 35:790-806

Firestone P, Peters B, Riviere M, Knights RM 1978 Minor physical anomalies in hyperactive, retarded and normal children and their families. J Child Psychol Psychiatry Allied Discip 19:155-160

Goldsmith HH, Campos JJ 1981 Toward a theory of infant temperament. In: Emde RM, Harmon RJ (eds) Attachment and affiliative systems. Plenum Press, New York

Oettinger L, Evans H, Harris S 1979 Minor physical anomalies: a review with special reference to family incidence. Learn Disab: Audio J Cont Educ. Grune & Stratton, New York

Quinn P, Renfield M, Burg C, Rapoport J 1977 Minor physical anomalies: a newborn screening and one year follow-up. J Child Psychiat 16:662-669

Rapoport JL, Quinn PO, Lamprecht F 1974 Minor physical anomalies and plasma dopamine-β-hydroxylase activity in hyperactive boys. Am J Psychiatry 131:387-390

Rothbart MK, Derryberry D 1981 Theoretical issues in temperament. In: Lewis M, Taft L (eds) Developmental disabilities; theory, assessment and intervention. SP Medical and Scientific Books, New York

Sameroff AJ, Chandler MM 1975 Reproductive risk and the continuum of caretaking casualty. In: Horowitz FD, Hetherington M, Scarr-Salapatek G, Siegel G (eds) Review of child development research. University of Chicago Press, Chicago

Schexnider VYR, Bell RQ, Shebilske WL, Quinn P 1981 Habituation of visual attention in infants with minor physical anomalies. Child Dev 52:812-818

Strelau J 1975 Reactivity and activity style in selected occupations. Pol Psychol Bull 48:1184-1199

Thomas A, Chess S 1977 Temperament and development. Brunner/Mazel, New York

von Hilsheimer G, Kurko V 1979 Minor physical anomalies in exceptional children. J Learn Disabil 12:462-469

Waldrop MF, Halverson C 1971 Minor physical anomalies and hyperactive behavior in young children. Except Infant 2:343-380

Waldrop MF, Pedersen FA, Bell RQ 1968 Minor physical anomalies and behavior in preschool children. Child Dev 39:381-400

Waldrop MF, Bell RQ, McLaughlin B, Halverson CF Jr 1978 Newborn minor physical anomalies predict short attention span, peer aggression, and impulsivity at age 3. Science (Wash DC) 199:563-564

Werner EE, Smith RS 1977 Kauai's children come of age. University of Hawaii Press, Honolulu

Werner EE, Bierman JM, French EE 1971 The children of Kauai: a longitudinal study from the prenatal period to age ten. University of Hawaii Press, Honolulu

DISCUSSION

Carey: What are the teratogenic agents you mentioned that seem to affect the central nervous system in the first trimester?

Bell: Much of this information is in the paper by C. Blackard & K. Tennes (unpublished paper, 1981 Bienn Meet Soc Res Child Dev, Boston, Mass). Viruses are implicated. We also know that the fetal alcoholism syndrome produces these specific anomalies as well as others. However, alcohol consumption among the mothers entering hospital for delivery, in that metropolitan area, was not enough to produce the minor physical anomalies. Nor was drug use or smoking among the mothers within a dangerous range. The agents must therefore be used at a high level.

Plomin: Did they look at the age of the mother as a risk factor?

Bell: Blackard & Tennes did not mention relationship to the mother's age. I cannot recall any relevant findings from our own studies, but there should be a relationship to age because of its association with Down's syndrome.

Hsu: Has influenza during pregnancy been examined as a risk factor?

Bell: I have not seen any study of that. All in all, we know little about teratogenic agents, except that we have an idea of the range.

Carey: What effect does malnutrition have?

Bell: The range of nutrition of the subjects in our study is not wide enough to answer that.

Werry: You mentioned that Schexnider et al (1981) noted an increased rate of habituation with fatigue. This draws together some of the threads in Dr Berger's paper. He described Eysenck's concepts of extraversion, which relate to speed of habituation. Herb Quay (1979) described psychopathy as attention-seeking behaviour on the thesis that because of rapid habituation these people need to keep stimulating themselves. Somewhat analogously, Virginia Douglas (1974) has shown with hyperactive children that the effects of stimulant drugs are most marked when the child has started to fail. Thus, studies of hyperactivity (and the effects of stimulants) suggest that there may be some relationship between this childhood trait and later extraversion.

Bell: Yes. Incidentally, I thought it important to include the concept of regulation of arousal in a definition of temperament because the Virginia Douglas (1980) theory of hyperactivity suggests that the child's central problem is the maintenance of level of arousal. This explains why hyperactive children do surprisingly better in conditions where they have a lot of background stimulation. Returning to the findings of Schexnider et al (1981) on rate of habituation, the more rapid rate shown in the fatigue condition does not square with the published work that Michael Lewis (1975) has summarized on the slower habituation that takes place in the presence of brain pathology (e.g. in decorticate infants).

Werry: When hyperactive children are given stimulants, the rapid level of habituation is slowed though not in all cases (Sykes et al 1971, 1972). This is because hyperactivity is almost certainly heterogeneous aetiologically.

Robinson: Jenny Dennis (1979) showed that the outcome from neonatal fits was universally bad if the neonate had a number of minor physical anomalies. I am not sure whether these minor physical anomalies were the same as those that you described. In addition, it may be wrong to consider that these anomalies are necessarily genetic because they are related to male sex. Perhaps the male fetus is simply more vulnerable to whatever interventions cause the anomalies, so that the normal chromosomal transcription processes are disrupted in some way.

Bell: I don't think that suggestion, by itself, explains the particular pattern of the sex differences—i.e. the aggressive and impulsive behaviours that reveal sex differences, according to C. F. Halverson's work (unpublished paper, 1981 Bienn Meet Soc Res Child Dev, Boston, Mass), to which we referred in our paper. Males are more vulnerable to complications of pregnancy and delivery, but without Halverson's hypothesis we would not have an explanation of how this vulnerability is related to the pattern of sex differences in preschool behaviour.

Robinson: Well, perhaps the intervention that causes the visible minor physical anomalies also affects the more vulnerable male fetal central nervous system, so producing this characteristic behaviour subsequently.

Graham: Perhaps the teratogenic agent is linked with some environmental phenomenon present in one society and not in another. It would be interesting to know the frequency of anomalies in different settings. This poses a challenge to epidemiologists.

Bell: In our paper we mentioned the summary of Price's work by von Hilsheimer & Kurko (1979). Price recorded his observations on anomalies of the skull in populations subjected to military occupation and to consequent changes of diet. He recorded details from various generations—before, during and after the change and restoration of diet. He found a different number of anomalies in these generations. The results suggested that the consumption of highly preserved and processed food increased the number of minor physical anomalies.

Rutter: In a clinic sample (Sandberg et al 1978) we found little association between hyperkinesis and minor physical anomalies, but this does not necessarily conflict with your results in that the non-hyperkinetic children had other forms of disordered conduct, whereas your categorization combined the aggressive/impulsive behaviour with the overactivity. Nevertheless, we found no difference between disorders that were and were not associated with hyperactivity. Similarly, Sandberg and her colleagues (1980) in their general population study (which would be more relevant to your findings) found little association between minor physical anomalies and hyperkinesis or conduct disturbance. Many children with high scores on minor physical anomalies showed no form of disorder. Presumably your 'no false positives' result has to take into account temperamental style as well as disorder: that is, some children with anomalies who showed no disorder had a hyperactive temperamental style.

Bell: One might think that if there is a small number of false positives, there can be no room for associations of anomalies with any other form of pathology. This could be confusing because minor physical anomalies are also related to learning disability, autism, and other behaviour disorders. However, autism is very uncommon and a substantial number of learning-disabled children are also hyperactive.

Plomin: We have been discussing teratogenic agents, but recent high-power banding techniques for chromosomes suggest that many essentially random, minor chromosomal abnormalities are common (Yunis 1976). It would be fascinating to correlate the extent, quantity and quality of minor chromosomal anomalies with the extent of minor physical anomalies. The physical anomalies could be indirect manifestations of minor chromosomal abnormalities, themselves the possible product of environmental teratogenic agents.

Bell: That work is certainly worth exploring in more detail.

Robinson: Those chromosomal abnormalities would have to be located on the Y-chromosomes, surely, to explain the sex difference?

Plomin: The sex differences in the normal dimensions of temperament are much over-rated (Plomin & Foch 1981), although there is a much greater incidence of males with psychopathology. Dr Bell, however, was dealing with the more normal dimensions of temperament.

Bell: Yes, results from the longitudinal study were based on a normal sample.

Wilson: You mentioned that the *number* of minor physical anomalies remains constant but their *nature* may change. What does this imply, in a developmental sense, about the underlying processes responsible for the anomalies at a given age?

Bell: Morphological development is the key here. A helpful example is the structural change in the nature of the palate during development. At some stages it cannot be used as an indicator. The structures have to reach a certain point of development before the anomalies can be identified. In cerebral palsy, similarly, the damage is possibly done during delivery but the effects are not apparent until age 2 or 3 years because motor performance has not developed sufficiently until then.

Carey: Every investigator uses a different definition of *hyperactivity*, so the data from one study can hardly be compared with those from another. This

word is used to mean practically anything. I think it should [   ]
better or abandoned (Carey & McDevitt 1980). How did j

Bell: First, it doesn't necessarily involve minimal brain d[   ]
clinical studies, the definition involves a deficit of attentioi
children, high activity and aggressive–impulsive behaviou
and throwing, and taking toys away from another child.

Carey: But these general impressions make it hard to apply the definition to different individuals clinically. When is it there, and when isn't it there?

Bell: There is a situational problem. Children are often placed in the hyperactive category because their *level of activity* is such that it begins to wear people out. This is because of the demands that the intense and frequently changing behaviour places on them.

Hsu: Do you have normative data on these components of the high-demand behaviour?

Bell: Yes, we have data on the distributions for normal approximations of these features. When we have used clinical samples we have taken whatever the clinical facility has provided.

REFERENCES

Carey WB, McDevitt SC 1980 Minimal brain dysfunction and hyperkinesis. A clinical viewpoint. Am J Dis Child 134:926-929

Dennis J 1979 The implications of neonatal seizures. In: Korobkin R, Guilleminault C (eds) Advances in perinatal neurology. SP Medical and Scientific Books, New York, vol 1:205-224

Douglas V 1974 Differences between normal and hyperkinetic children. In: Conners C (ed) Clinical use of stimulant drugs in children. Assoc Sci Pub (Elsevier/North Holland) Amsterdam

Douglas VI 1980 Higher mental processes in hyperactive children: implications for training. In: Knights RM, Backer DJ (eds) Treatment of hyperactive and learning disordered children. University Park Press, Baltimore

Lewis M 1975 The development of attention and perception in the infant and young child. In: Cruickshank WM, Hallahan D (eds) Perceptual and learning disabilities in children. Vol 2 Research and theory. Syracuse University Press, Syracuse, New York

Plomin R, Foch TT 1981 Sex differences and individual differences. Child Dev 52:383-385

Quay HC 1979 Classification. In: Quay HC, Werry JS (eds) Psychopathological disorders of childhood, 2nd edn. Wiley, New York

Sandberg ST, Rutter M, Taylor E 1978 Hyperkinetic disorder in clinic attenders. Dev Med Child Neurol 20:279-299

Sandberg ST, Wieselberg M, Shaffer D 1980 Hyperkinetic and conduct problem children in a primary school population: some epidemiological considerations. J Child Psychol Psychiatry Allied Discip 21:293-311

Schexnider VYR, Bell RQ, Shebilske WL, Quinn P 1981 Habituation of visual attention in infants with minor physical anomalies. Child Dev 52:812-818

Sykes D, Douglas V, Weiss G, Minde K 1971 Attention in hyperactive children and the effect of methylphenidate (Ritalin). J Child Psychol Psychiatry Allied Discip 12:129-139

Sykes DH, Douglas VI, Morgenstern G 1972 The effect of methylphenidate (Ritalin) on sustained attention in hyperactive children. Psychopharmacologia 25:262-274

von Hilsheimer G, Kurko V 1979 Minor physical anomalies in exceptional children. J Learn Disabil 12:462-469

Yunis JJ 1976 High resolution of human chromosomes. Science (Wash DC) 191:1268

Infant temperament, maternal mental state and child behaviour problems

S. N. WOLKIND and W. DE SALIS

The Family Research Unit, The London Hospital Medical College, Turner Street, London E1 2AD, UK

Abstract In a longitudinal study of firstborn children, interview-based measures of temperament were obtained when the infants were aged four months. From the individual items an 'easy–difficult' scale was constructed. The scale showed a fair internal consistency and reasonable test/retest reliability, and the obtained scores appeared to be independent of previous and current maternal attitudes and mental state. A wide range of scores was obtained. Four-month temperament, as reflected on this scale, related to the presence of behavioural problems when the children were aged 42 months, with 'difficult' children developing higher rates of problems. Problems at 42 months also related strongly to the mother's mental state *at that time*, with the children of depressed mothers showing more problems. When all three items—four-month temperament, 42-month behavioural problems and 42-month maternal depression—were examined, a strong interaction effect was found. Maternal depression was associated with behavioural problems only if the child had been in the extreme quartiles on the temperament measure. Some evidence suggested that an infant's temperament could affect its mother's later mental state.

The need to understand how a child's personal traits or temperament contribute to the development of behavioural difficulties has been stressed by clinicians from the very earliest days of child psychiatry (Miller 1933). The first major research effort relevant to this question was that of Thomas et al (1963) who described how 'they had become increasingly impressed with the contribution made to behavioural development by reactive characteristics of the child'. They added that 'an *exclusive* concern with environmental influences could not explain the range and variability in developmental course exhibited by individual children'. They found relatively persistent differences in temperament (or the 'how' of behaviour) amongst a group of children whom they followed up longitudinally. The general importance of individual differences during childhood has been strongly supported by work in related

1982 Temperamental differences in infants and young children. Pitman Books Ltd, London (Ciba Foundation symposium 89) p 221-239

areas. Laboratory studies have demonstrated persisting variation in reactivity in neonates (e.g. Birns 1965) and observational investigations have shown how, in infant–caretaker interaction, the infant can influence the amount, timing and quality of that interaction (e.g. Bell 1971).

The concept of temperament has been increasingly accepted as useful within child psychiatry. It provides a tool that can explore the often seen phenomenon whereby different children can easily, or only with difficulty, cope with the same situation (Wolff 1969, Rutter 1975). Even more important, however, is the fact that in a number of systematic studies *early* temperament has been found to relate to the *later* development of behavioural problems (Thomas et al 1968, Graham et al 1973, Maurer et al 1980). Most workers are cautious about the origins of temperamental differences, but some evidence implicates a genetic component (Torgersen & Kringlen 1978). It has never been suggested that a 'difficult' temperament will in itself cause a behavioural disturbance, but that problems may arise when a child with this characteristic is mishandled or confronted by stress. One analogy has been that of the temperamental contribution as a 'fault line' and of the family or other stress as the 'strain'. Both are needed to produce the behavioural difficulty, or earthquake (Cameron 1977).

Such a model is attractive, but the data supporting it are limited. Work in this field raises many methodological problems. Vaughn et al (1980) showed how infant temperament could be predicted from maternal attitudes during pregnancy. This raises the possibility that the association between temperament and behaviour problems is an artifact. Parents with continuing adverse attitudes could perceive an average infant as 'difficult' and could also use child-rearing practices that eventually produce problems. If this is not so, and if certain measures of temperament are truly reflecting, at least partially, infant differences, there are various explanations. Perhaps certain children are, because of their temperament, vulnerable to stress that is randomly present in the environment or perhaps a child's temperament will actually help to produce the type of stress that will, in turn, affect the child.

In a study of first children born to a randomly selected sample of mothers from a predominantly working-class inner-city area, we found an association between a measure of infant temperament at four months and behavioural difficulties at 42 months. This association is presented here, and is used to examine the issues mentioned above.

The study

The sample

During 1974 all British-born primiparous women attending the antenatal booking clinics serving a deprived inner London borough were contacted and screened for possible inclusion in a longitudinal study of them and their children. The 534 women seen represented 97% of all eligible women. Amongst the groups selected were random samples of married and single women (Wolkind & Zajicek 1981). Part of the single group, randomly chosen, was added to the married group to give a sample of women representative of the population as a whole. The results presented here were obtained from this true random sample.

Methods

Mothers were seen in late pregnancy and at four, 14, 27 and 42 months after the birth of their child. Mothers were never seen consecutively, and were seen only rarely more than once, by the same interviewer. At all stages maternal attitudes and child-rearing practices were assessed using semistructured interviews. All such items used had at least 85% inter-rater reliability. For the children, a measure of temperament was obtained at four months (described in more detail below) and a measure of behavioural difficulties at 42 months (Richman & Graham 1971). At each stage of the study the mother's mental state was assessed with a systematic and standardized examination of mental state. In 29 cases the mothers were given an entire interview four months after the birth of both their first and second babies.

The measure of temperament

The original work of Thomas et al (1963) used measures of temperament based on a content analysis of detailed interviews with mothers, who were asked to describe their infants' reactions to a variety of situations, e.g. during a feed and at bath time. The descriptions were then rated, to obtain measures of how each child reacted in these different settings. This procedure has been simplified by Carey (1970) who converted the interview into a 70-item self-rating questionnaire for mothers. With women from the district in which our study was taking place, pilot work demonstrated that many had difficulties with this instrument. We decided, therefore, to insert items from the questionnaire into the detailed semi-structured interviews, questioning the mother systematically until the interviewer felt that he or she had sufficient information to rate the child's reaction. As an example, in the assessment by the mother about the child's regularity in requiring a feed she was asked 'How regular has he/she been in his/her being ready for a feed?'. To give the mother a focus she was asked initially to consider the first feed of the day over the past week and then other feeds. It was then determined whether those seven days had been typical of the previous four weeks. On the basis of this detailed questioning the reply was rated as:

(1) Generally ready for a feed at the same time. Not over one hour variation. (Regular.)

(2) Sometimes the same, sometimes different times. (Intermediate.)

(3) Hungry times quite unpredictable. (Irregular.)

It could be argued that the essence of temperament is a child's 'usual' behaviour and that our study should not have been so focused on a particular period of time. In fact, of course, four weeks represented 25% of the child's life to that time.

All interviews were tape-recorded and this information showed that inter-rater reliability for individual items was high: in all cases it was over 85%, and usually it was over 90%. We decided not to include all 70 items from the Carey questionnaire and only 40 were retained. The major reasons for excluding individual items were:

(a) Some described situations not experienced by a substantial proportion of infants in the previous four weeks, e.g. reaction to the doctor; and

(b) for some questions a number of mothers found difficult in answering, e.g. estimating the strength of suck during feeding.

Results

On the 131 families in the random sample, seven were excluded from the study by the 42-month stage because of stillbirth, death of the child and, in one case, death of the mother. Of the remaining 124, 106 (85%) mothers were successfully interviewed at both four and 42 months after the birth of the child.

The dimensions of temperament

Both Thomas et al (1963) and Carey (1970) used nine dimensions of temperament (activity, rhythmicity, approach, adaptability, intensity, threshold, mood, distractibility and persistence). Since only 40 questions were used in our study it is perhaps not surprising that we found little evidence for the nine dimensions. We also noted, however, that where several questions were apparently aimed at eliciting the same characteristic there was often little support for a particular dimension. As an example,

rhythmicity in timing of bowel movements correlated negatively with rhythmicity of feeds and waking. Many items appeared to be totally unrelated to
any others. However, from a correlation matrix of the 40 individual items,
two distinct clusters were noted. Using these clusters, we drew up two scales
and obtained a standardized item alpha reliability coefficient for each (Specht
& Hohlen 1976). Table 1 shows the items with, in parentheses, the direction

TABLE 1 Items in scales 1 and 2 for assessment of temperament at four months of age

Scale 1	Scale 2
(1) Hunger cry (intense)[a]	(1) Threshold to wet nappy (high)[a]
(2) Amount of food taken (irregular)	(2) Activity on nappy change (low)
(3) Time of feeding (irregular)	(3) Activity in bath (low)
(4) Time of sleeping (irregular)	(4) Activity during sleep (low)
(5) Time of washing (irregular)	(5) Activity when playing (low)
(6) Persistence at play (poor)	(6) Threshold to soiled nappy (high)
(7) Distractibility when hungry (poor)	(7) Threshold to light and sound (high)
(8) Mood when food interrupted (negative)	
(9) Mood when wet (negative)	
(10) Mood when soiled (negative)	
(11) Mood when nappy being changed (negative)	
(12) Mood when hair being washed (negative)	
(13) Mood on being put to bed (negative)	
Standardized item alpha 0.68	Standardized item alpha 0.54
Mean score 22.68 ± 4.19[b]	Mean score 11.58 ± 2.67[b]
Range of scores 13–33	Range of scores 7–19
Boys' mean score 22.48	Boys' mean score 11.71
Girls' mean score 22.75	Girls' mean score 11.48

[a] Brackets contain the aspect of each item that scored highly. [b] Standard deviation.

of each reply that contributed to a high score; the alpha values, mean scores,
range and standard deviation are also shown. For four children, insufficient
questions had been answered to permit scale 1 to be constructed.

The alpha values suggested that each scale had sufficient internal consistency to be useful. On each scale there were no sex differences in mean
score. The scales 1 and 2 were not totally independent and a significant
($P<0.05$) but weak correlation of -0.2 (Pearson) was found between them.

In a pilot study 20 mothers were given the full interview on two occasions
separated by an interval of three to six weeks. The interviews were done by
different research workers. Scales 1 and 2 were constructed from each

interview, and Spearman rank-order correlations were done. For scale 1 this was 0.60 ($P<0.01$) and for scale 2, 0.92 ($P<0.001$).

Four-month temperament and forty-two-month behavioural difficulties

For further analysis of temperament the children were grouped on each scale according to quartile position, the two extreme quartiles being kept separate and the two middle quartiles being combined. Forty-two month behavioural difficulties were measured on the Behavioural Screening Questionnaire (BSQ) (Richman & Graham 1971). We obtained a score from an interview with the mother by adding a rating given for the absence (0), or presence in mild (1) or severe form (2), of 13 items of behaviour which caused difficulties or concern, e.g. sleep disorder, temper tantrums. Richman et al (1975) have suggested that children with scores of 10 or more on the BSQ are likely to be showing signs of a definite behaviour disorder. Table 2 shows the mean BSQ scores for the children in the quartile groupings on scales 1 and 2.

TABLE 2 Scores on the Behavioural Screening Questionnaire (BSQ) at 42 months for children in different quartiles of scales 1 and 2 at the four-month temperament assessment

Scale in the four-month temperament assessment	Mean BSQ scores at 42 months[a] Low quartile[b]		Middle two quartiles[b]		High quartile[b]	
Scale 1	5.33	(24)[c]	6.35	(54)	7.72	(24)[d]
Scale 2	6.57	(30)	6.29	(50)	6.14	(26)[e]

[a] SD = 3.197. [b] Quartiles of the scores in the four-month temperament assessment. [c] n values in brackets. [d] Scale 1, F (variance) ratio = 3.56; degrees of freedom 2/101; $P<0.05$. [e] Scale 2, F ratio = 0.13; degrees of freedom 2/105; $P>0.1$.

There was no association between quartile position on scale 2 and the 42-month score. Scale 2, predominantly a measure of activity, will not be considered further in this paper. Scale 1 was related significantly to the BSQ score. This scale appears from Table 1 to be predominantly a measure of mood and regularity. In further discussions the infants in the high-score quartile will be referred to as Negative Mood/Irregular, and those in the low-score quartile as Good Mood/Regular.

Before looking for possible mechanisms behind this association, we decided to examine whether the score in scale 1 related to any particular items of behaviour at 42 months. A score of 2 (indicating a severe problem) was uncommon for most items whereas a score of 1 (a mild problem) was extremely common. In Table 3 items of any degree of severity have been used. Soiling, which occurred only rarely, has been omitted from Table 3. Items indicating day or night wetting, which did not contribute to the total score, have been included for interest.

TABLE 3 Percentages of children showing (mild or severe) features of each item in the 42-month behavioural assessment. The children are grouped into the quartiles for scale 1 at the four-month temperament assessment

42-month behaviour items	Four-month temperament quartiles			χ^{2a}	τ c
	Good Mood/Regular (n = 24)	Middle two quartiles (n = 54)	Negative Mood/Irregular (n = 24)		
Poor appetite	40%	54%	62%	2.44	0.16
Food fads	36%	45%	62%	3.54	0.19*
Sleep problems	44%	56%	73%	4.48	0.21*
Management problems	44%	70%	73%	6.07*	0.21*
Temper tantrums	40%	61%	69%	4.48	0.21*
Dependency	56%	57%	69%	0.56	0.09
Mood	36%	46%	46%	0.83	0.07
Worrying	44%	45%	44%	0.02	0.01
Activity	72%	78%	72%	3.09	0.01
Concentration	18%	23%	31%	4.64	0.14
Fears	56%	53%	58%	0.4	0.01
Relationship with peers/siblings	76%	52%	72%	4.86	0.01
Day wetting	4%	0%	23%	8.24*	0.07
Night wetting	15%	7%	25%	4.57	0.08

* $P<0.05$. [a] Degrees of freedom: 2.

Management problems were significantly less common in the Good Mood/ Regular group, and day wetting was significantly more common in the Negative Mood/Irregular group. A number of other items—food fads, sleeping problems and temper tantrums (and to a lesser extent poor appetite and poor concentration)—showed trends over the three groups, with the Negative Mood/Irregular group showing in all cases the highest rate of problems. Emotional items—fears, poor mood and worries—were not related to the measure of temperament.

Maternal characteristics that could influence the perception of child temperament

In looking for potentially biasing maternal characteristics we felt that the mother's mental state at the time she was asked about her child's temperament was the most important. This, plus the mothers' mental state during pregnancy, whether or not she was a teenage mother, and a number of items measuring her attitude to pregnancy and child-rearing taken from the pregnancy interview, are examined in relation to the child's temperament in

Table 4. In addition, two pre-pregnancy measures, thought to be of potential importance to mothering, are also included: pre-pregnancy psychiatric difficulties and a disrupted family of origin (see Wolkind et al 1977).

TABLE 4 Numbers of children in each temperament quartile (at four months) whose mothers showed particular characteristics and attitudes at various times

	Four-month temperament quartiles			
Maternal characteristics	Good Mood/Regular (n = 24)	Middle two quartiles (n = 54)	Negative Mood/Irregular (n = 24)	χ^{2a}
Pre-pregnancy measures				
'Disrupted' family of origin	8 (33%)[b]	14 (27%)[b]	7 (29%)[b]	0.46
Psychiatric difficulties	0 (0%)	4 (7%)	6 (25%)	6.68*
Pregnancy measures				
Mother teenager at birth	8 (33%)	16 (33%)	8 (33%)	0.16
Psychiatric disorder	5 (21%)	14 (27%)	7 (29%)	0.45
Planned pregnancy	14 (58%)	33 (61%)	13 (54%)	0.33
Positive about being pregnant	16 (67%)	39 (72%)	15 (63%)	0.79
Resents restriction of pregnancy	6 (25%)	13 (24%)	5 (21%)	0.13
Fearful of labour	1 (4%)	9 (17%)	4 (17%)	2.42
Worried about child care	13 (54%)	26 (48%)	14 (58%)	0.75
Intending to breast feed	14 (58%)	27 (50%)	11 (46%)	0.79
Concern over getting up at night for baby	7 (29%)	11 (20%)	5 (21%)	0.79
Believes children should never be left to cry	6 (25%)	14 (27%)	9 (38%)	1.28
Effect on life of motherhood will be definitely positive	13 (54%)	26 (48%)	12 (50%)	0.24
4 months post partum				
Psychiatric disorder	7 (29%)	17 (31%)	9 (37%)	0.42

*$P<0.05$; [a] Degrees of freedom: 2. [b] Percentages of children in that temperament quartile.

Psychiatric disorder during pregnancy and at four months post partum, whether the mother was a teenager, pregnancy attitudes and disrupted family of origin were unrelated to the description given by the mother of her infant's temperament at four months. Women with a pre-pregnancy psychiatric history were more likely to have a child in the Negative Mood/Irregular group. The effect of this on the results will be discussed later.

A further biasing factor could be the mother's degree of confidence in her child-rearing abilities, with a confident mother seeing her child as 'easy' irrespective of its temperament, and vice versa. A problem in assessing whether this does happen is that a 'difficult' child could rapidly undermine a mother's confidence. It was possible, however, to examine this issue through investigation of the second child born to some of the mothers in the study. In these 29 cases the mother was given the identical interview, including questions on attitudes, child-rearing and the child's temperament, four months after the birth of her second child.

The general picture obtained from this second interview was that the mothers had fewer difficulties and were more at ease than they had been after the birth of the first child (see Table 5). Despite these differences in

TABLE 5 Sleep pattern and mothers' handling of first and second babies at age four months

Measured item	First child[a]	Second child[a]	χ^{2b}
Professional advice needed for feeding child	8	3	2.80
'Flexible' feeding schedule	7	18	8.51**
'Flexible' nappy schedule	11	19	4.23*
Baby sleeping full night before eight weeks	11	21	7.01**
Worries over bathing baby	6	0	$P = 0.02^c$

[a]29 pairs of siblings. [b]Degrees of freedom = 1. [c]Fisher exact probability test. *$P<0.05$. **$p<0.01$.

experience and handling there was no tendency for mothers to rate their second child as more regular or as having a better mood than the first child. The mean score on scale 1 for the first child in the group was 22.66, and for the second child, 23.07. Two sets of siblings had scores equal to each other; in 14 cases the second baby had a higher score and in 13 a lower score. There was no evidence to suggest 'sexual stereotyping' with, for example, the mothers seeing boys as less easy than girls. If the first child was a boy and the second a girl ($n = 8$) the mean scores were respectively 23.13 and 21.88, with only minimally lower scores for the girls. For the reverse case (first child a girl, second a boy; $n = 6$) the scores were 22.00 and 25.00. This difference was non-significant and was largely accounted for by one second child having a very much higher score than his older sister. In only three cases out of the six was the change in this direction.

Temperament, stress and behavioural problems

In the search for a stress at 42 months that might be acting in conjuction with a child's temperament to produce behavioural problems, our most obvious choice was maternal psychiatric disorder at 42 months.* In virtually all cases

---

* On the basis of the systematic examination mothers were rated as having: no disorder ($n = 65$); a disorder, but without impairment of daily functioning ($n = 12$); or a disorder accompanied by definite impairment ($n = 25$). For this analysis women with any degree of disorder are combined together to provide a 'psychiatric' group.

the maternal disorder was one of depression, usually with associated anxiety. In our study current maternal depression has proved to related strongly to child behavioural difficulties. In Table 6 the mean 42-month BSQ score of the

TABLE 6 Child scores at 42 months on the behavioural screening questionnaire (BSQ) in relation to maternal depression at 42 months and child temperament at four months

	Four-month temperament quartiles (n)			
	Good Mood/Regular (24)	Middle two quartiles (54)	Negative Mood/Irregular (24)	All (102)
No Maternal depression at 42 months				
Mean BSQ score (n)	4.412 (19)	6.230 (34)	5.742 (12)	5.608 (65)
n with score >10[a]	(1)	(6)	(0)	(7)
Maternal depression at 42 months				
Mean BSQ score	8.800 (5)	6.564 (20)	9.689 (12)	7.879 (37)
n with score >10[a]	(2)	(1)	(8)	(11)
Overall mean score	5.326	6.353	7.716	

[a] A score of 10 or more is the cut-off point on the BSQ.

Analysis of Variance (see Nie et al 1975): *Grand mean* = 6.43; s^2 (variance estimate) = 10.22.

Degrees of freedom			
3	Main effects	$F = 5.47$	$P = 0.001$
2	Temperament	$F = 2.33$	$P > 0.1$
1	42-month psychiatric state	$F = 11.01$	$P = 0.001$
2	Interaction between the above two factors	$F = 4.87$	$P = 0.01$

children is given according to their mothers' mental state at that time *and* to their original temperamental group. A number of significant differences between various groups is shown in Table 6. Within the Negative Mood/ Irregular and Good Mood/Regular groups, children with depressed mothers had significanctly higher scores than children whose mothers were not depressed ($P<0.001$). There was no association between maternal depression and child behaviour in the middle two quartiles ($P>0.1$). The children in the Good Mood/Regular group with non-depressed mothers had significantly lower scores than the remaining children with non-depressed mothers ($P<0.1$). For depressed mothers, the mean score of the Negative Mood/ Irregular children was higher than that of the middle group ($P<0.02$). The difference between this latter group and the Good Mood/Regular children with depressed mothers was not significant ($P>0.1$). Over 40% of the children who scored 10 or more on the BSQ came from the 12% of children with both a Negative Mood/Irregular temperament and a depressed mother.

Mothers' pre-pregnancy psychiatric illness

It was shown earlier (Table 4) that the one possibly biasing maternal variable relating to a child's temperament was psychiatric difficulties prior to the mother's pregnancy. This factor also related to psychiatric disorder at 42 months and to the BSQ score. The analysis of variance was therefore repeated, to exclude the 10 women with such a history. Current psychiatric state remained significantly related to the child's behaviour, at $P<0.01$; temperament alone was non-significant ($P>0.1$); but the interaction effect remained significant, at $P<0.05$. With this group of 92, we found that five of the seven Negative Mood/Irregular children with a depressed mother scored at or above the cut-off point of 10 on the behavioural scale, as opposed to only nine of the remaining 85 children ($P = 0.001$; Fisher exact probability test). In an analysis of the individual behavioural items for the 92 cases, we found an almost identical pattern as previously found (Table 2) when the 10 women were included.

Effects on mothers of infant temperamental characteristics

During the interview at four months, mothers were also asked about the effects on them of looking after their child and, in particular, about their physical and emotional tiredness (two separate questions).

Emotional tiredness at four months was unrelated to child temperament at four months (see Table 7) but women with Negative Mood/Irregular children

TABLE 7 Numbers of children in each temperament quartile (at four months) whose mothers showed tiredness at four months or depression at 14 months

Maternal characteristics	Four-month temperament quartiles			
	Good Mood/Regular	Middle two quartiles	Negative Mood/Irregular	χ^{2a}
Four-month tiredness[b]				
Physical	7/25 (28%)	16/62 (26%)	16/29 (55%)	8.09 ($P<0.05$)
Emotional	6/25 (24%)	19/62 (31%)	9/28 (32%)	0.50 (N/S)
14-month maternal depression[c]	0/18 (0%)	5/37 (13%)	5/14 (31%)	8.17 ($P<0.05$)

[a] Degrees of freedom: 2. [b] Includes 14 women interviewed at four months but not at 42 months post partum. [c] Includes only those mothers free of depression at four months.

were significantly more likely to report physical tiredness than women with children in the other three quartiles. To examine whether the temperament of the infants could have lasting effects on their mothers, we examined mental state at the 14-month interview, for the women who had had no disorder at four months. As shown in Table 7, women with Negative Mood/Irregular babies were more likely than the remainder to have developed a disorder during the intervening 10 months.

Discussion

The easy–difficult scale of temperament used in this study can be seen as a relatively crude instrument based, as it is, on only 13 individual items. It does, however, have sufficient internal validity and retest reliability to suggest that it is a useful measure. We obtained a wide range of scores in a random sample of healthy infants from a deprived area. When one considers the items that comprise the scale, it is clear that children at each end of the scale could have a very different impact on those caring for them.

An important question that we have examined is the extent to which an infant's score on the scale represents not his or her temperament but the attitude and feelings of the mother. The item used to illustrate the method of questioning, regularity of hunger, demonstrates how a measure based on interviews with mothers must reflect some aspects of her personality, behaviour and attitudes as well as the temperament of her baby. Some mothers may never have allowed an infant to show any innate regularity or irregularity of hunger pattern. They may have totally imposed their own pattern on the child. Despite this possibility, the findings presented here from the studies of both first and second babies do suggest that the temperament scores are relatively independent of maternal attitude. Of particular importance is the fact that the mother's mental state at the time of questioning does not seem to have biased her description of her baby. It may be that in measurement of temperament the method of obtaining data is important. The self-rating questionnaire used by Vaughn et al (1980) may be more liable to tap maternal attitude than will a method based on obtaining detailed descriptions of the infant's reactions and behaviour. The one maternal characteristic in this study relating to infant temperament is the presence of a pre-pregnancy psychiatric disorder. This is puzzling: it does not seem to be acting through the mother's mental state after the birth of the child, and the basic pattern of results is consistent even when mothers with such disorders are excluded. It is possible at this stage only to speculate on the nature of this association.

The overall findings do seem to support a 'stress/fault line' model (Cameron 1977) with, in this study, temperament as the fault line and current maternal psychiatric disorder as the stress. What is particularly interesting is that this study has identified a large group of children—in the two middle quartiles—whose behaviour at 42 months seems strikingly unaffected by depression in their mothers. The very similar patterns found for the Negative Mood/Irregular and for the Good Mood/Regular children indicate that the scale may not be measuring a linear dimension of easy–difficult temperament. Perhaps each end of the scale represents a normal variation in temperament that can, possibly in different ways, leave a child more vulnerable to the effects of later stress.

The findings presented in Table 7 suggest that one group of children—those at the Negative Mood/Irregular end of the scale—make their own contribution to the environmental stress that may, in turn, affect them later. Their mothers are more likely to be tired, specifically in a physical and not an emotional capacity. This, and a possible loss of self-esteem caused by problems in looking after a 'difficult' baby, could well contribute to the development of a psychiatric disorder during the following year. The findings lend support to a transactional model of development, with patterns of mutual influence between child and caretaker leading to the eventual outcome. This model must, however, be seen as taking place in a much wider context, and not as suggesting a mother and child locked together isolated from the rest of their family and society. Depression in mothers, for example, will affect and be affected by many other family characteristics, not the least of which will be the quality of the parents' marriage.

These results suggest the possibility of techniques of intervention. These could be designed to try to prevent the establishment of mutually reinforcing maladaptive behaviour patterns on the part of parents and children. Before this is contemplated, however, far more needs to be known about how both mother and father cope with children at each end of the temperamental scale and, in particular, whether certain types of handling can lead to an apparently 'difficult' temperament emerging as a positive attribute of a child. In addition, we need to know more about the basic nature of infant temperament. Is it a characteristic that shows a wide range of normal variation or are other factors involved? Even in a sample such as the one described in this paper, where severe handicapping disabilities were absent, could an extreme score at either or both ends of the scale be related to adverse circumstances at or before birth? Such questions clearly have both theoretical and clinical relevance.

Acknowledgements

The work reported in this paper was supported by generous grants from the Medical Research Council. The second-baby study was funded by a contract from the DHSS/SSRC programme on Transmitted Deprivation. We wish to thank our colleagues in the Family Research Unit for their many helpful comments on the draft.

REFERENCES

Bell RQ 1971 Stimulus control of parent or caretaker behaviour by offspring. Dev Psychol 4:63-72

Birns B 1965 Individual differences in human neonates' responses to stimulation. Child Dev 36:249-256

Cameron JR 1977 Parental treatment, children's temperament and the risk of childhood behavioural problems. Am J Orthopsychiatry 47:568-576

Carey WB 1970 A simplified method for measuring infant temperament. J Pediatr 77:188-194

Graham PJ, Rutter M, George S 1973 Temperamental characteristics as predictors of behavior disorders in children. Am J Orthopsychiatry 43:328-339

Maurer R, Cadoret RJ, Cain C 1980 Cluster analysis of childhood temperament data on adoptees. Am J Orthopsychiatry 50:522-534

Miller E 1933 Temperamental differences in the behaviour disorders of children. Br J Educ Psychol 24:222-236

Nie NH, Hadlai HC, Jenkins JG, Steinbrenner K, Bent DH 1975 SPSS—Statistical package for the social sciences, 2nd edn. McGraw Hill, New York

Richman N, Graham PJ 1971 A behavioural screening questionnaire for use with 3 year old children: preliminary findings. J Child Psychol Psychiatry Allied Discip 12:5-33

Richman N, Stevenson JE, Graham PJ 1975 Prevalence of behaviour problems in 3-year-old children: An epidemiological study in a London Borough. J Child Psychol Psychiatry Allied Discip 17:75-78

Rutter M 1975 Helping troubled children. Penguin, Harmondsworth

Specht DA, Hohlen M 1976 SPSS Reliability: subprogram for item and scale analysis. Vogelback Computing Center, Northwestern University, Illinois

Thomas A, Chess S, Birch HG, Hertzig ME, Korn S 1963 Behavioral individuality in early childhood. New York University Press, New York

Thomas A, Chess S, Birch HG 1968 Temperament and behavior disorders in children. New York University Press, New York

Torgersen AM, Kringlen E 1978 Genetic aspects of temperamental differences in infants. J Acad Child Psychiatry 17:434-444

Vaughn B, Deinard A, Egeland B 1980 Measuring temperament in pediatric practice. J Pediatr 96:510-514

Wolff S 1969 Children under stress. Penguin, Harmondsworth

Wolkind S, Zajicek E 1981 Pregnancy, a psychological and social study. Academic Press, London

Wolkind SN, Hall F, Pawlby S 1977 Individual differences in mothering behaviour: A combined epidemiological and observational approach. In: Graham PJ (ed) Epidemiological approaches in child psychiatry. Academic Press, London, p 107-124

DISCUSSION

Thomas: Your modification of the standard questionnaire (Carey 1972) for this specific population is a key issue and brings up the pertinent question of the suitability of the questionnaire for different populations with different social or cultural or class problems. Your findings link with those on the association between the temperamentally difficult child and other high-risk factors (Chess & Korn 1970, Chess et al 1971). Children with both mild mental retardation and physical handicap (related to congenital rubella) who were also temperamentally difficult had a greater risk of developing behaviour disorders.

Chess: In trying to ascertain a child's actual behaviour, we started first with the concept of a Pavlovian model and by the time we found it was not suitable we realized that we could obtain great detail of the child's behaviour from maternal reports. In deciding whether to use a questionnaire or scheduled observations, one returns to the argument about which of these techniques really captures the child. The Carey questionnaire (Carey 1972) arose from the need to provide the paediatrician, for practical purposes, with a means of using the temperament data. Your slight reversal of this approach, with the return to a semi-structured interview, makes a great deal more sense than the blind use of questionnaires in different populations. One must take into account whether the person one is questioning has had the social exposure as well as the intellectual ability to understand not only the language used but also the concepts behind the questions, and your approach helps to tackle this essential issue.

Kohnstamm: How did you standardize your assessments of maternal depression?

Wolkind: We used a standardized clinical interview that is used widely in British psychiatric research. We don't score items as such but we ask about each symptom. The mothers are asked about various aspects of anxiety and depression, and if there is any evidence for these items, one carries on questioning, to find the frequency, the severity and (most important) the impact of these symptoms on the woman's life. On this basis one makes a diagnosis and a severity rating for each woman.

Kohnstamm: Can you then rank the whole group of women on the severity rating?

Wolkind: We originally rated in terms of the degree of handicap, but our numbers are small. We used the categories of: no disorder; disorder with symptoms, but no impairment of everyday life; and disorder with a definite impairment of everyday life in terms of the ability to make relationships, to work or to look after the child.

Dunn: How do you interpret the association between depression and the two extremes of temperament?

Wolkind: Perhaps totally different mechanisms operate, and at the 'difficult' end may be a group of children who really are difficult. In the relationship between child behaviour and maternal depression one gets the picture of a constant feedback. For example, the babies of depressed mothers were less likely than the rest in our sample to have started sleeping right through the night before four months of age. No matter what the direction of cause and effect, this is just one more burden on a mother which could make her more depressed. Children of depressed mothers become dry at a later age, which equally could reinforce the mother's depression. At the 'easy' end of the spectrum is a group of benign and emotionally undemanding babies. It could be that they are truly easy in certain circumstances, but lack the capacity to cope with stresses should these arise.

Rutter: How confident are you about the results on the easy children?

Wolkind: These findings must be treated with caution. Only a very small number of children in this group had depressed mothers and the difference in behavioural scores within the easy group is not statistically significant.

Stevenson: The study by Naomi Richman, Philip Graham and myself carries on from where your data leave off. We had a curious result that may relate to your finding about the easy end of the sample being associated with maternal depression. But our result also creates a problem for your use of the Behaviour Screening Questionnaire (BSQ) as a continuous measure. We used the rates of deviance on the Rutter teacher questionnaire at age eight and we found that the girls at highest risk for showing a disturbance at this age were those who were virtually symptom-free at age three. The rates of deviance at age eight, when plotted against the scores on Naomi Richman's questionnaire (see Richman & Graham 1971) at age three produced a U-shaped function: the low-scoring girls and the high-scoring girls were the ones who showed the greatest deviance at eight. There was a similar but less marked effect for boys. This phenomenon parallels the opposite effects on the 'difficult–easy' dimension that you described. But it also rather undermines the BSQ score as a measure on which one can sensibly calculate means.

Werry: One needs to be cautious about using the generic term 'maternal depression' as if it were nosologically homogeneous. The distinct disorder of unipolar-type depression is susceptible to effective medical intervention, and as a result the implications for preventive measures for improved mental health in some children are important. One should distinguish clearly between something like battle fatigue and the development of depression as a distinctive clinical disorder. Management of the two will be different: battle fatigue is difficult to deal with in this sort of population, while clinical depression, in theory, should be relatively simple! How many of these women were depressed when the child was four months old and were still depressed when the child was four years of age?

Wolkind: Quite a few. Interestingly, at least 75% of the group of women who were depressed before they ever became pregnant (i.e. those who reported 'trouble with their nerves') were depressed also on at least two of the later stages in the study. One group of women became depressed for the first time at four months after the birth, and virtually all of them were still depressed at the next two interviews (14 and 27 months). And so it went on.

A number of children in this sample were therefore exposed to a depressed mother for the first years of their lives.

Werry: Were any of the mothers treated?

Wolkind: Some had been given diazepam by their general practitioners, but otherwise little treatment had been offered. We used a total non-intervention approach. However, my colleague, Mary Burd, and I have started a small intervention study by screening for depressed mothers in infant-welfare clinics. We are finding a dramatically high rate of depression but, paradoxically, the mothers clearly don't see themselves as depressed, or as needing or wanting help.

Hsu: Nobody has been talking about the father. The development of family interactions between father–child and father–mother is very complicated. For example, if the mother is depressed, how is the father coping, and does this change if she is mildly or severely depressed?

Wolkind: This is an important missing dimension. If one compares the women who became depressed for the first time after the birth with those who had been depressed before the birth, the first group was more likely to report that their marriages were deteriorating afterwards. The relationship between maternal depression and child behaviour becomes complex because the quality of the marriage gets mixed up in this. It was not only the role of fathers that we needed to examine. We found that the maternal grandmother was possibly more important than the father. Single teenage mothers seem to have few problems, and this is likely to be due to the role of the maternal grandmother. In our study it is extremely difficult to pin down truly causal factors; we seem to be finding constellations of predisposing factors.

Thomas: How did the non-depressed mothers correlate with the easy children?

Wolkind: The non-depressed mothers with easy children had a very low score on the behaviour disorder scale (mean, 4.4); this was significantly different from the mean score of the remaining children.

Thomas: We found (Thomas et al 1968) that easy children who developed behavioural disorders between 4–7 years of age tended to be in families where the parents' system of values, practices or demands on the child were idiosyncratic and contradictory to what the child met in the outside world among its peer group or at school. The child had adjusted well at home but then came into conflict with the outer world. Easy children whose mothers are depressed may adapt easily at home to the demands of the home environment but, because of the mother's depression, they may later come up against dissonant expectations in the outer world, or even in the home environment at a later stage.

Carey: So the child's being easy may tend to work against the child's well-being?

Thomas: Yes; being easy is a disservice if the expectations of the parents are in some way dissonant or non-adaptive for what the child needs in subsequent years or in the outside world.

Rutter: This information may not be consistent with Dr Wolkind's results because his data were taken at four months, and in the New York study there were no associations with disorder when temperament was measured as early as that (Rutter et al 1964, Thomas et al 1968). What mechanisms could be involved? Presumably, as in other studies, there will be little continuity of temperament from the four-month period to later childhood. Were the temperamental attributes associated with, for example, the patterns of observed mother–child interaction?

Wolkind: Within the observational data Hall & Pawlby (1981) found quite interesting continuities, but there was no relationship at all between four-month temperament at interview and four-month observations of the babies. There are two possible mechanisms. In the data linking temperament, tiredness and later depression, one might be seeing the start of a vicious circle that exaggerates the child's temperamental difficulties and makes even further difficulties for the mother. Secondly, the relationship between individual temperament questions and the child-behaviour items at 42 months is interesting, and supports the model I have suggested. Eating difficulties at 42 months relate significantly to several of the eating questions in the four-month temperamental scale but to virtually none of the other items. An area of difficulty may arise, and then somehow become enshrined within the family mythology, so that it carries on as such. There is a similar pattern with sleeping. These effects could exacerbate the temperamental differences.

Kolvin: Perhaps the differences between the populations studied explain the importance of social factors in your sample as against the relative lack of importance of social factors in the New York study.

Thomas: I would agree with that.

Bates: At 42 months Dr Wolkind is not looking at diagnosed behavioural problems but at a behavioural problem score, unlike the New York study. We found a similar relationship between perceived temperament at six months and perceived behaviour problems at three years in an ordinary population (J.E. Bates et al, unpublished paper, 1981 Bienn Meet Soc Res Child Dev, Boston Mass). The difficult infant seems to be coercive, and to demand attention from the parent, and this is also one of the elements in behavioural problems. So that might provide the link-up between early perception of temperament and perceived behaviour problems.

Wolkind: The nature of our sample may be important here. I don't want to over-stress the deprivation of the people—in fact the majority are able to cope with all sorts of difficulties—but, on balance, they have fewer resources to cope with strains than do people in more middle-class areas. The difficult child thus presents a special problem both physically and emotionally to the people in our sample as, for example, when a crying baby can be heard in all the surrounding flats. These environmental factors may produce a greater continuity in this sample than one might find in a middle-class population.

Rutter: But you haven't actually demonstrated continuity; rather, you have shown links between one measure and a different measure, which isn't quite the same thing.

Thomas: This may explain why the temperamentally difficult child in our sample in the first year did not predict later behaviour disorders, although it did in Dr Wolkind's sample. The mothers in our sample were middle class.

Berger: A child who is classified as easy may have some difficulty in one area of functioning. One problem with rating through the interview measures is that items with a high degree of salience are unweighted in the accumulation of results. This might link to maternal depression. A child who has a basic problem about settling at night, and thus causes the mother's sleep to be interrupted, would come out on the simple summation measure as an easy child, and yet the mother becomes depressed.

Dunn: Some years ago we did a longitudinal study on early predictors of sleep disturbances, though we didn't include an equivalent measure of maternal depression (Bernal 1973). Our study supported the notion that the predictability of a continuing sleep problem depended on the social circumstances in which the family was living. Nick Blurton-Jones et al (1979) did a model simulation showing how that might work; it was quite effective, and the basic conclusion makes good intuitive sense.

REFERENCES

Bernal JF 1973 Nightwaking in the first 14 months. Dev Med Child Neurol 15:760-769

Blurton-Jones N, Woodson RH, Chisholm JS 1979 Cross-cultural perspectives on the significance of social relationships in infancy. In: Shaffer D, Dunn J (eds) The first year of life. Wiley, Chichester.

Carey WB 1972 Measuring infant temperament. J Pediatr 81:414

Chess S, Korn S 1970 Temperament and behavior disorders in mentally retarded children. Arch Gen Psychiatry 23:122-130

Chess S, Korn S, Fernandez P 1971 Psychiatric disorders of children with congenital rubella. Brunner/Mazel, New York

Hall F, Pawlby SJ 1981 Continuity and discontinuity in the behaviour of British working-class mothers and their first born children. Int J Behav Dev 4:13-36

Richman N, Graham PJ 1971 A behavioural screening questionnaire for use with 3 year old children. J Child Psychol Psychiatry Allied Discip 12:5-33

Rutter M, Birch H, Thomas A, Chess S 1964 Temperamental characteristics in infancy and the later development of behavioural disorders. Br J Psychiatry 110:651-661

Thomas A, Chess S, Birch HG 1968 Temperament and behavior disorders in children. New York University Press, New York

On the continuity, change and clinical value of infant temperament in a prospective epidemiological study

MATTI O. HUTTUNEN and GÖTE NYMAN*

*Department of Psychiatry and *Department of General Psychology, University of Helsinki, Helsinki, Finland*

Abstract The temperament of 1855 children born in Helsinki during 1975–76 was recorded at the age of 6–8 months by parental questionnaires. In 1980–81 the continuity of temperamental dimensions was studied in a group of these children by using a temperament questionnaire for 3–7-year-old children. In addition, the clinical usefulness of infant temperament was assessed by analysing the infant temperament of the children who were later treated for a variety of paediatric problems. A significant positive correlation was found between seven of the nine temperamental dimensions studied at 6–8 months and at 5 years. However, the individual stability of the temperamental dimensions used was almost negligible, because less than 10% of the total variance of each dimension could be explained by the corresponding dimensions at the infant age.

The clinical usefulness of infant temperament questionnaires in prospective epidemiological studies was supported by the observation that children with later paediatric problems (behavioural problems, colic spasms, accidents) had had significantly different temperamental styles at the infant age from those without problems. The results support the importance of negative mood and high intensity of infant's behavioural style as risk factors for later paediatric problems.

Children are known to be born with marked individual differences in their styles of behaviour (Thomas et al 1963, Korner 1971, Buss & Plomin 1975, Thomas & Chess 1977, Kagan et al 1978). During the last few years there has been a growing interest in the potential importance of these inborn temperamental differences in the aetiology of various psychiatric and psychosomatic disorders (Thomas et al 1968, Rutter 1970, Graham et al 1973, Carey 1972, 1974, Cameron 1977, 1978, Carey & McDevitt 1978). Interest in temperamental research has been especially stimulated by the development of simple

1982 Temperamental differences in infants and young children. Pitman Books Ltd, London (Ciba Foundation symposium 89) p 240–251

questionnaires that use parental rating of their children's behaviour as a measure of different temperamental dimensions (Carey 1970, McDevitt & Carey 1978, Bohlin et al 1981). The greatest potential value of these simple questionnaires possibly lies in their application to unselected children in groups large enough for prospective epidemiological studies.

The validity of temperamental research and especially research using simple questionnaires rests heavily on the ability of the obtained data to predict consistently at least some aspects of the children's future tempera- ment, behaviour problems or psychosomatic illnesses. There is already some evidence for the general stability of infant temperament over the first years (Thomas & Chess 1977, Carey & McDevitt 1978, Hagekull & Bohlin 1981). However, many recent reviews do not support the notion of individual stability in the areas of cognitive and temperamental development (Kagan et al 1978, Rutter 1970).

Many of the issues concerning the clinical value of temperament research could be answered if a group of unselected children large enough for epidemiological studies were followed up over the years. This idea was the stimulus for the start of our prospective study of a large group of unselected children born in 1975–76 in the city of Helsinki. The original sample consisted of a total of 1855 children, whose parents completed the infant temperament questionnaire (Arajärvi & Huttunen 1981, Nyman et al 1982). This paper presents some preliminary findings from the follow-up studies of these children, concerning the stability and predictive value of infant temperament.

Subjects and methods

The data base of our study consists of the temperament data on 1855 babies born in Helsinki during 1975–76. The Carey (1970) infant temperament questionnaire was translated and modified for independent parental scoring. This questionnaire was then given to all the mothers visiting the Helsinki well-baby clinics when their children were 6–8 months old. Of the 4000 questionnaires distributed in the clinics, 1855 completely filled questionnaires were received for analysis (Arajärvi & Huttunen 1981, Nyman et al 1982). Temperamental category scores were calculated according to Carey (1970) and each baby was thus characterized by a temperament profile consisting of the nine dimensions (activity, regularity, approach/withdrawal, adaptability, threshold, intensity, mood, distractibility and persistence). In Carey's infant temperament questionnaire each dimension is represented by means of a number of questions scored between 0 and 2. A score close to zero in the Carey questionnaire indicates that the baby is easily adaptable, positive in mood, positive in its first reaction (approach), regular in biological functions, intensive in reactions, active, persistent, not easily distractible and has a high sensory threshold.

In addition to this information on infant temperament we have collected detailed data on the social class and pregnancy and birth complications of the same children. The social class distribution of the families of the 1855 children does not differ significantly from that of the whole population in Helsinki. We are currently doing the detailed analysis of the relations between infant temperament, social class, and pregnancy and birth complications.

During 1980–81 the translated version of the temperament questionnaire for 3–7-year-old children (Thomas & Chess 1977) was sent to the parents of the 1855 children of the original sample. In this questionnaire, the nine temperamental dimensions are represented by a mean of a number of questions scored between 1 and 7. In contrast to the Carey infant temperament questionnaire, high scores (close to 7) on this questionnaire indicate that the child is adaptable, positive in mood and approach (reaction), regular, intensive, active, persistent, has a high sensory threshold, but *is* easily distractible. As the present paper describes the correlation analysis between the scores of the temperament questionnaires of the same children at 6–8 months and 5 years of age, significant *negative* correlations would indicate some stability within the dimensions of activity, regularity, approach/withdrawal, adaptability, sensory threshold, intensity, quality of mood, and persistence; whereas a *positive* correlation would indicate stability for distractibility.

The present paper describes the correlation analysis for the first 299 children of the original sample. The correlation coefficients (Pearson's *r* values), which measure the association between the variables, were calculated between the means of the scores of the nine temperamental dimensions at the ages of 6–8 months and 5 years. The statistical significance of *r* values has been tested at present by the Student's *t*-test, even when the general distribution pattern of the data was unknown. A more detailed analysis of these results is currently under way.

Helsinki has a large central paediatric hospital (Aurora Hospital) to take care of all the acute somatic and behavioural illnesses and crises of children under the age of 15 years. In order to study the clinically predictive value of the infant temperament data we decided to analyse the temperament data of those children from our original sample who had already been seen or treated in this paediatric clinic. At the time of this preliminary analysis (autumn of 1980) a total of 270 children (15%) of the total sample had visited the clinic for various reasons. Here we describe the infant temperament data of the groups of children with acute behavioural problems, and who had the following hospital diagnoses: excitability, pneumonia, acute colic spasms and various accidents (contusions, fractures, wounds, intoxications and burns).

Results and discussion

We have tried to examine the validity of the infant temperament question-naire by two different approaches—by studying the individual stability of the nine temperamental dimensions across the two age-groups, and by examining the possible predictive value of infant temperament scores for a few paediatric problems.

Table 1 shows the correlation matrix between the individual means of the nine temperamental dimensions at the ages of 6–8 months and 5 years, with the stability coefficients in the diagonal. Owing to the inverse scoring system on the questionnaires for the two different age groups, the negative correlation coefficient stands for some continuity in eight of the nine temperamental dimensions (activity, regularity, approach/withdrawal, adaptability, sensory threshold, intensity, mood and persistence). There was a modest degree of continuity in seven of the nine temperamental dimensions ($r = -0.21$– -0.32) with the exception of intensity ($r = -0.15$) and distractibility ($r = 0.02$). Even if the predictive value of the individual infant temperament score is quite small, so that it explains less than 10% of the total variance of the same dimension at the later age, the statistical significance of these correlations is high ($P < 0.01$ or 0.001), which points to some meaningful relations between the infant and 5-year-old temperament dimensions.

By reading across Table 1 one can also judge whether the stability of a particular scale is discriminative in the sense that behavioural style measured by it at the older age is better predicted by the supposedly similar category of behaviours than by any other temperamental dimensions at the infant age. In this way one may also see, to some degree, the directions in which infant behavioural style is changing over the following 4 to 5 years.

Thus, a high intensity at the infant age is significantly correlated with a low sensory threshold at the later age ($r = 0.24$, $P < 0.001$). Could a high score in intensity at the infant age reflect a low sensory threshold to environmental stimuli? Similarly, a low persistence score seems to have a significant correlation ($r = 0.21$, $P < 0.01$) with a high activity level at the later age, which finding may only show the multifactorial origins of the general activity level observed and rated by the parents. It is certainly not surprising to find that positive quality of mood, positive approach reaction and high adaptability are significantly correlated with each other.

Another way to validate the use of the infant temperament questionnaires is to try to analyse the predictive power of the various temperamental dimensions for the later development of behavioural or somatic disorders in these children. In our opinion the possible relation of the infant temperament dimensions to somatic illnesses may be especially important in aetiological

TABLE 1 Correlation coefficients of the mean scores of the nine temperamental dimensions at the ages of 6–8 months and 5 years, in 299 children

6–8 months old	5 years old								
	Activity	Regularity	Approach	Adaptability	Threshold	Intensity	Mood	Distractibility	Persistence
Activity	−0.24	−0.05	−0.07	−0.01	0.12	−0.26	0.09	0.07	−0.12
Regularity	−0.01	−0.32	−0.10	−0.14	0.14	0.04	−0.16	−0.04	−0.13
Approach	−0.01	−0.02	−0.29	−0.26	−0.01	0.14	−0.21	−0.17	0.17
Adaptability	−0.00	−0.06	−0.23	−0.30	−0.01	0.04	−0.12	−0.13	0.17
Threshold	−0.01	0.05	−0.06	−0.02	−0.23	−0.04	0.03	0.10	0.08
Intensity	0.01	−0.19	−0.11	−0.15	0.24	−0.15	−0.10	−0.01	−0.17
Mood	0.12	−0.08	−0.24	−0.33	0.05	0.16	−0.26	−0.20	0.13
Distractibility	0.03	−0.03	−0.00	0.01	0.13	−0.11	0.03	−0.02	0.05
Persistence	0.21	−0.17	−0.01	−0.15	0.06	0.04	−0.13	0.03	−0.21

$P < 0.01$ if $|r| > 0.18$; $P < 0.001$ if $|r| > 0.23$

TABLE 2 Infant temperamental characteristics of children with acute behavioural problems, acute colic spasms and pneumonia

Temperamental dimensions	All children n = 1855	All children in the hospital n = 235	Diagnosis		
			Excitability n = 14	Abdominal pain/functional n = 51	Pneumonia n = 41
Activity	0.49 ± 0.26	0.50 ± 0.26	0.50 ± 0.35	0.50 ± 0.26	0.50 ± 0.24
Regularity	0.56 ± 0.42	0.60 ± 0.43	0.74 ± 0.44	0.64 ± 0.43	0.60 ± 0.40
Approach	0.55 ± 0.29	0.56 ± 0.28	0.59 ± 0.27	0.62 ± 0.30	0.55 ± 0.26
Adaptability	0.35 ± 0.24	0.37 ± 0.25	0.49 ± 0.29	0.41 ± 0.28	0.35 ± 0.22
Threshold	0.97 ± 0.33	0.92 ± 0.28	0.91 ± 0.29	0.97 ± 0.32	0.90 ± 0.28
Intensity	0.81 ± 0.24	0.71 ± 0.28	0.63 ± 0.29*	0.68 ± 0.29**	0.77 ± 0.27
Mood	0.55 ± 0.19	0.65 ± 0.19	0.73 ± 0.22**	0.70 ± 0.19**	0.60 ± 0.17
Distractibility	0.37 ± 0.21	0.35 ± 0.21	0.23 ± 0.19**	0.34 ± 0.25	0.37 ± 0.20
Persistence	0.90 ± 0.30	0.88 ± 0.32	0.87 ± 0.20	0.96 ± 0.33	0.86 ± 0.27

Means and standard deviations of the nine temperamental dimensions. * $P < 0.05$; ** $P < 0.01$; (Student's t-test).

studies of inborn temperament traits, as the roots of these traits are supposedly related to some specific differences in the neurobiological functions of the children, the contribution of which might increase the vulnerability of the child to various somatic illnesses as well as to behavioural problems.

As a group, the children treated in the paediatric clinic of Helsinki by the time of examination did not differ in their temperamental dimensions from those of the original sample of 1855 children (see Tables 2 and 3). However,

TABLE 3. Infant temperamental characteristics of children with various forms of accidents

Temperamental dimensions	All children n = 1855	All accidents n = 35	Contusions, fractures, wounds n = 17	Poisoning n = 7	Burns n = 9
			Diagnosis		
Activity	0.49 ± 0.26	0.42 ± 0.24	0.43 ± 0.26	0.43 ± 0.47	0.43 ± 0.27
Regularity	0.56 ± 0.42	0.65 ± 0.46	0.76 ± 0.49	0.49 ± 0.46	0.51 ± 0.39
Approach	0.55 ± 0.29	0.65 ± 0.34	0.75 ± 0.28**	0.63 ± 0.30	0.54 ± 0.43
Adaptability	0.35 ± 0.24	0.40 ± 0.31	0.45 ± 0.36	0.36 ± 0.13	0.36 ± 0.32
Threshold	0.97 ± 0.33	0.93 ± 0.32	0.88 ± 0.34	0.88 ± 0.31	1.07 ± 0.28
Intensity	0.81 ± 0.24	0.67 ± 0.27**	0.73 ± 0.18	0.74 ± 0.24	0.58 ± 0.30*
Mood	0.55 ± 0.19	0.66 ± 0.21**	0.71 ± 0.20**	0.63 ± 0.19	0.59 ± 0.23
Distractibility	0.37 ± 0.21	0.41 ± 0.34	0.36 ± 0.29	0.42 ± 0.25	0.53 ± 0.49
Persistence	0.90 ± 0.30	0.99 ± 0.32	0.97 ± 0.30	0.69 ± 0.26*	1.13 ± 0.27***

Means ± standard deviations. * $P < 0.05$; ** $P < 0.01$; *** $P < 0.001$; (Student's t-test).

we found rather modest, but statistically clearly significant, differences between the temperamental dimensions of some diagnostic categories and those of the original total sample of children. Thus, the children with acute behavioural crisis ('excitability') had had a more negative mood, a higher intensity and had been less easily distractible at the age of 6–8 months. In addition, the children with acute colic spasms had been more negative in their mood, and generally more intense in infancy, while children with pneumonia did not differ in any significant way from the original sample of 1855 children (Table 2).

The possible importance of the negative mood and high intensity in increasing the vulnerability of children to later problems was further supported by the finding that the children treated in the hospital after various accidents had had these characteristics of temperament more often than the 'average' child of the entire birth cohort. The children with various forms of accidents seem to have differed from each other at the infant age. Thus, the children with 'impulsive' accidents (contusions, fractures, wounds) had had a more negative mood and first reaction (approach/withdrawal), while the children with poisoning possibly ($P < 0.05$) had been more persistent, and the children with burns less persistent, than the means of the entire sample would predict. However, these differences are only suggestive, owing to the relatively small number of children in each diagnostic group. Furthermore, even if the observed differences were real and replicable, the predictive power of the presently used dimensional scores is far too low to give us any practical help beyond general education in the prevention of children's accidents.

Generally, the results are in good agreement with previous observations about the stability and predictive value of infant temperament data. The relationship between the 'difficult child' temperament (negative mood, high intensity, irregularity, slow adaptability and negative first reaction) and children's behavioural problems has been repeatedly reported (Thomas & Chess 1977, Carey 1972, 1974, Cameron 1977, 1978). Acute colic spasms have been previously associated with a low sensory threshold, and lacerations with the difficult temperament (Carey 1972, 1974). The present data seem to support the possible importance of negative mood and high intensity of the infants as temperamental risk factors for later paediatric problems. The physiological background of these characteristics, and the extent to which the observed high intensity is physiologically more related to, for example, a low sensory threshold of the infant remains to be answered.

On the whole, even at this preliminary stage of analysis, the data also support previous findings about the clustering pattern of the nine temperamental dimensions. As in our study, positive mood, approach and high adaptability have been repeatedly shown to be closely associated with each other, as well as high activity with high intensity and/or low persistence (Buss & Plomin 1975, Bohlin et al 1981).

In conclusion, even if the present data seem to give an almost negligible stability for the nine temperamental dimensions, they still generally support the usefulness of temperamental questionnaires as a research tool, at least in groups of children large enough for epidemiological purposes. It is certainly true that at least some of the rather modest correlations between the infant temperament scores and the scores at 5 years old could be explained as a consequence of a long-standing and disturbed parent–child interaction or of a fixedly biased parental view of a child's behaviour. The specific pattern of the observed correlations of temperamental differences in infancy with paediatric problems later in childhood suggests a more specific relation between the infant temperament and the child's later development. Finally, it must be pointed out that a more careful statistical analysis of the relative importance of individual items in the questionnaires may considerably improve the (as yet) weak predictive value of temperamental features in infancy for the outcome of the child's development.

REFERENCES

Arajärvi T, Huttunen MO 1981 Pregnancy and birth complications in the aetiology of psychiatric disorders with special reference to the temperament of children: a description of the Finnish prospective epidemiological study. In: Mednick SA, Baert AE (eds) Prospective longitudinal research: an empirical basis for the primary prevention of psychosocial disorders. Oxford University Press, Oxford, p 43-47

Bohlin G, Hagekull B, Lindhagen K 1981 Dimensions of infant behavior. Inf Behav Dev 4:83-96

Buss A, Plomin RA 1975 Temperament theory of personality development. Wiley-Interscience, New York

Cameron JR 1977 Parental treatment, children's temperament, and the risk of childhood behavioral problems. 1: Relationship between parental characteristics and changes in children's temperament over time. Am J Orthopsychiatry 47:568-576

Cameron JR 1978 Parental treatment, children's temperament, and the risk of childhood behavioral problems. 2: Initial temperament, parental attitudes, and the incidence and form of behavioral problems. Am J Orthopsychiatry 48:140-147

Carey WB 1970 A simplified method for measuring infant temperament. J Pediatr 77:188-194

Carey WB 1972 Clinical applications of infant temperament measurements. J Pediatr 81:823-828

Carey WB 1974 Night waking and temperament in infancy. J Pediatr 84:756-758

Carey WB, McDevitt SC 1978 Stability and change in individual temperament diagnoses from infancy to early childhood. J Am Acad Child Psychiatry 17:331-337

Graham P, Rutter M, George S 1973 Temperamental characteristics as predictors of behavior disorders in children. Am J Orthopsychiatry 43:328-339

Hagekull B, Bohlin G 1981 Individual stability in dimensions of infant behavior. Inf Behav Dev 4:97-108

Kagan J, Kearsley RB, Zelazo PR 1978 Infancy: its place in human development. Harvard University Press, Cambridge, Mass.

Korner AF 1971 Individual differences at birth: implications for early experience and later development. Am J Orthopsychiatry 41:608-619

McDevitt SC, Carey WB 1978 The measurement of temperament in 3–7-year-old children. J Child Psychol Psychiatry 19:245-253

Nyman G, Nyman M, Huttunen MO 1982 Measurement of infant behavior and temperament. The Helsinki Longitudinal Study. Psychiatria Fennica, in press

Rutter M 1970 Psychological development—predictions from infancy. J Child Psychol Psychiatry 11:49-62

Thomas A, Chess S, Birch HG, Hertzig ME, Korn S 1963 Behavioral individuality in early childhood. New York University Press, New York

Thomas A, Chess S, Birch HG 1968 Temperament and behavior disorders in children. New York University Press, New York

Thomas A, Chess S 1977 Temperament and development. Brunner/Mazel, New York

DISCUSSION

Wilson: In our early work (Matheny et al 1971) we interviewed the mothers of twins and found, almost inevitably, that where one twin was described as being more temperamental or more impulsive, that child was the one who collected a history of accidents—falls and broken bones—during childhood. This is similar to your results.

Thomas: Jim Cameron (unpublished results) has also found a correlation between accidents and the early characterization of the 'difficult child' constellation.

Carey: During what interval did these illnesses and accidents take place? Was it any time up to seven years of age?

Huttunen: The accidents recorded could have happened at any age before our examination.

Carey: It would be interesting to run off all the subjects against the later questionnaire too. You might find similar correlations.

Huttunen: Yes, I agree. Our aim is to use our cohort and our data to help improve the predictive validity of the individual scores and items. This is now possible as we have independent measures (clinical cases) in our hands to use for multiple regression analyses etc.

Torgersen: Your tabulated results are interesting because they show a similar pattern to my results from the infancy period up to six years of age. I found only one or two barely statistically significant correlations between individual temperamental categories at the two age-periods, but each temperament category in infancy correlated more significantly with that same temperament category at six years of age than it did with any of the other temperamental categories at six years.

Carey: As a researcher I find these results (which are similar to data that we have) fascinating; as a clinician I find them frustrating because I simply don't know how to translate them into a practical programme of accident prevention. What does one do with information of this sort, as a paediatrician or as a parent, to reduce the rate of accidents?

Huttunen: I really don't know, but one needs to have considerably higher correlations before putting these kinds of research findings into practical use. Nevertheless, the observed statistical significances should encourage us to go more deeply into the details of this sort of study.

Rutter: One implication is quite important. If children with head injuries (who constitute a prominent group among those suffering accidents) are behaviourally different before the accident (as suggested by several different studies—see Rutter et al 1982) then one must be very cautious about assuming that the behavioural difficulties seen afterwards are a result of the head injury. Our findings (Rutter et al 1982) suggest that, so far as mild head injuries are concerned, there is usually a simple continuity between behaviour before and after the accident, with the head injury playing little, if any, causal role. In contrast, with severe head injuries (i.e. those in which the post-traumatic amnesia exceeded one week), there was a marked behavioural change after the injury—a change that was caused in part by brain damage.

Chess: The social context can sometimes reinforce the behavioural context. For example, high-activity children in the middle-class group of the New York longitudinal study tended not to have behavioural problems clinically. More resources are available to enable the family to baby-proof the home or to move to a larger apartment where there is a closed-in yard, for example. However, the Puerto Rican families that we selected lived in public housing in which the size of the apartment was legislated by the housing authority. The apartments were small, the mothers did not have much assistance, and they had more children. Far from the high-activity children in this group being provided with *more* space and safer space, they were kept at home, where their mothers could watch them more carefully. The mothers didn't have time to sit with them in the playground; they couldn't send the children down to play in the street for fear that they would be run over; and so they kept them 'safe'. As a result, behaviour disorders within the family grew because the children were always getting into everyone's way, or breaking their siblings' toys. When the children went to school, and were 'released' from the house, they brought their high activity into the school and presented problems to the teacher. This example highlights the meaning of differences between lower and middle socioeconomic class, in terms of the functional life of the child and the parents.

Berger: We have learnt from life-span studies something about the question of cohort effects in this sort of design: will the data be replicated with a new cohort? Part of the inherent fascination of temperament is that, for example, for any cell of your correlation table for temperament and accidents that lead to hospitalization one could think up several plausible explanations. That is both the danger and the strength of a correlational approach and the reason why theoretical predictions are so important. Nevertheless, the consistency of the data on brain injury constitutes a form of replication which increases our confidence in the association. But we must remain cautious until we have a good theoretical basis for our explanations.

Kohnstamm: Some of Rembrandt's etchings of children at play show them wearing a kind of a helmet, which presumably prevented them from head injuries if they fell down. In ordinary road traffic nowadays all sorts of preventive safety measures, such as motor bike helmets, are used by drivers, whether they are accident prone or not. It might not be too far-fetched to suggest that boys (who have an accident rate at least twice as high as girls) with a high score on difficult temperament and a certain number of minor physical anomalies should wear a life-saving vest or a helmet when playing outdoors or near water! This would be a very simple preventive measure. One might, I suppose, object to this because it would immediately label the child as accident prone.

Wolkind: One would have to lock the child into such a device!

Chess: Not if one gave the garment some prestige value.

Kohnstamm: Something like a space helmet might be suitable!

Huttunen: As Dr Berger has already pointed out, the correlations between temperament and later development must be considerably higher before one even begins to think of such measures.

Thomas: Because you have such a large sample you could perhaps identify subgroups in which the correlations are much higher. Advice to specific groups with particular predispositions, rather than an attempt at a global strategy, might therefore be feasible.

Rutter: At present, the strength of association is such that one would wrongly predict many times more often than one would correctly predict, even if the correlations were much higher than they are already. Very high correlations would be required if one were to predict correctly more than 50% of the time.

Plomin: This might be a situation where multivariate analysis would be useful. From the low autocorrelations and multiple regressions, given that many of the nine dimensions are fairly independent, one might pick up substantial predictive power for some categories. Multivariate analysis could be valuable, say, in predicting from early temperament to later adjustments.

Bell: A theoretical prediction would not help to identify risk groups but would help to give a better idea of what the true correlation might be, if one were able to attain it.

Rutter: In practice, the best way to obtain a true prediction is not to correct by statistical manipulation but rather to obtain multiple measures of the same attribute, as Epstein (1979) has shown. This not only increases one's power of prediction but provides an increase in power that actually has some practical meaning.

Berger: In an epidemiological study, it is not very easy to adopt that approach.

Wilson: It might help to use factor scores which are composites of several variables pulled together in the most powerful way. One could then look at a correlation of factor scores at time 1 and at time 2. This would pick up some additional predictive variance because one will have sampled across several variables simultaneously. The use of multiple-regression procedures is another way to proceed. We have just begun to look at the pattern of temperament scores, in a canonical correlation sense, at time 1 and time 2. We look at the extent to which these two patterns are duplicated. This is linked to the multivariate way of trying to appraise stability of score profiles over time.

REFERENCES

Epstein S 1979 The stability of behavior. I: On predicting most of the people much of the time. J Pers Soc Psychol 37:1097-1126

Matheny AP, Brown AM, Wilson RS 1971 Behavioral antecedents of accident injuries in early childhood: a study of twins. Pediatrics 79:122-124

Rutter M, Chadwick O, Shaffer D 1982 Head injuries. In: Rutter M (ed) Behavioral syndromes of brain dysfunction in childhood. Guilford Press, New York, in press

Temperamental patterns in aggressive boys

I. KOLVIN, A. R. NICOL, R. F. GARSIDE, K. A. DAY and E. G. TWEDDLE

Nuffield Psychology and Psychiatry Unit, University of Newcastle upon Tyne, Fleming Memorial Hospital, Great North Road, Newcastle upon Tyne NE2 3AX, UK

Abstract Four groups of aggressive boys (and one group of controls) were studied, on the basis of: clinical referrals to a hospital clinic; teacher reports of assaultive behaviour in school; teacher reports of severe aggressive behaviour in school; and peer reports of aggressive behaviour. Questionnaire techniques were used to study behaviour and temperament. The last three groups proved to have rather similar patterns of behaviour and temperament and, therefore, they have been combined to give rise to an 'any school criterion' group. We compared three main groups: (i) clinical referrals; (ii) 'any criterion' (school-identified); and (iii) controls. On behaviour, the clinical group had the most adverse scores, especially on antisocial behaviour. The school-identified group also had a higher score than the controls on this dimension, and differed in degree from the clinical referral group. On temperament, the clinical referral group had a significantly more adverse score on all dimensions than both the controls and the 'any criterion' group. The 'any criterion' group scores were intermediate between the other two sets of scores. The differences on temperament between the control and the 'any criterion' groups appeared to be one of degree but not of type. Moreover, no specific type of temperament was associated with the different kinds of aggression we have studied. Principal components analysis supports the notion of no qualitative temperamental differences between the 'any criterion' and the control groups.

In their longitudinal study of temperament in childhood, Thomas et al (1968) have reported that they were able to predict aggressive behaviour in childhood from a number of temperamental patterns, which were detectable at an earlier stage of development. However, although certain temperamental clusters are stable during the first five years of life, this stability is not necessarily fixed, but evolves 'through continuous parent–child and child–environment interactions' (Carey & McDevitt 1978). These authors conclude that certain temperamental characteristics appear to predict stability of diagnostic groupings—namely, high activity and negative mood. However, from all accounts, even infants with a difficult temperament appear eventually to shift towards lesser degrees of difficulty (Thomas & Chess 1977).

1982 Temperamental differences in infants and young children. Pitman Books Ltd, London (Ciba Foundation symposium 89) p 252-268

The question arises of whether, in adolescence, despite modifications and adaptations of both behaviour and temperament, aggressive behaviour is generally associated with a particular pattern of temperament and also whether types of aggression are likewise associated.

In this paper we address two fundamental questions. First, can we identify patterns of temperament in groups of individuals who are characteristically aggressive? This may provide a clue as to why they respond aggressively to a wide range of environmental stimuli. For instance, it would be helpful to know whether aggressive boys identified as such within the community have temperamental characteristics, based on reports from other sources e.g. from parents, which set them aside from non-aggressive boys. A second, and allied, question is whether any intrinsic characteristics within children could be exaggerated or unleashed by life circumstances, such as the often reported harshness and punitiveness in family backgrounds of aggressive children.

Well known sex differences exist for aggressive behaviours in childhood and adolescence, with males far more likely to be aggressive than females (Maccoby & Jacklin 1974). Some workers consider this to suggest a constitutional determinant of aggression (Shaffer et al 1980), but social pressures cannot be overlooked. This was one of the main reasons for confining our study of temperament and aggression to males alone.

In this paper we focus on two major groups of aggressive boys—one identified within the school setting, and the second constituting clinical referrals to a child and adolescent psychiatric department. These are compared with a random control group.

Classification and aetiology of aggressive behaviour

We were particularly interested to ascertain whether certain temperamental patterns were characteristic of different types of aggression. Clearly, adolescent aggression is not a homogeneous phenomenon and we therefore surveyed the published work to identify systematic approaches to classification. One main approach to classification has been a clinical one.

Clinical approach to classification

McCord et al (1961) classified aggressive boys into those with serious overt aggression and those who were normally assertive. Those showing *overt aggression* participated in a whole range of aggressive acts, including assault; *normally assertive* boys had hostile responses that were sporadic exceptions to the general pattern of their lives.

Megargee (1970) has advanced the hypothesis that assaultive individuals can be divided into two quite distinct personality types—the undercontrolled and the overcontrolled. The *undercontrolled* aggressive male has quite low inhibitions against aggressive behaviour and responds with aggression whenever he is frustrated or provoked. The *chronically overcontrolled* type has strong inhibitions against the expression of aggression, but the instigation to aggression gradually summates until it exceeds his inhibitions, and he may then lash out and release his aggression in one serious act. Thus, not all extremely assaultive persons are necessarily continuously aggressive. This may account for the paradoxical outbursts of violence seen in usually quiet and inoffensive individuals.

While the study by Megargee (1970) only partly validates the above distinction, a later study of violent subjects in a Borstal (or older juvenile delinquent) population indicates that these were mainly of the undercontrolled type (Nicol et al 1972).

Megargee & Hokanson (1970) also classify aggression according to severity: *extreme*, reserved for physical assault of homicidal intensity; *moderate*, used for lesser degrees of physical aggression; and *mild*, used for verbal aggression and physical aggression not likely to injure the victims seriously.

Kolvin et al (1967) produced a classification based on a clinical study of aggressive delinquents. This is, in a sense, also hierarchical as it classifies aggression into two broad groups—assertive and non-assertive. The *assertive* group are hostile 'thugs' who wander around in groups, not quite aimlessly, having a sense of expectation of trouble. They appear to obtain a kind of satisfaction and enjoyment from their hostility and aggressive episodes. The *non-assertive* aggressive group has a number of subgroups: *paranoid* aggressives, who are continuously unapproachable, hostile youths; *catastrophic–impulsive* aggressives, whose catastrophic outbursts must, almost inexorably, run their course; *family-directed* youths, whose aggressiveness manifests itself only within the family; and youths who show a *cold* or *sadistic* streak.

The assertive and, possibly, the paranoid groups resemble the Megargee (1970) undercontrolled group, while the catstrophic–impulsive group resembles the Megargee overcontrolled group.

Aetiological approach

Another approach is that of Moyer (1968), who classified aggression in various animal species on the basis of a stimulus that elicited aggression, and who then sought evidence for a neurological or endocrinological basis for each of these types. He tentatively suggested the following types: inter-male; predatory; territorial; maternal; fear-induced; irritable; and instrumental.

While it is not easy to extrapolate from animals to humans, this work does emphasize the importance of biological factors. It is therefore not surprising that other workers have preferred to use an aetiological classification in clinical settings, e.g. chromosomal, hormonal, organic brain dysfunction, etc. However, such classifications encompass only a small proportion of individuals who are aggressive.

When surveying the major theories about the roots of aggression and violence in young adulthood, Lefkowitz and colleagues (1977) concluded that such questions can best be answered 'within a sociocultural model provided by learning theory'. They admitted, however, that environmental variables may interact with a widely ranging biological substratum. In a similar vein, Shaffer et al (1980) conclude, in their review, that there is no evidence that purely biological factors make a wide contribution to aggressive behaviour. They favour, instead, social and cognitive influences.

Classification according to source of reports

Finally, another way of classifying aggressive individuals is according to the source of reports about their behaviour. In our research this consists of: *clinical referral* to a hospital clinic; *teacher* reports of *assaultive* behaviour; *teacher* reports of *aggressive* behaviour; and *peer* reports of *aggressive* behaviour.

Methods

Screening among the school groups. Stage 1—Classroom screening. Fifty per cent of male pupils in all the classes in the second, third, fourth and fifth years of all secondary schools in Newcastle were randomly selected for survey by our screening techniques. For these screening purposes we used two techniques—a teacher behaviour questionnaire, and sociometry based on peer ratings of aggression using a 'guess-who' technique. We selected for study the boys with extreme (high) scores on these screening measures, and these constitute the screen positives.

Stage 2—Group testing. This was undertaken on two groups of boys—screen positives and controls. The procedure used will be described elsewhere.

Stage 3—Individual assessments. Clinical assessments were undertaken on subsamples of the above groups. For the controls we reduced the number of boys randomly. For the aggressive cohort we selected those who had the most extreme scores on the screening measures.

Clinical case study. A group of boys was gathered who had been referred for assessment because of violent or seriously aggressive behaviour. These boys were assessed by similar group and individual techniques as those applied in stages 2 and 3 above.

Groups studied. In this paper we describe the behaviour and temperament of the groups of boys selected for study. The numbers have been reduced by previous sampling as described in stage 3 above, by further random selection according to the numbers that we considered manageable by our research team, plus a small per cent of loss. Poor cooperation and losses were less of a problem in interviews of the parents than when we were seeking boys for individual assessment. Using parental interview, we studied 41 boys who were identified as aggressive by teacher questionnaire, 54 boys who were recorded as being assaultive on the teacher questionnaire, 32 boys who were identified by using classroom sociometry, 87 boys who were identified on any of the previous three criteria, 38 boys who were referred for clinical assessment, and 92 controls. There is, of course, a degree of overlap between the first three groups.

Assessment. The parents were interviewed without the interviewer being aware of the group to which the children belonged, but this did not always prove possible with those children referred for clinical assessment. Two types of parent questionnaire were used: a modified version of a behaviour questionnaire (Kolvin et al 1975); and a modified version of a temperament questionnaire (Garside et al 1975).

The interviewer went through an inventory of specified questions in a set order so as to elicit from the mother descriptions of *what* the youth did and *how* he did it in a series of specified situations. The answers were rated according to a clearly defined unipolar five-point scale. The questions were open-ended, in that they allowed the interviewer, if necessary, to explore the mothers' answers more deeply, in order to achieve a satisfactory rating.

The measurement of temperament at this age is difficult, because of the increasing variation in activities and interests of boys throughout adolescence (Thomas & Chess 1977). This creates problems in the development and standardization of questions or probes and, of course, in scoring. We have specifically looked at this, using three people who did their interviewing in pairs. Difficulties in eliciting information and in scoring were examined, and ways of obtaining meaningful responses and agreement between interviewers were sought. Our experience has led us to conclude that a briefer initial probe followed by an open-ended approach caters best for such variations. Where the standard question, beyond the initial probe, was modified, the interviewer would then enquire about other customary day-to-day activities relevant to the theme of the probe. In addition, it was emphasized that the interviewer should ensure that any questions should emphasize *how* the youth behaved rather than *what* he did. For instance, with the probe that was intended to elicit information about intensity of reactions at bedtimes, the object was to rate the intensity of reactions or feelings shown during whatever activities were customarily engaged in by the youth before sleep.

Behaviour interview. Thirty-eight items were used but, because of lack of spread, four items were discarded. The 27 items were grouped into three main dimensions:

(A)	Anxiety/neurotic	(9 items)
(B)	Antisocial	(9 items)
(C)	Psychosomatic/vegetative	(9 items)

In addition, the above items were reorganized into five mutually exclusive separate dimensions relating to physical/physiological aspects of behaviour in order to provide a more fine-grain picture:

(D)	Sleep problems—restlessness, awakening, etc.	(4 items)
(E)	Psychosomatic—health worries, headache, abdominal pain, etc.	(4 items)
(F)	Appetite—poor appetite and finickiness	(2 items)
(G)	Motor—tics, etc.	(2 items)
(H)	Bowel/bladder—wetting, soiling, constipation	(4 items)

Finally, a 'sum' score was derived as follows:

(I)	Sum of (A) + (B) + (C)	(27 items).

The items were so organized that A–C were mutually exclusive; this was true of D–H as well. The items contributing to the main groups A–C and to the discrete groups D–H were common.

Temperament interview. Thirty-one items contributed to six relatively clear-cut dimensions of temperament. The items were checked by cross-reference to ensure that the conceptual decisions had empirical endorsement. Four of the items were excluded because of insufficient spread (scatter) at this age.

The dimensions consisted of the following:

(A) Withdrawal   (4 items)
(B) Activity   (6 items)
(C) Irregularity/poor malleability   (7 items)
(D) Mood   (5 items)
(E) Intensity   (2 items)
(F) Assertiveness   (3 items)

Finally, a main activity–intensity–assertiveness dimension was derived, similar to that obtained in our previous component analysis (Garside et al 1975), as follows:

(G) Sum of (B) + (E) + (F)   (11 items).

Analyses. We confine ourselves here to simple analyses (*t*-tests) in which we compare each of the subgroups with the controls and each of the school-identified groups of boys with the group referred for clinical assessment. It was not possible to compare with each other the groups of boys selected on the basis of information from the schools because the groups overlapped; e.g. a boy could be identified both by teachers and by peers.

Results

Our major groups were school-identified aggressive children, clinical referrals and a control group. The school-identified group contained three overlapping subgroups—teacher-identified, peer-identified and assaultive. We first ascertained whether the distinction of being identified by different types of school information would be evident in any way when we examined behavioural data (parent interviews) from the home. We examined the profiles, i.e. mean scores, of the three school-identified groups on the various dimensions of both the behaviour and temperament scales. The profiles proved very similar on six of the behaviour dimensions and, on the two where they were not, the teacher-identified group had the highest scores on the anxiety–neurotic and antisocial dimensions, with the assaultive group having the lowest scores.

On temperament, the profiles proved similar on four of the seven scales. Where they were not so similar (two dimensions), the teacher-identified group had a higher adverse temperament score but, on this occasion, it was the peer-identified group that had the lowest score. Another way of representing this is to study comparisons with controls and, on three of the dimensions, both the teacher-identified group and the assaultive group had higher scores than the controls, but only on two of the dimensions did the peer-identified group have higher scores than the controls.

In these circumstances, we decided to combine the three school-identified groups for purposes of comparison, to constitute an *'any criterion'* school group.

Comparison of the three major groups

Behaviour. Fig. 1 shows that the shapes of the behaviour profiles are similar except in relation to the antisocial dimension. (This is true irrespective of

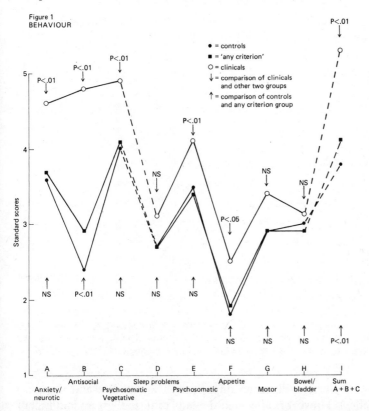

FIG. 1. Standard scores on each dimension (A–H) in the *behavioural* interview for control boys, 'any criterion' school-identified boys, and clinically referred boys. The data were re-analysed after the meeting, in the light of discussion (see p 267), before presentation in this way. Score for I is the sum of A + B + C.

whether 'raw' or standard scores are used.) The clinical group always had the most adverse behaviour scores, while the school-identified group and the controls had similar scores, except in terms of antisocial behaviour, where the school-identified group had a significantly higher score than the controls. It therefore seems that the school-identified group differ from the clinical referral group only in degree, that is, quantitatively but not qualitatively.

Temperament. The clinically referred group (see Fig. 2) had a significantly more adverse score than both the controls and the 'any criterion' group on

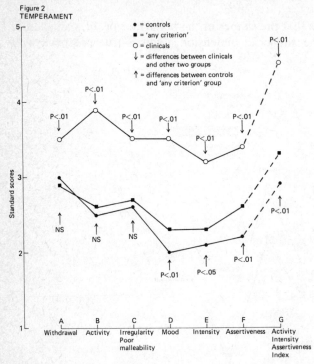

Figure 2
TEMPERAMENT

● = controls
■ = 'any criterion'
○ = clinicals
↓ = differences between clinicals and other two groups
↑ = differences between controls and 'any criterion' group

FIG. 2. Standard scores on each dimension (A–F) in the *temperament* interview for control boys, 'any criterion' school-identified boys, and clinically referred boys. The data were re-analysed after the meeting, in the light of discussion (see p 267), before presentation in this way. Score for G is the sum of B + E + F.

every dimension studied; (the same qualification about raw and standard scores applies here). However, although the 'any criterion' group had higher scores than the controls on most of the dimensions studied, the differences achieved statistical significance on only four of the seven dimensions—mood, intensity, assertiveness and the activity–intensity–assertiveness index. As the shapes of the curves of the controls and the 'any criterion' group are similar, it seems reasonable to suggest that on temperament the difference between these groups is, again, one of degree. However, the clinical group has particularly high peaks on activity and mood.

Principal components analysis on the temperament data. Another way of exploring underlying differences in the data of the groups studied is to undertake principal component analysis (PCA) (see Table 1). The numbers in

TABLE 1 Principal component analyses of temperamental items for control and 'any criterion' groups of boys

Principal components	Control group (n = 92)	'Any criterion' group (n = 87)
Component I		
Variance	21%	20%
Eigen value	6.3	5.5
Type	General component	General component
Description	Adverse temperament	Adverse temperament
Component II		
Variance	11%	9%
Eigen value	3.4	2.6
Type	Bipolar	Bipolar
Description	Withdrawal (adults/ children), poor adaptability, and moodiness	Poor adaptability, moodiness, and withdrawal (situations)
	versus Assertiveness and moodiness	*versus* Assertiveness, withdrawal (adults), and moodiness

the clinically referred group, however, were not sufficient for these purposes. In separate principal component analyses for the other two groups the *first* component was one of adverse temperament with high loadings as follows:

PCA Controls—mood, intensity, irregularity, activity
PCA 'Any criterion'—intensity, activity, irregularity, mood.

The *second* component in each group—both groups were bipolar—was also similar, but the similarities were less clear-cut. For the controls, the contrasting poles were: withdrawal (adults and children), social dependence, poor adaptability and moodiness (during dressing) *versus* dominance, assertiveness and moodiness (before and after sleep, during activity and meals). For the 'any criterion' group, the poles were: poor adaptability, moodiness (during dressing), poor malleability and withdrawal (situations) *versus* spontaneous assertiveness, dominance, moodiness (during activities and meals) and withdrawal (adults).

We appeared to have a fairly stable first component and a similar, but less stable, second component. Different kinds of moodiness appear at each pole of the second component and the loadings on withdrawal give rise to an inconsistent picture. We checked this by ranking the factor loadings on the temperamental items for each of the two groups. These ranks were correlated and we achieved a correlation of 0.73 for the first component and 0.57 for the second. We were therefore able to confirm the stability previously described—more variations are to be expected on a second component.

Discussion

One of the reasons for including temperament in our battery of assessments was based on the possibility that predictors of vulnerability to later aggressive behaviour would become evident. However, ours was not an ideal strategy for studying this—what is necessary is a longitudinal method, as used in New York and London research programmes. In the New York longitudinal study (Rutter et al 1964), temperamental patterns of irregularity, mood and poor adaptability were found to differentiate children who were likely to develop psychiatric problems. Graham et al (1973), in London, had broadly similar findings on children who had at least one parent who had received psychiatric treatment. As ours was a cross-sectional strategy, it can, at best, provide clues to possible predictors and allow us to offer hypotheses. But the method does not allow firm statements about causation nor are we able to say anything about stability and change in temperamental individuality.

There is evidence that aggressive behaviour tends to be persistent across later childhood and adolescence (Farrington 1978), which Shaffer (1978) suggests constitutes empirical support for the concept of an 'aggressive character trait'. He goes on to point out that many people consider persistent aggression to be constitutionally determined.

One of the other questions that this paper addresses is whether there are underlying patterns of temperament in different types of aggression which might be considered to be more basic and enduring than aggressive behaviour itself. Earlier research findings indicate that temperamental characteristics make an important contribution to children's vulnerability to developing psychiatric disorder (Graham et al 1973).

In brief, children with adverse temperamental characteristics are at higher risk for developing psychiatric disturbance. Furthermore, Rutter (1971) has reported that children with adverse temperamental characteristics were twice as likely as those without such characteristics to be the target of parental criticism.

Our research demonstrates an association between severe aggressive behaviour and greater degrees of temperamental adversity, in all the areas of temperament that we have investigated—the patterns are regular, with the shapes of temperamental profiles being similar. It is important to understand such associations and we therefore speculate that:

(i) greater degrees of adverse temperament may lead to greater criticism by peers and adults, and to retaliation;

(ii) as adverse temperament involves the dimension of poor adaptability and hence poorer social skills, this may form the basis of a greater likelihood of aggression; and

(iii) temperament may involve a constitutionally determined factor which, in addition, makes children more likely to produce aggressive behaviour.

We have not been able to demonstrate any association between a particular pattern of aggression and a particular type of temperament, but we have so far used only a crude classification based on the source of information about the behaviour. The only clear association identified is between 'clinical referral' and a general pattern of temperamental adversity, that is, significantly adverse scores on all the dimensions studied. This may be because clinical referral reflects severity. One possible, more specific, pattern relates to the peaks of high activity and negative mood in the 'clinical referral' group; the same two dimensions have proved predictive in diagnostic studies (Carey & McDevitt 1978). Nevertheless, the question remains of whether it is worthwhile pursuing this theme. In 1968 Moyer pointed out that as yet there had been no satisfactory systematic attempt to sort out the various kinds of aggression in order to indicate a reasonable basis for classification. While important advances have been made over the last ten years, these have not proved dramatic. Perhaps the search for clinical syndromes of aggression has been unsuccessful because the syndromes do not exist or account for only a small percentage of the total cases of aggression. Perhaps we should be seeking ways of studying profiles on a wide number of dimensions of behaviour rather than trying to place cases of aggressive behaviour into clinical pigeon-holes; or we should be highlighting factors (including temperament) that make a major contribution to aggression, rather than trying to identify more discrete syndromes.

One question that remains is whether it is possible to distinguish temperament from behavioural disturbance in adolescence. Thomas & Chess (1977) point out that, as the child grows older, it becomes increasingly difficult to measure and to categorize separate elements of behaviour—i.e. behaviour, temperament and motivation—because there are increasingly complex interactions between these facets of behaviour. Hence, it remains possible that at more extreme levels of deviance temperament and behaviour converge at this age, and one can do nothing more than report a variety of global dimensions of behaviour. We believe that this is unlikely, as our main groups differ widely on temperament but less widely on behaviour itself.

Acknowledgements

This research was supported by grants from the Northern Regional Health Authority and the Department of Education and Science. We are grateful to Mrs M. Davidson for secretarial help in preparing the manuscript, table and figures.

REFERENCES

Carey WB, McDevitt SC 1978 Stability and change in individual temperament diagnoses from infancy to early childhood. J Am Acad Child Psychiatry 17:331-337

Farrington DP 1978 The family backgrounds of aggressive youths. In: Hersov LA et al (eds) Aggression and anti-social behaviour in childhood and adolescence. J Child Psychol Psychiatry Allied Discip, Suppl 1

Garside RF, Birch H, Scott DMcI et al 1975 Dimensions of temperament in infant school children. J Child Psychol Psychiatry Allied Discip 16:219-231

Graham P, Rutter M, George S 1973 Temperamental characteristics as predictors of behavior disorders in children. Am J Orthopsychiatry 43:328-339

Kolvin I, Ounsted C, Lee D 1967 Aggression in adolescent delinquents. Br J Criminol 7:245-249

Kolvin I, Wolff S, Barber LM et al 1975 Dimensions of behaviour in infant school children. Br J Psychiatry 126:114-126

Lefkowitz MM, Eron LD, Walder LO, Huesmann LR 1977 Growing up to be violent: a longitudinal study of the development of aggression. Pergamon Press, New York

Maccoby EE, Jacklin CN 1974 The psychology of sex differences. Stanford University Press, Stanford, USA

McCord W, McCord J, Howard A 1961 Familial correlates of aggression in non-delinquent male children. J Abnorm Soc Psychol 63:493-503

Megargee EI 1970 Undercontrolled and overcontrolled personality types in extreme antisocial aggression. In: Megaree EI, Hokanson JE (eds) The dynamics of aggression. Harper and Row, New York

Moyer KE 1968 Kinds of aggression and their physiological basis. Commun Behav Biol Part A Orig Artic 2:65-87

Nicol AR, Gunn JC, Foggitt RH, Gristwood J 1972 The quantitative assessment of violence in adult and young offenders. Med Sci Law 12:275-282

Rutter M 1971 Parent-child separation: psychological effects on the children. J Child Psychol Psychiatry Allied Discip 12:233-250

Rutter M, Birch H, Thomas A, Chess S 1964 Temperamental characteristics in infancy and the later development of behaviour disorders. Br J Psychiatry 110:651-661

Shaffer D 1978 Introduction to the volume. In: Hersov LA et al (eds) Aggression and anti-social behaviour in childhood and adolescence. J Child Psychol Psychiatry Allied Discip, Suppl 1

Shaffer D, Meyer-Bahlburg HFL, Stokman CLJ 1980 The development of aggression. In: Rutter M (ed) Scientific foundations of developmental psychiatry. Heinemann Medical Books Ltd, London

Thomas A, Chess S 1977 Temperament and development. Brunner/Mazel, New York
Thomas A, Chess S, Birch H 1968 Temperament and behavior in children. New York University Press, New York

DISCUSSION

Chess: Did you use a selection of specific items in the principal component analysis?

Kolvin: No. We used all the items in the component analysis and consequently in the correlations.

Huttunen: I am interested in the differences in the reported level of appetite that you observed. We have recently studied the glucose-tolerance test among young offenders. We found that the offenders with a long history of aggressive behaviour who fulfilled the DSM-III diagnostic criteria (American Psychiatric Association 1980) for antisocial character disorder had functional hypoglycaemia significantly more often than a group of non-offenders (Virkkunen & Huttunen 1982). Even a small dose of ethanol in these subjects could induce hypoglycaemia. This observation may also be relevant to the physiological mechanisms of negative mood among the difficult children: small children with a tendency to negative mood may show functional hypoglycaemia. I hope that someone will repeat this work.

Kohnstamm: Olweus (1979) from Norway found a strong longitudinal stability in aggressive behaviour. Do you have any similar information?

Kolvin: No. We would like to make this a longitudinal study, but we haven't done this yet so I cannot answer your question. Other studies have indicated a continuity of aggression over adolescence and we wondered whether we could identify a temperamental pattern which would predict continuity of aggression in adolescents. As a first step we have undertaken a cross-sectional study.

Robinson: Did you include any girls?

Kolvin: No. When we started the research we decided to concentrate on boys. There has been a lot of published work on sex differences in relation to aggression. We were surprised when the schools told us that the girls rather than the boys were much more of a problem nowadays. Hence, we have now looked at head teachers' reports on percentages of boys and girls who are aggressive, and on types of aggression. These reports suggested that aggression was a much more common phenomenon in girls in the 1970s than before then. The reported sex differences, although not obliterated, are certainly diminished.

Stevenson-Hinde: I found your interview with nursery-school children (Garside et al 1975) very helpful because it was semi-structured, behaviourally based, and permitted the observer rather than the mother to do the rating. However, I wonder if a unipolar rating scale is preferable to a bipolar one. In this study, did you continue to use a skewed rating scale?

Kolvin: Yes. We continued to use a unipolar scale when rating items of temperament. We have, however, for the purposes of studying adolescents, reduced the length of the probe (i.e. the standard questions) and given the interviewer much more latitude in deciding what kind of adolescent activity to focus on when enquiring about different facets of temperament. One has to do this because it's not easy to find activities and interests that are consistent across all ages.

Werry: Were the temperament ratings made by the parents?

Kolvin: No. We undertake detailed interviews with the parents and the judgement about rating is made by the interviewer and not by the parents.

Werry: Was the identified group in your clinic present mainly because their parents had agreed for them to come?

Kolvin: No. Some of them were sent because of gravely difficult behaviour in the community, and others at the request of social agencies or even courts.

Werry: So is the identification of the boys as patients independent of the parents?

Kolvin: In a number of the cases, where the children were committing assaults in school, the parents were called to the school and the behaviour was discussed with them. This was similar to what transpired with the cases who were referred for clinical assessment except that the assaultive behaviour tended to be occasional rather than frequent.

Stevenson: I see a logical problem in your attempts to explore the different ways of classifying behaviour. The methods you have used have confounded the possibility of identifying patterns because you have mixed together two classification schemes. You identified groups in terms of sources of referral or places of aggressive behaviour and, taking those as fixed, you then tried to identify patterns or profiles of temperament that conform to this classification. This method puts two things together and assumes that the classification based on referral source would be isomorphic with a pattern based on temperament. Would it not be better to establish whether, by pooling all the subjects, and using cluster analysis on your present data, one could identify certain patterns of temperament? Having identified those patterns one could then see whether they were more frequently found in a particular sample from a specific referral source.

Kolvin: Yes—we have thought of this as a useful next step, but wondered whether it was legitimate to pool the clinical referrals and the school-identified cases for such purposes.

Keogh: Were there significant social-class differences in the referral rates?

Kolvin: Yes. In our preliminary work we found considerable differences in school-identification rates which merely reflected differences in social class distribution of the families of the pupils. These differences re-emerged when we did our major survey.

Thomas: Was there any social-class difference between the *clinic*-referred cases and the *school*-referred cases?

Kolvin: The school-referred cases resemble the controls in having a much wider spread of social class then the clinic-referred cases, which were notably from the less privileged classes.

Thomas: The identification of aggression as a problem of adolescence is often related to social class. The upper-middle and middle-class families have many, more discreet ways of dealing with a disturbance caused in the community by an aggressive youngster than do poorer parents, and do not have to resort to a clinic or court as frequently.

Carey: I am puzzled about your conclusion that aggressive adolescents were merely different in degree of temperament rather than having a specific profile. If results from the children with behaviour problems in the New York longitudinal study were plotted in the same way as your results, and compared with results from the children without behaviour problems, I wonder if a similar difference in degree would be apparent, but which in that study was *called* a difference in quality or temperament grouping. If you did a diagnostic profile, using means and standard deviations to categorize certain individuals as 'difficult', etc., your findings might be similar to those produced by the New York study.

Plomin: In your temperament profiles was the ordinate standardized; i.e. did you adjust the values for the mean and standard deviations of your different individual scales? That would be one way to evaluate the profiles a bit more clearly; the ups and downs of the profiles look very similar but are confounded with the means of the various categories.

Kolvin: That is a good point*.

Werry: You have used as your criterion a single kind of social behaviour. From a rather different frame of reference—a psychiatric diagnostic point of view—would your clinical group (who, presumably, have been studied in some detail and would have a psychiatric diagnosis) be diagnostically homogeneous for conduct disorder?

Kolvin: Yes. All these children have been diagnosed and rated in the same way using a number of different classifications applicable to them. Joan Stevenson-Hinde's suggestion (p 265) is useful here. An important question is whether we should combine all the identified cases and subject them to a cluster analysis. We have thought of doing this but have been reluctant to

---

* This analysis was done after the meeting, and Figs 1 and 2 (p 259 and p 260) are now presented in this form.

pursue it both because of the previously mentioned question of legitimacy and also because we have so far found little, apart from differences in severity, between the groups.

Werry: You alluded to some of the widespread data about aggressive behaviour in adolescents. The history of delinquency suggests that there are at least two qualitatively different types: those who are normal within the sub-culture (which happens to be abnormal with respect to the prevalence of the power structure of the society) and those who are abnormal in whatever sub-culture they find themselves. We would identify only the latter group as having conduct disorders. In the school-identified groups you are bound to have a heterogeneous group, which will dilute the possibilities of finding anything useful.

Rutter: The distinction between socialized and non-socialized aggression has been difficult to confirm in many studies. It sounds plausible, and there are certain pointers towards its validity but it remains doubtful whether it constitutes the most satisfactory way of subdividing conduct disturbances. Some subdivision is needed but the empirical findings so far (see Rutter & Giller 1982) do not indicate which of the various competing forms of categorization should be adopted.

Kolvin: An alternative approach would be not to try to categorize these subjects but to place them along a series of clinical dimensions relating to such themes as socialized and unsocialized delinquency and then to correlate these clinical dimensions with temperamental dimensions.

REFERENCES

American Psychiatric Association 1980 Diagnostic and statistical manual of mental disorders, 3rd edn. Task force on nomenclature and statistics. American Psychiatric Association, Washington DC

Garside RF, Birch H, Scott DMcI et al 1975 Dimensions of temperament in infant school children. J Child Psychol Psychiatry Allied Discip 16:219-231

Olweus D 1979 Stability of aggressive reaction patterns in males: a review. Psychol Bull 86:852-875

Rutter M, Giller H 1982 Juvenile delinquency: trends and perspectives. Penguin, Harmondsworth, Middlesex

Virkkunen M, Huttunen MO 1982 Evidence for abnormal glucose tolerance test among violent offenders. Neuropsychobiology, in press

Children's temperament and teachers' decisions

BARBARA K. KEOGH

Department of Education, University of California, Los Angeles, California 90024, USA

Abstract Findings from a series of studies of the educational implications of children's temperament patterns are summarized. This research has been guided by three hypotheses: (1) that there are real individual differences among children in behavioural styles or temperament; (2) that individual variations in children's patterns of temperament influence the nature of their interpersonal interactions; and (3) that perceived variations in temperament become especially powerful influences on adults' decisions when children are handicapped or at risk. Based on these assumptions, the study of temperament has followed two primary lines of research. In the first we have attempted to delineate the hypothesized link between perceived temperament variations and teachers' educational decisions. In the second we have attempted to determine the influence of perceived temperament variations on children's personal–social competence within intervention settings. Findings support a relationship between children's temperament and their achievement and adjustment in school. Temperament was related to measures of children's academic performance and to teachers' perceptions of other aspects of children's school adjustment. Further, teachers' ratings of children's temperament were related to their classroom management decisions. The results suggest that teachers' responses to children in the classroom are mediated by their perceptions of the children's temperament.

Background and rationale

The study of individual differences has been a major stream in the history of psychology and is of fundamental concern to educational and developmental psychologists. Given its historical importance, it is surprising that the major preoccupation of psychologists who study individual differences has been with cognition. From the educational perspective it is likely that a number of individual differences are important in children's educational performance. We propose that temperament is such a variable and that it has a significant impact on children's achievement and adjustment in educational settings

1982 Temperamental differences in infants and young children. Pitman Books Ltd, London (Ciba Foundation symposium 89) p 269-285

(Keogh & Pullis 1980). The study of temperament variability within an educational context has been a major focus of research in the Special Education Research Programmme at the University of California, Los Angeles (UCLA).

The UCLA programme of research has been guided by several major hypotheses and assumptions. We assume first that there are real individual differences among children in their temperament patterns and that these individual differences, while situationally sensitive, have some stability across situations and over time. Second, we assume that individual differences in children's temperament are perceived by adults and peers who interact with the children and, specifically, that these perceptions influence the nature of interpersonal interactions. In our view, adults' perceptions of children's temperament are particularly important in educational settings because instructional, management and placement decisions may be influenced. Third, we hypothesize that perceived variations in temperament are especially powerful influences on adults' decisions when children have some handicapping or limiting condition in physical or cognitive development. In other words, we propose that the impact of temperament increases with the severity of impairment. The practical consequence of this hypothesis is that temperament is a particularly important individual variable within groups of handicapped children.

With these assumptions and hypotheses providing a framework, we have approached the study of temperament in two primary lines of research. In one we have attempted to delineate the hypothesized link between children's temperament and teachers' educational decisions. In the other we have tried to determine the influence of temperament on children's personal social competence within intervention settings. In both lines of work we have studied handicapped and non-handicapped children. My focus in this paper is on the influence of individual differences in children's temperament on teachers' expectations and decisions.

Theoretical orientation

UCLA work on children's temperament and teachers' expectations has drawn heavily on the temperament work of A. Thomas and S. Chess and their colleagues (Thomas & Chess 1977, Thomas et al 1968, 1963) and on the decision-making model developed by Shavelson (1976). As the frame of reference proposed by the Thomas & Chess group is well known, it will not be detailed in this paper. The decision-making work requires brief discussion. Shavelson (1976) conceives of teaching as decision making, assuming that teachers have an array of strategies that can be selectively accessed when working with different pupils: 'In choosing a particular strategy, teachers attempt to achieve a desired outcome by matching events—both within the student (for example, attention, learning, motivation) and within the classroom (for example, distractions, facilities)—with a particular strategy. Since these events, called states of nature, are not certain but occur with different probabilities, the teacher must subjectively estimate the probability of a particular state' (p 412 in Shavelson 1976). Shavelson suggests further that probability estimates are built up in part from teachers' perceptions of children's behavioural characteristics; that is, teachers integrate selected information when making probability estimates about children's school competencies and their educational needs. Within Shavelson's model, teachers' estimates may be viewed as 'simplifying strategies' or heuristics (Tversky & Kahneman 1974) in the selection, processing and integration of information. Shavelson's approach has clear ties to the achievement attribution work of Weiner (1974, 1977) and to expectation theory.

As documented in reviews by Braun (1976), Cooper (1979), Dusek (1975) and West & Anderson (1976), there is considerable evidence attesting to the power of teacher expectancy on teacher–pupil interactions within the classroom. However, the basis for teachers' expectations is still uncertain. Dusek (1975) argues that teacher-generated expectancies have more effect than artificially or experimentally induced expectations, a point consistent with that of Mendels & Flanders (1973), who found 'naturalistic factors' more potent than contrived ones in expectation research. A variety of naturalistic factors may lead to different expectations, such factors including sex of child (LaVoie & Adams 1974, Kehle 1974), physical attractiveness (Clifford & Walster 1973, Kehle 1974), social class (Cooper et al 1975) and ethnicity (Gay 1975). In our view, temperament or behavioural style is another.

Temperament may be an especially potent influence on expectation if the temperament pattern is negative. As noted by Braun (1976, p 195): '. . . teachers are more influenced by negative information about students than by positive or neutral information'. Given the clinical picture of the 'difficult child' from the Thomas & Chess work, it is reasonable to hypothesize that particular temperament patterns may be viewed as noxious by classroom teachers, and that these perceptions are the basis for generalized expectations. The hypothesis is especially appealing given Cooper's (1979, p 406) suggestion that teachers' expectations '. . . influence teacher perceptions of control over student performance'. Although Cooper's focus was on educational performance, it seems likely that children's attributes influence teachers' perceptions of control in behavioural and social as well as academic areas.

The expectation model, along with Shavelson's (1976) decision-making model, provides a rationale for interpreting the impact of temperament variation on teachers' decisions. Of particular importance for this paper is Shavelson's argument that teachers' estimates of probability, rather than children's behaviours, determine management and instructional decisions. Shavelson's work provides a direct link between teachers' perceptions and teachers' educational decisions, and is of particular use in our work on temperament where we have attempted to identify the influence of children's temperament on teachers' estimates and decisions.

Aspects of measurement

Some aspects of measurement require review before I discuss the UCLA research findings. The Thomas & Chess (1977) Teacher Temperament Questionnaire (TTQ) has been found appropriate for clinical research, yet its use in schools in our studies presented serious problems. The 64-item TTQ proved time-consuming for teachers and not feasible for rating large numbers of children. There were also problems of item statement and questions of factor structure for the age range involved in our studies. As a first step, therefore, in collaboration with M. E. Pullis and J. Cadwell, we examined the psychometric properties of the TTQ, especially its reliability and factor structure; our analyses were based on data from samples of 35 teachers and over 300 children. Rate-rerate reliability of dimensional scores on a subset of children was high (mean Pearson $r = 0.69$–0.88); agreement between teachers' ratings of the same children was moderate but significant (mean $r = 0.33$–0.73). The eight dimensions of the TTQ were found to factor out into three primary dimensions. The first, which we called Task Orientation, was made up of persistence, distractibility, and activity. The second, identified as Personal Social Flexibility, tapped approach/withdrawal, positive mood, and adaptability. The third, identified as Reactivity, was composed of negative mood, threshold of response, and intensity of response. The third factor is essentially negative. The factor structure was found to be similar and stable across ages 3–6 years.

Because of the practical considerations of collecting temperament data on large numbers of school children, the 64-item scale was reduced to 23 items. Each item was weighted from 1–6 (1 = hardly ever; 6 = almost always). Items in the short form were selected to be factorially consistent with the longer form. The 23 items were grouped according to factor location and the item scores were summed to yield three factor scores for each child. These scores were found to be consistent and stable and to represent temperament variability in the age groups from preschool through the primary grades (Pullis 1979). Overall, the consistency of findings using the 23- rather than the 64-item TTQ suggested that the 23-item TTQ is a feasible substitute for the longer form. Our research on temperament reported here is based on findings from the 23-item short form of the TTQ.

Research findings to date

UCLA studies of temperament and teachers' perceptions and decisions have been carried out using two primary methods: vignette (word-picture) studies and research with children and teachers. In the vignette studies we have systematically manipulated the nature of the informational cues, characteristics of subjects and specific educational decisions in order to test a series of hypotheses about temperament and teachers' decisions. This paradigm also takes into account the effects of selected moderator variables (i.e. teacher characteristics) which may influence decisions. The vignette method has been shown by other investigators (Borko 1978, Shavelson et al 1977) to yield reliable and interpretable data; it provides a relatively direct way of determining the influence of particular kinds of information on teachers' decisions.

In the present work, information about the child from the vignette profiles included sex, ability, temperament patterns and handicapping conditions. In the first study, conducted with B. Yoshioka-Maxwell and J. Cadwell (unpublished report) teachers were presented with vignettes describing hypothetical pupils. Children were identified as boys or girls and as normally developing or developmentally delayed. Their temperament profiles were varied so that all possible combinations of temperament factors were represented. Scores on the three primary temperament factors already defined (Task Orientation, Flexibility and Reactivity) were presented graphically so that every temperament profile appeared in every boy/girl and normal/handicapped pairing. Teachers were asked to read each profile and to make a series of decisions about each hypothetical child in terms of readiness for kindergarten, likelihood of need for special services, and expectations of management problems in the classroom.

In a second related study with J. Cadwell, A. G. Wilcoxen, and B. Wright (unpublished report), we tested directly the influence of the degree and kind of handicap on teachers' decisions. In this study teachers were presented with descriptions of hypothetical children, all boys, some of whom were described as hearing-impaired, others as physically impaired. Handicapping conditions were selected because of their relative visibility. In addition to type of handicap, the severity of handicapping conditions (mild or moderate) was described. Findings from both studies allow several generalizations. There is a significant effect of children's temperament, especially Task Orientation, on teachers' decisions. Children with negative temperament patterns are viewed as requiring supervision and direction, and as being potential problems in the classroom. Handicapped children with negative temperament patterns are likely to elicit referral for special placement. Severity of handicap, rather than type of handicap, was associated with temperament in influencing teachers' decisions.

Findings from the vignette studies were encouraging but the real test of the influence of temperament on teachers' decisions clearly required work in actual classrooms. We have, therefore, extended this research in a series of studies working with preschool and primary-grade children and their teachers. As part of our research programme Pullis (1979) and Pullis & Cadwell (1981), examined the relationships between children's temperament, other pupil attributes, and teachers' decisions about classroom management and placement recommendations. The goal in this research was to determine if individual differences in temperament were associated with children's actual ability, their achievement in school subjects, and their behavioural adaptability. A second goal was to determine if perceived characteristics of children influenced teachers' classroom decisions about instructional strategies, referral for psychological services or expectations for future performance. Thirteen teachers of the primary grades rated over 300 children on the 23-item temperament questionnaire and also provided estimates of children's ability, expectations for performance, and management and instructional information. The latter decisions focused on management strategies in five typical classroom situations: individual deskwork, group activity, academic transitions, non-academic transitions and free play. Objective information about children was provided by the school district and included Intelligence Quotient (IQ), achievement test results and grades from previous school years.

In brief, Pullis (1979) found that the three temperament factors, particularly Task Orientation, were significant influences on teachers' classroom decisions, but had little influence on placement recommendations. The relationships between teachers' ratings of temperament and children's IQ, achievement scores and grades were significant. After controlling for the effect of IQ, Pullis found Task Behaviour and Flexibility to relate significantly to teachers' estimates of pupils' ability, the children with more positive temperament patterns being rated higher than those with less positive characteristics. In relation to test-determined IQs, teachers overestimated the ability of children with positive temperament characteristics. Taken as a whole, these findings support relationships between children's temperament and their achievement and adjustment in school. Specifically, teachers' ratings of children's temperament were significantly related to other measures of children's academic performance, to teachers' perceptions of other aspects of children's school behaviour, and to teachers' classroom management decisions. On the basis of these findings, we infer that teachers' responses to children in the classroom are mediated by their perceptions of the children's temperamental characteristics. We have replicated Pullis's (1979) findings in further UCLA work within the same school district (M. E. Pullis 1981, unpublished report) and with preschool and learning disabled children in other sections of the United States (Keogh 1982a).

Temperament and teachability

While vignettes and classroom research provided evidence that children's temperament influenced teachers' decisions, the basis of the mediating or organizing 'estimate' was unclear. We have hypothesized that teachers interpret pupil information, including temperament, within the context of their views of children's 'teachability'. The notion of teachability is consistent with the Thomas & Chess (1977) description of 'easy' as opposed to 'difficult' children. It is also consistent with the teacher–child interaction work described by J. E. Brophy and T. L. Good and their colleagues (Brophy & Evertson 1981, Brophy & Good 1970, 1974, Good & Brophy 1973).

In earlier work within the UCLA research programme we had demonstrated a strong agreement amongst teachers in their views of children's teachability. Maddox-McGinty (1975) used a paired-comparison technique in which four teachers compared every child in the classroom to every other child in response to the question: Who is more teachable? The paired-comparison technique yielded a quantitative distribution, with high scores representing high teachability and low scores representing low teachability. The actual range of aggregated scores was 9–289; there was absolute agreement as to rankings in the top and lower third of the distribution and some minor rearrangement, depending on the teacher, within the middle range. Importantly for this discussion, classroom observation data supported the generalization that teachers interacted differently and in differing amounts with children whom they viewed as high or low in teachability, their perceptions apparently converted into actual instructional behaviours. Maddox-McGinty's (1975) study supported other work on teachers' classroom behaviour and added further to the notion that teachability is a reasonable synthesizing construct within which to interpret temperament patterns.

Teachability research

In an effort to provide a more differentiated understanding of teachers' views of pupils' teachability UCLA researchers developed and tested a 33-item

'Teachable Pupil' scale, basing the teachable pupil attributes on teacher-generated descriptions (Kornblau 1982). The scale has been found to be reliable in terms of rate/rerate and teacher agreement. The items cluster into three primary dimensions, one tapping cognitive autonomous behaviours, a second defining school-related behaviours, and a third reflecting personal social characteristics. Kornblau (1982) has devised two forms of the scale, one to define teachers' views of 'model' or 'ideal' pupils, and a second to describe actual pupils in classrooms. The scale has been used with teachers from preschool through junior high school, and has factorial stability, although weighting of items varies somewhat according to the grade of teacher and child.

In a series of studies (see Kornblau & Keogh 1980, for review) we have demonstrated that teachers have *a priori* views about the attributes of model pupils. We have also shown that pupils whose characteristics are similar to the *a priori* model are viewed as highly teachable, but as less teachable the more they are discrepant from the model. In a recently completed study 49 teachers each rated 10–15 pupils on a 1–8 global teachability scale and on the differentiated 33-item Teachable Pupil Attribute Scale. The teachers also completed a 33-item ideal or model pupil scale. Comparison of the dimensional scores on the ideal and actual pupil ratings yielded a discrepancy distribution (range 19–38). The discrepancy scores were found to be significantly but inversely related to the teachers' overall ratings of children's teachability ($r = 0.55$). Of interest to the present paper was the finding that children who were viewed as less teachable were characterized by negative temperament patterns although not necessarily by low IQ or by academic deficiences. A multivariate analysis of variance across the discrepancy distribution yielded significant F values for all three temperament factors (Task Orientation, $F = 20.06$, Flexibility, $F = 10.91$, and Reactivity, $F = 6.5$; the overall value of F was 10.32). Discrepant children were described as high in Reactivity (over-reactive) and low in Flexibility and Task Orientation. In contrast, highly teachable pupils had positive temperament profiles. They were described as high in Task Orientation, high in Flexibility, and moderately Reactive.

The impact of children's temperament on teachers' views of teachability is well illustrated in a study of 80 preschool children, in 1979-81, in four preschools in Southern California. At the beginning of the study, all the children were four years old; they represented a broad range of socio-economic and ethnic backgrounds. Thirteen teachers or classroom aides provided temperament and teachability ratings; independent measures were taken of the children's cognitive ability, their readiness for school, their motivational characteristics, and their interactions with peers, the latter data gathered through classroom observations. Selected findings are of particular interest to this symposium. Teachers' ratings of children's teachability were significantly related to children's social class, the values of r ranging from 0.23 to 0.40 according to teachability dimensions; temperament factor 1 (Task Orientation) was modestly related to social class ($r = 0.27$). Teachability dimension scores were also related to children's IQ, although the relationships between temperament factor scores and IQ were non-significant. Correlations between the three teachability dimensions and the three temperament factors ranged from 0.14–0.69, with eight of nine values being statistically significant. Temperament factor 1 (Task Orientation) had the highest relationship to the overall teachability rate ($r = 0.47$). Regressing the various child characteristics (three temperament factors, IQ, sex, ethnicity, socio-economic status) onto the overall teachability rating accounted for 17% of the variance. Temperament factor 1 (Task Orientation) made the largest single contribution (13%). IQ and temperament factor 2 (Flexibility) contributed only an additional 3%, despite our expectation that cognitive ability would be a potent influence on teachers' views. Clearly, teachability is a complex perception which is not synonymous with intelligence.

Findings from other work (Keogh 1982b) demonstrate that within a group of children with relatively similar general ability but with educational problems (e.g. special schools for learning disabled pupils) teachability ratings vary. Teachers in special education programmes are able to make reliable and consensual differentiations about children's teachability; there are consistent relationships between these ratings and children's temperament patterns. These findings suggest that teachers' perceptions are built up from a variety of child attributes representing a number of aspects of children's personal competence. Temperament appears to contribute to this perception.

On a clinical note, it is interesting that the teachers who have participated in our research have reported that consideration of pupils' temperament has made them more sensitive to their own perceptions of individual children. The temperament dimensions apparently provide a differentiated framework for viewing children. Recognition of temperament patterns is particularly helpful in anticipating problem situations and allows teachers to modify their own behaviour in order to get a better approximation of the 'goodness of fit' suggested by Thomas & Chess (1977) in their work with clinical populations.

Summary

Taken as a whole, UCLA research on temperament and teachability suggests that individual differences in children's temperament are important contributors to children's success at school. Despite methodological and measurement limitations, it is possible to describe children's temperament patterns with some reliability. These variations in patterns are clear contributors to teachers' views of pupils' teachability, to the estimates they make of pupils' abilities, and to the kinds of expectations they have for pupils' educational performance. Recognition of the stylistic differences in children's behaviour is important for teachers as these variations are the basis of many instructional and management decisions.

Acknowledgements

This research was supported by Project REACH (Research on Early Abilities of Children with Handicaps) under contract between the US Office of Special Education and the University of California, Los Angeles. I wish to thank Dr Carol E. Smith of the System Development Corporation for consultation and editorial assistance in preparation of this manuscript. I also thank Alexander Thomas and Stella Chess for their continuing interest and consultation throughout this project. Their generosity in sharing ideas has added immensely to our work.

REFERENCES

Borko H 1978 Factors contributing to teachers' preinstructional decisions about classroom management and long-term objectives. Doctoral dissertation, University of California, Los Angeles

Braun C 1976 Teacher expectations: sociopsychological dynamics. Rev Educ Res 46:185-213

Brophy JE, Evertson CM 1981 Student characteristics and teaching. Longman, New York

Brophy J, Good T 1970 Teachers' communication of differential expectations for children's classroom performance: some behavioral data. J Educ Psychol 61:365-374

Brophy JE, Good TL 1974 Teacher–student relationships: causes and consequences. Holt Rinehart and Winston, New York

Clifford MM, Walster E 1973 The effect of physical attractiveness on teacher expectations. Sociol Educ 46:248-258

Cooper HM 1979 Pygmalion grows up: a model for teacher expectation communication and performance influence. Rev Educ Res 49:389-410

Cooper H, Baron R, Lowe C 1975 The importance of race and social class in the formation of expectancies about academic performance. J Educ Psychol 67:312-319

Dusek J 1975 Do teachers bias children's learning? Rev Educ Res 45:661-684

Gay G 1975 Teachers' achievement expectations of and classroom interactions with ethnically different students. Contemp Educ 46:166-172

Good TL, Brophy JE 1973 Looking in classrooms. Harper and Rowe, New York

Kehle TJ 1974 Teachers' expectations: ratings of student performance as biased by student characteristics. J Exp Educ 43:54-60

Keogh BK 1982a Temperament: an individual difference of importance in interaction programs. Top Early Child Spec Educ 2(2): in press

Keogh BK 1982b Individual differences in temperament: a contributor to the personal-social and educational competence of learning disabled children. In: McKinny JD, Feagens L (eds) Current topics in learning disabilities. Ablex Publishing Corp, New Jersey, in press

Keogh BK, Pullis ME 1980 Temperament influences on the development of exceptional children. In: Keogh BK (ed) Adv Spec Educ 1:239-276

Kornblau BW 1982 Teachable pupil survey: a technique for assessing teachers' perceptions of pupil attributes. Psychol Sch, in press

Kornblau BW, Keogh BK 1980 Teachers' perceptions and educational decisions. In: Gallagher JJ (ed) New directions for exceptional children. Jossey-Bass, San Francisco

LaVoie JC, Adams GR 1974 Teacher expectancy and its relation to physical and interpersonal characteristics of the child. Alberta J Educ Res 29:122-133

Maddox-McGinty AM 1975 Children's nonverbal behavior in the classroom and teachers' perceptions of teachability: an observational study. Doctoral dissertation, University of California, Los Angeles

Mendels GE, Flanders JP 1973 Teachers' expectations and pupil performance. Am Educ Res J 10:203-212

Pullis ME 1979 An investigation of the relationship between children's temperament and school adjustment. Doctoral dissertation, University of California, Los Angeles

Pullis ME, Cadwell J 1981 The influence of children's temperament characteristics on teachers' decision strategies. Am Educ Res J, in press

Shavelson RJ 1976 The psychology of teaching methods. In: Gage N (ed) Yearbook of the national society for the study of education. University of Chicago Press, Chicago, 75(1):372-414

Shavelson RJ, Cadwell J, Izu T 1977 Teachers' sensitivity to the reliability of information in making pedagogical decisions. Am J Educ Res 14:83-97

Thomas A, Chess S 1977 Temperament and development. Brunner/Mazel, New York

Thomas A, Chess S, Birch HG, Hertzig ME, Korn S 1963 Behavioral individuality in early childhood. New York University Press, New York

Thomas A, Chess S, Birch HG 1968 Temperament and behavior disorders in children. New York University Press, New York

Tversky A, Kahneman D 1974 Judgment under uncertainty: heuristics and biases. Science (Wash DC) 185:1124-1131

Weiner B 1974 Achievement, motivational and attribution theory. General Learning Press, Morristown, NJ

Weiner B 1977 An attributional approach for educational psychology. Rev Res Educ 4:179-209

West CK, Anderson TH 1976 The question of preponderant causation in teacher expectancy research. Rev Educ Res 46:613-630

DISCUSSION

Plomin: In one study you had 49 teachers rating hundreds of children, and in some studies you had teacher variance as well as child variance. Given that these should be relatively random samples, how much of the variance is actually between teachers?

Keogh: At one stage we thought we might have to transform all the rating data to some sort of standardized score because of that problem. We examined the distributional characteristics of the teachers' ratings and did not find a lot of variance: the teachers seemed to use the scales in similar ways.

We had similar ranges and closely matched means. Occasionally a teacher was very different from the rest, and I don't know how to explain it. To date we have not transformed the data, and we hope not to, arguing that the distributional characteristics, teacher by teacher, are comparable.

Bates: Teacher ratings are certainly useful and important. We should consider how the temperament ratings can be differentiated from other ratings that the teacher might make. One should have discriminability as well as convergence in order to understand the meaning of a scale. Do you have any data relevant to that?

Keogh: Our immediate plans are to try to identify the child's behavioural characteristics that allow us to understand why teachers rate as they do. We are in the process of collecting observational data which we can relate to the ratings (N. D. Burstein, unpublished work).

Bates: The problem is that a teacher might interpret general behaviour of the child in certain ways, so that a behaviour problem questionnaire might contain the teacher's same observations as a temperament questionnaire would.

Keogh: We have some objective, non-teacher-generated data from our observational studies (in progress). My colleagues K. Chan and D. Stipek are also gathering social competence and motivational data on the same children, their findings being independent of the teachers' perceptions. The additional child information may allow us to identify some behavioural bases for the teachers' ratings.

Bates: One perhaps should be able to discover particular variables that do *not* correlate with something called temperament.

Bell: One could probably tap, to a certain extent, variation due to a high incidence of minor physical anomalies. High-anomaly children are non-preferred sociometrically—e.g. other children don't want to sit next to them. But despite problems like that, at least one would pick up a different source of variance than the teacher's perceptions.

Hsu: Here again I would stress the importance of cross-cultural and sub-cultural studies on the impact of temperament on teachers (see also p 17 and p 113). In the same country, within different subcultures, the teacher's approach may be different. Even the main goal of teaching may be different in different cultures. In Taiwan it is normal to have 50 children in one classroom, and getting the children to remain quiet is emphasized. Most of the teaching is done by didactic lectures and the children are supposed to be listening. The goal of the teacher is for more children to succeed in entrance examinations for higher education.

Graham: Is it possible to look at the longitudinal interaction between temperamental characteristics, or the teacher's perception of them, and academic progress over a period of time? It would be interesting to know what academic failure does to temperamental characteristics and also how temperamental characteristics can predict academic progress.

Keogh: The closest information we have in relation to that comes from Michael Pullis' work on youngsters originally in the first grade and now about to enter the fourth grade. He found that teachers overestimated the IQs of children with positive temperament patterns and also tended to give them higher grades (see p 274-275).

Robinson: Can you tell, from your data, how much of the variance in academic progress is due to the teacher's perception of the pupil's temperament and how much is due to the learning styles of the children themselves?

Keogh: I cannot answer that. We would need a measure of learning style that was independent of teachers' perceptions.

Robinson: When teachers have been told what to expect about children's IQ, this is heavily reflected in the children's subsequent academic progress. Could the same effect apply here?

Keogh: In collaborative data collection on 4–5-year-olds with D. Stipek and K. Chan, we have been obtaining independent ratings of behaviour during testing along with measures of social competence, including peer sociometrics. Stipek's observational data assessing 'persistence' may be an objective aspect of at least one temperament variable which could be related to progress or achievement and which might help sort out the teacher-perception effects on children's performance.

Robinson: This is a central question.

Keogh: I agree absolutely. We must move towards some more objective, teacher-independent information in order to determine the relative impact of the teachers' perception. That's partly what I hope our observational data will do for us.

Kolvin: Is it possible for you to change the focus in your analysis from *how* children do things—in other words, temperament—to *what* they do. You have adjustment data as well. You could then see what contribution this makes to teachers' decision-making.

Keogh: Yes. We would be able to do that with our classroom observation data.

Bell: It seems to me that, from your previous efforts to predict learning disability from kindergarten data, you do have longitudinal data. There should be some convergent validity.

Keogh: The samples for which we have temperament information were very small.

Bell: I was thinking that one of the predictors of second- and third-grade disability from the kindergarten period was the ability to follow instructions, and another was social relations with the other children. So it does seem that you have some longitudinal data.

Keogh: They are not tied directly to this data base, although they allow the argument.

Berger: I would like to consider your behavioural observations. In our work of helping teachers with management of classroom difficulties, one can draw a set of distinctions between the teacher's views about a child, what the teacher thinks she does with that particular child, and what she actually does. The association between these may not always be strong. That is, they may not be congruent. Your results seem to account for some of the variance in terms of teachers' perceptions of what is going on, but the real issue is on the behavioural side—what do they actually do with the children? Is teachers' behaviour consistent with what they think they do?

Keogh: We obtained (A.M. Maddox-McGinty, unpublished work) a distribution of children's 'teachability' as perceived by teachers, and then selected pupils within each third of that distribution to observe the nature of the teacher–pupil interaction. We found that teachers spent just about the same amount of time with high-teachable and low-teachable pupils, but the kind of interchange was dramatically different. With low-teachable pupils, the interaction was directive, instructional, serious, sometimes punitive, but seldom fun. With the high-teachable pupils, there was instruction and considerable social interchange. Interestingly, the low-teachable youngsters, when not involved with the teacher in the classroom, were not involved with anybody, but spent a lot of time sitting alone. High-teachable children, on the other hand, interacted socially a lot with other pupils (even though they were perhaps not supposed to do that) and the behaviour was tolerated by the teacher. They spent very little time sitting doing nothing. I agree with you that what the teacher thinks she does and what she actually does can be very different, and we also know that the teacher interacts very differently with different pupils.

Berger: Have you used a behaviour modification framework which looks at things like praise or reprimanding for academic work? We find, clinically, that this is crucial: the teachers think that they praise the children or reprimand them in certain ways, but observations give an entirely different picture. We find low rates of positive comments about academic work and behaviour. Most of the interactions tend to be neutral or negative.

Keogh: In A. M. Maddox-McGinty's work the low-teachable children received a much higher rate of negative comments and instructional directions, and very little praise; the teacher variability was striking. We have also looked at the behaviour of teachers in kindergarten classrooms, and have found stylistic differences in the teachers' interactions with children. As an example, some teachers have a lot of verbal interaction with the children, either positive or negative, but relatively little physical contact. Other teachers are very physical—there is a lot of touching, patting, hair-ruffling, and that sort of thing. In a two-week period one teacher was observed never to praise a child.

Carey: You said that temperament was related to measures of children's academic performance. Would children with a certain amount of learning disability, but with a high score in your dimensions of Task Orientation and Flexibility (which in my mind translate into high attention-span and adapt-ability), do better than similarly disabled children with less of these two qualities?

Keogh: According to M. E. Pullis's data (unpublished results, 1979) and from our preliminary analyses of temperament in a group of learning-disabled pupils (Keogh 1982, in press) there is a positive correlation between the Task Orientation factor and academic performance. There may also be a tendency for teachers to overestimate the abilities of Task-Oriented children. Given the ability to persist and the teacher's positive attitude, we would expect such a child to get along fairly well in school, and to be an achieving pupil within a learning-disabled class.

Werry: Which temperamental characteristic had the highest loading (on multiple regression) with academic success in your results?

Keogh: Within the learning disabilities group the dimension of Reactivity contributed significantly to *progress* as assessed by a senior-teacher adminis-trator in the school. The temperament dimensions of Task Orientation and Flexibility were important contributors to the teachers' views of the pupils' teachability.

Werry: Isn't that the exact opposite of what you were proposing?

Keogh: Not really, but nonetheless it was a surprise, and I can only speculate about the reasons. This group of learning-disabled children in-cluded a number of pupils with serious behaviour/conduct problems. Progress may be related to an improved ability to moderate and control behaviour rather than to a better academic achievement *per se*. In general, teachers tend to value the child who is high in Task Orientation, who persists, and who is not distracted. In a group of children who have both academic and teacher problems, however, the attributes making up Reactivity may override the other influences.

Kolvin: Do you think age matters in this exercise? Perhaps the number of teachers who are teaching the child at a particular time is also important. Could you not strengthen the associations by combining data from various sources so as to produce pooled teacher–teacher or parent–teacher ratings?

Keogh: That is a good point. Occasionally we have been able to look at several teachers who work with the same children and we get reasonable agreements there. Ideally one would use a Junior High School, where the pupils go from class to class. My own interests have been with younger children in particular.

Hsu: Do you have any correlational data between teachers' rating scale and parents' rating scale?

Keogh: From our original sample of 300 or so youngsters, (B. K. Keogh et al, unpublished results) we obtained both mother's and father's ratings on as many children as we could (about 70). On those children we had ratings from several teachers and from each parent. The correlations between parents were generally good (range of *r*: 0.254–0.734; mean correlation, 0.579), but those between parents' and teachers' ratings were much lower, many statistically non-significant. There were differences, too, in the factor structure (based on ratings from 126 mothers). The Task Orientation factor (distractibility, persistence and activity), clearly defined in the teacher data, did not emerge as directly from the mothers' ratings. We interpreted this as reflecting a situational influence; that is, Task Orientation is a more important set of attributes in school than at home.

Rutter: Is the prediction of progress—academic, social, or behavioural—better with teachers' ratings of temperament or with pooled mother–father–teacher ratings?

Keogh: Our data do not allow us to answer that question.

Rutter: It would be interesting to try that, I think, in that you have an interesting comparison. On the one hand, the teacher is obviously much more closely related to the situation; on the other hand, by pooling data from different sources one can assess a more pervasive characteristic. Schachar et al (1981), dealing with the Isle of Wight data, found that pervasive over-activity (i.e. on teacher *and* parent ratings) was a better predictor of both cognitive impairment and the persistence of behavioural problems, than were either teacher or parent ratings alone.

Keogh: We might be able to analyse selected subsets of our data but we have not done so.

Rutter: I was struck that Personal Social Flexibility was much more important, in the teachers' views, in your learning disorder group. But that characteristic had a very low relationship to any of the outcome measures. What do you make of that?

Keogh: Perhaps we are dealing with such extreme youngsters in the learning disabilities sample that the relationships are idiosyncratic to that group. We shall have to look at the same kinds of variables in less handicapped groups. We can't make direct comparison between the two samples we have talked about today because one set of findings is for four- and five-year-old non-handicapped children, the other for older learning-disabled pupils. In the learning disabilities study, age and handicap are confounded.

REFERENCES

Keogh BK 1982 Individual differences in temperament: a contributor to the personal-social and educational competence of learning disabled children. In: McKinny JD, Feagens L (eds) Current topics in learning disabilities. Ablex Publishing Corp, New Jersey, in press

Schachar R, Rutter M, Smith A 1981 The characteristics of situationally and pervasively hyperactive children: implications for syndrome definition. J Child Psychol Psychiatry Allied Discip 22:375-392

General discussion II

Different approaches to the study of temperament and its disorders

Chess: This symposium has brought together people with different areas of interest in temperament, and has covered various aspects of the work that we have seen developing over the 25 years since we started our New York longitudinal study. From our early attempts to categorize children through our observations on them, we moved to using other people—i.e. the parents—as continuous observers, next to using standardized observations by trained observers, and then we became interested in observations that can monitor characteristic interactions without the presence of an observer distorting the situation.

Our core of agreement at this symposium is that we wish to elucidate the functional aspects of temperament development, whether to improve health-care or to help manage behavioural difficulties, or to increase our basic understanding of the developmental process. I shall go away from this symposium reassured that our initial study of temperament was a worthwhile area of research, and pleased that so many people from different disciplines are now working on the subject. We can all learn from each other's approaches.

Despite our arguments about whether questionnaires or interviews or observations are best, we are all fundamentally interested in using these tools to help us to know real children and what they do, and what potential each child may have for developing his or her temperamental style.

Kolvin: I am interested in the implications of the work we have been discussing here for management of children. We study the child's temperamental profile and also the child's interaction with the mother and then inevitably we move on to consider treatment. The crucial question is whether we can modify temperament by intervention and, if so, what kinds of intervention are effective.

Chess: As a psychiatrist I treat a large number of difficult children. I have great faith in attempts to turn a dissonant parent–child interaction into a more consonant one. But this consonance has been misunderstood and has led to the hypothesis that, provided the child's and the parent's temperaments match, functioning will be optimal. However, a highly intense child and a highly intense parent would not generally produce a good outcome. Even parents with the best will in the world can be sorely tried by a child who has a difficult temperament, especially if the child is a withdrawer, adapts slowly and has negative moods. Such a child may also be intense and irregular in rhythm, the latter especially important in the early months when parents need sleep. The parents can try love and then discipline, but even those who behave consistently with their other children can become inconsistent with a difficult child. Demoralized parents often need reassurance that they have acted responsibly by coming for treatment. When they feel less guilty about their own actions, they can begin to follow advice on management of the child, improving one situation at a time; and the evidence of a first success will breed further successes.

Practical uses of temperament research

Rutter: Your comments echo some of the points Professor Carey made in his paper (p 191-205). Let me for a moment take a cynical position, and ask him some questions about evidence. In so far as the clinician makes this sort of approach, does he or she actually need to know anything about the child's temperament? It may be helpful to introduce the parents to the notion of temperament in order to help them deal with the child better but, scientifically, what use does this information have in parent guidance? We know that there are robust and well established associations between temperamental variables and disorder; we know that temperamental variables are associated with certain patterns of parent–child interaction; and we know that temperament can change over time. That is important knowledge. But what evidence do we have about the best parental style for particular child temperaments? In other words, do we know how to use the information on temperament to advocate a particular mode of handling? Secondly, do we have any evidence about what causes temperament to alter over time? Thirdly, apart from the general finding that stresses are likely to be worse for the child with difficult temperament, what are the occasions when particularly adverse or difficult temperamental characteristics lead on to a disorder, and how can we translate that knowledge into clinical action?

Carey: The two anecdotes in my paper (p 197, 198) give a partial answer to your questions. In both cases, knowledge of the child's temperament told me two important things: it explained why a child developed a behavioural problem so rapidly when the surrounding situation became stressful, even though the child had been apparently doing well up to that point; and it set realistic goals for professional management by indicating the part of the child's symptoms that I should try to help the parents to alleviate i.e. the reactive aspects rather than the pre-existing temperament.

Graham: Apart from anecdotal information, we have no scientific evidence that a consideration of the child's temperamental style makes any difference to effective treatment. Indeed, it would be difficult to devise an experiment to demonstrate this because it's difficult to imagine a therapy that doesn't take the child's circumstances and personality into account. One might assume that child psychoanalytic forms of treatment, or family therapy, do not involve the children's characteristics but one knows from the observations of practitioners of each type of treatment that they do take account of the ways in which children differ from one another, though perhaps to different degrees. The piece of work nearest to a trial was reported by Cullen (1976), who suggested that child-centred parent counselling reduces the number of behaviour problems.

The second and third questions that Professor Rutter has raised are perhaps best considered as one question. We have evidence from our longitudinal study of 3–8-year-old children that characteristics within the family (e.g. marital disharmony) can turn non-difficult (non-symptomatic) children into difficult (symptomatic) children (Richman et al 1982). I am here talking about what I would call *severe* problems of temperamental characteristics or mild to moderate disorders of behaviour. One might expect children who are only slightly difficult, or who have minor behavioural problems, to be responsive to the same family influences and to the same types of therapy.

Bell: A feasible research goal, to produce something that might be useful for parents, would be to determine the effects on parents of children with these difficult characteristics at each of the major developmental phases. One could simply advise the parents on what they may encounter. How they *manage* the interaction with the child will be largely a matter of their own proclivities. If parents are told about the general characteristics of the difficult child, though without labelling the child with such a term, and how such a child affects adults, then they have all the information that they could expect to find useful.

Wolkind: It is important not to see temperament as a concept that is inevitably opposed to the views and practice of family therapists (see also p 205). Child psychiatric practice differs greatly from paediatrics, and because of the referral processes we predominantly see patients who have many difficulties within their families. In these cases the evaluation of the child's temperament can still be extremely useful. We can acknowledge the problems that a difficult temperament can cause for families in the same way that we acknowledge the problems associated with a physical handicap. This can often remove a weight of guilt from the parents and allow us to look more easily at the family dynamics.

Fulker: I speak not as a clinician, but as someone considering the sorts of things that I would like to hear if I were taking myself and my child to a clinician because of a temperament problem. We have discussed on several occasions the problem of prediction and the teasing out of relationships in longitudinal studies. These relationships are often moderate to weak, with correlations of only about 0.3, and we need to consider what a parent can usefully be told in this context. One might more usefully take the normative data and express them as statements about 'relative risks' which parents might then be able, subjectively, to get to grips with. For example, if my child were in the top 10% of a group that was associated only weakly (say $r = 0.3$) with some later problem, it might be useful to explain to me that if the child were in the lower 10% of the group his risk of later problems would be four or five times less. Such a relative risk statement might be more use to the parent than correlational statements.

Measurement and categorization of temperament (see also p 111-113)

McNeil: We have discussed measurement and categorization throughout the symposium, and I think it would be useful to summarize these discussions. We seem to agree more about the problems than about the solutions. Opinions are polarized. Psychometricians, for example, believe that there is no reason to free the clinical methods from the usual requirements for psychometric studies. Clinicians have justifiable fears that computer analysis will destroy their clinically meaningful patterns and yield a homogeneous composite that is tight and clean but of no clinical interest.

The reasons we do this kind of research are also different: some people want to apply it clinically; some to study the development of psychopathology; some to examine the evolution of the parent–child relationship; some to investigate the effects of potentially significant social or somatic events. There is also the interesting question of where temperament is important: is it, in a large sample, the 5% that has a unique and interesting temperament characteristic or is it, for example, the specific amount of the difficult trait in each child that is most important?

A general sentiment here has been that interviews are better than questionnaires. An important point is, for whom are we developing these instruments—for ourselves, where we have control over how they are used, or for more general scientific investigators? A well planned interview is probably much better than a questionnaire but a poorly done interview may be much worse than a well constructed questionnaire. Furthermore, there are different interview techniques and great differences between questionnaires, particularly in how anchored they are to specific behaviours (Persson-Blennow & McNeil 1979, Buss & Plomin 1975). Our instinctive feelings do not provide an adequate basis for assessing the relative advantages and disadvantages of questionnaires, observations and interviews. We must test what works best for what purposes. I would like to know, for example, what interviews can reveal that questionnaires cannot. One undoubtedly cannot measure interactions with a questionnaire. People will continue to use different methods. We need more studies like that of Wilhoit (1976), who compared two methods (interview and questionnaire) systematically *within the same study*. A vital direction for further research will be to set up studies like this, comparing results across different types of assessment, with due consideration given to the relative merits of each for particular purposes. Funds for research are limited, and questionnaires are likely, for purely financial reasons, to be used more in the future.

We should try to think more constructively and creatively about how to combine the various techniques. Some people are now using questionnaires in their interviews. Can we, similarly, use more of an interview style in our questionnaires? We have started to do this in my department by leaving the mother free to describe the child in her own words if our choice of answers on the questionnaire is inadequate for her. In that way we collect data on behaviour that we then score according to the answer which we feel is most appropriate. Telephone enquiries can be used to follow up problems encountered with questionnaires. The next question is whether one can study temperament and interaction at the same time, even though one uses two different methods.

Regarding constructs, I can't see any good alternative to trying both old and new constructs, assuming that the base data that one gathers are about the same. Although I have been critical of certain aspects of the New York longitudinal study, I can't understand why anybody would want to throw out those variables that have now been studied for 25 years, and for which so much information exists. But at the same time it would be foolhardy not to try to find alternatives based on these data, to see if they can help us in other ways. For example, we have used factor scores in stability analyses and found that they show higher stability, as expected, than do our single variables. If our goal is to detect characteristics that are stable, then that is a better measurement strategy; but if our goal is to find categories that relate to given individual characteristics then perhaps we would want to stick with some of the established variables; we should use both strategies.

Thomas: There is no question that a poor interview is a disaster, and any interview involves many intangibles connected with the interaction between interviewer and subject. An interview in combination with a questionnaire has been used in other areas of clinical research. A questionnaire can act as a screen, especially with large populations, for cases at high risk or susceptible to particular difficulties. An interview could then be used; for example, if the mother's and father's answers seem confused or are contradictory, this would provide a focus for the interview.

I have a final point about our own temperament categories. We have continued to be satisfied with them, as we have used them, primarily because they continue to indicate functional significance in our study and in others. Nevertheless we are delighted when other, new, categories that have functional significance are suggested. Barbara Keogh's discussion (this volume, p 269-285) of Task Orientation in school seems highly relevant here. A sure sign that the work we have tried to stimulate on temperament was coming to an end would be if no new categories or combinations of categories were being developed or found to be useful.

Developmental issues

Hinde: I have learnt from these few days that some temperamental characteristics may be constitutional and others may not; if they *are* constitutional, they may or may not have a genetic basis; if they have a genetic basis, it may or may not be heritable; if the genetic basis *is* heritable, it may not be consistently so; and the appearance of any characteristic itself may not be consistent with age. These findings must lead to a greater sophistication in the questions that we ask about the constitutional basis of temperamental characteristics. Now I understand that whether or not they are constitutional issues matters very much to the clinician; it affects whether or not she or he can reassure parents by telling them that they have, say, a very active child. But if one is concerned with the role of temperamental characteristics in personality development, then it doesn't matter so much because one starts at a particular developmental stage with certain individual characteristics and assesses whether they have consequences for later development.

In general, I believe that it is dangerous to consider us all as temperament researchers because this aspect of our work will become all the more valuable if its results are integrated with our other research interests. Temperamental characteristics are only part of the total picture, and their importance in development lies not just in their consistency over time but also in how they affect, and are affected by, other characteristics of the individual. Those effects are mediated through relationships with other individuals. One of the characteristics of a relationship between two individuals is that interactions of one type may be affected by interactions of quite different types; so the sequelae that we find may not be those that we would have predicted at first glance. For example, assessment of a child's rhythm or regularity depends on quite different issues from the behavioural data that we took when watching mother–child interaction. Yet there were strong and meaningful correlations between the assessments of Irregular and of how the mother and child behaved together, as I mentioned in my paper (p 66-86). Retrospectively, this makes sense, because in these mother–child dyads there was a good deal of maternal control. But one could not necessarily have predicted this from the sorts of questions on which the assessment of Irregular is based. The maternal control might be expected to have further consequences on temperamental characteristics or on other characteristics of the individual.

Because of the complexity in these mutual influences between temperamental characteristics and other aspects of personality we have to be wary about ascribing things that turn up at a particular age to timed gene action. We can climb onto that bandwagon too quickly by thinking that we are using the most recent findings from behavioural genetics and so on, but this could block the way to the analysis of what is actually going on in the course of interaction.

My final point is that if we are interested in the relations between temperamental characteristics and what goes on in interactions and relationships, we have to recognize that this depends on other variables—sex, sibling status, and so on. We need to know whether these are due to correlated characteristics in the child or due to other individuals treating, say, boys high on mood differently from girls high on mood. One way to answer Michael Rutter's second and third questions—about what makes temperament alter with time and what determines when adverse temperamental characteristics lead on to disorder—will be in the analysis of how temperamental characteristics affect behaviour and relationships. We must be careful not to let those sorts of studies get divorced from other more epidemiological studies about the long-term sequelae of particular patterns of temperamental characteristics.

Temperament and family interactions

Stevenson-Hinde: The dialectic between temperament and relationships has come up throughout the meeting, not only in the papers by myself (p 51-65), Hinde et al (p 66-86), Dunn & Kendrick (p 87-105) and Wolkind & De Salis (p 221-239), who have addressed it directly, but also in Robert Plomin's work (p 155-167) on behavioural genetics and the importance of E_1—the within-family variance—in the development of temperament. How can we best conceptualize and crystallize what is going on within a family? We seem to agree about certain steps. I realize that whether we do sums or not with our nine or eleven temperamental characteristics depends on our purpose. For this particular question, however, we really need to get down to four or five variables. In particular we should aim for summary characteristics such as Difficult or Slow-to-Warm-Up, which may be predictive of behaviour problems or settling into school. Assessments need to be made not only of the focal child, but also of siblings, mother and father. What would then be important would be the *pattern* of characteristics within each family. For example, an intense mother and an intense child will certainly interact differently from a low-intensity mother and an intense child. It is not just a matter of the child's characteristics but of how they fit with the characteristics of the rest of the family. This reflects Professor Carey's point that a Difficult child will not necessarily have difficult family interactions and be brought to him as a problem.

Both observations and interviews can add slightly different aspects to a study of family interactions. Having used interviews myself, I feel that they have an advantage in that the mother is free to talk about difficult scenes, perhaps in a way that she would be unwilling to act out in front of an observer. One therefore should not think that observations are necessarily more valid or true to life than interviews.

Finally, within the dialectic between characteristics and interactions, the idea of feedback has come up several times. It would be good if we eventually could make better use of models such as regulatory negative feedback and positive feedback. For the latter, I'm thinking of Stephen Wolkind's example of a difficult infant producing an extra burden on the mother which therefore influences her mood and behaviour and in turn influences the child's characteristics. It may be best not simply to look for high correlations but to look as well for 'flexible continuity' over time.

REFERENCES

Buss AH, Plomin R 1975 A temperament theory of personality development. Wiley, New York
Cullen KJ 1976 A six-year controlled trial of prevention of children's behavior disorders. J Pediatr 88:662-667
Persson-Blennow I, McNeil TF 1979 A questionnaire for measurement of temperament in six-month-old infants: development and standardization. J Child Psychol Psychiatry Allied Discip 20:1-13
Richman N, Stevenson J, Graham P 1982 Preschool to school: a behavioural study. Academic Press, London
Wilhoit P 1976 Assessment of temperament during the first months of life. Doctoral dissertation, Florida State University. (Available from University Microfilms, Ann Arbor, Michigan, No 76-29498)

Chairman's closing remarks

MICHAEL RUTTER

Department of Child and Adolescent Psychiatry, Institute of Psychiatry, De Crespigny Park, Denmark Hill, London SE5 8AF, UK

In our discussions about temperament it is striking that we have been able to take for granted the resolution of many issues that would have provoked controversy a mere 20 years ago. We have assumed the importance of behavioural individuality; it is well demonstrated, and it was unnecessary for us to discuss it further. Moreover, it was possible for us to start with the presumption that these differences *matter*; that they predict future disorders, patterns of personal interaction and responses to life change or stress.

Also, we have accepted as established that we can measure temperamental attributes. Of course, there has been argument about the most appropriate means of measurement and a recognition that continuing methodological difficulties have yet to be overcome. Nevertheless, we have at our disposal a variety of instruments that have proved 'workable. Instead of disputing these basic premises, we have focused on some of the more difficult issues that stem from their acceptance. Both the many matters that we could take for granted and the complexity of those that we actually discussed mark the progress made in temperament research over the last two decades.

The problems involved in measurement have been well aired in our discussions. It is accepted that many improvements could be made in our techniques of questionnaire, interview and direct observational assessment; further work is required into the issues of scaling and, most especially, into the conceptualization and grouping of variables; and much has to be learned about the comparability of measures across different age periods. Nevertheless, it is clear that we have enough instruments available for the moment. Rather than each of us making our own idiosyncratic modifications or improvements (which would remove the possibility of direct comparison across studies), we all need to utilize the existing measures in the *same* way,

1982 Temperamental differences in infants and young children. Pitman Books Ltd, London (Ciba Foundation symposium 89) 294-297

so that we can determine which findings are replicable and which patterns of associations remain stable across sexes, age groups, varying social circumstances and contrasting cultures.

If we proceed in this way, we shall have to decide which composite variables to employ. At present there is both a lack of agreement on the most appropriate composites and a lack of evidence about when such agreement might be established. Nevertheless, certain constellations of behavioural attributes keep recurring. These include the 'easy–difficult child' dimension with its characteristics of mood, adaptability, intensity (and sometimes regularity and approach/withdrawal) in various permutations; the 'slow-to-warm-up' dimension; and 'task orientation' as reflected in the characteristics of activity, attention and, perhaps, persistence. It seems highly likely that dimensions of this kind will prove to be the most useful—both theoretically and practically—although there is continuing uncertainty about just how these composites should be constructed and about what modifications in the concepts are required.

We have heard about a variety of research strategies that may be used to tackle these questions. Some have sought reliance on factorial structure; others have depended on associations with other variables of potential aetiological importance (such as minor congenital anomalies, neuro-developmental dysfunction, or genetic transmission); and yet others have urged the value of considering which temperamental variables constitute the best predictors. Of course, many different sorts of prediction may be considered in this connection—prediction to: the development of emotional/behavioural disorder or of learning difficulties; the child's response to stressful circumstances or life change; patterns of parent–child interaction; the child's response to a chronically depriving environment; or, simply, consistency in temperamental functioning over time. We have many ways of determining the most appropriate grouping of temperamental variables. We are not yet ready to close the issue of composite variables. We need further studies that will compare and contrast different composites in terms of these several proposed criteria. In this way we shall learn how to conceptualize and measure temperament more effectively. But in doing so we shall also learn a great deal about the ways in which temperament operates: measurement issues and substantive issues are closely intertwined.

Clinical applications of an understanding of temperamental individuality and the quest for knowledge on the role of temperament in personal development have tended to be seen as separate endeavours requiring quite disparate approaches. But the research on both fronts has given rise to much the same set of messages. We know that there are reasonably robust, although only moderately strong, associations between temperamental variables and children's responses in a variety of life situations. Many of these have been well discussed during the symposium. The principal need now is for a better discrimination of the *mechanisms* involved.

Some important lessons derive from what has been done already in this connection. Perhaps most crucial is the suggestion that the way forward lies in marrying the study of temperament to the study of other aspects of development and disorder. Indeed, that is what was undertaken in most of the research reported at this meeting. We have heard about some of the ways in which temperamental attributes are associated with other measures of children, their families and the sociocultural environment. In particular, attention has been focused on the role of temperament as a regulator of parent–child interaction in the family and of teacher–child interaction at school. The research issues in the two environments—intra- and extra-familial—are closely comparable, but certain kinds of investigation are more effectively conducted in the one than in the other. The two should be seen as complementary, with each being needed to test hypotheses deriving from investigations in the other.

This approach is being used most effectively in short-term longitudinal studies, but the concepts of personality development that underlie this research are different from those that prevailed when temperamental studies were first conducted. At that time there was a belief in strong continuities in development, with major dispositions or traits being established early and persisting throughout the period of growth with relatively little change. According to this 'trajectory' view of development (Rutter 1975), a child's innate disposition thrusts him or her forth on a course of personality development that is substantially set early in life, although the environment may retard, facilitate or distort its progression. With these concepts, it was natural to seek fundamental traits and to assess consistencies in development largely by means of correlations over very long time spans. However, research has shown that the correlations from the preschool years to adolescence or adult life are generally low and that the theoretical notion of fixed temperamental dispositions was mistaken. As a result, 'interactive' views of development have come to the fore. The concept of some meaningful continuity in personality growth remains but there is no longer a supposition of a persistent, innate inner core of personality. A child's personal qualities are most important in terms of their influence on social interactions and experiences, which in turn help shape personality growth. But throughout the course of development each interaction influences the next and in so doing may thereby change the temperamental style. Rather than high correlations being sought between temperamental measures at three months, three years and 30 years, there is an emphasis on the need to study the many steps that intervene and the many mechanisms that operate. The study of temperament constitutes an essential part of that investigative process but it has to be seen in terms of a very much broader set of variables and mechanisms than those reflected in consistencies between traits or internal dispositions. We are far from having answers to the many questions that arise from this approach to development, but certainly we are making progress down the road to an understanding of individual differences in personality.

REFERENCE

Rutter M 1975 Helping troubled children. Penguin Books, Harmondsworth, Middlesex

Index of contributors

Subject index